T0358214

*Routledge Library Editions*

# PRICING AND EQUILIBRIUM

ECONOMICS

# ECONOMIC THEORY & ECONOMETRICS
## In 6 Volumes

# PRICING AND EQUILIBRIUM

## An Introduction to Static and Dynamic Analysis

ERICH SCHNEIDER

Routledge
Taylor & Francis Group
LONDON AND NEW YORK

First published in 1952
Reprinted in 2003 by
Routledge
2 Park Square, Milton Park, Abingdon, Oxon, OX14 4RN

Transferred to Digital Printing 2007

*Routledge is an imprint of the Taylor & Francis Group*

© 1962 Routledge

*British Library Cataloguing in Publication Data*
A CIP catalogue record for this book
is available from the British Library

Pricing and Equilibrium
ISBN 0-415-31319-8 (hbk)
ISBN 0-415-31313-9 (set)

Miniset: Economic Theory & Econometrics

Series: Routledge Library Editions – Economics

Printed and bound by CPI Antony Rowe, Eastbourne

# PRICING AND EQUILIBRIUM

## An Introduction to Static and Dynamic Analysis

By

## DR. ERICH SCHNEIDER

*Professor at the University of Kiel*

*English Version by*
ESRA BENNATHAN
*University of Birmingham*

Routledge
Taylor & Francis Group

LONDON AND NEW YORK

FIRST PUBLISHED IN ENGLISH IN 1952

THIS SECOND EDITION FIRST PUBLISHED IN 1962

*This Edition © Routledge, 1962*
*is a revised translation based on 6th revised German edition*

*The German Original*
WIRTSCHAFTSPLÄNE UND WIRTSCHAFTLICHES GLEICHGEWICHT
*is Volume II, first published in 1949 by J. C. B. Mohr Verlag*
*(Paul Siebeck), of Professor Schneider's*
EINFÜHRUNG IN DIE WIRTSCHAFTSTHEORIE

*English Translation by T. W. Hutchison published 1952*

# PUBLISHER'S PREFACE

Since the first edition of Professor Schneider's *Wirtschaftspläne und Wirtschaftliches Gleichgewicht in der Verkehrswirtschaft* appeared in 1952 with the English title *Pricing and Equilibrium*, in the translation of Professor T. W. Hutchison (William Hodge and Company), the book has gone through five further German editions. In most of these, the author introduced substantial changes and as a result, the book, as it now appears, is more than one-third longer than when it was first published in English.

There are many additions, but the main ones are in Chapters II and IV. The theory of production has been given a much more extensive treatment which now includes the essence of the author's *Teoria della Produzione* (Milan, 1942). A section on location and the sales area has been included as an example of heterogeneous competition. The section on price discrimination has been re-written, and a new one added on long-run supply. And in re-casting his sections on the cost and profit plans of multi-product firms, the author has included an introduction to the theory of linear programming.

The present translation of the book's sixth edition is based in part on Professor Hutchison's earlier translation, revised and corrected where necessary. The translator has sought to conform to English notational conventions, and where the author differs from common English usage, algebraic or definitional, the reader's attention has been drawn to this in notes marked with an asterisk.

References to Volume III are to its English version, in the translation of Mr. Kurt Klappholz, with the title *Money, Income and Employment*.

# CONTENTS

# FROM THE FOREWORD
## TO THE FIRST EDITION

This second volume of the "Introduction to Economic Theory" deals with the economic plans of the household and of the firm and with the theory of economic equilibrium. In writing it I was guided by the principles which I outlined in the foreword to the first volume and in my essay *Das Gesicht der Wirtschaftstheorie unserer Zeit* (*Tübingen*, 1947). Thus, in the first place, my exposition emphasizes again the unity of economic theory. Secondly, in the discussion of the problems of partial equilibrium, dynamic analysis has been given the extended treatment which is its due. Dynamic analysis occupies so prominent a position in modern theory that the beginner ought to become acquainted with it at the earliest possible stage. If the nature of dynamic analysis has first been understood in relation to the comparatively simple problems of partial equilibrium, then it becomes much easier to examine the theory of the expansion and the contraction of the economy as a whole, which will be dealt with, along with problems of money and employment, in the third volume[1]. Though recognizing the great importance of dynamic analysis in modern economics we must not, in our teaching, neglect the static analysis of partial and total equilibrium. The important problem of how the individual plans in an exchange economy are coordinated cannot be fully explained and understood except in the context of both a static and a dynamic theory of economic equilibrium. I have, therefore, in this book laid special emphasis on an exhaustive treatment of this branch of theory.

Erich Schneider

Kiel, September, 1948

[1] *Money, Income and Employment.* (English translation by Kurt Klappholz.) London, Routledge 1961.

# INTRODUCTION

The course of the economic process through time results from the dispositions of the individual economic units engaged. With these different units acting in a particular way, a particular result will emerge from the interplay of these individual dispositions. This result has been studied in a previous volume on social accounting for an already completed period of time. The treatment was of an *ex-post* character.

We now wish to turn our attention to the actual plans and dispositions which are the forces shaping the course of the economic process through time. This is to shift our angle of vision. Previously we were looking back at the past, now we are asking how the economic process will develop in the future from a given initial position if the economic units behave in a particular way. Only thus is it possible to make a causal analysis of economic events and to predict the course to be expected on particular assumptions. If we are to explain the actual course of historical development by means of a causal analysis, we have to start with an analysis of the economic plans of the responsible individuals. For an exchange economy we must analyse, therefore, the economic plans of the households, of the firms, and of the state, because every actual disposition which comes about is the result of a particular economic plan or calculation. Every economic plan is based on particular objectively given conditions, and on expectations. At the same time, the dispositions of an economic individual result from an economic plan based on particular expectations. Whether these expectations are fulfilled will only be known at the end of the economic period for which the plan was drawn up. Generally the actual events resulting from the interaction of the individual dispositions will differ from the assumptions on which those dispositions were based, so that an individual unit in the course of, or at the end of, the planning period will be forced to revise its plans. The divergencies between the expectations on which the particular dispositions were based, and the actual course of events, are the motive force behind the constant revision of economic plans and, therefore, behind changes in dispositions and actions. Consequently, it is not sufficient for the purposes of a genuine causal analysis to ask what the course of the economic process as a whole will be, if the individual units behave in a particular way. It is necessary, rather, to study, in addition, what factors determine these dispositions and actions. To use an expression of the Swedish economist J. Åkerman, a causal analysis requires an analysis of the "model calculations" of households, firms, and the state, that is, an analysis of models of the calculations which the individual units make in arriving at their dispositions. The analysis of these model calculations is logically the first link in the chain of our investigations, and the first task on which we shall be engaged. We shall first of all be concerned with a closed economy with no state activity. The changes which are brought about by the activity of the state, and by relations with outside economic systems, will be discussed elsewhere. In the first place we are simply concerned to prepare the necessary intellectual tools, and to show how by using them we can solve the simplest forms of problem in the case of an exchange economy. We are, therefore, only concerned with households and with firms. We have to show how the economic plans of these two groups of units are shaped, and how their particular dispositions emerge from them (Chapters I and II). These questions are of a micro-economic character, that is, they relate to the single economic unit. In the case of the business enterprise they belong with the theory of the firm and the study of business administration. We must study these problems here because the central problems of economic systems cannot be answered except by studying the interactions of the dispositions of the individual units. The close connexion between the economics of the firm and of the economy as a whole will be particularly clear at this point. On the one hand, the theory of the firm provides us with an important basis for economic theory. On the other hand, the dispositions of firms, and especially changes in them, can only be fully understood from the point of view of the economy as a whole.

After analysing the economic plans of the households and the firms we then have to answer the question about the interplay between the dispositions of the individual units. This question will lead us to develop the theory of economic equilibrium (Chapter IV). In volume III we will study the general theory of processes of expansion and contraction of the economy as a whole.

# CHAPTER I

# The Economic Plan of the Household

## 1. The Determinants of the Household's Consumption Plan

1. The consumption plan of the household consists of decisions about the quantities of the different goods it desires which it will buy in the coming period, and about the sums of money it will devote to the purchase of these different goods. If we assume that the household faces given prices, which it cannot alter, then the decision about *the physical quantities of the different goods* to be purchased, is one and the same as the decision about *the sums of money* to be devoted to their purchase. This is a realistic assumption and we shall be making it in what follows.

2. The extent of the purchases which a household can make in a particular period is limited by *the purchasing potential* for that period, which is determined as follows:

(a) by the expected income for the period;
(b) by the cash holding at the beginning of the period and the possibilities of changing into cash claims which are not legal tender;
(c) by the credit possibilities available during the period.

The expected income is, therefore, only one of the factors determining the purchasing potential in a period, though, of course, it is the most important factor.

3. If the sum of money to be devoted in the coming period to the purchase of consumers' goods is less than the expected income for the period, then the household is planning a *positive* level of savings during that period. We shall describe such savings as "*planned*" or "*ex-ante*" savings as contrasted with the actual *realized* savings resulting at the end of the period.

If the sum of money to be devoted to consumption in the coming period is greater than the expected income then negative savings are being planned.

The planned saving of the household is, of course, simply the inverse expression of its planned consumption. The decision about

1

the level of consumption-spending is at the same time a decision about the level (positive or negative) of *ex-ante* savings. *Vice versa* the decision about the level of savings determines the sum of money available for the purchase of consumption goods.

In which order the household makes its decision is a question of fact. For households which plan to add a particular sum in each income period to their total savings, *ex-ante* savings is the primary quantity. By subtracting this quantity from the expected income one arrives at the sum of money available for consumption purposes (or "total consumption-spending", as it might be called), which is then the residual quantity in the plan. On the other hand, for households which fix their consumption-spending first, savings is the residual quantity. In both cases the level of consumption-spending, and of saving, is determined in one single decision. No doubt households exist which do not determine in advance their level of consumption-spending, living simply from day to day and leaving their individual purchases more or less to their spontaneous habits and whims. The sums devoted to consumption will then be determined accidentally. The level of savings will be simply an unintended residual, the household discovering at the end of a period that a particular positive or negative saving has been made. One cannot speak in this case of a consumption *plan* for a particular period. But in what follows we are concerned only with households which make definite decisions for the forthcoming period which are part of a definite economic plan.

4. The consumption-spending planned for a coming period consists of the total of the sums to be devoted to the purchase of the different individual goods. We have to ask what determines these partial sums. We can answer straightaway that given the situation in which it must act, and with free consumers' choice, the household will purchase those goods in those physical quantities which will afford it a maximum of subjective satisfaction, or, to use Pareto's term, a maximum of *ophelimity*.* Since the nature and urgency of the tastes to be satisfied are a subjective problem of the household we may regard them as requiring no further analysis by the theoretical economist. The purchasing plans for particular goods, and the quantities of goods and of money they involve, or, in other words, the allocation of consumption-spending quantitively and qualitatively, can be taken as data needing no further study at this stage. If a household in the coming period allots 100 dollars for accommodation, 80 dollars for clothing, 20 dollars for bread, etc. this is simply taken to imply that the household obtains the maximum of ophelimity by this combination of expenditure. For the

* The term normal in English literature is *utility*. [*Tr.*].

course of economic events it is the purchases of goods that are relevant, that is, what the household does and not what it feels. As Lexis put it: "The subjective order of preferences and the use of income by each individual must be *postulated*. For the theoretical economist it is only the results of the overt actions of large groups which have to be studied. Tastes and satisfactions appear to him simply as quantitative expressions, the former as effective demand for a particular quantity of goods, and the latter as a particular quantity of goods possessing a particular price."[1] What are relevant are the sums of money devoted to the purchases of the goods desired by the household, that is, the *effective monetary demand*. We might add that this monetary demand, given the scale of preferences, depends on the expected level of prices and the purchasing potential. Our discussion of the character of the consumption plan of the household, and of its determinants, can be illustrated by the following classification made by Zwiedineck-Südenhorst.[2]

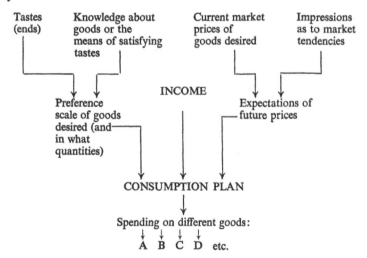

The modern theory of the consumption, or demand, of the household, is not content with these propositions alone. If the object is simply to explain the course of the economic process in a period of time as resulting from the interplay of individual dispositions, then it is enough to know the different sums of money devoted to the different goods by the individual households in their economic plans.

[1] W. Lexis: *Allgemeine Volkswirtschaftslehre*, Leipzig, 1913, p. 18.
[2] O. v. Zwiedineck-Südenhorst: *Allgemeine Volkswirtschaftslehre*, 2nd ed., 1948, p. 45.

The question as to how the course of the economic process is shaped in a particular period is answered by examining the actions of the different economic units, and the economic plans on which these actions are based. The dispositions of the economic units are, however, based on expectations which may well not be fulfilled. For the household, for example, expectations about prices and incomes determine its decisions for the coming period, and these expectations may, in the course of, or at the end of, the period, as a result of the interplay of the independent dispositions of all the other economic units, be seen to have diverged from the *ex-post* facts to a greater or lesser extent. These divergencies, as we have already explained, will cause revisions in plans, leading in their turn to fresh dispositions. To understand and explain the course of the economic process from period to period it is necessary to know how the divergencies between the actual facts, and the expectations on which the plans are based, cause changes in the dispositions of the economic units. For this purpose it is necessary to study the relationships between the dispositions or plans and the elements which determine them. It is therefore necessary to study how changes in tastes, in total consumption-spending, and in the structure of prices, alter the household's dispositions, or its effective physical and monetary demand for particular goods. A knowledge of these relationships is also indispensible in the study of problems of economic control, for example of the question as to how, and to what extent, the physical and monetary demand of the household may be influenced by variations in prices, or how consumption-spending may be affected by changes in income. The theoretical economist is forced, therefore, to analyse on the one hand the quantitative relationships between the physical and monetary demands of the household, and on the other hand, prices, consumption-spending and tastes. We must now turn to the study of these relations.

### 2. The Quantitative Relationships between Demand, Tastes, Prices and Total Consumption-Spending

1. The consumption plan of a household, as we have seen, depends on:

(a) tastes, that is, its psychological attitude towards different goods;
(b) the quantity of money to be devoted to consumption purposes;
(c) the expected prices of goods.

If these factors are known, the household can tell us what goods will be purchased and in what quantities, and what sums of money will be devoted to the purchase of particular goods. Of these three factors only the level of consumption-spending and the prices of goods can be objectively ascertained. Tastes are subjective. Our theory is concerned with quantitative relationships, and there are different ways in which this subjective element can be introduced. Much of the controversy over the theory of value has been devoted to the question as to how subjective tastes are to be introduced into the theory of demand. These controversies have their place in the history of economic thought, but we do not wish to go into them here. We shall simply expound our theory of demand in the form which has become usual at the present day.

2. We start from the empirical fact that with given tastes the quantities of goods demanded by a household depend on the level of planned consumption-spending, and on the prices of all the goods desired by the household. If the household desires simply bread, potatoes and meat, then clearly the quantity of bread demanded (total consumption-spending being fixed) depends not only on the price of bread but on the prices of potatoes and meat. Correspondingly for the prices of potatoes and meat. All the quantities involved in the consumption plan (tastes being given) are interdependent.

If there are $n$ goods desired by the household and the prices of these $n$ goods are $p_1, p_2, \ldots, p_n$, the physical quantities to be purchased $x_1, x_2, \ldots, x_n$, and the sum of money to be devoted to consumption is $c$, then the quantities of each good to be demanded (that is, $x_1, \ldots, x_n$) (if tastes are given) is a function of (or depends on) the prices of the goods $p_1, \ldots, p_n$, and the sum of money $c$ which is to be devoted to consumption. The consumption plan of the household can be expressed by the $n$ demand functions for the $n$ goods:

$$
\begin{aligned}
x_1 &= f_1(p_1, \ldots, p_n, c) \\
x_2 &= f_2(p_1, \ldots, p_n, c) \\
&\cdot \quad \cdot \quad \cdot \quad \cdot \quad \cdot \\
&\cdot \quad \cdot \quad \cdot \quad \cdot \quad \cdot \\
x_n &= f_n(p_1, \ldots, p_n, c)
\end{aligned}
\tag{1}
$$

These functions tell us the physical demand of the household for the different goods, when prices and total consumption-spending are given. For each level of prices and of consumption-spending these functions will give a particular physical quantity of goods as the physical demand. We may assume that we have obtained these functions by questioning the households at the beginning of the economic period.

The corresponding monetary demand for the different goods results from multiplying the physical quantities demanded by the prices obtaining. That is, it is given by the mathematical products $p_1 \cdot x_1, \ldots, p_n \cdot x_n$. The total of monetary demand for the different individual goods naturally equals the total of consumption spending.

$$p_1 \cdot x_1 + \ldots + p_n \cdot x_n = c \qquad (2)$$

This equation is usually described as the "*budget equation*" of the household. The demand functions (1) have the further important characteristic that the physical demand for the individual goods remains unchanged if the prices and the total of consumption-spending are all multiplied by 2 or 3, etc. This implies that the physical demand depends simply on the *relations between prices and their relation to total consumption-spending*. Following Irving Fisher, this circumstance can also be expressed by saying that *the households are free from money illusion*. The Theory of Demand is as a rule based on this assumption.[1]

We have assumed, in setting out the demand function of the household, that the level of demand for the individual goods depends simply on the prices expected in the forthcoming planning period. Generally, as experience shows, the development of prices in the near future, or of the tendency of prices, is a factor in the decision as to quantities to be purchased. At first, however, we shall disregard this factor, but we shall come to discuss it in Section 8 below.

3. It is of great interest and also of great practical importance to ask how the household will alter its physical demand if the prices of goods and/or the total of consumption-spending alter, while tastes remain the same. There are three questions we have to put here:

(a) How does the physical demand for a good change with the price of this good, if the prices of all other goods desired by the household, and total consumption-spending, remain unchanged: or, briefly, how does $x_i$ change *ceteris paribus* with changes in $p_i$ $(i = 1, 2, \ldots, n)$?

(b) How does the physical demand for a good change when the price of *another* good desired by the household changes, all other prices and total consumption-spending remaining the same: that is, how does $x_i$ change *ceteris paribus* with changes in $p_k$ $(k \neq i)$?

(c) How does the physical demand for a good vary with total consumption-spending, the prices of all goods desired by the household remaining constant: that is, how does $x_i$ vary *ceteris paribus* with $c$?

[1] See Vol. III, (Money, Income and Employment, London, 1961) p. 96 for demand functions for which this assumption does not hold.

4. Let us take the first question. Three types of reaction are conceivable: the demand for the good may fall as the price rises, or it may increase, or it may remain the same (Fig. 1). Experience tells us that the type of reaction portrayed in Fig. 1A is the rule, and that in Fig. 1B is the exception. We shall refer to the exceptional case as the *Giffen case*, for it is said to have been Sir Robert Giffen who observed that the consumption of bread in the poorer English households *ceteris paribus* increased with an increase in the price of bread.

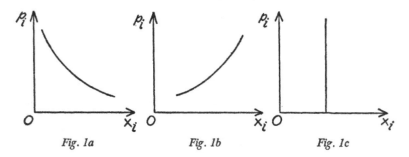

Fig. 1a          Fig. 1b          Fig. 1c

5. The same types of reaction are conceivable in answer to the second question. With complementary goods, for example tobacco and pipes, the demand for the *first* good will decline with a rise in the price of *this first* good, and *also* the demand for the *other* complementary good will decline. With goods which may be substituted for one another, on the other hand, a *rise* in the price of the *first* good (the price of the substitute remaining the same) will lead to an *increase* in the demand for the *second* good. Finally, these three types of reaction are each possible answers to our third question: it is quite conceivable that an increase in the total of consumption-spending may *ceteris paribus* lead either to a decrease or to an increase in the physical demand for a particular good. Similarly, the demand for a good may remain entirely unaffected by alterations in the total of consumption-spending. Goods the demand for which declines with a rise in total consumption-spending are usually described as *inferior goods*.

6. Up till now we have expressed the consumption plan of the household in terms of the demand functions, which state the physical quantities demanded of each particular good desired by the household, as functions of the prices of these goods and of the level of total consumption-spending. It is often convenient to start from the income of the household rather than from the total of its consumption-spending, so that the physical quantities of a good

demanded are made to depend on prices and on the income $y$:

$$x_1 = f_1(p_1, \ldots, p_n, y)$$

$$\cdot \quad \cdot \quad \cdot \quad \cdot \quad \cdot \tag{3}$$

$$\cdot \quad \cdot \quad \cdot \quad \cdot \quad \cdot$$

$$x_n = f_n(p_1, \ldots, p_n, y)$$

The difference between the income and the total monetary demand of the household for consumption goods (given by the total of consumption-spending $p_1 x_1 + \ldots + p_n x_n$), gives the level of planned saving, positive or negative:

$$y - (p_1 x_1 + \ldots + p_n x_n) = s \tag{4}$$

When $s = 0$ the total of consumption-spending equals the income. Equation (3) is then identical with equation (1).

If it can be assumed that the relation between consumption-spending and the level of income is uniquely determined so that consumption-spending increases with an increase in income, which is an assumption that corresponds with experience, then, of course, the same propositions can be made about the functional dependence of the demand for particular consumers' goods on the level of income, as can be made about the dependence of that demand on the level of consumption-spending.

### 3. The Derivation of the Individual Demand Function from the Indifference Map of the Household

1. Before we deal further with these different types of reaction, we have to show how the demand function is determined by tastes, prices, and the total of consumption-spending. Modern economic theory deduces these relations with the aid of the analysis of choice developed by Pareto, who made use of a construction of Edgeworth's. For the sake of simplicity we shall deal with the case where there are only two goods desired by the household.

We shall measure on a pair of coordinates the different quantities $x_2$ of good No. 2 along the horizontal axis, and along the vertical the different quantities $x_1$ of good No. 1. A particular quantity-combination of goods $x_1$, $x_2$ will, therefore, be represented by a point $P$ somewhere within this system of coordinates (Fig. 2). This combination gives the household a particular satisfaction, or possesses for it a particular ophelimity. We now ask the household what other combinations of quantities of the same goods have the same ophelimity for it as the combination represented by the point $P$, that is, between what other combinations and the combination represented by *P* the household is *indifferent*. It is obvious at once that the combination represented by point *Q* will be preferred to that represented by point *P*. Any combination which is *not* preferred to point *P* can only be one in which, if the quantity of *one* of the goods is *larger*, that of the *other* is *smaller* than the quantity represented by point *P*. The question which we have to put to the household can therefore be formulated as follows: starting from point *P*, by how many units must the quantity of good No. 2 be increased (or diminished) in order that the ophelimity of the household shall

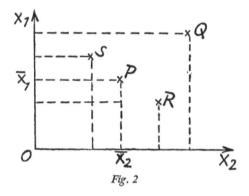

*Fig. 2*

remain unchanged when the quantity of good No. 1 is diminished (or increased) by one unit (that is, if the new combination is not to be preferred to the former one or *vice versa*). Let us assume that the points *R* and *S* have this characteristic. Then, in the estimate of the household, points *R*, *P* and *S* have the same value. The household is indifferent between these combinations of goods. We can now take the points *S* or *R* as our starting point and repeat our question. In this way we shall obtain all the points between our two coordinates (that is, all the combinations of the two goods) between which the household is indifferent. The curve traced out by these points was termed by Pareto *the indifference curve* of the household. It is clear that every point within this system of coordinates must lie on an indifference curve. Each curve traces out all the points which possess, in the estimate of the household, the same value, and these curves can be arranged according to an index of ophelimity. Any curve for which there are points that are preferred to all the points on a second curve, will have a higher ophelimity-index than this second curve. It is obvious that a curve with a higher ophelimity-index can never cut one with a lower index. In Fig. 3 curve I (passing through *P*) is an indifference curve with a particular ophelimity-index. Curve II, which passes through the point $Q$, has a higher index because point $Q$ is preferred to the point $P$. In this case curve II cannot cut curve I. If it did, as is assumed in Fig. 3, a contradiction would result. The point $R$ would then have to be preferred to the point $S$. This is

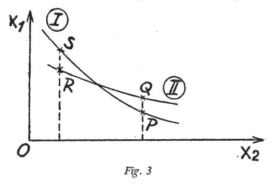

*Fig. 3*

impossible because point $R$, as compared with point $S$, represents the same quantity of $x_2$, but a smaller quantity of $x_1$. The system of coordinates, therefore, is covered by a family of non-intersecting indifference curves. Any combination that is preferred to another combination lies on an indifference curve further from the two axes.

We now have to clear up the question of *the shape* of indifference curves, that is, whether they are concave to the origin (Fig. 4A), or convex to the origin (Fig. 4B). Only the empirical facts can answer

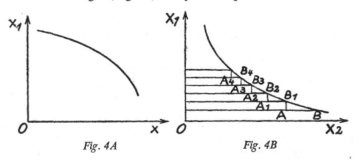

*Fig. 4A*          *Fig. 4B*

this question. Experience tells us that the quantity of good No. 2 which would be given up for each increase of one unit in good No. 1 (*if there is to be no change in the ophelimity-index*) is smaller, the greater the quantity of good No. 1 that is already possessed. This is simply to say that indifference curves must be convex to the origin (Fig. 4B). From Fig. 4B it is immediately obvious that the distances

$AB$, $A_1B_1$, etc., representing the decrease in the quantity of $x_2$ compensated by successive increases of one unit in the quantity of $x_1$, must get smaller as $x_1$ increases. As the reader can easily convince himself, this would not be the case with a curve concave to the origin.

The quantity of good No. 2 the loss of which would exactly be compensated by the addition of one unit of good No. 1, in the estimate of the household (that is, in Fig. 4B the distances $AB$, $A_1B_1$, etc.),

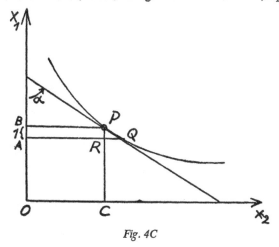

*Fig. 4C*

is termed *the marginal rate of substitution* of good No. 2 for good No. 1.* The marginal rate of substitution of good No. 2 for good No. 1 depends, as one can see, on the particular combination of the two goods which the household happens to possess. Geometrically the marginal rate of substitution of good No. 2 for good No. 1 (starting from the combination represented by $P$) is given by the tan of the angle between the tangent to the indifferent curve (at $P$) and the $x_1$ axis (Fig. 4C). The marginal rate of substitution at point $P$ is

* The definition of the marginal rate of substitution which is commonly accepted in Anglo-Saxon literature is the inverse of this: using the above notation, *the marginal rate of substitution is the quantity of good No. 1 which would just compensate the consumer for the loss of a marginal unit of good No. 2.* This is called variously the marginal rate of substitution "*of good No. 2 for good No. 1.*" (e.g. by Hicks and Allen) or "*of good No. 1 for good No. 2.*" (e.g. by G. J. Stigler).

    Geometrically, the marginal rate of substitution thus defined would, in Fig. 5, be the *cotg* and not the *tan* of the angle $\alpha$ (i.e. OA/OB instead of OB/OA).

    In translating, I have rendered what in the German text is literally "the marginal rate of substitution of No. 2 by No. 1" as "the marginal rate of substitution of 2 for 1". [*Tr.*]

represented by $QR$. For small changes in $x_1$ the arc $PQ$ can be taken as equivalent to the tangent to the curve at $P$, so that

$$\frac{QR}{PR} = \frac{QR}{1} = \tan \alpha$$

The concept of the marginal rate of substitution allows us to give yet another formulation to the fact, founded in experience, that led us to draw the indifference curve convex to the origin:

*The marginal rate of substitution of good No. 2 for good No. 1 decreases with the increased substitution of good No. 1 for good No. 2. This proposition is also known as the law of the diminishing marginal rate of substitution.*

2. We are now able to deduce the individual demand function of a household from its tastes, prices and total consumption-spending. The theory of choice provides us with a system of indifference curves for the household which is a quantitative expression of its tastes. In place of the expression "with given tastes" we can now substitute the expression "with a given indifference map or system of indifference curves". If its tastes and total consumption-spending are given, the household will so distribute its expenditure between the two goods that the maximum of satisfaction will be obtained. From all the possible distributions of its expenditure given by the budget equation:

$$p_1 x_1 + p_2 x_2 = c \qquad (2a)$$

it will choose that combination which corresponds to the highest index of ophelimity on its indifference map.

As can easily be recognized, the budget equation (2a) can be represented on our coordinates by the straight line which marks off the distance $\frac{c}{p_1}$ on the ordinate axis, and the distance $\frac{c}{p_2}$ on the abscissa (Fig. 5).[1] The distance $\frac{c}{p_1}$ represents the quantity of the first good which could be purchased if *the whole of* consumption-spending was devoted to the first good. Correspondingly, $\frac{c}{p_2}$ represents the quantity of the second good which could be purchased if the whole of consumption-spending was devoted to the second good. From Fig. 5 it is clear $\tan \alpha = \frac{c}{p_2} : \frac{c}{p_1} = \frac{p_1}{p_2}$. The slope of the budget

[1] To see this it is only necessary to write the equation (2a) in the form:

$$\frac{x_1}{c/p_1} + \frac{x_2}{c/p_2} = 1$$

line is therefore determined simply by *the relation between the prices of the two goods.*

In order to find out which of the points on the budget line *AB* has the highest ophelimity-index, we must draw in the budget line on

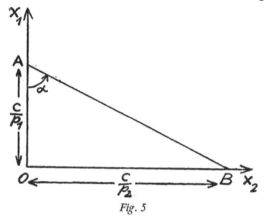

*Fig. 5*

our diagram of an indifference map (Fig. 6). A glance shows at once that that point on the budget line (or that combination $x_1$, $x_2$) has the highest ophelimity-index which *just touches* one of the curves of the indifference map. With given tastes, given prices and a given total of consumption-spending, the household will buy in a particular planning period the quantity of the two goods represented by the

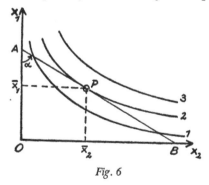

*Fig. 6*

coordinates of the point *P*. The quantities corresponding to point *P* represent the physical demand of the household in the coming period according to the plans it has worked out. With given tastes, given prices, and a given total of consumption-spending, these two quantities (of demand in physical terms) are uniquely determined.

We have shown already that the marginal rate of substitution of good No. 2 for good No. 1, given a particular combination of the two goods (or a particular point on the indifference map), is measured geometrically by the tan of the angle ($\alpha$) formed by the tangent to the indifference curve through the point $P$, and a line parallel to the $x_1$ axis (Fig. 4c). At the point with the highest ophelimity-index ($P$ in Fig. 6) this tangent coincides with the budget line. For the budget line it holds, however, that

$$\tan \alpha = \frac{p_1}{p_2}$$

Therefore the quantity-combination of goods which the household will elect to have has the characteristic that the marginal rate of substitution of good No. 2 for good No. 1 is the same as the ratio of the price of 1 to the price of 2:

Marginal rate of substitution of good No. 2 for good No. 1

$$= \frac{\text{Price of good No. 1}}{\text{Price of good No. 2}}$$

We can say then that with a given total of consumption-spending, and given prices, the household will so distribute its spending between the two goods that the marginal rate of substitution will fulfil this condition.

It is easy to see what this condition implies. If the price of good No. 1 is 4s. per unit, and that of good No. 2 2s. per unit, there is the price relationship of $\frac{p_1}{p_2} = 2$. This implies that at the ruling prices two units of good No. 2 can always be exchanged for one unit of good No. 1. The price relationship represents the *objective* exchange relationship between the two goods. If, therefore, the household in formulating its plans starts from a combination $x_1, x_2$ where the marginal rate of substitution of good No. 2 for good No. 1 is greater than the objective exchange relationship, this means that the *subjective* valuation of a unit of good No. 1 is higher than the *objective* valuation as expressed by the ruling price relation. The household will, therefore, substitute good No. 1 for good No. 2. This substitution benefits the household (or it increases its ophelimity), up to the point at which its own subjective valuation of a unit of good No. 1 exactly equals the price relation expressing their objective values. Similarly, if the household starts from a combination where its marginal rate of substitution of good No. 2 for good No. 1 is below the objective exchange relation (or market price), it is clear that it will pay the household to substitute good No. 2 for good No. 1 until the subjective marginal rate of substitution equals the objective exchange relationship.

3. We have shown how the demand of a household can be deduced from a system of indifference curves, if prices and total consumption-spending are given.

It is now obvious from Fig. 6 that the level of demand for a particular good will alter if one or more of its three determinants (tastes, prices and total consumption-spending) alter. If the tastes of the household alter, then the system of indifference curves will change and (*ceteris paribus*) the point *P* will shift. The same happens

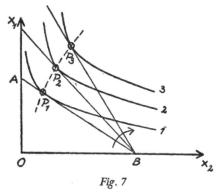

*Fig. 7*

if (*ceteris paribus*) prices or total consumption-spending change. We now want to work out some of these dependencies by using the constructions developed above. We shall find out by using the indifference curve technique what can be said about the character-istics of the demand functions (1) of a household, with given tastes.

4. Let us study, first, the functional relation between the demand for a good and the price of this good, all other prices and total consumption-spending remaining constant. We shall confine our-selves to the case of two goods and study what quantities of good No. 1 the household will demand at different levels of the price $p_1$. Assuming $p_2$ and $c$ constant, we shall be giving different alternative values in the budget equation (2a) to the price $p_1$. Then every value of $p_1$ corresponds to a new budget line which, with $p_2$ and $c$ constant, must go through the point *B* (Fig. 5). As $p_1$ falls the length of *OA* (Fig. 5) increases, and so one arrives at the decreasing values for the price $p_1$ by turning the budget line *AB* on the point *B* like the hand of a clock. The level of demand at each price will then be given by the point of tangency of the corresponding budget line with an

indifference curve (Fig. 7). Thus the coordinates of the points $p_1$, $p_2$ and $p_3$ correspond to three alternative levels of the price $p_1$. It can be seen from Fig. 7 that for any assumed structure of tastes, represented by the shape and position of the indifference curves, the quantity demanded of the first good will increase as the price of this good falls. This is the regular case which we have already discussed.

A structure of tastes, however, is possible which will lead to an abnormal reaction of demand. This case is illustrated in Fig. 8. Here the quantity demanded of the first good falls with a fall in the price of this good.

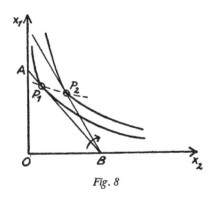

*Fig. 8*

5. Let us consider now the functional relation between the physical quantity demanded of a good and the size of the total of consumption-spending, all prices remaining constant. In the budget equation (2a) total consumption-spending is now given different values, while the prices $p_1$ and $p_2$ are held constant. Geometrically this means that the budget line shifts to and fro with each new line parallel to the others. The larger the total of consumption-spending the further the budget line moves from the origin. The quantities of goods demanded at each level of consumption-spending will be given in the usual way by the coordinates of the point of tangency ($P_1$, $P_2$ and $P_3$) of the budget lines with the indifference curves (Fig. 9). The totality of these points of tangency lies on a curve from the slope of which can at once be seen how the quantities demanded change with changes in total consumption-spending. If the indifference curves are as in Fig. 9, then it is clear that the quantities demanded of *both* goods increase (*ceteris paribus*) with an increase in total consumption-spending. That is the usual case. Another reaction to changes in total consumption-spending may occur if the indifference curves are shaped as in Fig. 10. Here it is clear that the quantity demanded of

the *first* good *decreases* with an increase in total consumption-spending, while that of the *second* good *increases*. In this case the first good is an inferior good.

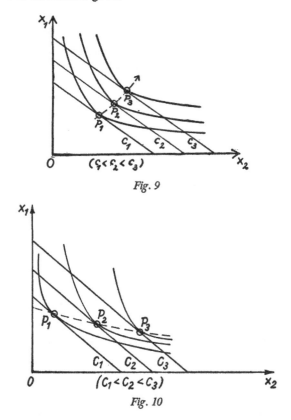

Fig. 9

Fig. 10

6. By making use of the results obtained above as to the relation between the quantities demanded and the total of consumption-spending (all prices remaining constant), we can also clarify the conditions determining whether the quantity demanded of a good (*ceteris paribus*) falls or rises, if there is a rise in the price of this good. In Fig. 11 we have the normal case. The quantity demanded of $x_1$ increases with a fall in the price $p_1$ from $OA_1$ to $OA_2$. With a fall in the price of $p_1$ the household moves on to an indifference curve with a higher index of ophelimity (II). This higher index can be reached by the household if, with prices unchanged, the total of consumption-spending is appropriately raised, that is, by an amount which increases

B

consumption-spending to the sum represented by the budget line
$S'T'$ (parallel to $ST$), which touches the indifference curve II. With
given prices, the quantities demanded at the higher level of consumption-spending (given by the coordinates of the point $Q$) are, of course,
different from those at the point $P_2$. From point $Q$ the household
can, however, get to the point $P_2$ by substituting for the second good
a compensatory quantity of the first good, assuming that, with a fall
in the price $p_1$, total consumption-spending is simultaneously lowered
to its original level. Therefore, the change in the quantities demanded

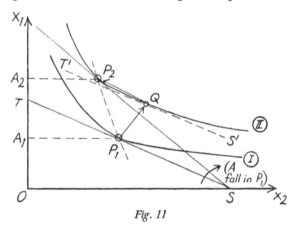

*Fig. 11*

of the two goods resulting from the fall in price $p_1$ (that is, the movement from point $P_1$ to $P_2$) can be looked upon as consisting of two
stages: (a) one from $P_1$ to $Q$ and (b) one from $Q$ to $P_2$. The *first* stage
corresponds to an increase in the total of consumption-spending
with prices remaining constant. This increase is equivalent in
ophelimity to a fall, by a particular amount, in the price $p_1$, with $p_2$
and total consumption-spending remaining constant. The *second*
stage corresponds to a substitution of the first good for the second
good along the indifference curve II. The first stage is purely the
effect of an alteration in total consumption-spending, and following
Allen and Hicks may be called *the income effect*. The second movement from $Q$ to $P_2$ is solely the consequence of substitution and may
be called the *substitution effect*. The effect of a fall in the price of a
good on the quantity demanded can, therefore, always be represented
as the sum of an income effect ($P_1$ to $Q$) and of a substitution effect
($Q$ to $P_2$). Now every substitution of the first good for the second is
represented by a movement along the indifference curve in the direction of increased quantities of $x_1$. The income effect (that is, the

movement from $P_1$ to $Q$) may not always lead to an increase in the quantity demanded of $x_1$. It was shown above that the quantity demanded usually increases (*ceteris paribus*) with an increase in total consumption-spending, and that the exceptional case is that of inferior goods. In the usual case a fall in the price of a good leads to an increase in the quantity demanded *both* through the income effect *and* through the substitution effect. As far as the substitution effect is concerned a fall in the price of a good *always* leads (*ceteris paribus*) to an increased demand for this good. But with inferior goods, owing to the income effect, a fall in the price of the good may lead to a *decrease* in the quantity demanded. It is therefore possible in this case that the *decrease* in $x_1$, owing to the income effect, is larger than the *increase* corresponding to the substitution effect, so that *altogether* the fall in the price of the good $x_1$ (*ceteris paribus*) leads to a decrease in the quantity demanded.

7. This derivation of the individual demand function and its properties from the household's indifference curve system needs to be precisely understood. The upshot of our examination was that the demand functions are determined if the indifference curve system is given. But conversely it can also be proved, given certain assumptions, that for each system of demand functions of a household there exists one and only one indifference curve system[1]. *For the theory of demand it is thus immaterial whether one starts from the preference system of the household in the shape of the indifference functions or from the preference system in the shape of demand functions. The two points of departure are equivalent.*

#### 4. Elasticity of Demand with Respect to Price and Income

1. In paragraph 3 we examined some of the characteristics of the demand functions (1) of the household. It was shown how the physical quantities demanded of a good vary *ceteris paribus* (a) with the price of this good and (b) with total consumption-spending (or income). For many purposes it is quite sufficient simply to know the direction of this variation, that is, to know whether the physical quantity demanded rises or falls with a fall in price or an increase in income. For other purposes it is essential to know not only, for

---

[1] The reader will find the proof of this in the latest comprehensive treatment of the theory of demand by H. Wold, *Demand Analysis. A Study in Econometrics.* (Stockholm, New York, 1952); and also in H. v. Stackelberg, *Zwei kritische Bemerkungen zur Preistheorie Gustav Cassels.* (Zeitschrift für Nationalökonomie, vol. 4, 1933).

example, that the physical quantity demanded (*ceteris paribus*) falls with a rise in price, but also the *quantitative* effects of a change in price or income. *How much* does the demand for a good increase if its price falls by *a particular amount*? It might appear that the question as to the quantitative effects of a particular change in price or income can be answered if we know (a) that at a price of 10s. for the good X (the prices of all other goods and the total of consumption-spending being given), 100 units are demanded, and at a price of 9s. this demand (*ceteris paribus*) increases to 110 units; and similarly (b) that at a price of 5s. (*ceteris paribus*) 250 units of the good X are demanded, and at a price of 4s. this demand increases (*ceteris paribus*) to 270 units. A fall in price of one monetary unit results, therefore, in the first case in an increase of 10 units in the quantity demanded, and in the second case of 20 units. This statement, however, tells us little. The two reductions in price are certainly the same *absolutely*, but not *relatively* or *percentually*. In the first case the fall in price is one of 10%, in the second case one of 20%. In order to get an idea as to whether the demand in the second case reacts more strongly or less strongly to a fall in price than in the first case, it is necessary to consider a *relatively* equal fall in price if we are to make a satisfactory comparison. Correspondingly, it is necessary for purposes of comparison to give the *percentual* change in the quantity demanded. It is for this reason that economists measure the strength of the reaction of demand to a change in price or income by *the elasticity of demand with respect to price or income*, that is, by the percentual change in the quantity demanded when the price or income (*ceteris paribus*) alters by a particular percentage.

The concept of the elasticity of a variable in relation to another variable, which is of such great significance in economic theory, was developed by Alfred Marshall. We must make ourselves thoroughly familiar with all its different applications, as it is one of the economist's most important concepts.

2. Let us consider first the elasticity of demand in relation to income. We start from the individual demand function of the household for a particular good No. $i$:

$$x_i = f_i(p_1, \ldots, p_n, y)$$

where $p_1, \ldots, p_n$ are the prices of the goods desired by the household, and $y$ its income. With given prices and a given income the quantity demanded, $x_i$, will be of a definite magnitude. In order to find out how elastic the demand is in relation to a small (strictly speaking, infinitely small) change in income (all prices remaining unchanged) we vary the given income $y$ by a small amount $dy$[1].

This variation in income results in a change in the quantity demanded, $x_i$, by the amount $dx_i$. Now an absolute change of $dy$ in the income $y$ results in a percentual change in the income $y$ of the quantity $\dfrac{dy}{y}$ . 100. Corresponding to this we have a relative change in demand of the quantity $\dfrac{dx_i}{x_i}$ . 100.

*We define the elasticity of demand for the good No. i with respect to income, to be the relation between the relative change in the quantity demanded and the relative change in income.* This *income elasticity* of demand ($Y_i$) for the good No. $i$ is, therefore, measured by the quotient:

$$Y_i = \frac{dx_i}{x_i} \cdot 100 : \frac{dy}{y} \cdot 100$$

$$= \frac{dx_i}{x_i} : \frac{dy}{y} = \frac{y}{x_i} \cdot \frac{dx_i}{dy} \tag{5}$$

Though not quite exact for all purposes, it would usually be adequate to say that the income elasticity tells us by how much per cent the quantity demanded changes with an alteration (*ceteris paribus*) of 1% in income. From the way the concept is formulated it is clear that the income elasticity is a pure number. Its magnitude also, as can be seen at once, is independent of the units of money and weight in which the income and the quantity demanded are measured. The reader should notice the assumptions on which the concept of income elasticity is based. All prices are treated as fixed. Only the income is changed by a small percentage. We then ask by how much per cent demand changes. It must also be noticed that an income elasticity of a particular amount is always related to a particular level of income, and generally varies with the level of income. If a household has an income of £500 per year, then the income elasticity for the good No. $i$ will generally be different from what it would be if the same household, with prices unchanged, had an income of £1,000 per year. We have already shown that the quantity demanded usually increases (*ceteris paribus*) with an increase in income, and decreases only in the exceptional case of inferior goods. By using the concept

---

[1] The symbol $dy$ signifies a small (strictly speaking an infinitely small) change in the variable quantity $y$.

of income elasticity we can now formulate this relation as being such that, in the regular case, income elasticity is positive, and in the exceptional case negative. The exact magnitude of income elasticity at a particular level of income is, of course, specially significant. For the usual case there are two different possibilities to be distinguished:

(a) If the income elasticity is positive and greater than 1, then one says that *demand is elastic with respect to income*. A change in income of 1% then corresponds to a change in the quantity demanded of more than 1%.

(b) If the income elasticity is positive but smaller than 1, then we say that *demand is inelastic with respect to income*. An income change of 1% then corresponds to a change in demand of less than 1%.

Positive income elasticities smaller than 1 are found in the case of important consumers' goods the need for which is already met to a considerable extent by small or moderate incomes (e.g. housing requirements).

(c) If the income elasticity is nil, then we say that *demand is perfectly inelastic with respect to income*.

The size of the income elasticity for particular goods can be taken as a criterion for distinguishing between essential and non-essential goods, if we define as essential goods those with an income elasticity smaller than 1, and as non-essentials those with an income elasticity greater than 1. We must notice here that the size of the income elasticity of a household's demand for a particular good varies with the level of its income, and, therefore, the dividing line between the two kinds of goods is not clear-cut. A good which is "non-essential" at a particular level of income can become "essential" at another level.

Previously we have spoken of the elasticity of the physical demand for a good in relation to income. It is equally important to know how the monetary demand reacts to changes in income. The monetary demand is arrived at simply by multiplying the physical demand by the price. Since prices can be considered constant as income varies, it is obvious that the absolute change in the monetary demand for a good is equal to the change in the physical demand multiplied by the price. The relative change in the monetary demand, as a consequence of a change in income, is therefore the same as the relative change in the physical demand. This fact is important if we are determining income elasticities on the basis of household budgets, because these may only tell us about the sums of money devoted to the purchase of particular goods, and not about the quantities of goods bought. For example, Danish investigations have shown that for incomes between 2,000 kr. and 5,000 kr. per year the expenditure on rent increases by 0·7% when income increases by 1%; which is to say that both the physical and the monetary income elasticity of demand for housing accommodation equals 0·7. The fact that the income elasticity of demand for housing is smaller than 1 was first discovered by the German statistician Schwabe in the law he formulated as follows: *Within the same social stratum the expenditure on housing accommodation declines relatively with increases in income*. The rule established by the German statistician Engel, according to which the expenditure on food *increases absolutely* with a rise in income, but *decreases relatively*, can also be formulated with the aid of the concept of elasticity by saying that the income elasticity of demand for food is smaller than 1.

3. Just as we measure the reaction of the physical demand to changes in income (prices remaining constant) by the income elasticity of demand, so in the same way we can measure the reaction of the quantity demanded to changes in price, when all other prices and income remain constant, by the *price elasticity*. Here two questions have to be distinguished:

(a) What is the change in the quantity demanded of a good if the price of *this* good (*ceteris paribus*) varies by a small (strictly speaking, infinitely small) amount?

(b) What is the change in the quantity demanded of a good if the price of *another* good (*ceteris paribus*) varies by a small (strictly speaking, infinitely small) amount?

The measurement of changes in demand is made in the first case by the *direct price elasticity* and in the second case by the *cross price elasticity*.

By the *direct price elasticity* we mean the relation between the relative change in the quantity demanded of a good and the relative change in the price of *this* good (income and the prices of all other goods desired by the household remaining constant).

By the *cross price elasticity* we mean, correspondingly, the relation between the relative change in the quantity demanded of a good and the relative change in the price of *another* good desired by the household (income and all other prices remaining constant).

If we describe the absolute change in the price $p_i$ as $dp_i$, and the corresponding absolute change in the quantity demanded $x_i$ of good No. $i$ as $dx_i$, then the direct price elasticity is given by the quotients

$$\eta_{x_i p_i} = \frac{dx_i}{x_i} : \frac{dp_i}{p_i} = \frac{p_i}{x_i} \cdot \frac{dx_i}{dp_i} \tag{6}$$

In the usual case the quantity demanded of a good falls with an increase in the price of this good; that is, in the usual case the direct price elasticity is negative.*

Correspondingly, the cross price elasticity is given by the expression:

$$\eta_{x_i p_k} = \frac{dx_i}{x_i} : \frac{dp_k}{p_k} = \frac{p_k}{x_i} \cdot \frac{dx_i}{dp_k}$$

where $x_i$ again signifies the physical quantity demanded of good No. $i$ and $p_k$ the price of the good $K$.

These two price elasticities are, like all elasticities, pure numbers.

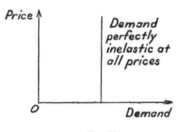

*Fig. 12*

Their value is independent of the units chosen for measuring prices and quantities.

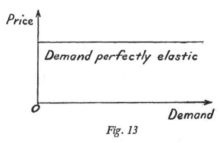

*Fig. 13*

---

* In order to obtain a *positive* number for the direct price elasticity in the normal case, Alfred Marshall introduced the convention of writing the direct price elasticity with a negative sign, thus:

$$\eta_{x_i, p_i} = -\frac{dx_i}{x_i} : \frac{dp_i}{p_i} = -\frac{p_i}{x_i} \cdot \frac{dx_i}{dp_i},$$

where $\eta$ is the conventional symbol for the price elasticity (of demand), $x$ stands for quantity and $p$ for price, of the $i$th good. Since, in the "usual case", quantity increases as price falls, $dp_i/p_i$ is negative in this "usual case" and Marshall's convention yields a positive value for the entire expression. This convention is generally accepted in English textbook literature which, for example, gets a price elasticity greater than $+1$ for elastic demand, while on Professor Schneider's usage it would be less than $-1$. [*Tr.*]

If at a particular price the price elasticity is absolutely (i.e. neglecting the signs) greater than 1, then one says that the demand at this price is *elastic*. If the price elasticity at a particular price is absolutely smaller than 1, then demand at this price is said to be *inelastic*. If the price elasticity is nil, then the demand at this price is said to be *perfectly inelastic*. If, finally, price elasticity at a particular price is infinite, then the demand is said to be *perfectly elastic*.

If price elasticity at every price is equal to nil, this means that the same quantity of the good will be demanded at every price. The relation between demand and price may then be represented by a line parallel to the price axis (Fig. 12). If the demand at a price is perfectly elastic, this means that the household is ready to buy indefinitely large quantities at this price. In this case the relation between price and demand may be represented by a line parallel to the quantity axis (Fig. 13).

The relations between price and demand given in Figs. 12 and 13 are limiting cases. In general, the quantity demanded and the price elasticity vary at different levels of the initial price. The exact understanding of this relationship is of great importance, and must be studied in some detail. Let us consider how the demand for a good depends (*ceteris paribus*) on the price of this good, and let us imagine different alternative values for the price $p$ of a good, corresponding with different levels of demand $x$ for this same good. In the usual case $x$ will decrease as $p$ increases. The functional relationship might take the form represented in the following table:

| Price | Quantity demanded |
|-------|-------------------|
| 0     | 20                |
| 1     | 18                |
| 2     | 16                |
| 3     | 14                |
| 4     | 12                |
| 5     | 10                |
| 6     | 8                 |
| 7     | 6                 |
| 8     | 4                 |
| 9     | 2                 |
| 10    | 0                 |

At the price nil the quantity demanded will be 20 units per unit of time. That quantity can be described as the saturation demand. The price 10 at which demand completely disappears may be called the "maximum" price. As the price increases from nil to the "maximum", so the quantity demanded falls from the saturation quantity to nil.

At a price of 2 the demand is 16 units per unit of time. If this price is raised by 1, then the demand falls off by 2 units. The direct price elasticity at the price 2 amounts, therefore, approximately to:

$$\eta = -\frac{2}{16} : \frac{1}{2} = -0.25.$$

Correspondingly, if $p = 5$:

$$\eta = -\frac{2}{10} : \frac{1}{5} = -1.$$

If $p = 8$:

$$\eta = -\frac{2}{4} : \frac{1}{8} = -4.$$

It is clear that the price elasticity depends on the level of the initial price, and that it increases as the price increases.

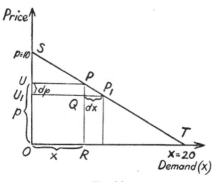

Fig. 14

In order to study this relationship more closely we may portray our demand table on a diagram. The resulting curve (Fig. 14) may be described as *the individual demand curve of the household*, and we must emphasise that this curve is drawn up under the *ceteris paribus* assumption. The curve, it must be noted, is *hypothetical*, in that it shows what quantities the household *would* buy at different prices for the good in question, other things remaining equal. The curve makes it clear, in contrast to the table, how the quantity demanded changes as the price increases through *all* values from nil to 10.[1] Let us assume that the initial price $p = OU$, with the corresponding quantity demanded being $OR = UP = x$. Let us lower this price by

[1] The equation for the demand curve is $p = 10 - \frac{1}{2}x$.

a small sum $dp = UU_1$, then the quantity demanded increases by the amount $QP_1 = dx$. The price elasticity at the price $OU$ is, therefore, given by:

$$\eta_{xp} = \frac{p}{x} \cdot \frac{d_x}{d_p} = \frac{OU}{UP} \frac{QP_1}{QP} \qquad (7)$$

As the triangles $PQP_1$ and $SUP$ are similar:

$$UP : SU = QP_1 : PQ.$$

Therefore substituting:

$$\eta_{xp} = \frac{OU}{UP} \cdot \frac{UP}{SU} = \frac{OU}{SU} = \frac{PT}{PS} \qquad (8)$$

For the case of a straight-line demand curve the price elasticity at a particular price $OU$ is given by the quotients

$$\frac{OU}{US} = \frac{PT}{PS}$$

This rule, formulated by Marshall, has general validity. Within

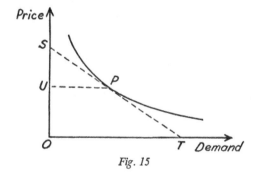

Fig. 15

an infinitely small neighbourhood of the point $P$ a curve can be replaced by the tangent to the curve at point $P$ (Fig. 15). Therefore, to find geometrically the price elasticity at a particular price $OU$ the following general rule holds: We draw the tangent $ST$ to the demand curve at point $P$ corresponding to the price $OU$; the price elasticity at that price is then given by the quotient

$$\frac{PT}{PS} = \frac{UO}{US}$$

A glance at the figure shows (a) whether the price elasticity at a particular price is larger, smaller, or equal to $-1$, and (b) how the price elasticity varies with the level of the initial price. It is at once clear that the price elasticity (a) increases indefinitely as the price approaches the "maximum" price; (b) approaches the value nil as the price approaches nil; and (c) between the price nil and the maximum price increases from nil to infinity. In our example of a straight-line demand curve the following relationships hold:

| Price | | Price Elasticity |
|-------|------|------------------|
| $p = 0$ | $0$ | Perfectly inelastic demand |
| $0 < p < 5$ | $> -1$ | Inelastic demand |
| $p = 5$ | $-1$ | |
| $5 < p < 10$ | $< -1$ | Elastic demand |
| $p = 10$ | $-\infty$ | Perfectly elastic demand |

The price elasticity increases as the price increases and passes through all values from nil to infinity.

It is therefore again clear that one can never speak simply of an elastic or inelastic demand, but only of an elastic or inelastic demand *at a particular price*.

### 5. The Relation between Individual Monetary Demand and Physical Demand

1. In Section 4 we considered demand in terms of physical quantities. We must pass now to an analysis of the relation between monetary demand and price. The concept we have developed of price elasticity will prove useful here. As we know, the monetary demand for a particular good in a particular period of time is given by multiplying the physical quantity demanded by the corresponding price:

Monetary Demand = Price × Physical Quantity.

Monetary demand, therefore, in our picture of the demand curve (Fig. 16) can, at the price $p$, be represented by the area of the rectangle formed by the distance representing price ($OU$) and that representing the quantity demanded ($OQ$). We now have to ask how, on our diagram, monetary demand varies as prices change, that is, how the area of the rectangle $OUPQ$ varies when the price $OU$ changes. The reader will see at once that the direction in which the monetary demand changes with a fall or rise in price depends essentially on the magnitude of the price elasticity at the initial price. If, taking an infinitely small reduction, the price decreases by a particular percentage and the demand increases by a particular percentage, then, whether the monetary demand increases or decreases depends on the percentage of the price fall as compared with the percentage increase in demand. If the percentage increase in demand is larger than the percentage fall in price, then monetary demand must on balance increase. That is to say, monetary demand

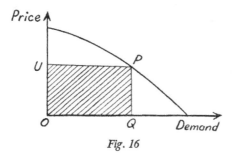

*Fig. 16*

increases with a small fall in price if the price elasticity is absolutely (neglecting the sign) greater than 1. If the price elasticity equals 1, then monetary demand remains unchanged with a small fall in price. Instead of saying that price elasticity at a price $p$ is absolutely larger than (or smaller than, or equal to) 1, one can also say that monetary demand increases (or decreases, or remains unchanged) if the price falls by a small amount; or, finally, monetary demand increases decreases or remains unchanged, if the household decides (*ceteris paribus*) to buy, instead of the quantity $x$, a slightly larger quantity at a correspondingly lower price. We have, therefore, relationships which can be set out in the following table:

|  | Inelastic demand $\eta > -1$ | $\eta = -1$ | Elastic demand $\eta < -1$ |
|---|---|---|---|
| Rise in Price | Monetary demand increases | Monetary demand unchanged | Monetary demand falls |
| Fall in Price | Monetary demand falls | | Monetary demand increases |

In short: *If demand is elastic, the physical quantity demanded and the monetary demand move in the same direction, and if it is inelastic, they move in opposite directions.*

In Fig. 17 the monetary demand corresponding to the demand curve $DD'$ is represented as a function of the physical quantity demanded. The monetary demand corresponding to the physical demand $OX$ is $XY$, and is obtained by multiplying the physical quantity demanded $OX$, by the corresponding price $XZ$; that is, it corresponds to the area of the rectangle $OUZX$. Where demand is elastic, monetary demand increases as physical demand increases: where demand is inelastic, monetary demand decreases as physical demand increases: where elasticity equals $-1$, the curve of monetary demand attains its maximum. The curve of monetary demand is often known as the *outlay curve* of the household for the particular good, because the monetary demand represents the sum of money which the

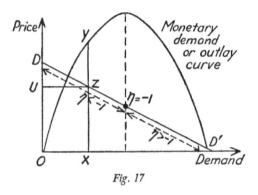

*Fig. 17*

household intends to devote to the purchase of a particular physical quantity of a good. Of course, the outlay curve may have several maxima according to the shape of the demand curve.

If the outlay for a particular good is (*ceteris paribus*) constant over a particular price range, that means that the price elasticity within this range is equal to $-1$. Between price and the physical quantity demanded the following relationship must obtain over this price range:

$$\text{Price} \, (\times) \, \text{Physical Quantity Demanded} = \text{const.}$$

or:

$$\text{Price} \, (p) = \frac{\text{const.}}{\text{Physical Quantity Demanded} \, (x)}$$

The shape of such a demand curve is that of a rectangular hyperbola. Following Marshall we may call it a constant outlay curve. The constant outlay curve is a special case in the family of so-called *iso-elastic demand curves* (that is, demand curves with constant elasticity), and has played an important part in the statistical investigation of the structure of households' demand.

2. We have shown that the direction in which expenditure or outlay on a good changes, with a small variation in the physical

quantity demanded, depends on the price elasticity. It is of great importance, therefore, to measure the size of the change in outlay which follows a change in the physical quantity demanded. The concept of *the marginal outlay* may be introduced as a measure of the quantity of this change in outlay. This concept is arrived at as follows: the outlay corresponding to the physical demand $OA$ is $AB$ (Fig. 18).

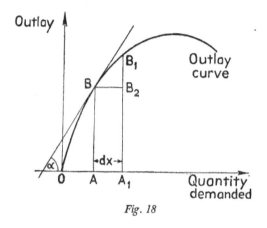

*Fig. 18*

Let us suppose that the quantity $OA$ increases very slightly by the amount $AA_1 = dx$. This increase in demand corresponds to an increase in outlay of the quantity $B_1B_2$ (Fig. 18). By the marginal outlay we understand the quotient:

$$\frac{\text{Increase in Outlay } (B_1B_2)}{\text{Increase in Physical Quantity Demanded } (BB_2)}$$

that is, the additional outlay resulting from the addition of 1 unit to the quantity demanded. As the increase in the physical quantity demanded must be taken to be infinitely small, the marginal outlay is given geometrically by the slope of the tangent to the outlay curve at the point $B$; that is, by tan $\alpha$, the angle formed by the tangent to the outlay curve at point $B$ and the horizontal axis (Fig. 18). It would be not quite exact, but would be satisfactory for most purposes, to say that the marginal outlay may be defined approximately as *the change in outlay corresponding to an increase in the quantity demanded of 1 unit*. We shall often be coming across the sort of reasoning which has led us to the concept of marginal outlay. Thinking in terms of margins, and the notion of the margin, is highly important in economic theory. Wherever it is a question of analysing the influence of small changes in economic quantities the instruments of marginal analysis must be applied. The reader must make himself thoroughly familiar with this concept.

3. It is clear from the foregoing analysis that the marginal outlay in relation to a particular physical quantity demanded is closely related to the size of the price elasticity. We must now deduce what this relation is. If the physical quantity demanded increases by a particular percentage, and the price decreases by a particular percentage, then the monetary demand (or outlay) increases by the percentage increase in demand, and decreases by the percentage fall in price. If we denote the absolute (infinitesimal) increase in demand as $dx$, the corresponding absolute (infinitesimal) fall in price as $dp$, and the change in outlay as $dA$, then:

$$dA = p \cdot x \cdot \frac{dx}{x} + p \cdot x \cdot \frac{dp}{p} \qquad (9)$$

$$= p \cdot dx + x \cdot dp$$

where the sign of $dx$ is positive, that of $dp$ is negative and *vice versa*. From (9) we obtain the following expression for the marginal outlay:

$$\frac{dA}{dx} = p + x \cdot \frac{dp}{dx}$$

$$= p\left(1 + \frac{x}{p} \cdot \frac{dp}{dx}\right) \qquad (10)$$

$$= p\left(1 + \frac{1}{\frac{p}{x} \cdot \frac{dx}{dp}}\right)$$

Now the expression $\frac{p}{x} \cdot \frac{dx}{dp}$ is simply the direct price elasticity $\eta$, so that we can write (10) in the form:

$$\frac{dA}{dx} = p\left(1 + \frac{1}{\eta}\right) \qquad (11)$$

This equation, which we shall refer to as the Amoroso-Robinson Relation, shows the relation between marginal outlay and direct price elasticity. It follows from it that the marginal outlay is positive if demand is elastic ($\eta < -1$), and negative if demand is inelastic ($\eta > -1$). We can see at once what the relationship is between marginal outlay and price. We only need to write the equation (11) in the form:

$$p - \frac{dA}{dx} = -\frac{p}{\eta}. \qquad (12)$$

From (12) it follows that *for every finite value of price elasticity marginal outlay is always smaller than price*. The difference between price and marginal outlay is larger the smaller is the price elasticity. If $\eta = -\infty$ marginal outlay equals the price. From (12) it follows also that the difference between price and marginal outlay increases as the absolute value of the price elasticity falls. The curve which represents the dependence of marginal outlay on the quantity

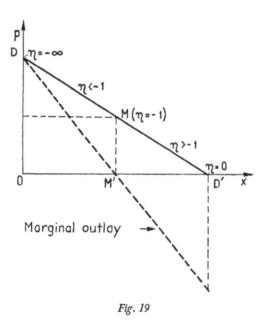

*Fig. 19*

demanded lies below the demand curve for all finite values of price elasticity, and falls as price elasticity decreases absolutely. If we consider the straight-line demand curve $DD'$ in Fig. 19, we know that the price elasticity at $D$ is infinitely small, that from $D$ to $M$ it is less than $-1$, that at the point $M$ it equals $-1$, that from $M$ to $D'$, it is greater than $-1$, and that at the point $D'$ it is nil. The curve of marginal outlay also begins at point $D$, and falls, as the quantity demanded increases, in the manner portrayed in Fig. 19. It can easily be shown that the curve of marginal outlay in the case of a straight-line demand curve is also a straight line.

From equation (11) one can also derive geometrically from a given demand curve the marginal outlay at any particular level of demand.

It was shown above that the price elasticity at point $P$ (Fig. 20) (that is, at the price $OU$) is given by the quotients $\dfrac{PT}{PS} = \dfrac{UO}{US}$. We may make use of this to derive from equation (11):

$$\frac{dA}{dx} = p + \frac{p}{\eta} = OU - OU \cdot \frac{US}{OU} = OU - US = PQ - US$$

The marginal outlay corresponding to the demand $OQ$ is arrived at by subtracting an amount equal to the distance $SU$ from the price $PQ$. This subtraction can be simply carried out by drawing from $U$ a line parallel to the tangent to the demand curve at $P$. Where this line cuts $PQ$ (that is, at $V$) is the point on the marginal outlay curve which we want. The distance $QV$ then represents the marginal outlay at the level of demand $OQ$.

To illustrate these relations further the following table is added. As the demand curve, the straight-line curve in the example on page 25 is used:

| Quantity Demanded | Price | Outlay | Marginal Outlay | Price Elasticity |
|---|---|---|---|---|
| 0 | 10 | 0 | — | |
| 1 | 9·5 | 9·5 | 9·5 | |
| 2 | 9 | 18 | 8·5 | |
| 3 | 8·5 | 25·5 | 7·5 | |
| 4 | 8 | 32 | 6·5 | |
| 5 | 7·5 | 37·5 | 5·5 | $\eta < -1$ |
| 6 | 7 | 42 | 4·5 | |
| 7 | 6·5 | 45·5 | 3·5 | |
| 8 | 6 | 48 | 2·5 | |
| 9 | 5·5 | 49·5 | 1·5 | |
| 10 | 5 | 50 | 0·5 | |
| 11 | 4·5 | 49·5 | −0·5 | |
| 12 | 4 | 48 | −1·5 | |
| 13 | 3·5 | 45·5 | −2·5 | |
| 14 | 3 | 42 | −3·5 | |
| 15 | 2·5 | 37·5 | −4·5 | |
| 16 | 2 | 32 | −5·5 | $\eta > -1$ |
| 17 | 1.5 | 25·5 | −6·5 | |
| 18 | 1 | 18 | −7.5 | |
| 19 | 0·5 | 9·5 | −8.5 | |
| 20 | 0 | 0 | −9.5 | |

4. We have seen that in the usual case the direct price elasticity is negative. Let us study now the sign for cross-elasticity. The cross-elasticity shows, as we have seen, by how much per cent the quantity

demanded of good No. i changes if the price of the good No. *k* changes (*ceteris paribus*) by 1%; that is, it tells us how much the quantity demanded by the household of a particular good is affected by a (*ceteris paribus*) price change in *another* good. For example: by how much does the demand for butter change if the price of margarine changes by 1%? Or, by how much per cent does the demand for envelopes change if the price of writing paper changes by 1%?

The cross-elasticity, therefore, describes the demand relationship

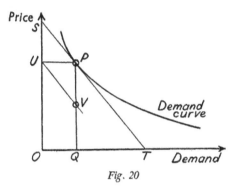

*Fig. 20*

between two goods. In general, two sorts of demand relation are possible: that of substitutability and that of complementarity. If the two goods are substitutes in the economic plan of the household, this means that the physical quantity demanded of the first good *increases* if the price of the second good (*ceteris paribus*) *increases*. This increase in the physical quantity demanded of the first good will be the greater, the greater are the possibilities of substitution between the two goods in the estimate of the household. If the price of butter rises, while that of margarine remains constant, then the quantity of butter demanded will fall and that of margarine will rise. If, on the other hand, two goods are complementary for the household, this means that the physical quantity demanded of each of the goods falls if the price of one of them (*ceteris paribus*) rises: the demand for envelopes will fall *together* with the demand for writing paper, if the price of writing paper (*ceteris paribus*) rises. This difference between substitute and complementary goods, and the relationships characterizing them, may obviously be expressed by the sign of the cross-elasticity. If two goods are substitutes then the cross-elasticity is *positive* (that is, a small rise in the price of good No. 2 leads to an *increase* in the physical quantity demanded of good No. 1). If, on the other hand, two goods are complementary, then the cross-elasticity is *negative* (that is, a small rise in the price of good No. 2 leads to a *decrease* in the physical quantity demanded of good No. 1).

## 6. The Derivation of the Aggregate Demand Function from the Individual Demand Function

1. Up to now we have been studying the economic plan of the individual household over a particular period of time. This can be expressed by the system of individual demand functions given in equations (1) and (3), assuming that we may disregard the influence of expected price changes. From the individual quantities demanded by the household one can easily obtain the relevant total demand of all consumers. We simply have to add up the individual quantities demanded by each household. If we write the system of individual demand functions of the particular households in the form of equation (3), then the total physical demand for a particular good appears as the function of the prices of all the goods desired by all households, and of all the individual incomes. The total physical demand, therefore, depends, in so far as we are concerned with income as its determinant, *not only* on the total income of the economy, *but also on the distribution of that total income among the individual households*. With the total income of society remaining constant (and with constant prices), a change in the distribution of income will alter the physical demand for the different goods.

If we denote the prices of all the goods desired by the $m$ households in an economy as $p_1, p_2, \ldots, p_n$, and the income of the households for the planning period as $y_1, y_2, \ldots, y_m$, then the following functional relationships hold for the total physical quantities demanded $X_1, \ldots, X_n$:

$$X_1 = X_1(p_1, \ldots, p_n, y_1, y_2, \ldots, y_m)$$
$$\cdot \quad \cdot \quad \cdot \quad \cdot \quad \cdot \quad \cdot \quad \cdot \quad \cdot \quad \cdot \quad \cdot \quad \cdot$$
$$\cdot \quad \cdot \quad \cdot \quad \cdot \quad \cdot \quad \cdot \quad \cdot \quad \cdot \quad \cdot \quad \cdot \quad \cdot \tag{13}$$
$$X_n = X_n(p_1, \ldots, p_n, y_1, y_2, \ldots, y_m)$$

If it is assumed that individual demand depends only on the relation between prices and incomes (see p. 6) then the aggregate or total demand functions (13) will clearly possess the same property.

2. From the system of demand functions in equation (13) the corresponding total monetary demand for different individual goods is arrived at by multiplying the physical quantities by the corresponding prices. The total monetary demand for a particular good is,

therefore, dependent on all prices, on total income and on the distribution of income.

## 7. The Micro-Economic and the Macro-Economic Consumption Function

1. By adding all the monetary demands for the individual goods one arrives at the value of the total planned consumption for the coming economic period, $C$. The following relation holds:

$$C = p_1X_1 + p_2X_2 + \ldots + p_nX_n \tag{14}$$

where the prices are those expected for the coming period, and where $X_1, \ldots, X_n$ etc., represent the *total* quantities of the individual goods which the households plan to purchase. This total planned consumption is obviously also dependent on all prices, on total income, and on the distribution of income:

$$C = C(p_1, \ldots, p_n, y_1, y_2, \ldots, y_m) \tag{15}$$

We shall describe this important relationship as *the general macro-economic consumption function for the economy*, and we must study it now in more detail. But let us first investigate the general *micro*-economic consumption function of the *individual household* which is the fundamental element in the general macro-economic consumption function for the whole economy.

2. From equation (3) the total planned consumption $c$ of a household for a period is given as follows:

$$c = p_1x_1 + \ldots + p_nx_n.$$

As the quantity demanded of *each* good is a function of the prices of *all* the goods in the economic plan of the household, and of its income, the total consumption, therefore, is a function of all prices and of the income of the household:

$$c = c(p_1, \ldots, p_n, y) \tag{16}$$

We describe this relationship as the *general micro-economic consumption function* for the household. We can derive at once from it the general savings function of the household (that is, the function which tells us how, according to the economic plan of the household, planned savings depend on prices and on income):

$$s = y - c = y - c(p_1, \ldots, p_n, y) \tag{17}$$

If we know the consumption function, then we know the savings function and *vice versa*.

In order to discover the properties of the general individual consumption function we must have the answer to two questions:

(a) How does a change in the price of a good (*ceteris paribus*) influence the total of consumption-spending?

(b) How does a change in income influence the level of total consumption-spending, all prices remaining constant?

Of these two questions the second is of special importance in the theory of employment, and we shall discuss only it here. Let us imagine that the prices of all goods are given and "frozen". Let us, then, ask what the total sum will be which the household devotes to consumption purposes, when different alternative levels of income are at its disposal in the same planning period. We shall describe the resulting functional relation as the *special individual consumption function*. The reader must always keep in mind that we are not concerned here with historical relations, or with how in the past consumption has varied with the level of income of a particular household. We are concerned with a hypothetical planned relationship: that is, what sum would be devoted in the coming planning period (at given prices) to consumption purposes *if* income was alternatively £20, £30 or £40 per month?[1] If this question was put to a typical household the answer would give us a planned consumption function as portrayed in Fig. 21. The curve begins at point $A$; that is, the household, even if it has no income at all, must spend at least the sum $OA$ to maintain its existence, prices being taken as given. The sum devoted to consumption purposes would increase as the income of the household increased. The household, for every income below $y_0$ (Fig. 21), would be incurring debts, or, what comes to the same thing, would be indulging in negative saving. The sum devoted to consumption would be larger than the income. With an income of $y_0$ consumption would exactly equal income, and with an income larger than $y_0$ consumption would be smaller than income. If we were to start from the savings of the household, the same fact could be described as planned savings increasing with the level of income. For income, smaller than $y_0$ savings would be negative. At an income of $y_0$ savings would be nil. Let us describe this income $y_0$ as the *basic income* of the household, as Alvin Hansen has called it.[2] The basic income of the household can be arrived at graphically, as in the

---

[1] It is an important task for the econometrician to attempt an answer to the question as to what can be deduced from actual historical consumption functions as to the shape of hypothetical planned consumption functions.

[2] Alvin Hansen (*Fiscal Policy and Business Cycles*, New York, 1941, p. 285) coined this term for macro-economic quantities. It can, of course, be applied to micro-economic quantities.

diagram, by drawing in a line bisecting the right angle between the two axes. Dropping a perpendicular from where this line cuts the individual consumption curve, gives us on the abscissa the basic income. The vertical distance between the consumption curve and this bisecting line then gives us the quantity of planned savings. Thus with the help of this simple construction the savings curve can be drawn in, if we have the consumption curve (Fig. 21).

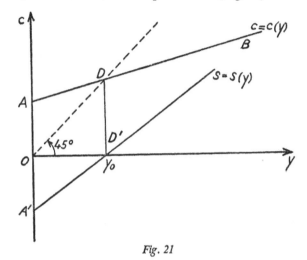

*Fig. 21*

The only empirical fact assumed so far is that the consumption of the household increases if its income increases in the same planning period. With an increase in its income the household plans (*ceteris paribus*) to increase its consumption. We have still to answer the question as to *how* consumption increases with the level of income. For this purpose let us ask what increase in consumption would result (*ceteris paribus*) from an increase in income of a particular quantity. *A priori* reasoning and experience both tell us that the increase in consumption corresponding to a particular increase in income would always be smaller than this increase in income.[1] Let us suppose now that there is a small increase in income (strictly speaking an infinitesimal increase), and describe this as $dy$; and let us

[1] "The fundamental psychological law, upon which we are entitled to depend with great confidence both *a priori* from our knowledge of human nature and from the detailed facts of experience, is that men are disposed, as a rule and on the average, to increase their consumption as their income increases, but not by as much as the increase in their income" (J. M. Keynes: *General Theory of Employment, Interest and Money*, London, 1936, p. 96).

describe the corresponding change in consumption as $dc$; then the consumption function has the following two characteristics: (a) $dy$ and $dc$ have the same sign; (b) $dc$ is smaller than $dy$. The quotient $dc/dy$ (or the change in consumption resulting from a change in income of 1 unit) is therefore, as a rule, positive and smaller than 1.[1] Let us describe the quantity $dc/dy$ as the measure of the *individual marginal propensity to consume*. In Fig. 21, for the sake of simplicity, it has been assumed that the marginal propensity to consume is

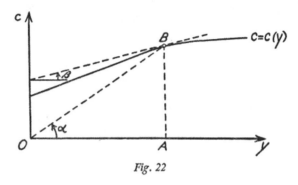

*Fig. 22*

independent of the level of income (i.e., that it is a constant). Usually, at any rate above a certain level of income, the marginal propensity to consume will decrease with a rise in income, so that the consumption curve will usually have the shape given in Fig. 22.

If one divides the consumption corresponding to a particular income, by that income, then this quotient $c/y$ gives us *the average propensity to consume* at this level of income. From the shape of the consumption curve it follows that the average propensity to consume decreases as income increases and for every level of income is larger than the marginal propensity to consume.

The average propensity to consume is then:

$$\frac{c}{y} = \frac{AB}{OA} = \tan \alpha$$

In order to study the alteration in the average propensity to consume as income increases, we simply have to ascertain how the angle $\alpha$ changes as income increases (that is, as the point $A$ moves to the right). A glance at Fig. 22 shows at once that the angle $\alpha$ decreases as income increases. The figure shows, too, that the slope of the tangent to the consumption curve at point $B$ (or the angle $\beta$) is always

[1] J. M. Keynes: *Op. cit.*, p. 96.

smaller than the slope of $OB$ (or the angle $\alpha$). Now tan $\beta$ represents simply the marginal propensity to consume, so that our statement above is proved.

The marginal propensity to save follows at once from the marginal propensity to consume. From the definition of the marginal propensity to consume:

Marginal Propensity to Save
$$= 1 - \text{Marginal Propensity to Consume} \quad (18)$$

The marginal propensity to save must also be smaller than 1. If the marginal propensity to consume *decreases* with an increase in income, so the marginal propensity to save *increases*. From the equation, income equals consumption plus saving, the average propensity to save is given as follows:

Average Propensity to Save
$$= 1 - \text{Average Propensity to Consume} \quad (19)$$

As the average propensity to consume decreases as income increases, so the average propensity to save increases as income increases.

We have been considering the planned consumption of a household, and therefore its savings, as dependent simply on the prices and the income expected in the planning period. With given prices, consumption and saving are then regarded simply as functions of income. Modern theory treats income, prices being given, as the most important variable for the level of consumption and saving. Our argument, as contrasted with the earlier theories, has completely disregarded the structure and level of interest rates as one of the factors influencing saving and consumption. The earlier theories laid decisive emphasis on the relation between the rate of interest and saving, *income being taken as given*. They held that savings from a given income increased and decreased as the rate of interest increased and decreased. It has been shown, and confirmed by experience, that a unique relationship of this kind between the rate of interest and savings (or total consumption spending) does not exist. It is equally possible when there is an increase in the rate of interest, for savings to be either increased or diminished; and it is also possible that savings are completely independent of the rate of interest. The level of interest rates is only one of the many different factors which influence saving. Saving is undertaken, for example, to form a reserve for emergencies, for the sake of one's children's education, in order to buy a house or a car, in order to accumulate a fortune for reasons of prestige, because income is too large to spend entirely on consumption, or, finally, in order to obtain interest.[1] Clearly, according to the different objects of saving, the influence of the rates of interest expected in the planning period on the level of savings, if it exists at all, may work in either direction. If, for example, the aim is to build up a particular sum for buying a house in five years, then it is possible that a *higher* rate of interest, if it is regarded as permanent, will lead to *smaller* annual quotas of saving, than would a *lower* rate of interest. It is equally possible that the annual savings would remain unchanged, and that the objective would be reached earlier. A definite *"ceteris paribus"* relationship between rates of interest and saving cannot be guessed at *a priori*. The only fact that is certain is that the rate of interest has only a secondary influence on consumption, and, therefore, on the savings of the household, in any particular period of time. It is simply the level of income, prices being given, which is, in the short run, of primary importance. The structure of interest rates certainly has an influence on the *form* of savings. Of that we shall come to speak in another volume.

3. If we consider prices as given constants, then we can write the individual consumption function of a household as follows:

$$c = c(y) \tag{20}$$

where $y$ is the income, and $c$ the consumption in the planning period. The characteristics of these functions were discussed in the previous section. If we suppose that the economy is made up of $m$ households, then there are altogether $m$ individual consumption functions:

$$c_1 = c_1(y_1)$$
$$\cdot \quad \cdot \quad \cdot$$
$$\cdot \quad \cdot \quad \cdot \tag{21}$$
$$c_m = c_m(y_m)$$

where $y_1 \ldots y_m$ represents a particular individual income and $c_1 \ldots c_m$ the total sums devoted by each individual to consumption. The total consumption $C$ for the community as a whole is arrived at by adding up the individuals' consumption, and is seen to be a function of the individual incomes:

$$C = C(y_1, y_2, \ldots, y_m) \tag{22}$$

As the total of individual incomes is the total income of the

[1] J. M. Keynes: *Op cit.*, pp. 107/8; A. Mahr: "Zinshöhe, Sparen und Kapitalbildung" in *Zeitschrift für Nationalökonomie*, Bd. X, pp. 362–76; H. C. Wallich: "The Changing Significance of the Interest Rate" in *American Economic Review*, 1946, p. 771; M. Ezekiel: "Saving, Consumption and Investment" in *American Economic Review*, 1942.

community, we could also say that the total consumption of a community depends on the size of, and the distribution of, the community's income. If we assume that the distribution of income depends in some way on the level of the community's income $Y$, then, prices being given, total consumption can be represented as a function of the level of the community's income:

$$C = C(Y) \tag{23}$$

This function may be described as the *special macro-economic consumption function*. We shall examine it in greater detail in Vol. III (Money, Income and Employment) (p. 95). Its characteristics are given directly by the characteristics of the individual (micro-economic) consumption function on which it is based[1]:

(a) An increase in the value of the national income brings (*ceteris paribus*) an increase in the value of consumption.

(b) An increase $dY$ in the national income corresponds (*ceteris paribus*) to an increase $dC$ in consumption, which will be smaller than the increase in the national income. The (macro-economic) marginal propensity to consume of the whole community is, therefore, positive and smaller than 1.

Statistical and econometric studies have shown that the assumptions we have made, in discussing the individual consumption function, about the significance of the level of interest rates for consumption, hold good also for the macro-economic consumption function. No particular influence of the level of interest rates on the total of savings (and hence on the total of consumption) could be found for the economy as a whole. A definite influence could hardly be expected in view of the numerous different motives which affect saving. The application of multiple correlation analysis to the relationships between consumption, interest, and income, yielded no significant correlation between the rate of interest and consumption. *It is, therefore, legitimate (prices being taken as given) to regard the level of national income as the sole relevant variable for the level of consumption and to write the special macro-economic consumption function in the form of equation (23).* If prices are assumed to change, then, of course, the consumption function changes. The same is true if the tastes of the household and its propensity to save alter. If the households, with prices constant, become thriftier, this means that out of every level of income less is consumed than before. The

---

[1] The reader is again reminded that in formulating these characteristics we are not concerned with historical relations, but with the relations between consumption and different levels of the national income in the same planning period.

consumption function would shift downwards (Fig. 23). It can be seen at once from this diagram that the basic income is smaller in a thrifty economy than it is in one that is less thrifty. It is essential to distinguish carefully between an increase in consumption out of a *higher* income, with the consumption function remaining the same

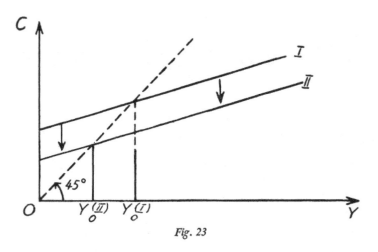

*Fig. 23*

(or, as Keynes puts it, with a given propensity to consume), and an increase in consumption out of a *given* income, *with a change in the consumption function* (or a changed propensity to consume).

### 8. The Long-Term Economic Plan of the Household (Dynamic Demand Functions)

Up to now, in analysing the demand of the household for a particular good in the coming period, we have always assumed that its plans take account only of the prices that it expects to be charged in that coming period for the goods which it desires (and of the level of total consumption-spending). In studying the way in which demand for good *A* depends (*ceteris paribus*) on its price, we asked what quantities of this good the household would demand in the coming period with the price at different levels. The magnitudes in this demand relation all related to this same period. For a number of goods, especially for those that are capable of being stored and which can be used by the household in subsequent periods, it will take into account, when planning its demand, not only the prices expected in *this* period, *but also the prices expected in subsequent periods*, and, in the case of storable goods, the existing stocks. The plan will relate not simply to a single period, but to several periods. It will be a *long-term* plan.

If we describe the expected price of a good in the coming period, $t$ until $t + 1$, as $p_t$, the price expected in the next period, $t + 1$ until $t + 2$, as $p_{t+1}$, and so on, and the level of stocks at time $t$ as $L_t$, then for the period $t$ until $t + 1$, planned demand, $x_t$, will depend (*ceteris paribus*) on $p_t, p_{t+1}, p_{t+2} \ldots$ and $L_t$:

$$x_t = f(p_t, p_{t+1}, p_{t+2}, \ldots, L_t) \qquad (24)$$

that is, demand in the coming period will depend (*ceteris paribus*) on prices in *this* period, on the *expected* prices in *subsequent* periods, and on the stocks at the moment of planning. How far into the future the expected development of prices is taken into account at the moment of formulating plans will depend on what Tinbergen has called the *economic horizon*. If we describe the expected development of prices (or the *tendency* of prices) approximately by the first derivative of the function $p(t)$, which tells us how in the judgment of the household the price will vary through time, we can write the equation (24) in this form:[1]

$$x_t = f\left(p_t, \frac{dp_t}{dt}, L_t\right) \qquad (25)$$

Such demand functions may be described as *dynamic* demand functions. We introduce this term here without going further into the characteristics of dynamic relationships. This will be done in Chapter III.

On the characteristics of this function the following remarks may be made:

(a) With a given price tendency $\left(\dfrac{dp_t}{dt}\right)$, and with a given level of stocks, the quantity demanded in the period $t$ until $t + 1$ depends simply on the prices in this period. The nature of this dependency has already been studied in detail. The usual demand function, relating simply to a single period, is therefore contained in equation (25) as a special case.

(b) With given prices in the coming period, and a given level of stocks, demand in the coming period depends on the expected price tendency: if a fall in prices is expected (*ceteris paribus*) the demand will decrease, and will decrease the more the greater the expected fall

[1] Cf. R. Frisch: "Statikk og Dynamikk i den Økonomiske Teori" in *National-økonomisk Tidskrift*, 1929, pp. 341–3. Also G. C. Evans: *Mathematical Introduction to Economics*, New York, 1930, p. 36. (Evans does not take stocks into account.)

in prices. If a rise in prices is expected (*ceteris paribus*) the demand will increase, and will increase the more the greater the expected increase in prices. An expected fall in price for the coming period, and a subsequent rising price tendency will, therefore, *both* have the effect of increasing demand.

(c) With prices for the coming period given, and with a given tendency for future prices, demand in the coming period will depend on the level of stocks: the higher the level of stocks at the beginning of the period the smaller, as a rule, will be the demand in that period.

The function (25) can be illustrated numerically in the same way as we have, several times in this chapter, illustrated the usual single-period demand functions. Following Frisch[1] we may take the example of the purchase of coke. The quantity demanded, $x$, represents the purchase planned for the following week, and the price tendency $\dot p = \dfrac{dp}{dt}$ gives the expected rise or fall in prices per week. In planning demand so as to take account of the future development of prices and of the level of stocks, no equality can be assumed between the amount purchased and the amount used up in a period. Parallel with the purchasing plans, a consumption plan must be drawn up. But we need not go any further into these relationships in this introductory chapter.

| | $L_t = 0$ cwt. | | | | | $L_t = 10$ cwt. | | |
| --- | --- | --- | --- | --- | --- | --- | --- | --- |
| | $\dot p = -0.5$ | $\dot p = -0.25$ | $\dot p = 0$ | $\dot p = +0.25$ | $\dot p = +0.5$ | $\dot p = -0.25$ | $\dot p = 0$ | $\dot p = +0.25$ |
| $p = 1$, $x =$ | | | 7 | 9 | 20 | | 6 | 8 |
| $= 2$ | | | 6 | 7 | 12 | | 5 | 6 |
| $= 3$ | 3 | 4 | 5 | 6 | 12 | 3 | 4 | 5 |
| $= 4$ | 2 | 3 | 4 | 5 | 6 | 2 | 3 | 4 |

## BIBLIOGRAPHY

J. Åkerman: *Ekonomisk Teori*, I. Lund, 1939.

K. E. Boulding: *Economic Analysis*. 3rd ed., New York, 1955.

A. L. Bowley: *Mathematical Groundwork of Economics*, London, 1923.

J. R. Hicks: *Value and Capital*, 2nd ed. London, 1946.

A. Marshall: *Principles of Economics*, 8th ed. London, 1946.

V. Pareto: *Manuel d'Économie Politique*, 2nd ed. Paris, 1927.

[1] *Op. cit.*, p. 342.

U. Ricci: "Klassifikation der Nachfragekurven auf Grund des Elastizitäts-begriffes." *Archiv für Sozialwissenschaft und Sozialpolitik*, 1932.

P. A. Samuelson: *Economics: An Introductory Analysis*, 4th ed. New York, 1959.

P. A. Samuelson: *Foundations of Economic Analysis*, 2nd ed. Cambridge, Mass, 1951.

H. Schultz: *The Theory and Measurement of Demand*, Chicago, 1938.

H. von Stackelberg: *The Theory of the Market Economy*, Transl. A. T. Peacock. London, 1952.

F. von Wieser: "Theorie der gesellschaftlichen Wirtschaft," *Grundriss der Sozialökonomik*, Abteilung I, Teil II. 2nd ed. Tübingen, 1924.

H. Wold: *Demand Analysis. A Study in Econometrics*, Stockholm, 1952.

F. Zeuthen: *Economic Theory and Method*, London, 1955.

O. von Zwiedineck-Südenhorst, *Allgemeine Volkswirtschaftslehre*, 2nd ed. Berlin, Göttingen, Heidelberg, 1948.

*The Theory of the Consumption Function:*

J. S. Duesenberry: *Income, Saving and the Theory of Consumer Behavior*, Cambridge, Mass. 1949.

M. Friedmann: *A Theory of the Consumption Function*, Princeton, 1957.

A. Hansen: *Fiscal Policy and Business Cycles*, New York, 1941.

A. Hansen: *Business Cycles and National Income*, New York, 1951.

A. Hansen: *A Guide to Keynes*, New York, 1953.

J. M. Keynes: *General Theory of Employment, Interest and Money*, London, 1936.

# CHAPTER II

# The Economic Plan of the Firm

The economic plan of a firm is made up, first, of decisions about what it has to purchase for its own productive activities *from* other economic units, and, secondly, of decisions about sales *to* other economic units. The firm is, therefore, linked in two directions with other economic units: on the one side it is a demander of labour and material factors of production from households and other firms; and on the other side it is a supplier of the products which are produced by its particular combination of labour and material factors of production, and which are in turn demanded by households and other firms. We now have to examine this part of the process of production as it takes place within the firm, and the forces motivating it. We have to ask what determines the kind and quantity of purchases which the firm makes *from* other economic units, and the kind and quantity of sales it makes *to* other economic units.

## Section A

## OBJECTIVES, MODES OF BEHAVIOUR, AND FORMS OF MARKET

### 1. The Objectives of the Firm

The first essential determinant of the kind and quantity of purchases and sales that a firm makes is the objective after which it is striving. In the theory of the free exchange economy we usually start from the assumption that the private firm, with which alone we are concerned, aims at the maximum profit under the conditions in which it is operating; that is, it aims at making as large as possible the difference between its revenue (or the selling value of the quantities of goods it plans to sell) and the (planned) costs of this quantity. As the amount of profit relates to a particular period of time, we have to ascertain the period over which the firm is aiming at maximising its profits. Here we have to distinguish between profits planned for a single economic period (for example, for the coming year) and the planning of a profit over several economic periods. In planning of the first kind (or "short-term" planning) a maximum revenue is being aimed at only for the single period, while in the second kind of planning (or "long-term" planning) the aim of the firm is to maximize profit over several periods. We shall be concerned with both kinds of planning and with both kinds of objective. Moreover, we shall have to examine the problems and plans of the firm which is aiming at other objectives (for example, a conventional rate of profit).

## 2. The Modes of Behaviour of the Firm

In addition to its objective, there is a second factor of fundamental importance for the quantity and nature of the purchases and sales that a firm makes: its *mode of behaviour*. Only when we know what mode of behaviour the firm is adopting to achieve its objective, can we tell how its production, supply, sales, and purchases are determined. It is only in the last twenty years that this fundamental fact, so important in understanding the course of the economic process in an exchange economy, has been understood and studied in full detail.[1] A precise study of the real world has taught us that in the modern exchange economy a large number of different modes of behaviour are adopted, and that the course of the economic process varies with the nature of the economic behaviour of the units involved. It is, therefore, necessary to survey systematically the main types of economic behaviour which actually occur.

### a. The Behaviour of the Quantity-Adjuster

There are some firms which take the prices of the goods they are selling, and (or) the prices of the factors of production, as given, and assume that they are unable to influence them. Such firms can only decide as to the quantities of goods they will sell or buy at the given ruling prices, that is, adjust the quantities of their sales or purchases

---

[1] The fundamental work on this family of problems was written by R. Frisch, "Monopoly, Polypoly, The Concept of Force in the Economy," (1933) translated in *International Economic Papers*, No. 1, 1951. See also F. Zeuthen, *Problems of Monopoly and Economic Warfare*, London, 1932, H. v. Stackelberg, *Marktform und Gleichgewicht*, Vienna, 1934. Among recent accounts are: F. Machlup, "Tipi di concorrenza nella vendita," *Giornale degli Economisti*, 1941; R. Triffin, *Monopolistic Competition and General Equilibrium Analysis*, Cambridge, Mass. 1941; E. Schneider, "Zielsetzung, Verhaltensweise und Preisbildung," *Jahrbücher für Nationalökonomie und Statistik*, vol. 137, 1943; F. Zeuthen, *Economic Theory and Method*, London, 1955; J. Tinbergen, *Beperkte Concurrentie*, Leyden, 1946.

according to the market prices. A firm behaving in this way may be described as a "quantity-adjuster". What the firm itself is fixing are quantities of goods, and these quantities may be described as its *action parameter*. By the action parameter of an economic unit we understand a variable in its plan which the economic unit can fix according to its own estimates and decisions.

### b. *Price-fixing on the Basis of an Expected Price-Sales Relation*

1. A seller may be in a position to fix the selling price of a good according to his own estimates, while the buyers decide how much

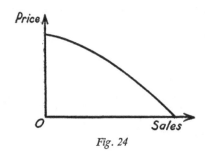

*Fig. 24*

they are ready to buy at this price. The seller in deciding about the price to fix must form an idea as to the quantities of the good which he believes himself able to sell at different prices. In his economic plan he will range against different prices the quantities he thinks that he will most probably sell at each price: if I fix the price at 10s. per unit, I expect that in the coming economic period I shall be able to sell 1000 units; if I fix the price at 9s. per unit, I may expect that in the coming period I shall be able to sell 1100 units, and so on. The functional relation given in this way between prices and expected sales may be described as the *expected individual price–sales function of the seller* (or demand as seen by the seller). The diagram (Fig. 24) represents this demand as seen by the seller. This sort of price–sales (or demand) curve is completely different from the individual demand curve of a household which we described in Chapter I. The individual demand curve of a household tells us something about the actual dispositions of the household based on its economic plan: if the price of bread is 5d., then the household *will buy* 10 loaves in the planning period; if the price of bread in the same period is only 4½d., then the household (*ceteris paribus*) *will buy* 11 loaves, etc. The individual price–sales curve of the seller contains simply a statement about the levels of sales *expected* at different alternative prices in one and the same period of time. The seller's action-parameter is the price, while the quantity to be sold is for him an *expectation parameter*. The reverse is the case for the household, for which the quantity is an action-parameter and the price an expectation parameter. The seller will base his decisions about the price in the planning period on the expected price–sales relation. We therefore describe this mode of behaviour as *price-fixing on the basis of an expected or conjectured price–sales relation*.

2. Let us now consider in greater detail how a seller plans his expected price–sales function. If the seller believes that his sales in the planning period depend simply on the price he fixes, that is, that the prices fixed by other sellers of the good in question are irrelevant for his sales and for the actions of the buyers, then we say that *the seller is acting as a monopolist*. More generally, we may say that *a seller is acting monopolistically if he calculates that his sales depend solely on his own action-parameters and not on the action-parameters of other sellers*. If the price is the action-parameter of the seller, then we describe this as *monopolistic price-fixing*, or more precisely as the fixing of prices according to the monopolistic mode of behaviour.

A different mode of behaviour occurs if the seller, in making his economic plan, calculates that his sales do not depend simply on his own action-parameters, but also on those of other sellers. Let us assume that seller No. 1 reckons that the sales $x_1$ of the good which he supplies, depend both on the price $p_1$ which he fixes for his good, and on the price $p_2$ which the seller of good No. 2 fixes. His expected price-sales function then has the form:

$$x_1 = f(p_1, p_2) \tag{1}$$

The seller No. 1 can, of course, only fix his own price $p_1$. But as he assumes that his sales also depend on the price $p_2$ of the other seller, he will take this fact into account in planning his price and sales. There are two cases to be distinguished:

(a) The seller No. 1 may assume that his sales also depend on the price of seller No. 2, but does not believe that the price fixed by seller No. 2 will be altered *as a consequence of* changes in $p_1$. Thus the seller No. 1, in considering his expected price–sales function, takes the price $p_2$ as constant. A mode of behaviour such as we have just described may be termed *polypolistic*. If the price is fixed by the seller, then one may speak of *polypolistic price-fixing*.

(b) The seller No. 1 may assume that his sales also depend on the price $p_2$ of the seller No. 2, and that the seller No. 2 will react in one way or another to changes in the price $p_1$. He will then, in drawing up his expected price–sales function, take account of the reaction which he expects from seller No. 2. The mode of behaviour described here of seller No. 1 may be termed *oligopolistic*. If the price is fixed by the seller then one may speak of *oligopolistic price-fixing*.

It is, of course, quite possible, that out of a number of sellers, the quantity of whose sales depends in the judgment of each one of them on the prices of all the others, *one* may act polypolistically and *another* oligopolistically, or all of them may act in either of the two ways.

A numerical example may help to make these two different modes of behaviour clearer. Seller No. 1 offers the good $X$, while seller No.

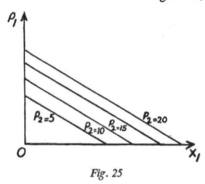

*Fig. 25*

2 supplies a competing good $Y$. The seller No. 1 reckons that the sales $x_1$ of his good depend in the following way on the prices $p_1$ and $p_2$ of the two goods, and on these two prices alone:

$$x_1 = 10 - 2p_1 + \tfrac{1}{2}p_2 \qquad (2)$$

The fact that the two goods are substitutes for one another is shown by the fact that, $p_1$ being given, $x_1$ increases with $p_2$. The cross-elasticity of $x_1$ in relation to $p_2$ is therefore positive. If the price fixed by seller No. 2 is 10, then with seller No. 1 acting polypolistically the following expected price–sales function results:

$$x_1 = 15 - 2p_1.$$

If, however, the price of seller No. 2 is 20 then polypolistic behaviour by seller No. 1 gives an expected price–sales function as follows:

$$x_1 = 20 - 2p_1.$$

The price–sales curves of seller No. 1 corresponding to different prices, on the assumption of polypolistic behaviour, are pictured in Fig. 25. The higher the price $p_2$ the further the conjectured price–sales function of seller No. 1 lies from the origin $O$.

If seller No. 1 behaves as an oligopolist, a different conjectured price–sales function results. Let us assume that the price combination at the end of the planning period for the seller No. 1 is $p_1 = 1$ and $p_2 = 2$. Then, with this combination of prices in the coming period, the expected sales of seller No. 1 will, according to equation (2), be 9 units. Seller No. 1 now plans a change of price. All price changes in the real world follow on the actual prices of the previous period. (This fact, which has been described by O. v. Zwiedineck-Südenhorst as the principle of price continuity, will concern us again later on.) If the first seller now plans a reduction in price from 1 to 0·9, and

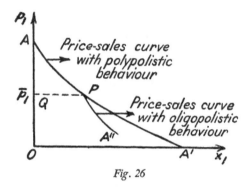

*Fig. 26*

reckons that the seller No. 2 will react by reducing his price from 2 to 1·8, then he will expect an increase of his sales from 9 to 9·1. If, on the other hand, he reckons that the second seller will reduce his price from 2 to 1·6, then he will not expect any change in sales. The price–sales function of seller No. 1 can, therefore, only be obtained *if we make an assumption as to how, in the judgment of seller No. 1, the second seller will react to price changes by seller No. 1.* An assumption about the behaviour of seller No. 2, which, in fact, often corresponds with oligopolistic behaviour in the real world, is as follows: seller No. 1 reckons that seller No. 2 will react to reductions in the price $p_1$ by reducing his price $p_2$, but will not follow increases in price. It is not difficult to see that the individual price–sales function of seller No. 1, so long as this assumption holds good, will be as in Fig. 26. In Fig. 26 $\bar{p}_1$ is the price of the first seller actually ruling at the beginning of the planning period. The sales expected at this price, and at the actually ruling price of seller No. 2 for $x_2$ will, in the coming period, be $PQ$. The expected price–sales function of seller No. 1 will be $APA'$ if we assume that he acts as a polypolist. If the first seller reckons that the price of the second seller will remain unchanged if the price $p_1$ is raised, then his expected price–sales curve (for prices where $p_1 \geqq \bar{p}_1$) may be represented by the arc $AP$. On the other hand, if he reckons that when he reduces his price the second seller will react in a parallel way, then his sales will always be smaller, at any price $p_1 \leqq \bar{p}_1$, than if he was counting on conditions of polypoly. The price–sales curve will for all prices below $\bar{p}_1$ lie to the left of the arc $PA'$. In Fig. 26 it has been assumed that the sales of seller No. 1 increase with a reduction in the price $p_1$ below its initial level $\bar{p}_1$. How large the increase in sales will be, or whether *any* increase can be expected, depends on the notion of seller No. 1 as to the strength of the reaction of seller No. 2, and as to the behaviour of the buyers. What is decisive is that if this assumption is made as to the behaviour of seller No. 2, the expected price–sales curve of seller No. 1 at the initial price (i.e., the actual price at the moment of planning) will have a kink. This kinky demand curve has a certain role in the modern theory of oligopoly which we shall have to discuss in due course. The kinky price–sales function also occurs, of course, if the first seller is confronted with two or more sellers of substitute goods, and reckons that they will all follow any reduction in price with a parallel reaction. The mode of behaviour which gives a kinky price–sales function for a seller under oligopolistic conditions is, of course, only one out of a number of different possibilities.[1]

### c. *Fixing the Quantity of Sales on the Basis of an Expected Price–Sales Relation*

The kind of behaviour discussed in the previous section also applies in the case where a seller, instead of fixing the price, fixes the quantity. The action-parameter of the seller is then the quantity, while the fixing of the price is in the hands of the buyers. The expected price–sales function of a seller then tells us what price the seller believes he can obtain for a particular quantity of a good in the planning period. In the firm's planning of its price–sales function we have again to distinguish between the quantity sold monopolistically, polypolistically, or oligopolistically.

### d. *The Fixing or Accepting of Options*

A seller may be said to be *fixing an option* if he simultaneously fixes both the price and the quantity and leaves it to the other party to choose between accepting or rejecting the option. The mode of

---

[1] For instructive examples of the observed behaviour of oligopolists see G. J. Stigler: "The Kinky Oligopoly Demand Curve and Rigid Prices" in *Journal of Political Economy*, vol. IV., 1947, p. 432.

behaviour of the other party may then be called that of an accepter or taker of an option.

### e. Economic Warfare: Strategy and Manœuvre

All the modes of behaviour we have mentioned up to now possess one common characteristic: they imply peaceful adaptation between economic units, that is, they exclude economic warfare or manœuvre. There are, of course, many different kinds of behaviour adopted either in open economic warfare, or in manœuvring between economic units. Recently these have come to be studied systematically.[1]

### 3. Competition Between Sellers

1. We said in Para. 2 above that the seller of a particular good behaves monopolistically if, in drawing up his economic plan, he reckons that his sales depend only on his own action-parameters (for example, on his own prices), and not on the action-parameters of other sellers (for example, the prices which other sellers fix for the goods they offer). That is, changes in price by other sellers are regarded as having no influence on a seller's own sales. A seller who behaves monopolistically feels that he is alone on the supply side. He reckons that, given his own action-parameters, his sales depend only on the behaviour of the buyers, and do not depend on the behaviour of other sellers.

2. When a seller thinks, or knows, that his sales do not depend only on his own actions and on the behaviour of the buyers, but also on the actions of other sellers, then one may say that *there is competition between these sellers*. If, for example, seller No. 1 of a good $X$ reckons that his sales depend on his own price, on the price of a seller No. 2, and on the behaviour of the buyers, whether the good $X$ is identical or not with that offered by seller No. 2, we may say that competition exists between these two sellers.

3. Let us now study more closely the nature of the competitive relationships between sellers. Let us suppose that seller No. 1 is offering a good $X$ and seller No. 2 a good $Y$. The prices of these two goods are the same. Prices being given, both sellers have a certain sales, revenue, and total profit per unit of time. Let us now assume that seller No. 1 slightly lowers the price of his good $X$, while seller

---

[1] Economic strategy has been studied especially by F. Zeuthen (*op. cit.*), and also: H. Möller: *Kalkulation, Absatzpolitik, und Preisbildung*, Vienna, 1941; K. W. Rothschild: "Price Theory and Oligopoly" in *Economic Journal*, 1947; and the great work of J. v. Neumann and O. Morgenstern: *Theory of Games and Economic Behaviour*, Princeton, 1947.

No. 2 retains his price unchanged. Then two cases are possible: (a) all the customers of seller No. 2 may move to seller No. 1, and seller No. 2 lose his entire sales; (b) seller No. 2 may only lose a part of his sales to seller No. 1.

(a) If seller No. 2 loses all his customers, that means that the customers are indifferent as between the two sellers, or that the buyers have no preferences between the two sellers. One may then say that *competition between the two sellers is perfect or "homogeneous"* (Triffin). The two goods offered by the two sellers are regarded by the buyers as economically identical. Perfect competition, of course, presupposes that the buyers know all the facts as to what is being offered by the sellers. The selling side of the market must, so to speak, be perfectly transparent to all the buyers. It follows from the character of the perfectly competitive relationship that at any one moment the same price must rule for all sellers (Jevons' Law of Indifference). Whether, therefore, perfect competition in fact exists between sellers can only be discovered by one seller trying to alter the price common to himself and all the other sellers.

(b) If all the customers do not move from seller No. 1 to seller No. 2 this means that some buyers have preferences between the two sellers. The goods offered by the two sellers are not, in the judgment of some of the buyers, economically identical. One may then say that the relation between the sellers is one of *imperfect or "heterogeneous" competition* (Triffin). With imperfect competition, different prices can exist at one and the same moment for the goods of competing suppliers, without all the purchasers moving to the cheapest seller. If the selling side of the market is not completely known to all the buyers, then it is, of course, possible that a competitive relationship which was imperfect at first may become perfect as knowledge increases. One may then speak of a *temporary imperfection of competition* (Zeuthen). With increasing knowledge or "transparency" of conditions, existing differences in prices will disappear.

The imperfection of competition between sellers depends mainly on the existence of preferences on the part of the buyers as between the different individual sellers, i.e. on the fact that the goods offered are not regarded as economically identical, which, of course, does not exclude their being physically identical. Where there is economic identity physical identity can usually be assumed, and, therefore, with perfect competition, the goods offered by all sellers will generally be physically identical. Economic heterogeneity of goods is, on the other hand, equally possible whether the goods are physically identical or not.

Reasons for the existence of consumers' preferences may be (1) the spatial distribution of buyers and sellers in a particular geographical area; (2) imponderable personal reasons (e.g. in the treatment of customers by the shopkeeper, etc.); (3) in actual or believed material differences in the particular goods.

4. From these remarks about the reasons for heterogeneous competition between sellers, it follows that homogeneous competition is bound up with the fulfilment of the following conditions: (a) no personal attachments between buyers and sellers; (b) a spatial distribution of buyers and sellers within a geographical area such that no preferences can arise for reasons of distance. This condition will, for example, be fulfilled if either buyers and sellers are placed at one and the same point geographically, or if the buyers are all at one point and the sellers all at another point.

If these conditions are not fulfilled, then there will be heterogeneous competition between the sellers. It is obvious that the case of heterogeneous competition is the one most frequently met with in reality. But the study of perfect competition is not without its value for real problems. In stock exchanges and other organized markets the conditions of perfect competition are completely, or approximately, fulfilled.

5. Before we consider further the kind of competitive relationships which may exist between sellers, we must dispose of a confusion which the reader might fall into owing to the usual associations of the terms "monopoly" and "competition". Monopoly means one sole seller. By a monopolist we mean the single seller of a good precisely defined according to its nature and quality, and sold in a particular geographical area. A seller, for example, who offers a vacuum cleaner "X" as the single supplier in some precisely defined economic area has a monopoly position in respect of this good. Whether a seller has a monopoly position in a particular area for a particular precisely defined good is a question, therefore, of the *number* of sellers of this good in this area. If there are several sellers, then the individual seller has not got a monopoly position; the single seller then has competitors. If, on the other hand, only a single seller exists, then there is a monopoly. We can see at once that "monopoly" in this morphological sense has no necessary connexion with the "monopolistic mode of behaviour" of a seller which we defined earlier. Monopolistic behaviour occurs if a seller in his economic plan reckons that his sales depend only on his own parameter of actions (for example, on his price) and on the behaviour of the buyers, but does not depend on the action-parameters of other sellers. As soon as a seller reckons that his sales also depend on the action-parameters of other sellers he is no longer behaving as a monopolist. He no longer feels himself alone on one side of the market. From this definition of the monopolistic mode

of behaviour it follows that a supplier A, who in the morphological sense (that is, according to the *number* of sellers) is a "monopolist", need not "act monopolistically". It might be that other sellers in the same geographical area are offering goods which might not be physically identical with his own good, but which are regarded by the buyers as substitutes, so that the sale of his own goods does not depend only on his own prices but on the prices of the goods of other sellers. There would therefore exist between seller A and the sellers B and C a competitive relationship, although A was the sole supplier of his good in his region. On the other hand, it is perfectly possible that physically the same good may be supplied by two sellers in the same area, so that judging by the number of sellers there is competition, although both sellers behave monopolistically in drawing up their economic plans. If, for example, the two sellers are spatially situated so far apart that their markets, even at a price of nil ex-works do not overlap, then neither seller, in fixing his own price, has any reason for taking account of the prices fixed by the other seller. The first seller will act as though the second was not there. He will consider his sales as depending only on his own prices and on the customers. If, according to the numbers in the market, a competitive relation exists between monopolistic suppliers of different goods, then one may suitably speak of *monopolistic competition between sellers*.

*There can be no doubt that for the course of the economic process through time it is only the mode of behaviour of the economic subject that is relevant.* The morphological structure of an economic area, or the numbers of sellers and buyers in it, plays no role in the first instance. It can only be of significance if particular modes of behaviour are bound to particular forms of supply and demand. Such a relationship does not necessarily hold, as we have seen above. A monopolistic supplier in the morphological sense may behave monopolistically, polypolistically, oligopolistically or in some other way: and a seller of what is physically the same good as that of other sellers can, as we have shown, behave differently according to the form of the selling side of the market, when he draws up his economic plan. This fact, that in general a definite relationship does not exist between the morphological structure of the demand or supply side of the market and the mode of behaviour which is adopted, justifies us in treating the morphology of the supply and demand in a particular geographical area as being of secondary importance. This, of course, is not to say that it is not of great interest to classify demand and supply according to the number and size of the particular suppliers and demanders, as well as according to the nature of the goods offered by the individual sellers and demanded by the individual buyers. But what is always decisive for the course of the economic process is simply the mode of behaviour of the individual economic subject.

6. We must now examine more closely the two kinds of competitive relationships, or competitive modes of behaviour, discussed above. Competition between sellers may be either homogeneous or heterogeneous, and the sellers may be acting either polypolistically or oligopolistically. We may speak, therefore, *of polypolistic (or oligopolistic) homogeneous (or heterogeneous) competition.* The question as to how the individual sellers in homogeneous or heterogeneous competition act in a particular case, is a question which can only be decided empirically. If a competitive relationship holds between a *large number of relatively small sellers,* then one can, *a priori,* regard a polypolistic mode of behaviour on the part of each seller as the most probable. As each seller is only, as it were, a drop in the ocean compared with *all* the sellers, we can speak in this case of *atomistic competition* instead of polypoly, and it can be assumed that the individual seller will not reckon that if he lowers his own price there will be a reaction from the other sellers. The loss of customers to the seller who lowers his price will be distributed among so many other sellers that no one of them will feel any appreciable change in sales. If, on the other hand, a competitive relationship holds between a *small number of relatively large* sellers, then it may be expected *a priori* that the individual seller will behave oligopolistically. He will have to assume, for example, under heterogeneous competition, that a reduction in his price will lead to so appreciable an alteration in the sales of his competitors that sooner or later they will react to his price-cut. Here again, there is no necessary relation between the morphological structure of the demand and supply side of the market on the one hand and mode of behaviour applied on the other. What is important for polypolistic and oligopolistic competition is *primarily* always the mode of behaviour of sellers, and not their number and relative size.[1] If we follow the usual terminology in describing polypolistic competition between sellers as a competitive relationship between a large number of relatively small sellers, it must always be remembered that we are only taking as an example one particular form of supply with which the polypolistic mode of behaviour can be regarded *a priori* as the most probable. In many of the writings on the subject, "oligopoly" or "polypoly"

---

[1] "The criterion of polypoly is not simply 'large numbers', but rather a way of planning and acting, usually associated with the existence of a large number of sellers in the market" (F. Machlup: "Tipi di concorrenza nella vendita" in *Giornale degli Economisti*, 1941, p. 141).

refer to the morphological structure of the supply side of the market. Oligopoly on the supply side then means the existence of a few relatively large sellers, duopoly on the supply side the existence of two relatively large sellers, and polypoly on the supply side the existence of many relatively small sellers. These concepts must be strictly distinguished from the corresponding terms for the different modes of behaviour.

What we have said here applies to heterogeneous as well as to homogeneous competition. But in respect of homogeneous competition there are one or two further special features to notice. We have already remarked that with homogeneous competition differences in price cannot exist, because the goods offered by the sellers are treated as identical by the buyers and no preferences exist between the individual sellers.

Let us examine, first, the case where the sellers decide on the amount to be sold while the buyers name the price (the same for all sellers) at which the sales will take place. The action-parameter in the economic plan of the individual seller is now the quantity to be offered. If there are a large number of relatively small sellers, so that the individual seller is not in a position to alter the price ruling for all sellers *by varying the quantity he supplies,* then one may speak of *atomistic (or polypolistic) homogeneous competition.* The individual seller in this case may be said to be an *autonomous quantity-adjuster.* In his economic plan he only has to decide what quantity he will offer at a price which he is unable to influence. This condition must be precisely understood. Only the *single* seller is unable to influence the price by varying the quantity he supplies. If *all* the sellers alter the quantity they offer, naturally the price ruling for all of them will change. The conditions are different if a small number of relatively large sellers offer goods which in the estimation of the buyers are the same. The individual seller will now be in a position, by varying the quantity he supplies, to alter the common price which the buyers fix. By diminishing (or increasing) his quantity, assuming that the quantities supplied by all the other sellers remain constant, he will be able to raise (or lower) the price obtainable, assuming, still, that one and the same price continues to be charged by all, so that the other sellers have to accept the rise (or fall) in price which he has brought about. In making his plans for a change in the quantity supplied, he will behave either oligopolistically or polypolistically, according as to whether he assumes that the other sellers will react to a change in the quantity he supplies or not. In the first case we may speak of oligopolistic (and in the second case of polypolistic) *quantity-adjusting under homogeneous competition.*

Let us now assume, on the other hand, that the sellers fix the price and the buyers determine what quantity they will buy. The action-parameter in the economic plan of the individual supplier is now the price common to all sellers. By definition, price differences cannot exist with homogeneous competition, so every seller must assume that a cut in price will be followed by all the other suppliers.

We have here been discussing, for the case of homogeneous competition, the different ways in which either the quantity supplied or the price may be acted upon, i.e. the possibilities of choosing either the quantity or the price as the action-parameter. This discussion can also, of course, be applied to the case of heterogeneous competition and to a seller acting as a monopolist.

7. The different modes of behaviour and of competitive relationships we have discussed for sellers can also be applied to buyers. We may say of a buyer that he acts as a *monopsonist* if in his economic plan he reckons that the price he has to pay depends only on his own action-parameters and not on those of other buyers. The monopsonist, in his economic planning, will consider only the behaviour of sellers, and not the behaviour of other buyers. We may define, correspondingly, homogeneous and heterogeneous competition between demanders, as well as polypolistic and oligopolistic behaviour on the part of buyers. It may be left to the reader to think out all the different cases.

8. Up to now we have discussed the competitive relationships between a given number of economic subjects, buyers or sellers. But a seller who acts as a monopolist, or who has other sellers as competitors, will have to take account of another factor in fixing his price and sales. He will have to consider whether or not there is *a possibility of new competitors*. We may say that competition is "free" if it is open to an economic subject to extend a particular existing network of competitive relationships. Competition, on the other hand, is "closed" if it is impossible to penetrate an existing network. Finally, competition is "restricted" if the existing network of competitive relationships can only be penetrated under particular conditions. The question whether entry, either on the demand side or the supply side, to a particular market is "free", "closed", or "restricted", is of the greatest importance in analysing the course of the economic process. It will be clear that with free competition an alteration in the mode of behaviour of existing competitors may be caused by the appearance of new competitors, and that this may decisively alter the course of the economic process. It is possible, for example, that oligopolistic competition may obtain between sellers, which turns into polypolistic competition when new competitors

appear. It is also possible that the former competitors may use every weapon of economic warfare to resist the penetration of new competitors.

9. We may describe as a *market* the totality of the economic relationships (exchange relationships, buying and selling relationships) between a group of sellers and buyers. The morphological structure of the supply and demand side of the market may be described as the *market form*. By the tobacconists' market in a particular geographical area we understand the network of economic relationships between the sellers and buyers of "tobacconists' goods". This concept is simply a collective term for a large number of very different sorts of goods (different brands of cigarettes and cigars, and different kinds of tobacco, etc.). To analyse the course of economic events we must, therefore, go back to the individual economic units, that is, to the particular sellers and buyers, and must examine in turn the partial markets for each particular precisely defined sort of "tobacconist's good", or each "*individual market*" (or "*Elementarmarkt*" to use Stackelberg's term). The individual market is always the primary concept, and it is always quite justifiable to limit the concept of a market simply to the individual market.

However, in studying the course of economic events through time the concept of the individual market is not essential. It must be recognized that it is the dispositions of the individual economic subjects which determine the course of the economy, and it is then clear that *what is relevant for study is simply the dispositions of the individual suppliers and demanders, and their interactions with regard to all the goods in a particular geographical area. Every supplier (or demander) of a precisely defined good is in more or less close economic relations with all other suppliers (or demanders) within a particular economic area* (Triffin). According to the problem which is being posed one can either study the complete network of supply and demand relationships, or only a section of them, i.e. engage in a "general" treatment as contrasted with a "partial" treatment. We shall be taking examples of these in Chapter IV.

### 4. The Location of Production and the Sales Area
### (An Example of Heterogeneous Competition)

1. Let us consider a seller who offers a certain good at a given price ex-works, denoted by $p$. The price which buyers of the good who are not located at the production centre must now pay for it equals the sum of its price ex-works and of the cost of transporting it from the centre of production to the point of sale. Let $p_e$ represent the price

for which the good sells at distance $e$ from the centre of production. Assuming for the sake of simplicity that transportation costs are directly proportional to the distance between the point of sale and the centre of production, we can determine this *local price $p_e$* from the equation

$$p_e = p + f \cdot e \tag{1}$$

where $f$ is the freight rate per physical unit and per mile (say, ton-mile). Assume, again for simplicity, that transportation always takes the geometrically shortest route between the centre of production and

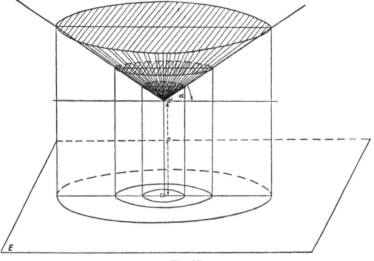

*Fig. 27*

the point of sale. It follows at once that all points of sale having the same local price for the good in question will lie on a circle centred on the production centre $C$ and having the radius $e$.

The influence of distance ($e$) upon the local price can be shown in striking fashion if above every point of sale we erect a straight line, perpendicular to the earth's surface, the height of which indicates the local price. We then obtain a kind of funnel (Fig. 27), called *Launhardt's* Funnel in honour of the scholar to whom we owe this construction.[1] On our assumptions it is shaped like an inverted cone

---

[1] Wilhelm Launhardt was professor at the Hannover College of Technology. He produced the construction of the funnel in his book *Mathematische Begründung der Volkswirtschaftslehre*, (Leipzig, 1885) and applied it most skilfully to problems of location and of the market economy.

of which the apex $C'$ lies at a distance of $p$, vertically above the centre of production $C$. The straight lines (or slant edges of the cone) which ascend in every direction from the point $C'$ all have the slope of $\tan \alpha = f$.

For many purposes we need consider not the funnel but only the section which results when the funnel is cut by a plane through $CC_1$ (Fig. 28).

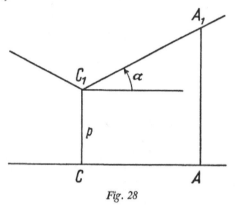

Fig. 28

Let us assume that the maximum price at which all demand ceases is the same whichever the direction of transport, say $AA_1$ (Fig. 28). The sales area of the production centre $C$ is then bounded by the circle about $C$ with radius $CA$. The size of the sales area appears at once as a function of the price ex-works and of the height of the freight rate.

2. Now let us consider two suppliers of goods that are substitutes (such as coals of different quality) and compare the situation of their sales areas. Such a comparison presupposes that the prices of the two goods refer to equivalent quantities, i.e. to quantities which the consumer regards as equivalent. If the buyer can get his coal from seller No. 1 or from seller No. 2 his choice between the two cannot be thought of as depending on a comparison of the prices per ton quoted by the two sellers. We ought instead to compare the prices of quantities of equivalent calorific value. Since such equivalent quantities would as a rule have different weights, the comparison would normally have to be based on different freight rates. When we speak below of the two sellers' ex-works prices $p_1$ and $p_2$ these prices will always refer to one physical unit of good No. 1 and the equivalent quantity of good No. 2; the latter quantity we shall define as the unit of good No. 2.

Seller No. 1 is placed in the production centre $C_1$ and seller No. 2 in production centre $C_2$. The distance between the two centres may, of course, be so great that the sales areas of the two suppliers will be completely separated whatever the freight rates and the prices ex-works. In that case the two suppliers will not behave competitively. The sales of each supplier will with a given freight rate depend solely on his price ex-works.

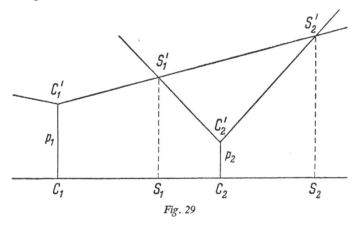

*Fig. 29*

A more significant and also more interesting case occurs where the sales areas of the two suppliers penetrate one another and the two suppliers thus compete. Launhardt's funnel serves to demonstrate this form of competitive relation very clearly.

Figure 29 represents the vertical section through the two funnels above the production centres $C_1$ and $C_2$. It can be seen (Fig. 29) that all points between $S_1$ and $S_2$ belong to the sales area of $C_2$, while those to the left of $S_1$ and to the right of $S_2$ belong to the sales area of $C_1$. The points $S_1$ and $S_2$ belong to the competition frontier, which means that they lie on the line of demarcation between those two areas. The competition frontier contains all those points (localities) where the local prices for equivalent physical quantities from the two production centres are the same. This competition frontier between the two centres is clearly the projection on the earth's surface of the curve formed by the intersection of the two funnels. Figure 29 offers a simple graphical method for determining all the points of the competition frontier, and hence its shape. We said already that $S_1$ and $S_2$ are readily identifiable as being points on the competition frontier. To find further points, we may draw parallel to $C_1C_2$ a family of horizontal straight lines $g_1, g_2, \ldots$ which cut the funnel over $C_1$ in $A_1', A_2' \ldots$, while cutting the funnel above $C_2$ in $B_1', B_2', \ldots$. Let $A_1, A_2, \ldots$ and $B_1, B_2, \ldots$ be the projections respectively of $A_1', A_2', \ldots$ and of $B_1', B_2', \ldots$ upon the horizontal line $C_1 C_2$. The circles around $C_1$ with the radii $C_1 A_1, C_1 A_2, \ldots$ and the circles about $C_2$ with the radii $C_2 B_1, C_2 B_2, \ldots$ are then the loci of points at which the prices of equivalent quantities from the two

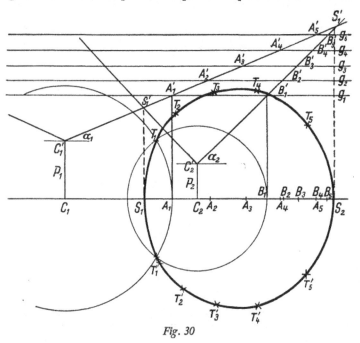

Fig. 30

centres are equal, namely $A_1 A_1' = B_1 B_1'$; $A_2 A_2' = B_2 B_2'$; etc. The points of intersection $T_1$ and $T_1'$, $T_2$ and $T_2'$ of such pairs of circles are points on the frontier of competition.[1] In the case presented in Fig. 30 the competition frontier is a curve about the production centre $C_2$. The competition frontier encloses the sales area of $C_2$ while $C_1$ has the rest of the area. The external boundary of $C_1$'s sales area is a circle round $C_1$ which has for its radius that distance from $C_1$ which corresponds to the maximum price.

The competition frontier in Fig. 30 was drawn on the supposition of different ex-works prices and freight rates. It will assume other shapes if the prices ex-works are the same and the freight rates different or equal. Their geometric construction is left to the reader.

[1] Figure 30 only shows the construction of points $T_1$ and $T_1'$.

Here we want to show how the shape of the competition frontier may be calculated for the different cases.

Any point on the competition frontier (such as $P$ in Fig. 31) must clearly fulfil the condition

$$p_1 + f_1 \cdot e_1 = p_2 + f_2 \cdot e_2. \tag{2}$$

In the case which we examined above, in which $p_1 \neq p_2$ and $f_1 \neq f_2$,

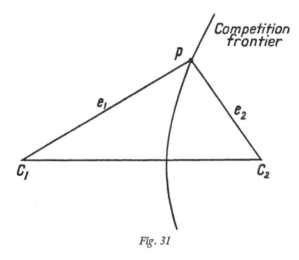

Fig. 31

the competition frontier was shown to be a closed curve surrounding the production centre with the lower ex-works price.[1]

If $p_1 \neq p_2 \; (p_1 > p_2)$ and $f_1 = f_2 = f$ we may write (2) in the form

$$e_2 - e_1 = \frac{p_1 - p_2}{f} \tag{3}$$

The points lying on the competition frontier now have the property that the difference between $e_2$ and $e_1$ is constant. The competition frontier is, therefore, a hyperbola, more particularly that portion of a hyperbola which is concave to the dearer production centre $p_1$. We should note that the competition frontier is now no longer a closed curve.

If $p_1 = p_2 = p$ while $f_1 \neq f_2$, it will follow from (2) that

$$e_2 : e_1 = f_1 : f_2. \tag{4}$$

[1] The computation of the competition frontier yields an equation of the fourth degree belonging to the family of ellipses of the fourth order.

The points on the competition frontier are now characterized by the fact that the ratio of the distances from the two production centres is constant. The competition frontier is accordingly a circle, more particularly that circle which divides the distance $C_1 C_2$ in the proportion $f_2 : f_1$ (Appolonius' circle). Where the difference between $p_1$ and $p_2$ is but small, a circle will approximate the competition frontier described by equation (2). A first approximation to the competition frontier in Figs. 29 and 30 is therefore the circle through $S_1$ and $S_2$, $S_1 S_2$ being its diameter.

Lastly, if $p_1 = p_2 = p$ and $f_1 = f_2 = f$, (2) becomes

$$e_1 = e_2, \tag{5}$$

which makes the competition frontier the perpendicular bisector of the straight line which joins the two centres.

The preceding analysis is directly applicable where more than two production centres are in existence. The sales areas of the different centres will then have the shape of polygons bounded by curve segments such as we found earlier on. The sales areas of the German centres of lignite production in 1924 are shown in Fig. 32.[1]

3. Our examination up to now has revealed that the competition frontiers depend for their position upon the level of the prices ex-works as charged in the production centres and on the height of the freight rates. Any change in an ex-works price or in a freight rate will produce an immediate shift or alteration of the competition frontier. The manner of this dependence is most clearly seen in Fig. 33 even though these relationships are only shown there by way of a vertical section through the production centres.

In the initial position we allow prices and freight rates to be equal in both centres. The competition frontier in this case is the perpendicular bisector of the distance $C_1 C_2$, and $S$ is one point on it. If the supplier at $C_1$ now lowers his ex-works price to $C_1 C_1''$ his sales area will *ceteris paribus* expand. Along the line $C_1 C_2$ he will penetrate to the point $S_1$ which hitherto lay within the sales area of the supplier at $C_2$. The competition frontier now becomes that portion of a hyperbola which is concave to $C_2$. Seller No. 2 will obviously not lose all his former customers. Competition and the market are imperfect precisely because of the preferences that result from the

---

[1] Taken from the study by P. Krebs, *Die Frachtgrenze der deutschen Braunkohle* (Technik und Wirtschaft, 1924, pp. 213–18). For details, the reader should turn to this study which computes the competition frontiers by means of Launhardt's funnels.

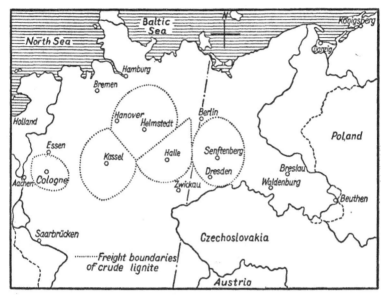

*Fig. 32*

geographic distance between seller and customer. This imperfection
of the competitive relationships between the two sellers is demonstrated very clearly in Fig. 33.

We can easily tell how the line $C_1C_2$ is divided between the two
sellers. If the distance of the point on the competition frontier from

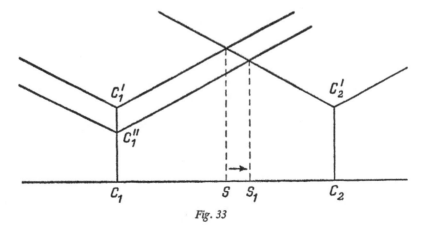

*Fig. 33*

$C_1$ or $C_2$ is written respectively as $x_1$ or $x_2$, it follows from equation (2) that

$$p_1 + f_1 \cdot x_1 = p_2 + f_2 \cdot x_2$$

where

$$x_1 + x_2 = c.$$

These two equations allow us to find $x_1$ and $x_2$. We get:

$$\begin{aligned} x_1 &= \frac{p_2 - p_1 + f_2 \cdot c}{f_1 + f_2} \\ x_2 &= \frac{p_1 - p_2 + f_1 \cdot c}{f_1 + f_2} \end{aligned} \tag{6}$$

The two equations (6) are examples of the price–sales function (1) which was discussed on p. 51 above and exhibit the manner in which the sales of the two suppliers stationed along $C_1 C_2$ depend upon the prices ex-works and the freight rates.

Since the two goods are substitutes, the cross-elasticity will be positive (see p. 35 above).

## Section B

## THE REVENUE PLAN OF THE FIRM FOR A SINGLE ECONOMIC PERIOD

We have described the two decisive influences on the purchases and sales of a firm as being its objective and its mode of behaviour. We now have to study how the firm's objective and mode of behaviour affect the economic plan and the dispositions which result from it. As objective we assume, first, the maximization of net profit for a single economic period.

We define the net profit of a period as the difference between the revenue for that period (that is, the sales proceeds of the quantity sold) and the costs of the quantity sold. The planning of a firm's net profit, therefore, requires the planning of the revenue from, and the planning of the costs, of the quantity that is to be sold. We shall take first the planning of revenue. The planning of costs will be considered in the subsequent section.

### 1. The Revenue Plan of a Seller acting as a Quantity-Adjuster

1. Let us take first the case of a single-product firm, that is, a firm which produces and supplies only a single good. As the price for a

quantity-adjuster is given, the revenue expected for a single period is the product of the quantity expected to be sold and the selling price per unit. Let us denote the sales expected in the planning period as $x$ (units per unit of time), the selling price as $p$, and the revenue as $R$, then:

$$R = p \cdot x \tag{1}$$

As the selling price is a constant the revenue will vary in direct proportion to the sales. The *revenue curve*, that is, the curve which portrays the relationship between revenue and sales, is in this case a

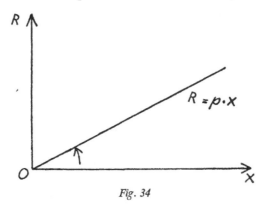

Fig. 34

straight line through the origin, the slope of which is the measure of the selling price (Fig. 34).

2. If we are dealing with a multi-product firm, then the planned revenue is the sum of the revenues from the individual goods. Let us describe the quantities expected to be sold of the $n$ goods as $x_1$, $x_2, \ldots, x_n$ and the prices of the goods as $p_1, p_2, \ldots, p_n$, then the revenue will be:

$$R = p_1 x_1 + p_2 x_2 + \ldots + p_n x_n \tag{2}$$

Revenue now becomes a function of the quantities of the $n$ goods that are to be sold.

## 2. The Revenue Plan of a Seller Facing an Expected Price-Sales Relation

1. Let us consider first a single-product firm. The firm is in a position to fix the selling price for the good it makes and offers. The consumers decide what quantities they wish to buy in an economic period at the fixed price. For the seller, therefore, the price is his

action-parameter and the quantity sold his expectation-parameter. The level of sales expected in the economic period will now obviously depend on the price that is fixed. The seller will have to try and form an idea as to the quantities that will be sold at the different prices. This expected price–sales function for the individual firm will be the basis for the supplier's revenue plan (see Section I, sub-section 2, 2). The shape of this function depends, as we have shown, mainly on whether the supplier acts as a monopolist, as a polypolist, or as an oligopolist. Let us assume that the supplier has planned his expected

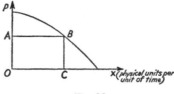

*Fig. 35*

price–sales function on the basis of past experience and his expectations as to the future. In general, the supplier will only plan the quantities to be sold around the price ruling in the previous economic period. In his plan he will try to find out what alterations in sales are to be expected from alterations upwards or downwards of the previous price. We want here to assume that the supplier plans the entire expected price–sales function (that is, the relation between the price and the expected sales at all prices from nil up to the price at which expected sales would be nil). The curve drawn in Fig. 35 represents an expected price–sales function:

$$p = f(x) \qquad (3)$$

in which $p$ is the price and $x$ the quantity that is expected to be sold during the planning period at this price.[1] From (3), the expected revenue at the price $p$ is immediately given as

$$R = p \cdot x = x \cdot f(x) \qquad (4)$$

Geometrically this revenue is represented by the area of the rectangle $OABC$ (Fig. 30). In order to study how the revenue varies with the planned price, i.e. what revenue is expected to correspond to different

[1] The reader will perhaps prefer to write the price–sales function in the form $x = F(p)$ so as to have the price as the independent variable and the sales $x$ as the dependent variable. But since Marshall it has been usual to write the price–sales relation as in (3). It is necessary only to be quite clear as to which variable is an action-parameter and which an expectation-parameter.

alternative levels of price, we simply have to find out the variation in the area of this rectangle *OABC*. Instead of the price we could, of course, take the expected sales as the independent variable. Then the plan would be drawn up in the following way: if a sale of $x_1$ is to be obtained in the planning period, then (in the judgment of the supplier) the price must be fixed at $p_1$; if a sale of $x_2$ is to be obtained then the price must be fixed at $p_2$, etc. For convenience we want to study the problem in this form. A whole series of theorems which we shall later be developing are more easily treated in this form. Nothing essential is altered thereby.

The form of relationship between the revenue and the planned sales depends on the nature of the price–sales function. The relationships are the same as those we have already studied when analysing the demand curve of a household. Everything said there regarding the outlay or expenditure curve derivable from a demand curve, can be applied word for word if in place of "expenditure" we substitute the word "revenue", and in the place of "demand" the word "sales". The individual price–sales function of a supplier is nothing else but the demand as seen by the seller, or the relation that is expected between price and demand. Let us, therefore, lay down the following propositions, once more contenting ourselves with a summary of the main conclusions:

(a) *If the elasticity of sales in relation to price is less than* −1 (*i.e. if sales are elastic*), *then revenue will increase with an increase in sales. Marginal revenue* (*i.e. the change in revenue corresponding to an increase in sales of* 1 *unit*) *is positive.*

(b) *If the elasticity of sales in relation to price is equal to* −1, *then the revenue will remain constant if the price is altered. Marginal revenue is then nil.*

(c) *If the elasticity of sales in relation to price is greater than* −1 (*i.e. sales are inelastic in relation to price*), *then revenue will fall with an increase in sales. Marginal revenue is then negative.*

(d) *The relation between marginal revenue, price, and elasticity of sales is given by the Amoroso-Robinson formula:*

$$\text{Marginal Revenue} = \text{Price} \times \left(1 + \frac{1}{\text{Elasticity of Sales}}\right)$$

(e) *Marginal revenue at a price where sales are nil is equal to the price. For every quantity of sales above nil marginal revenue is smaller than price.* This follows simply from the fact that increasing the sales by 1 unit increases the revenue by the price of this unit *minus* the mathematical product of the previous sales and the reduction in price necessary in order to sell one more unit.

In the case of a straight-line price–sales curve the marginal revenue curve is also a straight line as portrayed in Fig. 19.

The marginal revenue curve of an oligopolist may show a peculiarity in that he may calculate that his competitors will answer reductions in his price by corresponding reductions, but that they will not react to increases in his price by altering their prices. We have shown above (pages 53/54) that the expected price–sales curve of the individual firm will then show a kink at the ruling price (Fig. 36). It can easily

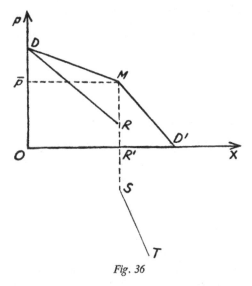

*Fig. 36*

be understood by constructing the marginal revenue curve corresponding to a particular price–sales curve (Fig. 36) that the marginal revenue curve will be discontinuous at the price $\bar{p}$ corresponding to the sales $OR'$; if falls vertically by $RS$. This fact will be shown to be important later on.

2. Let us turn now to the revenue plan of a multi-product firm. For the sake of simplicity let us assume that the seller produces and sells two goods, 1 and 2. The analysis can easily be applied to the case of more than two goods. The prices of the two goods are $p_1$ and $p_2$, and the quantities sold at these prices $x_1$ and $x_2$. The plans in respect of revenue involve the plans for the quantities it is expected will be sold at particular prices. Here we must distinguish a series of different cases:

(a) The seller may reckon with, or know, that the sales of each good do not depend on the price of the other good he is supplying.

If this is the case one may say that the two goods are "*independent*" in respect of demand, or that their sales are not related (for example, soap and walking-sticks). The expected price- and sales-functions of the two goods then have the following forms:

$$p_1 = f(x_1) \quad \text{and} \quad p_2 = g(x_2) \tag{5}$$

The sales plan may be expressed by the function:

$$R = p_1 x_1 + p_2 x_2 = x_1 \cdot f(x_1) + x_2 \cdot g(x_2) \tag{6}$$

which gives the total revenue as the sum of the partial revenues from the two goods.

(b) The seller may know, or assume, that the sales of one good depend also on the price of another good he is supplying. One may say then that the two goods are *dependent* in respect of demand, or that their sales are related (for example, butter and margarine, gas and gas-stoves). The expected price–sales functions of the two goods are now:

$$x_1 = f(p_1, p_2) \quad \text{and} \quad x_2 = g(p_1, p_2) \tag{7}$$

or

$$p_1 = F(x_1, x_2) \quad \text{and} \quad p_2 = G(x_1, x_2) \tag{8}$$

In the first form, particular prices fixed by the supplier are ranged against the expected sales of the two goods. In the second form, the functions answer the question as to what the prices must be, if expected sales are to be of a particular magnitude.

Let us base the revenue plan on the price–sales functions (7), then the revenue is given as a function of the two prices:

$$R = p_1 \cdot f(p_1, p_2) + p_2 \cdot g(p_1, p_2) \tag{9}$$

By using the price–sales functions (8) revenue is seen to be a function of both the quantities sold:

$$R = x_1 \cdot F(x_1, x_2) + x_2 \cdot G(x_1, x_2) \tag{10}$$

The characteristics of the price–sales functions and of the revenue functions depend on whether the two goods supplied are complementary goods or substitute goods. As we have shown already, the difference between *complementary* and *substitute* (or *competing*) goods is given by the sign of the cross-elasticity (page 35). If the two goods are complementary, then the sales of both goods decline if the price of one of them is raised, the price of the other remaining constant. The cross-elasticities of both goods are then negative:

$$\frac{\partial x_1}{x_1} : \frac{\partial p_2}{p_2} = \frac{p_2}{x_1} \cdot \frac{\partial x_1}{\partial p_2} < 0$$

and

$$\frac{\partial x_2}{x_2} : \frac{\partial p_1}{p_1} = \frac{p_1}{x_2} \cdot \frac{\partial x_2}{\partial p_1} < 0$$

The symbol $\partial$ signifies that the price of the good of which we are studying the change in sales, is held constant.

If the two goods are substitutes, then the sales of the first good decrease if there is an increase in the price of this good, while the price of the second good remains constant but the sales of the second good increase. The cross-elasticities then for both goods are positive:

$$\frac{\partial x_1}{x_1} : \frac{\partial p_2}{p_2} = \frac{p_2}{x_1} \cdot \frac{\partial x_1}{\partial p_2} > 0$$

and

$$\frac{\partial x_2}{x_2} : \frac{\partial p_1}{p_1} = \frac{p_1}{x_2} \cdot \frac{\partial x_2}{\partial p_1} > 0$$

If two complementary goods are being supplied, then we must take account of the fact that with a fall in the price of one good (the price of the other good remaining constant), an increase in the sales of *both* goods must be expected. In any case, with a fall in the price of the first good an increase in the revenue from the complementary good is to be expected. If the direct price elasticity of the first good is less than $-1$, then there will, in addition, be an increase in the revenue from the first good, so that in any case there is bound to be an increase in revenue. If the direct price elasticity of the first good is greater than $-1$, then the revenue from the first good will decrease. The nature and magnitude of the change in total revenue will then depend on whether the increase in revenue from the second and complementary good does, or does not, exceed the decrease in revenue from the first good.

If the two goods are substitutes, then a reduction in the price of the first good (with the price of the second good constant) will result in a decrease in the sales of the competing good, and, therefore, a decrease in the revenue from the sale of this competing good. Whether the total revenue from both goods increases or decreases again depends on the direct price elasticity of the first good, the price of which is being reduced in the firm's plan. According to the size of this elasticity the total sales may increase or decrease or remain unchanged.

The same considerations hold good if, instead of from prices, we start from the planned sales, that is, assuming that the price–sales functions on which the plan is being based are as in (8). We then have to ask how the alteration in the sales of a single good (i.e. an alteration in the sales of one good, the sales of the other good remaining constant) influences the total revenue.

The concept of marginal revenue can, of course, also be applied to the revenue plan of a multi-product firm. It is only necessary to distinguish between different possible sorts of marginal revenue. Let us confine ourselves again to the marginal revenue related to a particular quantity of sales, so that we then have to distinguish between the *partial* marginal revenue of a good (or the change in revenue corresponding to an infinitely small change in the sales of this good, with the sales of the second good remaining constant), and the *total* marginal revenue, that is, the alteration in revenue corresponding to an infinitely small change in the sales of *both* of the two goods. If the changes in the sales of the two goods are small, strictly speaking, infinitesimal, the total marginal revenue will be equal to the sum of the two partial marginal revenues.[1]

In this connexion there is another point of particular importance in understanding the price–sales and revenue plans of a multi-product firm. For the case of two goods the two price–sales functions (7) and (8) contained four variables: two prices and two quantities of goods. The system of equations of the two price–sales functions may, therefore, be satisfied by an infinite number of combinations of values for the prices and quantities. Only when the numerical values of two of the four variables are given, are the values of the two other variables determinable from the two price–sales functions. This fact may be expressed by saying that the system of equations for the two

---

[1] If we describe the dependence of revenue on the two levels of sales as $R = R(x_1, x_2)$, then the partial change in revenue resulting from a change in the level of sales $x_1$, by the infinitesimal amount $dx_1$ is given as:

$$dR_1 = \frac{\partial R}{\partial x_1} \cdot dx_1$$

Correspondingly, the partial change in revenue resulting from a change in the level of sales $x_2$ by the infinitesimal amount $dx_2$ is given as:

$$dR_2 = \frac{\partial R}{\partial x_2} \cdot dx_2$$

The total change in revenue resulting from a simultaneous change in both levels of sales by the infinitesimal amounts $dx_1$ and $dx_2$ is then:

$$dR = dR_1 + dR_2 = \frac{\partial R}{\partial x_1} \cdot dx_1 + \frac{\partial R}{\partial x_2} \cdot dx_2$$

price–sales functions possesses two *degrees of freedom*. The numerical values of two variables may be chosen at random; then the values for the other variables are determinate. It follows that it is impossible to answer such questions as the following: how do the sales of a good change if its price increases from 5s. to 6s.? Or: how do the sales of a good change if the price of a competing good is lowered from 10s. to 8s.? An answer is only possible if, in addition, the numerical value of a second variable is given. Let us take an example: A firm may be supplying both gas and electricity. It is not possible simply to say how the sales of gas will alter if the price of gas falls. We must know also whether the price of electricity remains constant, or falls by 10%, or whether the sales of electricity remain unchanged, etc. It must always be borne in mind that the system of equations for the two price–sales functions has two degrees of freedom.

### 3. The Revenue Plan of a Multi-Product Firm supplying "Made-to-Order" Goods

The case of the multi-product firm, which we have been studying in paragraph 2, was one where each good was being produced and offered in more than one unit at a time. If the firm is producing single articles, that is, only a single example of each good corresponding to the particular tastes of individual customers, then the planning of its revenue is very much simplified. There is no longer a price–sales function in the former sense. The total revenue is simply the sum of the prices of the single goods the sale of which is planned during the coming period. The prices are arrived at either by negotiation between seller and customers, or are fixed by the seller as an option to be taken or left. (See Chapter IV, Section II, sub-section 7).

### Section C

## THE COST PLAN OF A GOING FIRM FOR A SINGLE ECONOMIC PERIOD (THE SHORT-TERM COST PLAN)

The profits for a period are given by the difference between the revenue of the period and the costs of the quantity sold during the period. We now have to ask how these costs are planned.

### 1. The Cost Plan of a Single-Product Firm

1. Let us consider, first, a firm which produces and sells one single product. In the previous section we showed how the revenue for

the coming economic period was planned. It was shown how the different alternative levels of revenues corresponded to different levels of sales. Now in studying the planning of costs we have to answer the question as to what costs are necessary in order to produce and sell different alternative outputs in the economic period.

2. *By the costs of a particular output we understand the money value of the quantities of means of production necessary for producing and selling this amount of goods.* The quantities of means of production which are necessary to produce and sell, say, 1,000 units of a good in the planning period, may be described as the real costs of this output. They represent what *Rummel* has called the *quantity-structure* of costs. To find out the components of these costs is the first step in planning costs. It is necessary, for example, to ask: (a) what quantities of raw materials are necessary for the production of $x$ units; (b) how many hours of labour, how many machine hours, kilowatt hours, and quantities of auxiliary raw materials, etc., are necessary in the different departments to produce $x$ units of the good; and (c) what quantities of the means of production are necessary to sell these $x$ units in the planning period. It must be noticed that it is only the *necessary* quantities of the means of production which are involved in the definition of costs. After finding out what the real costs are, and the different physical quantities which go to make them up, then these must be valued in terms of money in order to arrive at the corresponding *money costs*. (The problems of valuation which arise belong to the field of business administration and take us outside the subject matter of this book.) Throughout the following analysis we shall mentally add to these costs the normal interest upon invested capital as a kind of "as-if-costs".

From our study of the composition of costs it follows at once that the cost corresponding to sales of $x$ units is made up of raw materials costs, transformations or "working" costs, and business and sales costs. The total of raw materials and manufacturing costs may be described as the *production costs*. It is clear that the firm will try to produce each quantity of product with that combination of the means of production which incurs the lowest costs. We shall later have to study more precisely the characteristics of this minimum cost combination (Chapter II, Section V). Here we simply assume that the management of the firm is always trying to plan for the minimum costs corresponding to any particular output.

3. The firm's planning requires it to find out the production and sales costs for different alternative outputs. How do the costs behave for the different alternative outputs which may be produced from the existing plant? That is the question which has to be answered. In

practice the planning of costs, just like the planning of revenue, will usually only cover a few alternative levels of output. But here we wish to assume, as we did in studying the revenue plans, that all possible alternatives are considered when costs are being planned. We suppose that the planning of costs is carried out for all the possible levels of output, given the existing plant. Every output from nil up to capacity output, $x_{max}$, must be allotted the planned total costs corresponding to it. If we measure along a pair of coordinates the alternative outputs

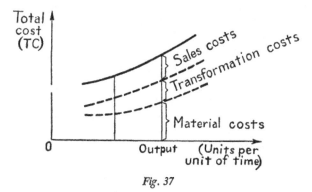

*Fig. 37*

on the abscissa, and on the ordinate the corresponding total costs of each output, then every possible alternative that may be planned corresponds to a particular point within this system of coordinates. The totality of these points lies on a curve which we may describe as the planned total cost curve, or simply as the *total cost curve*. We must now see what we can say about the shape of this curve and the particular components of which its ordinates are made up (Fig. 37).

4. It is immediately clear that the total costs will be greater, the greater is the output that is being planned. The question is simply as to how these total costs and their components alter, as the planned output increases. The answer which is usually given to this question is: the total costs are made up of (a) those costs which are independent of the level of output that is planned, (b) those costs which grow or vary with the level of output that is planned. The first kind of cost is described as *fixed costs* (*in relation to the output*), and the second kind as *variable costs*. It must be noted that this classification of the component parts of total costs, in accordance with their behaviour with changes in output, does not arise out of the nature of these particular kinds of costs themselves. It is not that certain kinds of cost by nature belong to fixed costs, while other kinds of costs by nature belong to variable costs. *Whether particular sorts of cost are*

*fixed or not in the cost plan of the firm depends on the dispositions of the manager.* These dispositions invariably determine the level of costs which are understood to be the money value of the quantities of the means of production which are needed for the production of a given amount of goods. There is no automatic way, according to which the individual components of cost each alter with the level of production that is planned. It is, for example, false to say that the depreciation of machinery is definitely a part of fixed costs. Whether it is so or not depends on the dispositions of the management. If the level of depreciation for machinery *is fixed as a constant* year by year on the basis of the depreciation plan for the machinery, then depreciation charges are fixed costs. If the depreciation charges for the period are treated as proportional to the number of machine hours necessary for the output planned, then depreciation charges for machinery will be variable costs. The same applies to other sorts of costs.[1] It is sometimes said that fixed costs are the costs of keeping the plant in readiness, or the costs which are incurred when nothing is being produced, though the plant is being held ready for production. To this it may be said that there is no *general* condition of readiness for a plant. The condition of machines, for example, in a particular period, may vary more or less in readiness from that of the personnel. One can always only speak of the preparedness of a *particular factor of production* or group of factors of production. Moreover, the costs of "readiness" for any particular group of factor, are by no means fixed. It is very well possible that certain services which are necessary for maintaining the machines if nothing is being produced, are not incurred when production is under way.

In classifying the planned costs of alternative quantities of product into the two groups of fixed and variable costs, we must never lose sight of the dependence of all costs on the dispositions of the firm. Only those costs are fixed which the manager plans as fixed for the period in relation to a particular quantity of product. *There is no absolute fixity of any particular cost.*

The reason for the fact that is is impossible to plan all costs as variable in relation to the output, is because certain factors of production are not related to particular single units of product, but to a total of present and future production. Every decision of the management is related to a particular time, i.e. it will be considered at a particular moment of time, and will relate to a particular future

---

[1] "The dependence of costs on a particular load or level of activity is not rigidly fixed. Costs depend very much on the dispositions of the different departments of the firm and the men running them" (Henzel: *Kostenanalyse*, Bühl, Baden, 1937, p. 36).

D

period of a particular length. It follows from this that according to the series of dispositions which have already been entered upon in the past, certain obligations will exist which will obstruct the free fixing of costs in the coming period. But it is never the case that there is any automatic relationship.

5. We now have to ask whether there is any further proposition which we can state beyond the proposition that total costs increase with the quantity of product that is planned. Can anything be said about the way in which this increase takes place? As the fixed costs are, by definition, independent of the level of production that is planned, we can limit ourselves to considering the dependence of variable costs on the output produced. The answer to the question as to how the variable costs depend on output can obviously only be given by empirical facts. The facts show, first, that there are costs which increase in a discontinuous way as the quantity produced increases. For example, the costs of a certain kind of supervisory labour may be planned as fixed for an output up to $x_1$. If the output exceeds $x_1$, then the costs of supervision have to be increased discontinuously, so that from an output of $x_1$ up to the capacity output they are again independent of the quantity produced. For simplicity we shall disregard the existence of this kind of discontinuously variable costs. By far the majority of all variable components of cost increase more or less continuously with the level of output that is planned. We will, therefore, only concern ourselves with these.

Let us suppose that the output planned is increased successively by one unit at a time, so that the total variable costs increase with each additional unit of product. Let us describe the increase in the total variable costs for each additional unit of product as the *marginal costs* of this unit of product.[1] Marginal costs tell us then by how much the total costs increase (or diminish) if the planned output is increased (or diminished) by one unit.[2]

Experience tells us that in a firm with given plant which is also faced with given prices for the variable factors of production, marginal costs may vary in different ways with increasing production:

(a) marginal costs may remain constant as output increases up to the limit of capacity (Fig. 38A);

---

[1] For the fixed costs, by definition, marginal costs is nil.

[2] Let $b(x)$ denote the dependence of aggregate variable costs on the quantity of output. Then marginal costs of the output $x$ are given mathematically by:

$$\text{Marginal Costs} = \frac{db}{dx} \cdot dx,$$

where $dx$ is the infinitesimal change in output.

(b) marginal costs may remain constant up to a point short of maximum capacity and increase thereafter up to the limit of productive capacity (Fig. 38B);

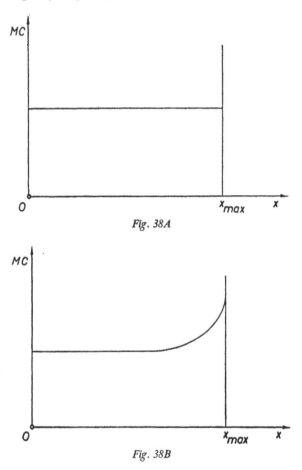

*Fig. 38A*

*Fig. 38B*

(c) marginal costs first decrease up to a level of output which is short of maximum capacity, and increase thereafter till maximum capacity is reached (Fig. 38C);

(d) marginal costs remain constant ($m_1$) up to output $x_1$ ($< x_{max}$), constant also (at $m_2$) but greater than $m_1$ for the outputs $x_1 < x \leq x_2$ (where $x_2 < x_{max}$), and for the outputs $x_2 < x \leq x_{max}$ they are again constant (at $m_3$) but larger than $m_2$ (Fig. 38D).

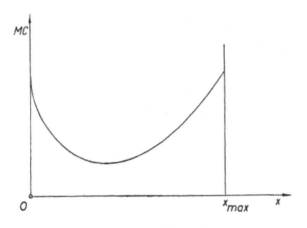

*Fig. 38C*

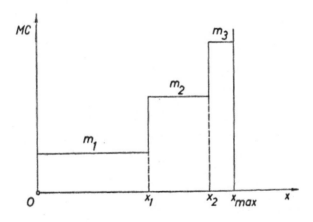

*Fig. 38D*

These four cases are represented in the following tables by numerical examples:

| Product per planning period | Marginal costs (shillings per unit) | | | |
|:---:|:---:|:---:|:---:|:---:|
| | Case *a* | Case *b* | Case *c* | Case *d* |
| 1 | 10 | 10 | 25 | 10 |
| 2 | 10 | 10 | 20 | 10 |
| 3 | 10 | 10 | 16 | 10 |
| 4 | 10 | 10 | 14 | 10 |
| 5 | 10 | 10 | 13 | 10 |
| 6 | 10 | 10 | 11 | 15 |
| 7 | 10 | 10 | 10 | 15 |
| 8 | 10 | 12 | 12 | 15 |
| 9 | 10 | 15 | 15 | 20 |
| 10 | 10 | 24 | 24 | 20 |

We shall examine in Section V upon what assumptions we ought to expect the behaviour of marginal costs to conform to type *a*, *b*, *c* or *d*. Here we limit ourselves to the description of the four forms which the marginal cost function can, in our experience, assume.

6. If one knows the marginal costs for particular levels of output, then one can find out at once the level of the total variable costs by a simple addition. For example, in our numerical example below the total variable cost for an output of four units is obtained by adding the marginal costs of the first, second, third, and fourth units. This calculation is carried out in the adjoining table. The corresponding curves showing the dependence of total variable costs on the quantity of output are portrayed in Figs. 39. The total variable costs increase with the level of output.

| Quantity of product | Total variable costs | | | |
|:---:|:---:|:---:|:---:|:---:|
| | Case *a* | Case *b* | Case *c* | Case *d* |
| 1 | 10 | 10 | 25 | 10 |
| 2 | 20 | 20 | 45 | 20 |
| 3 | 30 | 30 | 61 | 30 |
| 4 | 40 | 40 | 75 | 40 |
| 5 | 50 | 50 | 88 | 50 |
| 6 | 60 | 60 | 99 | 65 |
| 7 | 70 | 70 | 109 | 80 |
| 8 | 80 | 82 | 121 | 95 |
| 9 | 90 | 97 | 136 | 115 |
| 10 | 100 | 121 | 160 | 135 |

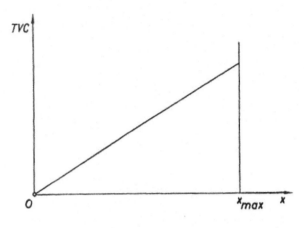

*Fig. 39A*

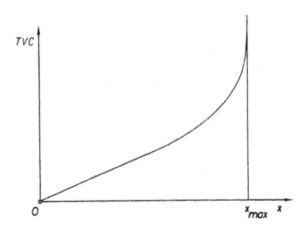

*Fig. 39B*

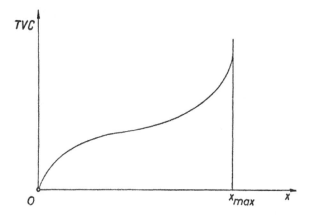

Fig. 39C

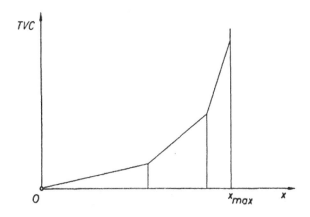

Fig. 39D

If we add the planned fixed costs to the total variable costs, then we get the total costs as a function of the level of output. In Figs. 39 we have a diagrammatic picture of the total cost curve. The curve of total variable costs is raised by the constant quantity equal to the fixed costs, to give the total cost curve.

7. So far we have discussed marginal costs, total variable costs, and total costs. In addition to these total and marginal cost concepts, the concept of *average (unit) costs* is of essential importance in the analysis and planning of costs. These are to be contrasted with the marginal costs which relate to simple units. If we describe the total costs for an output $x$ in a particular period of time as $C$, then one simply arrives at the unit costs or average cost by a simple division, calculating how much of the total costs are, on the average, to be allotted to each unit. If we describe the average costs as $AC$, then

$$AC = \frac{C}{x}$$

According as to whether in calculating the unit costs one takes into account only the fixed costs, only the total variable costs, or the total costs, one speaks of *average fixed costs (AFC) average variable costs (AVC)* or *average total costs (ATC)*. The relationship obviously holds that the average total costs are equal to the sum of the average fixed costs and the average variable costs. As the level of total cost is a function of output, the level of unit costs will also depend on the level of output. In the adjoining table we give these relationships, making use of the figures for case $c$ in the table on page 85 and assuming that fixed costs for the period are 50s.

| (1) Output | (2) Fixed Costs | (3) MC | (4) TVC | (5) TC | (6) AFC (2):(1) | (7) AVC (4):(1) | (8) ATC (5):(1) |
|---|---|---|---|---|---|---|---|
| 1 | | 25 | 25 | 75 | 50 | 25 | 75 |
| 2 | | 20 | 45 | 95 | 25 | 22·5 | 47·5 |
| 3 | 50 | 16 | 61 | 111 | 16·67 | 20·33 | 37 |
| 4 | | 14 | 75 | 125 | 12·5 | 18·75 | 31·25 |
| 5 | | 13 | 88 | 138 | 10 | 17·6 | 27·6 |
| 6 | | 11 | 99 | 149 | 8·33 | 16·5 | 24·9 |
| 7 | | 10 | 109 | 159 | 7·15 | 15·56 | 22·7 |
| ........ | ........ | ........ | ........ | ........ | | | |
| 8 | | 12 | 121 | 171 | 6·26 | 15·13 | 21·4 |
| 9 | | 15 | 136 | 186 | 5·56 | 15·11 | 20·67 |
| | | | | | ........ | ........ | |
| 10 | | 24 | 160 | 210 | 5 | 15·6 | 21·0 |

The relationships are still more easily apparent if we portray graphically the functional relationships between the variables concerned. In Fig. 40 the total cost curve (*TC*) is given for the same

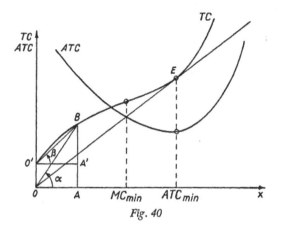

*Fig. 40*

case as that represented in Fig. 39c. The total costs corresponding to an output *OA* are *AB*. The total unit costs are then obviously equal to the tan of the angle $\alpha$, formed by the line *OB* and the abscissa:

$$ATC = \frac{AB}{OA} = \tan \alpha.$$

In order to find out how the total unit costs alter as output increases we simply have to follow how the angle $\alpha$ changes as the level of output increases.[1] It is clear from Fig. 40 that the total unit costs of an output, starting from nil, at first decrease, reach their minimum at a level represented in the figure by $ATC_{min}$, and then increase as the output increases. The curve of total unit costs, therefore, has the shape given in Fig. 40.

We may see, correspondingly, how average variable costs depend on output. The average variable costs are given by the equation:

$$AVC = \frac{A'B}{O'A'} = \tan \beta.$$

If one follows out the alteration in the angle $\beta$ as output increases from nil to $x_{max}$, then average variable costs first decrease as output increases; at an output of $AVC_{min}$ where the line $O'B$ touches the

[1] An angle and its tan change in the same direction.

total cost curve, they reach their minimum; and they then increase with each further increase in the level of output. From Fig. 40 it is immediately clear that the output at which average variable costs are at a minimum is always smaller than the output at which total unit costs are at a minimum. The curve of average variable costs lies completely below the curve of total unit costs. The difference between the total unit costs and the average variable costs equals the

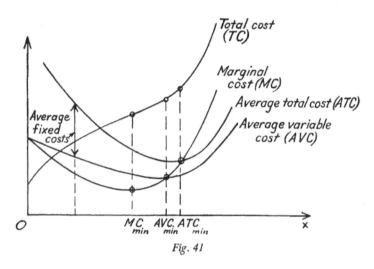

*Fig. 41*

average fixed costs for that particular level of output. Figure 41 gives both the marginal cost curve and the total cost curve corresponding to it, and includes also the curve of average variable costs and that of total unit costs. We must notice the order of the minima for marginal costs, average variable costs, and average total costs. The output at which marginal costs are at a minimum is smaller than the output at which average variable costs are at a minimum, and this again is smaller than the output at which total unit costs are at a minimum:

$$MC_{min} < AVC_{min} < ATC_{min}.$$

The average variable costs and the average total costs are therefore falling while marginal costs are already increasing.

The minima for the average variable costs and the total unit costs have an important characteristic which becomes clear when we notice that the marginal costs corresponding to a particular output are given geometrically by the slope of the total cost curve at this output, that is, by the slope of the tangent to the total cost curve at the point corresponding to the relevant output. The slope of the tangent can, of course, be measured by the tan of the angle formed by the tangent and the abscissa (Fig. 42). If we take into account this fact, we can see at once from Fig. 41 that at the minimum points of average variable cost and average total cost, average cost is equal to marginal cost. The marginal cost curve, that is, cuts the average variable cost curve at its lowest point, and also the average total cost curve at its lowest point.

8. The curves we have dealt with here for the case described in Fig. 39c can be used in the same way for the type of total cost curves

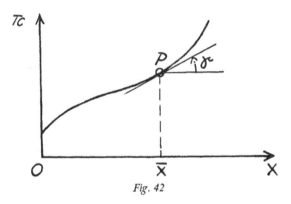

*Fig. 42*

portrayed in Fig. 39A, B, D. We may leave the details of this application to the reader.

In the case of constant marginal costs (case *a*) the analysis of the cost curves is a particularly simple matter. Total variable costs are then directly proportional to output. If we write marginal costs as *m*, and output in the period as *x*, then

$$TVC = m \cdot x.$$

We see at once that average variable costs are in this case equal to marginal costs:

$$AVC = \frac{TVC}{x} = m.$$

Total costs will be represented by the linear function

$$TC = f + m \cdot x$$

where *f* stands for the fixed costs. From this function one finds average total costs as

$$ATC = \frac{f}{x} + m,$$

which implies that average total costs decrease with increasing output and reach their minimum when $x = x_{max}$. Average total costs are in this case always greater than marginal costs and the analysis of costs thus leads to results different from those for the previously examined case $c$. The reader should analyse cases $b$ and $d$.

9. Up to now we have assumed that all costs corresponding to alternative levels of output in the cost plan of the firm depend solely on the level of output. This assumption corresponds with the facts for most kinds of costs. However, there are certain costs belonging to the sales side, the size of which does not depend directly on the planned sales, but on the planned *revenue*. We must therefore supplement our remarks in one respect. Under *sales costs* two different groups of costs are to be distinguished. The first group contains those costs which it is planned to incur in order to influence sales. We may describe these costs as the *costs of influencing sales* or *actual sales costs*. They may depend partly, as, for example, with advertising costs, on the sales and the selling price, assuming the firm is fixing the price at which it is selling, and partly on the revenue (e.g. commission). The second group contains those costs which are necessary in order to effect a particular quantity of sales (freight, packing, cost of transport, etc.). The costs in this group are partly dependent on sales and partly on revenue, and partly on the two together. We may describe this second group of costs as *passive sales costs*. Only for the case where passive sales costs alone are planned, which are in relation to the planned level of sales, will the total costs be dependent on output, and planned as increasing with the level of output. If the firm's plans include advertising costs with a view to influencing demand, then total costs may not always be representable as a function of the quantity sold. But we can only enter further into these relationships when we come to analyse the profit plan of the firm.

## 2. The Cost Plan of a Multi-Product Firm

1. If a firm produces several products, we must distinguish between the following cases:

(a) The products are wholly independent of each other as regards their production. If, for example, the two products 1 and 2 are made by entirely separate plants which allow, per unit of time, a maximum output of $x_1^{max}$ and $x_2^{max}$ respectively of the two products, then we can take all points within and on the rectangle $OABC$ (Fig. 43) as representing the aggregate of *possible* combinations of the quantities of the two products. At point $B$ the capacities of both plants are fully utilized.

(b) The products are made simultaneously or alternately by processes which utilize one or several common factors of production. In this case we speak of *common* production.

For instance: two processes can be carried out with one machine which will transform two different inputs each into a different product. Suppose that the production of one unit of the first (second) product requires $t_1(t_2)$ time units. It follows that maximum output,

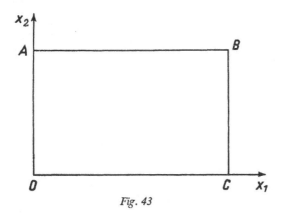

*Fig. 43*

in the available time $T$, only allows of the production of such quantities $x_1$ and $x_2$ of our products as will satisfy the condition

$$t_1 . x_1 + t_2 . x_2 = T. \qquad (x_1 \geqq 0; \quad x_2 \geqq 0)$$

Graphically, this condition is represented by a straight line (Fig. 44) called the *capacity frontier*.

The distance $OA$ ($OB$) is the measure of the maximum quantity of the first (the second) product obtainable when the machine is used solely for the first (the second) process. All other points of the capacity frontier between $A$ and $B$ represent those quantity combinations $x_1$, $x_2$ of the two products which are the maximum output obtainable from the machine in time $T$.

All the quantity combinations that are contained within the triangle $OAB$ may of course also be obtained. They satisfy the condition

$$t_1 x_1 + t_2 x_2 < T.$$

The condition

$$t_1 x_1 + t_2 x_2 \leqq T \qquad (x_1 \geqq 0; \quad x_2 \geqq 0)$$

therefore states all the quantity combinations of the two products that are attainable within the limits of available capacity.

There is, however, an essential difference between quantity combinations or points *inside* the area contained by the capacity frontier and those actually lying *upon* it:

Starting from a point *P* that lies *inside* the capacity frontier, it is possible to raise the output of each product without reducing that of

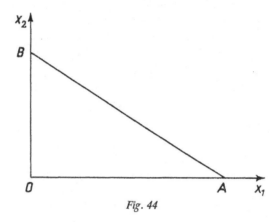

*Fig. 44*

the other, till the frontier is reached. But starting from a point *on* the capacity frontier, the output of one product can be expended only at the expense of the other.

The peculiarities of *common production* persist as we increase the number of products beyond the two we have discussed. There is of course no need for the capacity frontier to be a straight line. It can be a curve or can be composed of straight-line segments (Fig. 45). The following example will imply a capacity frontier shaped as in Fig. 45.

Let a firm produce two goods, 1 and 2. Production is carried on in four departments. Department I makes good No. 1 by combining the two intermediate products $A_1$ and $B_1$. Department II makes good No. 2 by combining the intermediate products $A_2$ and $B_2$. Department III makes the intermediate products $A_1$ and $A_2$, and Department IV makes the intermediate products $B_1$ and $B_2$.

Department I has a capacity of 30,000 units of product per unit of time (say, per day). The capacity of Department II is 20,000 units per day. The maximum output per day in Department III is as much of the intermediate product $A_1$ ($A_2$) as is needed for 45,000 units of good No. 1 (30,000 units of good No. 2). It follows that to make enough of intermediate product $A_1$ ($A_2$) for one unit of good No. 1 (one unit of good No. 2) one needs $\dfrac{1}{45,000}$ $\left(\text{or } \dfrac{1}{30,000}\right)$ of one day.

If we write $x_1$ (or $x_2$) for the quantities of good No. 1 (or No. 2) that are to be made per day we will find that Department III can in one day produce only such quantities of the intermediate products $A_1$ and $A_2$ as will satisfy the condition

$$\frac{x_1}{45,000} + \frac{x_2}{30,000} \leqq 1.$$

The equation

$$\frac{x_1}{45,000} + \frac{x_2}{30,000} = 1$$

describes the *capacity frontier of Department* III.

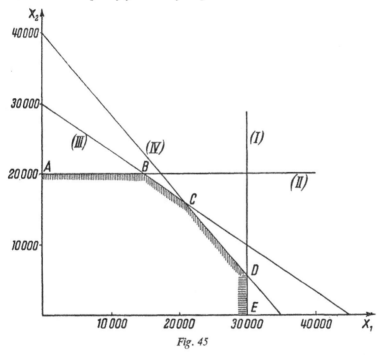

Fig. 45

In Department IV let the maximum output per day be as much of intermediate product $B_1$ ($B_2$) as will just suffice for 35,000 units of good No. 1 (or 40,000 units of good No. 2). It follows that the *capacity frontier of Department* IV is defined by:

$$\frac{x_1}{35,000} + \frac{x_2}{40,000} = 1.$$

We can now draw the capacity lines of the four departments into the system of co-ordinates $x_1$ and $x_2$ and discover at once the range of possible quantity combinations for the two goods 1 and 2 (Fig. 45). The capacity frontier for the four departments together is found to be the broken line $ABCDE$. All those quantity combinations ($x_1$ and $x_2$) are attainable that lie either within or upon this line. The capacity frontier determines the maximum quantity of good 1 (2) that is obtainable, given the quantity of good 2 (1). Over the range $BCD$ production of the two goods is *alternative* in the sense that a greater quantity of one good is achievable only if the quantity of the other good is simultaneously reduced.

(c) The products may be connected on the production side, so that one product cannot be produced without simultaneously, and of technical necessity, other products being produced. In this case one may speak of *joint production or inter-connected production*. There are two sub-cases between which we must distinguish:

($c_1$) The joint products may be produced in fixed unalterable proportions. In this case the production of two joint products is not possible without one unit of product $A$ being produced simultaneously with, say, three units of product $B$. There is a wealth of examples of joint production in constant proportions throughout the chemical industry.

($c_2$) The joint products may be producible in proportions alterable within certain limits. The older they are when slaughtered, the more wool sheep produce in proportion to the quantity of meat.

2. These purely technical relationships have important consequences in the planning of costs, which we must now consider. The question we have to ask is: what role do the cost concepts developed in respect of more simple production play in the planning of the costs of a multi-product firm?

(2a) Let us take first the case of complete *independence as regards production*. Consider a firm which plans to make and sell in the coming economic period $x_1$ units of good No. 1 and $x_2$ units of good No. 2, etc. The function which describes the dependence of total costs $C$ upon the quantity combinations $x_1, x_2, \ldots$ is then by definition of the following form:

$$C = a_1 + b_1(x_1) + a_2 + b_2(x_2) + \ldots,$$

where $a_1 + b_1(x_1)$ represents the total cost function for good No. 1, $a_2 + b_2(x_2)$ that for good No. 2, and so forth. The different goods have in this case *mutually independent total cost functions* so that marginal cost, average variable cost and average total cost can all be computed for each single good.

(2b) Not so in the case of *common production*. There, the total cost function is of the form:

$$C = a + b(x_1, x_2, \ldots, x_n).$$

Here, in contrast with case 2a, it is not possible to split variable costs into a series of components each of which depends on the quantity of one good alone. This implies that the marginal costs for a certain good depend not solely on the quantity of that one good but also on the quantities of all others:

$$\frac{\partial C}{\partial x_i} = \frac{\partial b(x_1, x_2, \ldots, x_n)}{\partial x_i}. \quad (i = 1, 2, \ldots, n).$$

They now measure the change in costs which comes about when the quantity of one good increases by one unit while the quantities of all other goods stay constant. *Along* the capacity frontier itself it is of course impossible to increase the quantity of one good while holding constant the quantities of all the others. For quantity combinations which lie on the capacity frontier one can only determine "*left-hand*" *marginal cost*, i.e. the change in costs which occurs when the quantity of one good *diminishes* by one unit, all other quantities of goods remaining constant.

Apart from the partial marginal costs it is possible to determine the *special variable costs* for every single good. Those are the costs which would disappear if the production of the good was to cease while nothing changed in the quantities of the other goods. Taking a two-product firm, the special variable costs $b_1$ of good No. 1 would be:

$$b_1 = b(x_1, x_2) - b(0, x_2).$$

For good No. 2, the special variable costs $b_2$ would accordingly be:

$$b_2 = b(x_1, x_2) - b(x_1, 0).$$

Normally, $b_1 + b_2 < b$, because with the complete cessation of production certain costs would disappear which are still necessary if the production of only one of two goods is stopped.

The special variable costs of quantity $x_1$ ($x_2$) of good No. 1 (good No. 2) depend upon *both* $x_1$ and $x_2$. The average special variable costs of one good, $\frac{b_1}{x_1}$ or $\frac{b_2}{x_2}$ similarly refer to a given quantity of good No. 1 *and* a given quantity of good No. 2.

Where one is faced with common production, one cannot determine average total costs for the single products because there are, by definition, costs which fall commonly on all of them. These *common costs* are not related to a single product and cannot in consequence be allocated to quantities of particular products. If, in practice, the common costs are nevertheless allocated between particular goods, this is only by introducing assumptions for which there is no logical foundation.

(2c) We pass now to the case of *joint production in fixed proportions*. A firm may be producing jointly two products $A$ and $B$ in a fixed proportion. For example, the production of 1 unit of $A$ is technically fixed with the production of 2 units of $B$. We may then obviously treat the firm as a single-product firm producing a complex good of which the unit is $1A + 2B$. It follows that all the costs can be planned and calculated for this complex good as we have described in the case of simple production. Partial marginal costs, special variable costs, and average total costs cannot, however, be calculated for each of the joint products separately.

If the quantitative relationship in which joint products are produced is variable within certain limits, then it is possible to increase the production of one of the goods by 1 unit, while holding constant the quantities produced of the other joint products, and so to calculate the partial marginal costs of each separate joint product. The special variable costs for the individual goods cannot be ascertained, because the cessation of production of one product results necessarily, for technical reasons, in the cessation of production of the other joint products. Only the variable costs of a particular combination of all the joint products can be ascertained.

## Section D

### THE PROFIT PLAN OF A GOING FIRM FOR A SINGLE ECONOMIC PERIOD
#### (The Short-Term Profit Plan)

The profit of a firm in a period may be defined as the difference between the revenue and the costs corresponding to this revenue. We now have to deduce the profit plan for a single period, corresponding to the sales and costs plan for the period.

### (i) THE PROFIT PLAN FOR A SINGLE-PRODUCT FIRM

#### 1. The Profit Plan of a Firm acting as a Quantity Adjuster

1. A firm may plan for the coming period the production and sales of $x$ units of a particular good. The selling price, which is treated by the firm as a given constant, is $p$. The planned revenue is then given

by the equation $R = p \cdot x$ (shillings per period). Its size depends on the planned level of sales, and this dependence may be portrayed graphically by the revenue line discussed earlier (Fig. 34). It may be assumed, further, that the firm can sell, at any given price, any quantity within its productive capacity without incurring any active sales costs (for example, advertising costs). Its costs consist, therefore, simply of production costs (i.e. manufacturing costs and passive sales costs). The manufacturing costs and part of the passive sales costs

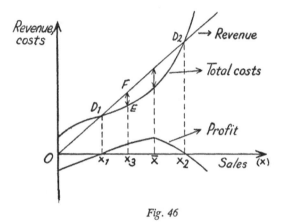

*Fig. 46*

depend, as we have shown, simply on the level of planned sales, while a part of the passive sales costs depends on the level of revenue. For simplicity's sake we want here to abstract from the case where there are passive sales costs dependent on the level of revenue. They can easily be fitted into our analysis by treating them as a deduction from revenue, and thus basing our analysis on this reduced revenue. We may, therefore, consider the level of the planned total production costs as depending simply on the level of planned sales. This dependence, which is expressed by the cost function, which we have already studied in the previous section, has the shape portrayed in Fig. 40, case c. Let us now draw in the diagram, along with the revenue line, the planned cost function, which will then show us at once the profit for each level of planned sales. In the case portrayed in Fig. 46, it is clear that the revenue line cuts the total cost curve at two points, $D_1$ and $D_2$, corresponding on the abscissa with $x_1$ and $x_2$. These two points may be described as the break-even points where cost is exactly covered by revenue. If the level of planned sales is smaller than $x_1$ or larger than $x_2$, then according to the plan a loss will result.

The revenue will be smaller than the total costs. If the planned level of sales is larger than $x_1$, but smaller than $x_2$, a profit will result. For example, if a quantity of sales equal to $x_3$ is planned, there will be a profit equal to $EF$. The level of the positive or negative profit depends, of course, on the level of sales which is planned. The nature of this dependence may be expressed by a profit curve which can be directly derived from Fig. 46. The profit at first increases with an increase in

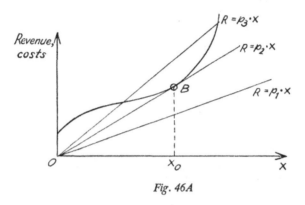

*Fig. 46A*

sales, reaches its maximum with a sales of $\bar{x}$, and decreases with any further increase in sales. Whether a positive profit is obtainable at any level of sales within the capacity of the firm, depends obviously on the total cost curve and on the selling price, which is a datum for the firm and is given geometrically by the slope of the revenue line. Figure 46A shows three different prices ($p_1 < p_2 < p_3$) corresponding to the three revenue lines. At a price of $p_1$ the revenue line lies entirely below the total cost curves. There is, therefore, no level of sales yielding a positive profit.[1] At a price of $p_2$ the revenue line touches the total cost curve at the point $B$. Again there is no level of sales yielding a positive profit. Only for that level of sales corresponding to the point of tangency $B$, is the revenue exactly equal to costs. The price $p_2$ is here equal to the minimum average cost. Only when the price is higher than this minimum of average total costs can there be levels of sales which yield a positive profit.

[1] In this case the attempt must be made so to reduce planned costs or, what is the same, so to lower the cost curve, as to obtain a range of positive profits. As was emphasised in the analysis of costs, the cost curve is not something rigid. The level of costs depends on the firm's dispositions in every case. The economic planning of the firm consists always in weighing up against one another all its "partial" plans.

We can also portray these relationships by using the curve of average total costs deducible from the total cost curve. As was shown earlier, the total cost curve in Fig. 46 has a unit cost curve corresponding to it, as shown in Fig. 47. In Fig. 47 we now draw in the price at which each quantity can be sold. As we start from the assumption that the selling price for the firm is a given constant, so the price–sales curve is in this case parallel to the abscissa. The firm

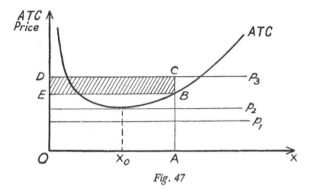

*Fig. 47*

then can sell any quantity at the given price and its sales are perfectly elastic in relation to price. Fig. 47 shows the price-lines corresponding to the three revenue lines in Fig. 46A. The difference between the average costs for a particular level of sales and the selling price, represents the profit per unit obtainable on that level of sales. The profit per unit obtainable at a price of $p_3$, with a sales of $OA$, therefore, equals $BC$. The total profit is given by multiplying unit profit by the quantity sold. In Fig. 47 it is, therefore, represented by the rectangle $EBCD$. From Fig. 47 it is clear that a positive profit per unit, and therefore positive total profits, can only be obtained if the selling price is higher than the minimum of average total costs.

2. We now have to ask the question as to which of the alternatives, within the range of possibilities open to it, the firm will choose; that is, which of the possibilities portrayed in Fig. 46 and Fig. 47 will be chosen. The answer to this, as we have seen earlier, can only be obtained if we make an assumption about the objectives of the firm. We first want to investigate what choice the firm will make, and how it will dispose of its resources, if it has as its objective *maximum total profit* in the period of time under consideration. From Fig. 46 it is clear at once that this objective is reached with a sale of $\bar{x}$. Therefore, in the coming period a quantity of $\bar{x}$ units will be produced and offered for sale.

How can this level of sales $\bar{x}$, which corresponds to the firm's objective, be discovered? The firm in making its plans will not, in practice, consider all the levels of sales within the limits of its capacity. It will, in the first place, consider the results of the previous economic period and its expectations as to the future, and then try to discover whether changes in the quantity to be sold, either upwards or downwards, will yield an increased total profit or not. Let us assume that the first plan proposed reckons with a sales of $x_3$ (Fig. 46). This plan would yield a profit equal to *EF*. In order to find out whether by this plan the firm will attain its objective, let us increase the sales by 1 unit over those proposed in the plan, and discover what effect this has on costs and revenue. If the sales are increased by 1 unit then the

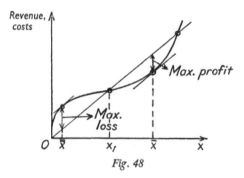

*Fig. 48*

revenue, in the case of a firm acting as a quantity-adjuster, will be increased by the price of this unit. The corresponding increase in costs will be measured by the marginal cost, which by definition tell us by how much costs increase if the quantity to be produced in the plan is increased by 1 unit. If, when the quantity to be sold in the original plan is increased by 1 unit, the marginal cost of this unit is less than the selling price, then it will be profitable for the firm to alter its plan accordingly. The same calculation can be made on the basis of this second amended plan. So long as the marginal cost corresponding to an additional unit of sales is smaller than the selling price, then it is profitable for the firm to increase the quantity sold. As the price is constant, a continued increase in the quantity sold will yield decreasing additions to profits as marginal cost begins to increase in the case portrayed in Fig. 46A. The addition to profits will be nil when marginal cost is equal to price. Any further increase in output will lead to marginal cost exceeding the price, so that the addition to profit will be negative. It follows from this that, under the conditions considered in Fig. 46, the maximum total profit will be obtained when the marginal cost is equal to the selling price. As we know, the marginal cost of a particular quantity of output is measured by the slope of the total cost curve at the point corresponding to this level of output. The point of maximum total profit, therefore, is given geometrically in Fig. 46 by that quantity of sales at which the tangent to the total cost curve is parallel to the revenue line (Fig. 48).

As may be seen from Fig. 48, there is also a particular level of output, between the levels of nil to $x_1$, where marginal cost is equal to price, but where a loss is made. This level of output corresponds to the maximum total loss. It is at once clear that the point of maximum total profit (or total loss) can only lie within the range of rising (falling) marginal costs. Immediately before the point of maximum total profit marginal cost must be less than price, while immediately

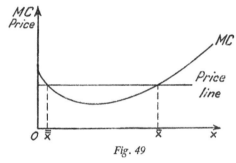

*Fig. 49*

after it must be greater than the price. *Vice versa*, immediately before the point of maximum total loss marginal costs must be greater than the price, while immediately after that point they must be less than the price. Figure 49, which shows the marginal cost curve and price line corresponding to the total cost curve in Fig. 48, makes these relationships quite clear.

3.  From the above arguments, particularly from Figs. 48 and 49, it follows that the level of output decided on by the firm, on our assumptions as to its mode of behaviour and objectives, depends on the given cost curve and on the level of the selling price. We must now look at this relationship more closely. We must ask *what levels of output the firm will produce at alternative levels of the selling price in its economic plan.* Let us now draw in the average total cost curve *ATC* on the diagram in Fig. 49, and the curve of average variable costs *AVC* (Fig. 50).[1] At a price of $p_2$ the firm will sell the quantity *OF* in the planning period the marginal costs of which are equal to this price $p_2$. If the price with which the firm is reckoning in its plan

[1] The relation between these curves was discussed earlier in the case of Fig. 41.

is lower (higher) than $p_2$, then the firm will produce and offer a smaller (larger) quantity in accordance with the shape of the marginal cost curve.

If the price is higher than the minimum $BD$ of average total costs, then the firm will make a positive profit equal to the area of the rectangle $IKHE$.

If the price equals the minimum average total cost, then (with the price line $p_1$) the total profit will be nil. The entrepreneur obtains

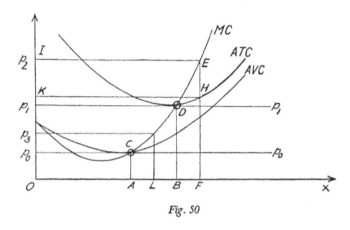

*Fig. 50*

only just the normal interest on invested capital and perhaps also entrepreneurial remuneration (the wages of entrepreneurship). The price $p_1$ represents the *lower price limit in the long run*. If the price falls permanently below this level, production ceases to pay.

In the short run, however, it may still pay the firm to supply at a price that stands between minimum average variable cost ($AC$) and minimum average total costs ($BD$).

If the firm produced the quantity $OL$ at the price $p_3$, it would make a loss. As this loss is obviously smaller than the loss it would make by ceasing production for that period (when it would suffer a loss equal to its fixed costs), it would therefore pay the firm to produce and offer the quantity $OL$. With this quantity the loss will be smaller than for any other quantity.

If the price is equal to the minimum average variable cost (with the price line $p_0$), then the production and sale of quantity $OA$ will exactly cover the variable cost. It is, therefore, a matter of indifference to the firm whether it produces at this level or closes down. Only if the price is less than the minimum average variable cost will *any* level of production lead to a loss greater than the loss of closing down. The price $p_0$ therefore represents the *lower* price limit in the short run.[1]

It follows from the above that the relation between price and the quantity supplied in the short run (that is, in the single economic period) is given by that part of the marginal cost curve which lies above the average variable cost curve (Fig. 51). This part of the marginal cost curve $CC'$ may be described as *the individual supply*

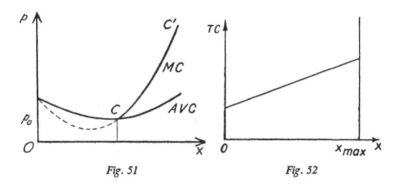

Fig. 51                          Fig. 52

*curve of the firm.* It tells us what quantities the firm will offer at different levels of price assumed in its plan. *The reader will observe that the existence of this curve is connected with the assumption that the firm on the supply side is acting as a quantity-adjuster.* Only on this assumption can a particular quantity of output be connected with a particular price.

4. Let us now enquire what modifications of our analysis are needed if the total cost curve is a straight line up to the point of full capacity (Fig. 52). Marginal costs are then equal to average variable costs and constant for all levels of output that lie within the limit of capacity (case $a$, p. 82/3). The marginal cost, which is now equal to the average variable cost, is then constant for all the levels of output within its capacity. The average total cost falls with an increase in output, and reaches its minimum at the point $x_{max}$. If the price is above the minimum of average total cost, then it is clear from Fig. 53 that the maximum total profit $AB$ is always obtained by using the firm's capacity to the full. The arguments of our previous section show that the quantity $x_{max}$ will at once be supplied when the price

[1] The reader might wish to consider how in the short run the lower price limit will shift if the costs of shutting down are less than the fixed costs.

equals or exceeds the level of average variable cost, which in this case is independent of the level of sales. The individual supply curve in this special case has the shape given in Fig. 54. It runs parallel to the

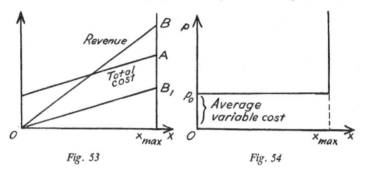

Fig. 53          Fig. 54

price axis and begins at the price $p_0$ equal to the average variable cost. The supply of the individual firm is here totally inelastic in relation to price if $p > p_0$.

The point of maximum profit fails, in this case, to satisfy the condition of equality between price and marginal costs. For $x_{max}$ there only exist left-hand marginal costs which, taken absolutely, are less than price.

5. Let us consider now a group of suppliers of products which are, in the judgement of the buyers, identical, who all behave as quantity-adjusters, and have as their objective the maximum total profit for the single period. The individual suppliers differ only in the structure

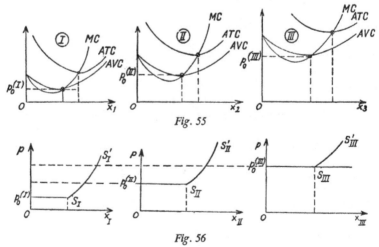

Fig. 55

Fig. 56

of their costs, as will be shown by the position and shape of their individual cost curves. Let us now put the individual firms in the order of the minima of their average costs. Figure 55 shows in this order the cost curves of the three firms. For each of them there is an individual supply curve (Fig. 56). A glance at the three supply curves shows that firm 1 will be the only supplier so long as the price lies between $p_0^{(I)}$ and $p_0^{(II)}$. Within this price range firm 1 may be described as the *marginal firm*. As soon as the price reaches a level of $p_0^{(II)}$, firm 2 will become a supplier. Within the range $p_0^{(II)} \leqq p < p_0^{(III)}$ the

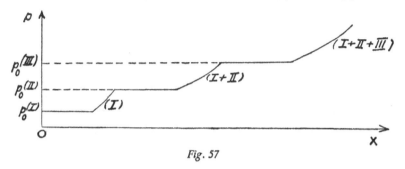

*Fig. 57*

total quantity supplied will, at each price, be equal to the sum of the individual quantities supplied by firms 1 and 2. In this price range firm 2 is the marginal firm. At a price of $p_0^{(III)}$, and at every price above this, firm 3 will appear as a supplier, so that at each price the total supply is obtained by adding the individual quantities supplied by the three firms. Figure 57 shows the *short-term total supply curve deduced in this way, of a group of going firms each supplying a product which in the judgement of the buyers is the same.* For the case where the individual supply curves have the shape given in Fig. 54, the total supply curve will be represented by a series of steps (Fig. 58), the width of the individual steps equalling the capacity of the firms, and the height of the steps their average variable costs. Which firm is the marginal firm depends on the level of the price.

6. Up to now we have assumed that the price is given to the individual firm for *every* level of output. This is a case which occurs where atomistic homogeneous competition exists between the supplying firms. In this case the firm does not have to reckon with active selling costs (for example, expenditure on advertisements). The case is different if there is imperfect competition between suppliers, though the goods they are selling are the same in the judgement of the buyers, and they are selling this good at the same price. Then the firm must reckon in its plans with advertising costs,

which will vary with the planned level of output, if it is to sell the quantity fixed in its plans. To the production costs and the passive selling costs there must be added now the *advertising costs*, which will increase with the quantity to be sold. Let us now assume that for each level of sales, and with given prices, the lowest advertising costs are planned. At a particular level of sales the marginal costs will be equal to the marginal production costs and the marginal advertising costs. We can see from our foregoing discussion that in

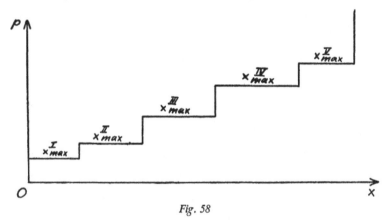

*Fig. 58*

the case of a quantity-adjuster the level of output at which total profits will be a maximum must be such *that the sum of marginal production costs and marginal advertising costs is equal to the selling price.*

7. Finally, we wish to consider what modifications are necessary in our results if the firm has other objectives in view. Maximum total profit in the planning period is only one of many possible objectives, especially in a controlled economy. Let us consider, for example, a case where the individual firm, because of official regulations, can only aim at a profit per unit of a particular percentage, for example, 20 % of the given selling price. This objective is, for a single-product firm, obviously identical with that of a total profit of 20 % of the revenue. As can easily be seen, this objective will be obtained at a level of sales where the average total costs, plus 25 %, are equal to the price. Given a U-shaped curve of average total costs (such as drawn in Fig. 47), and a price *greater* than the minimum of average total costs raised by one-quarter, the objective would in fact be obtained at each of two different levels of sales. But if we assume that the firm will always supply the larger of the two outputs then one definite level

of output can be associated unambiguously with each price. The individual supply curve now consists of the rising part of the average total cost curve which has been shifted upwards by one-quarter of its ordinal values (i.e. its height).

8. Finally, it should be noticed that even when the firm is aiming at maximum total profit, the level of output corresponding to this objective may not be realizable for *financial reasons*. Because of the sequence in which the firm has to make and receive its payments, it may be compelled to plan for a particular level of sales which will not fulfil the condition, price = marginal cost. Either the financial planning involved, or the difficulty of obtaining certain raw materials, may set limitations on the profit plan, and make impossible the achievement of maximum total profit given by the condition, price = marginal cost.

The various partial plans must always be co-ordinated, within the framework of the total plan. One can continue to take as the objective of the firm the maximum total profit, but "maximum profit" must be taken as satisfying certain other conditions, for example, the firm's liquidity requirements. Even so, an individual firm's supply curve can still, of course, be drawn up. It is still possible to estimate a particular level of output which will be sold at each level of prices in the period. The concept of the individual supply curve depends simply on the assumption that the firm is behaving as a quantity-adjuster, but not on any particular assumption as to the objective the firm sets itself. Of course, the supply curve of the firm will alter with the objective of the firm.

## 2. The Profit Plan of a Seller Facing an Expected Price–Sales Relation

1. In Section II, paragraph 2, we considered the revenue plan of a seller facing an expected price–sales relation, that is, of a seller who is in a position *either* to fix the price and to leave to the buyers acting as quantity-adjusters the fixing of the quantity sold, *or* to fix the quantity sold and leave it to the buyers to decide at what price they are willing to buy the quantity offered. Let us describe the planned individual price–sales function of the seller as

$$p = f(x),$$

where $p$ = the price and $x$ the sales of a seller who believes that this quantity can be sold in the planning period at the price $p$. Then the total revenue $R$ is obtained by multiplying the sales by the price:

$$R = p \cdot x = x \cdot f(x).$$

The shape of the revenue curve (which is the curve which shows how total revenue varies with the level of planned sales) depends on the form of the price–sales function. If the seller is acting as a monopolist, then he assumes in his plans that his sales depend solely on the level of *his own* price. The cross-elasticities of sales in relation to the prices of the goods offered by other sellers, will be considered as nil or approximately nil. If the seller is acting as a polypolist, then he assumes that his sales depend not only on the level of his own price, but *also* on the level of the prices fixed by other sellers for their goods.

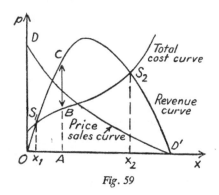

*Fig. 59*

But he assumes that changes in his own price will not lead to alterations in price by his rivals. Given the behaviour of the buyers, the shape of the price–sales curve which he draws up in his plans is then determined by the level of his rivals' prices. The curve will be constructed on the basis of the expected behaviour of the buyers and the expected prices of his rivals. If the seller is acting as an oligopolist, then he assumes not only that his sales depend both on his own price and on the prices of his competitors, but also that the competitors will react in one way or another to alterations in his price by altering their own prices. According to the assumption which the oligopolist seller makes in his plans about the nature of the reaction of rivals, the position and shape of the expected price–sales curve will be different. In every expected price–sales curve it is essentially the expectations of the seller as to the behaviour of the buyers and of possible rivals that are expressed. The relations have already been considered earlier.

2. Let us assume, first, that the expected price–sales curve, and the corresponding total revenue curve, have the shapes portrayed in Fig. 59. In order to discover the profits corresponding to different combinations of price and sales, that is, to different points on the

price–sales curve, we have to subtract total costs from the total revenue. We assume that the total cost curve, as worked out in the plans, has the shape given in Fig. 59. The profit corresponding to the sales $OA$ is then given by the distance $BC$. It is clear that in this case also there are two areas of losses and one of profits, exactly as in the case considered in the previous paragraph. A positive profit is only obtained if the sales lie between the quantities $x_1$ and $x_2$, at which costs and revenue are exactly equal. In the following table these relations are further clarified by means of a numerical example.

| (1) Price | (2) Sales | (3) Revenue | (4) Costs | (5) Profit | (6) Marginal revenue | (7) Marginal costs | (8) Marginal profit |
|---|---|---|---|---|---|---|---|
| 0 | 20 | 0 | 22 | −22 | | | |
| 1 | 18 | 18 | 20 | −2 | −9 | 1 | −8 |
| 2 | 16 | 32 | 18 | +14 | −7 | 1 | −6 |
| 3 | 14 | 42 | 16 | +26 | −5 | 1 | −4 |
| 4 | 12 | 48 | 14 | +34 | −3 | 1 | −2 |
| 5 | 10 | 50 | 12 | +38 | −1 | 1 | 0 |
| 5·5 | 9 | 49·5 | 11 | +38·5 | +0·5 | 1 | −0·5 |
| 6 | 8 | 48 | 10 | +38 | +1·5 | 1 | +0·5 |
| 7 | 6 | 42 | 8 | +34 | +3 | 1 | +2 |
| 8 | 4 | 32 | 6 | +26 | +5 | 1 | +4 |
| 9 | 2 | 18 | 4 | +14 | +7 | 1 | +6 |
| 10 | 0 | 0 | 2 | −2 | +9 | 1 | +8 |

A glance at Column 5 shows that a positive profit can only be obtained if the price is between 2 and 9 (that is, when sales are between 16 and 2). On the assumption that the seller is simply trying to maximize his profit in the single period for which he is planning, he will, in our numerical example, fix the price at 5·5 and will produce and offer for sale 9 units. The seller will, of course, not usually discover this (the most favourable price–quantity combination) in the first draft of his plan. His planning will start from the previous realized price, or from some price–quantity combination in the neighbourhood of the previous price. He will then try by altering his price or quantity to find out whether a rise in price (and a fall in sales) or a reduction in price (and an increase in sales) is profitable for him. What he has to consider is the same as what we found the quantity-adjuster had to consider in making his plans. He has to discover the relation between marginal revenue and marginal cost when he alters the quantity in his plan by one unit. The difference in the formation of their plans between a quantity-adjuster and a seller facing an expected price–sales function, consists simply in marginal revenue no longer in the latter case being independent of the size of the sales. For the quantity-adjuster marginal revenue (which is the increase in revenue from selling one more unit of output) was always constant and equal to the selling price. This relationship holds no longer. Rather, as we demonstrated in Section II, § 2, the marginal revenue for every level of sales above nil is always smaller than the price, and it decreases as sales increase and the price falls. It was shown that marginal revenue according to the Amoroso-Robinson formula is given by the equation:

$$\text{Marginal Revenue} = \text{Price} + \frac{\text{Price}}{\text{Elasticity of Sales}}$$

Marginal revenue diverges the more from price the smaller the elasticity of sales. Let us assume that in the first draft of the seller's plan marginal revenue is larger than marginal cost (i.e. that the increase in revenue from an increase of 1 unit in sales is larger than the corresponding increase in cost). Then it is obviously profitable for the seller to plan an increase in sales and a corresponding reduction in price. Further increases in sales will be profitable so long as marginal revenue is greater than marginal cost. But we know that for a price–sales curve of the shape given in Fig. 59 marginal revenue falls as sales increase, and becomes negative after the point of maximum revenue is reached. The difference between marginal revenue and marginal cost, i.e. the marginal profit, will, therefore, necessarily decrease with an increase in the quantity sold, and if we assume continuous variations in the quantity sold, will at a certain level of sales be nil, and beyond this will become negative. This only says that profit will have reached its maximum at a sales equal to $x_0$. At that point (a) *marginal revenue will be equal to marginal cost*; and (b) *immediately below that point marginal revenue will be greater, and immediately above less, than marginal cost.* If there are discontinuous variations in sales the point of maximum profit will obviously be at a level of sales for which the marginal profit is negative for any increase or decrease of one unit in the quantity sold; that is, with an increase (or decrease) in the quantity sold the marginal revenue will be smaller (or greater) than the marginal cost. In our numerical example profit reaches its maximum at sales of 9 units. In Columns 6, 7 and 8 we give the relevant magnitudes for marginal revenue, marginal cost, and marginal profit. A glance at these columns at once confirms the general rule we have given above. If we assume continuous variability of the quantity of sales, the quantity at which profit will be at a maximum must be such that the following two conditions are satisfied:

(1) Marginal Revenue = Marginal Cost,

or, making use of the Amoroso-Robinson relation,

(2) Price — Marginal Cost $= - \dfrac{\text{Price}}{\text{Elasticity of Sales}}$

*For a seller facing an expected price–sales function, profit will be at a maximum at that level of sales at which the difference between price and*

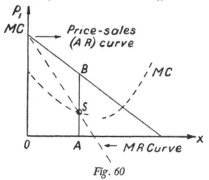

*Fig. 60*

*marginal cost is equal to the quotient of price and sales-elasticity (or the mathematical product of price and price-flexibility).* (We use here the term "price-flexibility", introduced by H. L. Moore, for the reciprocal value of the elasticity of sales in relation to price, that is, the "flexibility" of the price in relation to sales.) We shall designate this theorem "Cournot's Theorem" in honour of the economist who first treated the problems of the planning of prices on the above assumptions. The price–quantity combination which satisfied the (identical) conditions (1) and (2) above, or the point on the price-sales curve corresponding to it, may be described as the "Cournot point".[1]

Geometrically, the Cournot point is the point of intersection of the marginal revenue and marginal cost curves, or the price–quantity combination corresponding to this point (Fig. 60). If the maximum of profits occurs on the limit of the range over which output can vary (in Fig. 61, at the quantity $OA$ which represents full capacity

[1] Augustin Cournot (1801–1877) was a French mathematician, philosopher and economist. His main economic work, *Recherches sur les Principes Mathématiques de la Théorie des Richesses* (1838), contained the foundations of a considerable part of modern theory. Cournot, among other achievements, gave the first precise treatment of price formation under monopoly. The theory of price formation we have expounded above is often described as the theory of monopoly price. But this is too narrow a designation. The analysis holds for any seller facing an expected price-sales function, for polypolists and oligopolists as well as monopolists.

output) then we can only find left-hand marginal costs. At the point of maximum profit, left-hand marginal revenue will then always be greater than left-hand marginal costs.

3. As the elasticity of sales is normally negative, it follows from equation (2) that the most favourable price for the seller is always greater than marginal cost. The divergence of price from marginal

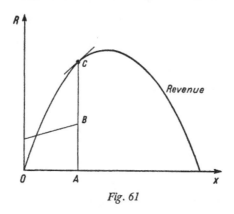

Fig. 61

cost is greater (or smaller) the smaller (or greater) is the elasticity of sales. The condition of maximum profit for a seller acting as a quantity-adjuster is that price equals marginal cost, which is simply a special case of the general relationship (2) when the elasticity of sales is infinite. For the quantity-adjuster, marginal revenue equals price.

4. From Cournot's Theorem (2) a series of other characteristics of the Cournot point may be deduced.

(a) It is clear, first, that for a given price–sales function and cost function, it is simply the *marginal* costs that are relevant for the position of the Cournot point. The level of fixed costs (for a quantity-adjuster as well as for a seller facing an expected price–sales function) has no influence on the Cournot point, or the most favourable price–sales combination for a seller. The level of fixed costs only influences the level of profit.

(b) As marginal costs are always positive, the elasticity of sales at the Cournot point must always be greater than 1. The most favourable price–sales combination for the seller must, therefore, lie on that part of the price–sales curve where sales are elastic in relation to price.

(c) From the fact that the Cournot point always lies on an elastic part of the sales curve, it follows that the quantity sold at the point of maximum profit will always be smaller than that quantity at which maximum total revenue is obtained.

5. To discover the Cournot point it is necessary to know the expected price–sales function and the cost function. It follows that the position of the Cournot point, given the cost function, depends on the form of the expected price–sales function. To each position of the expected price–sales function, there corresponds (with a given cost function) a particular optimum price–sales combination. It follows

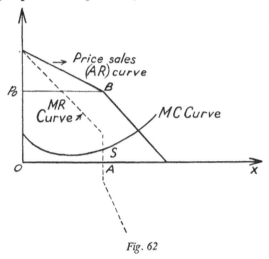

*Fig. 62*

from this that for a seller facing an expected price–sales curve, there can be no individual supply curve as there is in the case of a quantity-adjuster. The question as to what quantity will be offered at a given price has no sense in this case. The only possible question is: How will the seller react, with a given cost function, to movements in the expected price–sales function?

6. We wish to give a special treatment to the *case of an oligopolist seller* who has to reckon with his competitors following a reduction but not an increase in his own present price. It was shown previously that the expected price–sales curve for an oligopolist behaving in this way will show a kink at the prevailing price, with the consequence that the marginal revenue curve will be discontinuous at this price (Fig. 36). *When this is the case it may be profitable for the seller to stick to the previously prevailing price also for the coming period.* This will, in fact, be the case, if the marginal cost curve cuts the marginal revenue curve in the interval of discontinuity. With the curves as shown in Fig. 62 the previously prevailing price $p_0$ will also be the most favourable price for the seller in the coming period. The possibility we have here described may in some circumstances give

an explanation of oligopolists' behaviour, in so far as this often shows stability in prices.

7. Our previous investigation was conducted on the assumption that the seller has no active sales costs. We now have to study how the planning of prices and sales is carried on if the seller tries to influence the shape of the price–sales function by incurring *active selling costs* (*advertising costs*). In Fig. 63 the curve $D_0D_0'$ represents

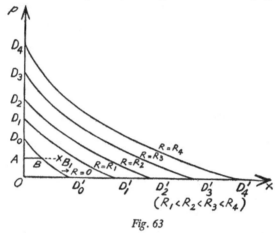

*Fig. 63*

the expected price–sales function of a seller if no advertising costs are being incurred. We now have to ask what are the minimum advertising costs which have to be incurred in order to sell the larger quantity $AB_1$ at a price of $OA$. These minimum advertising costs we may describe as $R$. Their level obviously depends on the price the seller is fixing and the quantity he wishes to sell at this price. The minimum advertising costs that have to be incurred are, therefore, a function of the price aimed at ($p$), and of the quantity which it is hoped to sell ($x$):

$$R = R(p, x)^{(1)} \qquad (3)$$

This function has these characteristics: (a) that with a constant price ($p$), $R$ increases with an increase in the sales in such a way that the advertising costs, above a particular level of sales, increase more rapidly than the sales; each further increase in sales by one unit requiring an increased amount of advertising costs; and (b) that with constant sales $X$, $R$ increases with an increase in price so that above a certain price further price-increases can only be achieved by incurring

---

(1) This function is the inverse function of the demand function which has $R$ as a parameter: $x = f(p, R)$.

increasing additions to advertising costs. To every price–quantity combination lying to the right of the price–sales curve $D_0 D_0'$ there corresponds a particular minimum level of advertising costs.

The totality of all the price–quantity combinations which, in the opinion of the seller, can be realized with the same advertising costs $R_1$ is represented by the price–sales curve $D_1 D_1'$, corresponding to this level of advertising costs (Fig. 63). Such a price–sales curve exists for

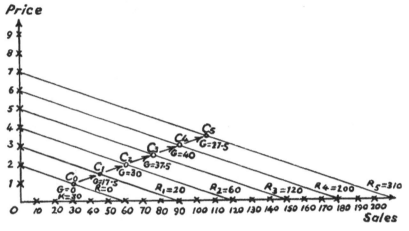

Fig. 64

every conceivable level of advertising costs. The higher the sum set aside in the economic plan for advertising costs, the further the price–sales curve shifts to the right. For every price–sales curve corresponding to a particular $R$ we can discover the appropriate Cournot point, and the maximum profit corresponding to this point (= revenue minus the production costs minus the advertising costs). The seller will then try to discover the Cournot point on that price–sales curve which corresponds to the absolute maximum profit (*maximum maximorum*). These relations are clarified in the numerical example of Fig. 64. In the diagram it has been assumed for simplicity that the production costs of the seller are independent of the level of sales, and are always at the level of 30 (shillings) for the period. It is further assumed that a rise in advertising costs results in a parallel shift in the price–sales curve. To every sales curve corresponding to a particular level of advertising costs there is a Cournot point ($C$) and a particular level of profit. It is clear that the incurring of advertising costs to a quantity of 20 (shillings) will make it profitable to offer instead of 30 units at a price of 1 (shilling), 45 units at a price 1·5. The profit thereby increases from 0 to 17·5. Similarly, it is profitable further to increase the advertising costs to 60 (shillings) and to offer 60 units at a price of 2 (shillings) whereby a further increase in profit of 12·5 (shillings) is obtained. In view of the characteristics of the advertising function (3) which we have described above, we finally reach a level of advertising costs at which a further increase leads to a diminution in profits. This level of advertising costs is obtained when $R = 200$. At this expenditure on advertisement 90 units will be sold at a price of 3 (shillings); this price–quantity combination results in a profit of 40 (shillings).

It will be noticed that when we introduce active sales costs both the price and the quantity become an action-parameter of the seller. The seller can choose price and quantity, whereby the production and advertising costs incurred are uniquely determined. If we designate the profit as $G$, and the production costs as $C(x)$[1], then the profit will be given by the equation:

$$G = p \cdot x - [C(x) + R(p, x)] \qquad (4)$$

where $p$ and $x$ are mutually independent variables. The seller will try in his economic plan so to fix price and quantity that the profit will be a maximum. If advertising costs are not incurred, the most favourable price–quantity combination is given by the condition that marginal revenue = marginal cost. In place of this equation, when advertising costs are incurred, two conditions are necessary, which result simply from the fact that every divergence from the most favourable price–quantity combination will lead to a diminution in profits. The two conditions (assuming the possibility of continuous variations of all the magnitudes) are:

(a) *With a variation in sales, while prices remain constant, the marginal revenue* (with respect to quantity) *must be equal to the sum of the marginal production cost and the marginal advertising cost* (with respect to quantity).

(b) *For variations in price with sales constant, the marginal revenue must be equal to the marginal advertising cost* (each taken with respect to price).[2]

---

[1] We assume, for the sake of simplicity, that there are no production costs dependent on turnover.

[2] We know revenue ($T$) to be $T = p \cdot x$. Hence, for case (a),

$$\frac{\partial T}{\partial x} = p.$$

Immediately before the optimum point is reached marginal revenue must furthermore be greater than marginal cost, and immediately after it must be smaller.

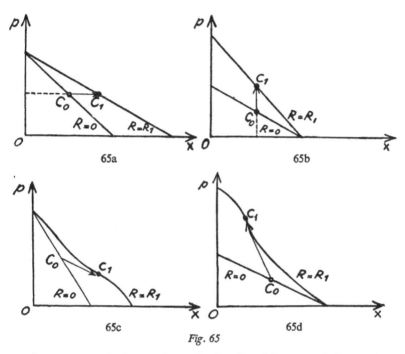

Fig. 65

In our numerical example, a rise in advertising costs led to a rise in price and in the quantity sold. That need not be so. How the most favourable price–quantity combination changes depends on how the

---

and for case (b),

$$\frac{\partial T}{\partial p} = x.$$

Condition (a) can accordingly be expressed as:

$$p = \frac{\partial C}{\partial x} + \frac{\partial R}{\partial x}$$

i.e. the sum of marginal production costs and marginal advertising costs must equal price.
Condition (b) reduces to:

$$x = \frac{\partial R}{\partial p}.$$

price–sales function shifts when advertising costs are incurred. Figure 65 shows different possibilities where, for simplicity, it is assumed that there are only fixed costs.[1]

A glance at Fig. 65 shows that if advertising costs are incurred, the price–sales curve may shift so that either (a) a larger quantity will be sold at an unchanged price, (b) the same quantity at a higher price, (c) a larger quantity at a lower price, or (d) a smaller quantity at a higher price.

### 3. The Problem of Price-Discrimination

We have assumed up to now that the seller of a good facing an expected price–sales curve offers this good in the forthcoming economic period at a price which is the same for all buyers. A seller, however, facing an expected price–sales curve, may under certain conditions have the possibility of offering the same good to different buyers at different prices; that is, he may be able to discriminate in fixing his prices for different buyers. We now wish to deal with the problems resulting from this possibility.

1. One may speak of *price-discrimination* if a seller in one economic period offers the *same* good to *different* buyers, or groups of buyers, at *different* prices.

For example, electric current is sold to households at a price different from that at which it is sold to firms: a doctor discriminates in fixing his fees in accordance with the level of income of his patients: an hotel at a holiday resort charges different prices in the season and outside it: telephone charges are different according to the time of day at which they are incurred.

A practice related to price-discrimination occurs if a seller fixes different prices in the planning period for two not completely similar goods (e.g. chocolate of the same quality in different packing, or passenger transport in second and third class, etc.).

There is no price-discrimination if, for example, a seller in one economic period sells a book at a price of 10 shillings and, owing to the small sales of the book, having changed his economic plan, reduces the price to 6 shillings in the next period.

[1] See F. Zeuthen: *Economic Theory and Method*, (London, 1955) p. 273. The problem of planning prices and sales where advertising is undertaken was first dealt with by E. Chamberlin in his book, of such seminal importance for modern price analysis, *The Theory of Monopolistic Competition*. Considerable progress with the problem was made in the studies of B. Barfod: *Reklamen i teoretisk-økonomisk Belysning*, Copenhagen, 1937, and F. Zeuthen: "Effect and Cost of Advertisement" in *Nordisk Tidsskrift for Teknisk Økonomi*, Copenhagen, 1935.

2. It is clear that a seller who is acting as a quantity-adjuster, and is therefore in a relation of atomistic and homogeneous competition with other sellers, is not in a position to indulge in price-discrimination. *A necessary condition for price-discrimination is that the seller faces an expected price–sales function for his goods.* He must be in a position to act either as a monopolist, a polypolist, or an oligopolist. The seller must have a market "of his own" for his good, which will be expressed in his plans by his assuming that a particular price–sales function holds good in his case.

3. The quantity of sales which the seller will expect to make at different prices can clearly be divided into partial quantities for the individual buyers, or groups of buyers, who are demanding the seller's good. In Fig. 66 it is assumed that the total sales $AC$, which the seller reckons to sell at a price $OA$, is divided into two partial quantities, $AB$ for Group 1 of the buyers, and $BC$ for Group 2. If we carry through this division of the total sales for every price, then the relevant price–sales function will be given for each of the two groups of buyers. In Fig 66 the curve $DD''$ represents the price–sales function of Group 1 of the buyers. The price–sales curve of Group 2 can be derived from the fact that each horizontal distance corresponding to $BC$ between the two curves $DD''$ and $DD'$ represents the quantity sold at each price. Figure 67 contains the partial price–sales functions of the two groups of buyers and the total price–sales function for the case of linear functions.

The process of price-discrimination consists in so dividing up the total price–sales curve as between different groups of buyers that it is profitable for the seller, instead of selling at the same price to all purchasers, to fix different prices simultaneously for the different groups of buyers. This sort of discrimination is, of course, only possible *if there is no possibility of communication between the two groups of purchasers.* It must be impossible for those purchasers who are to pay the higher price to join the other group for whom a lower price is fixed. It must also be impossible that the group of buyers with the lower price can by arbitrage make the good available to the buyers who are charged the higher price. There are a wide range of examples in practice of the ways and means by which this process of isolating different groups of buyers of one and the same good can be carried out, so that they have to pay different prices to the same seller. Often the process of isolating a particular group arises necessarily from the nature of the good offered (for example, the personal services of a doctor: freight charges for different kinds of goods). In other cases it has to be artificially brought about (for example, by tariffs, or a restriction on re-selling). The means used in effectively

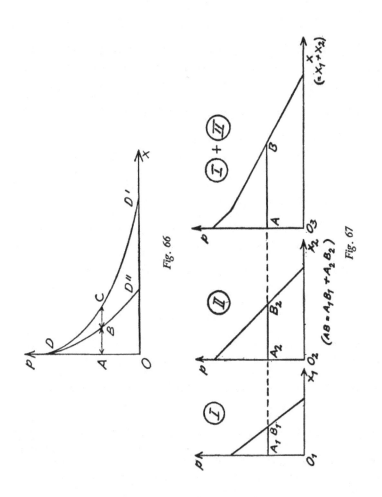

Fig. 66

Fig. 67

isolating a group of buyers depend on whether the objective is *discrimination on personal grounds*, that is, discrimination in respect of the personal position of the consumer (for the services of a doctor, or in school fees); or whether it is *discrimination on material grounds*, that is, discrimination in regard to the use to which the good is put (e.g. the use of electricity for domestic lighting and for industrial purposes); or whether it is *discrimination on geographical grounds*, that is, discrimination in respect of the geographical position of the buyer (for example, selling abroad and in the home market). A seller may discriminate on geographical grounds between home and foreign buyers, so that for the foreign buyers a lower price is fixed *ex-works* than for the domestic buyers. It must then be emphasised that discrimination is only occurring if the price is different for the two groups of buyers ex-works.[1] The kind of geographical price discrimination which is described as "dumping" can only be successfully carried out if the goods sold abroad at a lower price ex-works can be prevented from being returned to the original country. Often transport costs give a sufficient protection against the return of dumped goods. If the home market price at the factory is $p_i$, the export price at the factory $p_e$ (so that $p_e < p_i$), and the transport costs from the factory to the foreign buyer are $t$, then if

$$p_e + 2t \geqq p_i,$$

obviously the transport costs are sufficient to prevent the re-import of the dumped goods. If on the other hand

$$p_e + 2t < p_i,$$

then the difference between the home market and the foreign price ex-works is larger than twice the transport costs, so that if it is not to be profitable to reimport the good, a duty equal to $d$ will be necessary on the good in question, so that

$$p_e + 2t + d \geqq p_i.$$

The import duty must be so high that the difference between the

[1] If, for example, a seller sells the same good, at the same time, to all buyers in a particular geographical area, at the same *delivered* price (the so-called zonal price system), then there is discrimination for or against all buyers since their transport costs would be different according to their distances from the factory. Similarly the Basing-Point system is a form of geographical price-discrimination. The good is sold at a price calculated by adding the transport costs to the point of delivery, to the fixed price at some selected basic point. The price ex-works is then given by subtracting the transport costs from the factory to the buyer from the delivered price (Pittsburgh-plus system).

home market and the foreign price ex-works is not more than twice the transport cost, plus the duty.

4. Let us now assume that our seller has, either arbitrarily or in accordance with one of the different grounds for price-discrimination, divided a market for which he has previously fixed a single price on the basis of an expected price–sales function, into two groups of buyers, and has estimated the corresponding price–sales functions for the two groups. We have to ask which quantity of output, and which division of this output between the two markets offer the greatest total profit to the seller.

In Fig. 68, the price–sales functions of the two groups of buyers, I and II, are represented by the straight lines $S_1S_1'$ and $S_2S_2'$. The quantity of sales corresponding to one given price ruling on both markets is arrived at by adding together the quantities sold on the two sub-markets.

Let the equation of the price–sales function for sub-market I be:

$$p_1 = 10 - \tfrac{1}{2}x_1,$$

and that for sub-market II:

$$p_2 = 7 - \tfrac{1}{4}x_2.$$

If both markets are treated as one, and prices fixed uniformly, then the following equation gives the total sales function:

$$p = 10 - \tfrac{1}{2}x \quad \text{where} \quad 7 \leqq p \leqq 10;$$
$$p = 8 - \tfrac{1}{6}x \quad \text{where} \quad 0 \leqq p < 7.$$

For simplicity we shall assume marginal costs to be constant and equal to 2. A simple calculation will show that with uniform pricing in both markets, maximum profits are reached at a price $p = 5$. To this there corresponds a sale of 18 units, giving a revenue of 90 shillings and profits (neglecting fixed costs) of 54 shillings. The sales are divided between the two markets as follows:

$$x_1 = 10; \qquad x_2 = 8.$$

Figure 68 tells us at once that on sub-market I the marginal revenue corresponding to the quantity $x_1 = 10$ is nought, while on sub-market II there corresponds to the quantity $x_2 = 8$ a marginal revenue of 3. If, therefore, only one price is charged, marginal revenue on sub-market I (II) is less (more) than marginal cost. This being so, the seller will find it profitable to adopt a different allocation of his total sales of 18 units as between the two sub-markets, contracting (expanding) sales to sub-market I (II) or, which comes

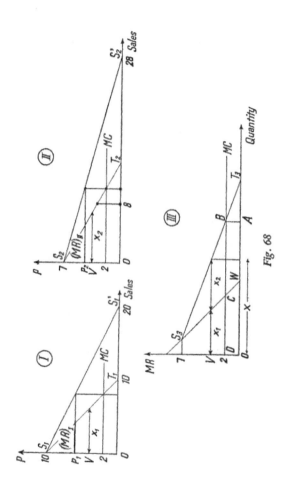

Fig. 68

to the same thing, raising the price on sub-market I and lowering it on sub-market II. More particularly he will find it profitable to keep raising the price on sub-market I (and lowering it on II) till the marginal revenues on the two markets are equal. While marginal revenue on one market remains above that in the other, profits can always be enlarged by reducing sales in the market with the lower marginal revenue and expanding them in the market with the higher marginal revenue. This proposition has general validity. The optimal distribution of a *given quantity of output* between several sub-markets must always satisfy the *condition of the equality of marginal revenues on all sub-markets*.

To obtain a simple diagrammatic presentation of the most favourable distribution of a *given* output between two sub-markets, we add the marginal revenue curves of the sub-markets horizontally. Diagram III in Fig. 68 shows this horizontal addition of the marginal revenue curves implied in our example.[1] Marginal revenue is $OV$ ($= 4$), and the corresponding sales are $x_1$ in sub-market I and $x_2$ in sub-market II. For each level of marginal revenue we plot in diagram III the sum of the corresponding sales in the two sub-markets. This yields the curve $S_3 T_3$ which, together with the curve $S_3 W$ (being the marginal revenue curve of sub-market I) allows us to read off the optimal distribution of a given output between the two sub-markets.

In our example, the quantity $x = 18$ ($= OA$) — at which maximum profits are earned when prices are fixed uniformly—is optimally distributed between the two markets if:

$$x_1 = 8; \qquad x_2 = 10.\text{[2]}$$

With this distribution, marginal revenue in both sub-markets equals marginal costs:

$$MR_I = MR_{II} = MC = 2.$$

It follows that the output of $x = 18$ is similarly the optimal total output for the discriminating supplier. The corresponding prices are $p_1 = 6$ and $p_2 = 4 \cdot 5$. Thus we see that it pays the seller to raise the price on sub-market I and to lower it on sub-market II. Profits are

---

[1] Figure 68 relates only to the price interval which is relevant to transactions on both markets, i.e. $0 \leqq p < 7$

[2] The marginal revenues in the two sub-markets are:

$$MR_I = 10 - x_1; \qquad MR_{II} = 7 - \tfrac{1}{2}x_2.$$

The optimal distribution of 18 units follows from the equations:

$$10 - x_1 = 7 - \tfrac{1}{2}x_2; \qquad x_1 + x_2 = 18.$$

greater by 3 shillings than they would be under uniform pricing.

In our example, total sales were the same whether there was price discrimination or not. This is always so if the price–sales functions are linear. If they are non-linear, the total quantity of sales under price-discrimination may be either greater or smaller than under uniform pricing. For instance, the output that is optimal under uniform pricing may be so divided as to make the marginal revenues in the two sub-markets equal to each other but greater (smaller) than marginal costs for the total quantity of sales. It will then pay to increase (reduce) the total quantity of sales and once again to distribute the new quantity between the two sub-markets so as to equate marginal revenues in them. The seller will find it profitable to increase the quantity of sales, or lower it, till marginal costs are equal to marginal revenue on each sub-market. Uniform pricing would in this case result in an optimal quantity of sales which is less (more) than that under price discrimination.

*In general, therefore, the quantity of sales in the two sub-markets, to be optimal, must satisfy two conditions:*

$$\text{Marginal Revenue I} = \text{Marginal Revenue II}$$
$$= \text{Marginal Costs.} \qquad (5)$$

*So long as marginal revenue differs from marginal costs for either of the two groups of buyers, the seller can achieve an increase in his total profits by expanding the quantity sold to the group for which marginal revenue is greater than marginal cost and contracting it where the marginal revenue is smaller than marginal cost.*

It is easy to determine graphically the two quantities $x_1$ and $x_2$ which satisfy condition (5). We have to look for the intersection of the curve $S_3T_3$ (Diagram III) which was arrived at by adding horizontally the marginal revenue curves of the sub-markets, with the marginal cost curve. In our example, which assumed constant marginal cost, this occurred at point $B$. The optimal total quantity of sales is therefore $OA$ of which $CD$ will be sold on sub-market I and $BC$ on sub-market II. For sub-market I, the seller fixes the price $p_1$, and for market II the price $p_2$.

The fact that discrimination must lead to a larger profit than uniformity is obviously the essential reason why a seller facing an expected price–sales function discriminates. But he can only carry this out successfully on an essential pre-condition, which is easily derivable from condition (5) if we remember that according to the Amoroso-Robinson formula

$$\text{Marginal Revenue} = \text{Price} \times \left(1 + \frac{1}{\text{Elasticity of Sales}}\right).$$

Let the prices for the two groups of buyers be $p_1$ and $p_2$, and the elasticity of sales at these prices be $\eta_1$ and $\eta_2$, then the condition of equality of the marginal revenues from both groups of buyers is given in the formula:

$$p_1 \cdot \left(1 + \frac{1}{\eta_1}\right) = p_2 \cdot \left(1 + \frac{1}{\eta_2}\right) \qquad (6)$$

or:

$$\frac{p_1}{p_2} = \frac{1 + \dfrac{1}{\eta_2}}{1 + \dfrac{1}{\eta_1}} \qquad (6a)$$

From this equation it is clear that the prices $p_1$ and $p_2$ for the two groups of buyers are only different if the elasticities of sales in relation to price are different for the two groups; and that the price will be higher for that group of buyers for whom the elasticity of sales in relation to price is absolutely lower. *It is now clear that the real reason why it pays a seller to fix different prices for different groups of buyers lies in the different elasticities of demand in relation to price-changes of the two groups of buyers.* With a uniform price it would be most profitable for the seller to charge a price $p = 5$ (Fig. 68). At this price the elasticity of sales for Group 1 is absolutely smaller than it is for Group 2. It is just for this reason that it pays the seller to lower the price for Group II and raise it for Group 1. It is, therefore, the task of the seller who is planning to discriminate, to form, or to choose, such groups of buyers as fulfil the condition of different elasticities of sales.

The important conclusion which we have obtained from the relation (6a) also provides the explanation for the fact that with geographical price-discrimination between home and foreign buyers the foreign price ex-works is usually lower than the home price. In general, the sales to home buyers are less elastic in relation to price than those to the foreign group of buyers. The reverse case does occasionally occur when the foreign price ex-works is higher than the domestic price, i.e. when sales at home are more elastic than the sales abroad.

5. Up to now we have been starting from a given division of the total sales-function and have asked what price-discrimination will then be most profitable in respect of the different groups of buyers. We come to the same results if we consider a seller who first delivers goods at a uniform price to a single group of buyers (for example, domestic buyers), and then introduces into his plans a second group

of buyers (for example, foreign buyers), and seeks to discriminate between the two groups in the prices he charges.

6. Another sort of question arises if the seller facing an expected price–sales curve has the possibility of dividing as he likes the total sales between the different groups of buyers. The total price-sales function can then be divided in a number of different ways into different partial price–sales functions for the different groups of buyers. To every possible division there corresponds a particular optimum price-discrimination based on our condition (5). The question then arises as to which of the possible ways of dividing the buyers will be most profitable for a seller with a given total price-sales function. This problem also is capable of exact treatment and solution, though we shall not go into it here.[1]

7. The possibility of price-discrimination also occurs if the seller has a different objective in view from that of maximizing the total profit for a single economic period. The possibility of price-discrimination is not bound up with the application of a particular mode of behaviour, but simply with the assumption that the seller faces an expected price–sales function which differs for different economically isolatable groups of buyers.

### (ii) The Profit Plan of a Multi-Product Firm

This problem is so many-sided that no exhaustive treatment is possible within the limits of an introduction. We confine ourselves to the examination of a few important cases.

1. Let us begin by considering the case of a firm which makes *two goods in common production*. Let the cost function be linear and of the form

$$C = a_1 x_1 + a_2 x_2 + b, \tag{7}$$

where $b$ denotes the fixed costs in the period, $a_1$ and $a_2$ the variable costs per unit of good 1 and 2, and $x_1$ and $x_2$ the output of good 1 and good 2 respectively.

1a. For a seller who acts as a quantity-adjuster, i.e. who considers the prices $p_1$ and $p_2$ of the two goods as given, profits within the period will be:

$$G = (p_1 - a_1) \cdot x_1 + (p_2 - a_2) \cdot x_2 - b. \tag{8}$$

If it is assumed that the seller aims at maximum profits, we have to discover those values of $x_1$ and $x_2$ for which the expression (8) is

[1] See J. Robinson: *The Economics of Imperfect Competition*, London, 1933 (Chapter 15).

maximized. The constant $b$ having no influence upon the position of the maximum, we may instead of (8) consider the expression

$$g = (p_1 - a_1) \cdot x_1 + (p_2 - a_2) \cdot x_2. \tag{8a}$$

Let us now look for those combinations $x_1, x_2$ which yield the same profit $g$. Clearly, these combinations will lie along a straight line which cuts off the distance $\dfrac{g}{p_1 - a_1}$ on the $x_1$ axis, and the distance $\dfrac{g}{p_2 - a_2}$ on the $x_2$ axis. Such a straight line we call an iso-profit line (Fig. 69). For each value of $g$ there exists one definite

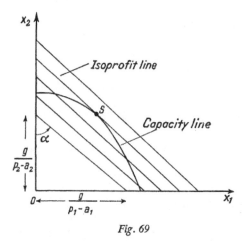

*Fig. 69*

iso-profit line. The greater is $g$, the further will the iso-profit line lie away from the origin. If we allow $g$ to assume all the values from 0 to $\infty$, we obtain a family of parallel straight lines which form with the $x_2$ axis (taken in its negative sense) the angle $\alpha$ such that

$$\tan \alpha = \frac{p_2 - a_2}{p_1 - a_1}.$$

We now recall that only those output combinations $x_1, x_2$ can be achieved by the seller which lie either inside the area bounded by the capacity frontier and the axes, or on the capacity frontier. As soon as we have drawn the capacity frontier on the diagram of iso-profit lines, we can determine those quantity combinations $x_1, x_2$ which are optimal for the seller. With a capacity frontier of the shape drawn in Fig. 69, this optimal combination $x_1, x_2$ is represented by the co-ordinates of the point $S$ in which the capacity frontier touches an iso-profit line. Any other quantity combination inside or upon the capacity frontier represents a smaller total profit. As the price of good 2 rises while that of good 1 remains constant, so the angle $\alpha$ will increase and the point $S$ moves to the left. It then becomes profitable to expand the sales of good 2 and to contract those of good 1. In each case the firm's capacity is always fully utilized. The

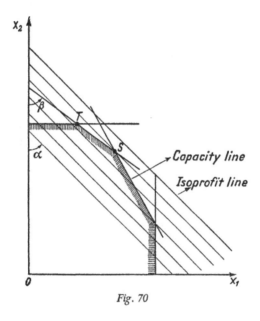

Fig. 70

manner of this utilization of capacity depends on the prices of the two goods.

The case of a capacity frontier shaped as in Fig. 70 possesses some distinctive features. The practical significance of such broken straight line capacity frontiers was discussed earlier on (see p. 94). Given the slope of the iso-profit lines in Fig. 70, given, that is, those prices of the two goods, we observe that the point $S$ marks the seller's optimal combination of the quantities $x_1$, $x_2$.

Imagine now that the price $p_2$ rises continuously while the price $p_1$ stays constant. In the case exemplified by Fig. 69 this price change would produce a continuous leftward shift of the point $S$, that is a continuous rise (fall) in the supply of $x_2$ ($x_1$). In the case illustrated in Fig. 70, however, the continuous rise in $p_2$ causes not a continuous but rather a discontinuous rise of $x_2$ (fall of $x_1$). If $p_2$ rises, the point

$S$ will continue to represent the optimal quantity combination until the angle $\alpha$ reaches the size of angle $\beta$. When $\alpha = \beta$, the seller's optimal combinations are all the output combinations on the line $TS$. If $\beta < \alpha < 90°$, the optimal quantity combination will be represented by the point $T$. Depending on the prices of the two goods, any of the points on the capacity frontier can represent the optimal combination of outputs.

For exercise, the reader should draw the curve of the supply functions $x_1 = x_1(p_1, p_2)$ and $x_2 = x_2(p_1, p_2)$ for each of the two cases portrayed in Figs. 69 and 70.

1b. If the firm is confronted by an *expected price–sales function* for its products, the iso-profit lines will cease to be straight lines. If, for instance, the price–sales functions are linear, the family of iso-profit lines will be represented by a family of ellipses of the position shown in Fig. 71. Each ellipse corresponds to a given level of profits and the higher the profit, the further does the corresponding ellipse lie from the co-ordinate axes.[1] The point $P$ represents that combination $x_1$, $x_2$ which yields the highest absolute profit. Figure 71 shows that in this case, exactly as in that of a single-product firm with linear cost functions, it is quite possible for the point of maximum profits to lie inside the area bounded by capacity frontier and axes.

2. The relationships which we examined in the preceding section can obviously also be phrased in the *language of marginal analysis*. If revenue in its dependence on the quantities of sales $x_1$ and $x_2$ be described by

$$R = R(x_1, x_2)$$

and if the total cost function is

$$C = C(x_1, x_2)$$

then the total profit, $G$, is given by

$$G = R(x_1, x_2) - C(x_1, x_2).$$

---

[1] Let the demand functions be:

$$p_1 = m_1 - n_1 x_1 \qquad (m_1 > 0, n_1 > 0)$$
$$p_2 - m_2 - n_2 x_2 \qquad (m_2 > 0, n_2 > 0)$$

implying the assumption that both goods are mutually independent as regards the demand for them.

Let the cost function be:

$$C = a + b_1 x_1 + b_2 x_2 \qquad (a > 0, b_1 > 0, b_2 > 0)$$

The profit function is accordingly:

$$G = (m_1 - n_1 x_1) \cdot x_1 + (m_2 - n_2 x_2) \cdot x_2 - a - b_1 x_1 - b_2 x_2$$
$$= (m_1 - b_1) \cdot x_1 + (m_2 - b_2) \cdot x_2 - n_1 x_1^2 - n_2 x_2^2 - a.$$

For $G$ = constant, this equation describes an ellipse.

Assume now that the firm's plan, in its first draft, is based upon the quantity combinations $\bar{x}_1$, $\bar{x}_2$. There results a profit in the amount of $\bar{G}$. The seller will now consider whether he can add to his profits by making a partial change in the quantity of one good while keeping the other quantity constant. He will thus, at every stage, compare the *partial marginal revenue* for each good (cf. p. 77, Section B, para. 2) with the corresponding *partial marginal costs* (cf. p. 97, Section C,

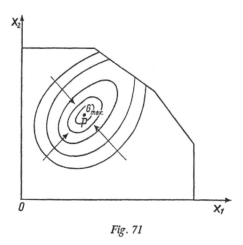

*Fig. 71*

para. 2). So long as partial marginal revenue for a good continues to exceed its partial marginal cost, the seller will find it to his advantage to sell more of that good. If, on the contrary, partial marginal revenue is less than partial marginal costs, it is profitable to contract the quantity sold of that good. *Provided that a profit maximum exists inside the region of capacity* an optimal quantity combination has to fulfil the two following conditions:

(a) partial marginal revenue must equal partial marginal costs; and

(b) the partial marginal revenue yielded by any smaller (greater) quantity of a good must exceed (fall short of) the partial marginal costs.

These conditions need to be modified if the point of maximum profits lies on the capacity frontier. Point $S$ in Fig. 69, for example, can be characterized thus: at the point of maximum profits, the marginal rate of substitution of $x_2$ for $x_1$ must equal the ratio $\dfrac{p_1 - a_1}{p_2 - a_2}$. In Fig. 70, even this proposition ceases to be valid for points like $S$ and $T$ because the marginal rate of substitution cannot be defined for these points.[1] But these facts do not entitle us to conclude that marginal analysis is inapplicable to these cases. Marginal analysis is not identical with the above two conditions (a) and (b). Nor is it conditional on the assumption either of profit maximization or of the relevant functions being continuous and differentiable. It cannot be sufficiently stressed that marginal thought means thinking in terms of changes, be they infinitesimally small or finite, in economic variables, or in terms of the relationships between such changes. Wherever thought proceeds in terms of changes in variables or of the relations between such changes—and thinking in terms of changes is of central importance for the science of economics—marginal analysis is called for.[2] This thesis does not conflict with the observation that the combination of linear profit functions and broken straight line capacity frontiers will not allow the profit maximum to be determined by the normal means of the differential calculus, and that therefore other methods must be employed. The mathematical technique of "linear programming" which was evolved to deal with this very case supplements rather than supplants marginal analysis.[3]

3. The same rules hold for the case of *joint production in variable proportions*. Special consideration must be given to the case of *joint production in constant proportions*. It was shown before (Section III, Para. 3) that we may treat a firm producing joint products in fixed proportions as a single-product firm with a complex product, so that the profit plan for a single-product firm can simply be applied to this special case of joint production.

(a) Let us consider first the case of a seller acting as a quantity

---

[1] There only exists a right-hand or left-hand marginal rate of substitution.

[2] cf. E. Schneider, "Der Realismus der Marginalanalyse in der Preistheorie." (*Weltwirtschaftliches Archiv*, vol. 73, 1954.)

[3] This technique, developed by Dantzig and others, deals with the determination of the maxima of functions in several variables whose range of variation is subject to certain restrictions. It is, therefore, concerned with the problem of how to maximize linear functions in several variables with side conditions in the form of inequalities.

cf. chiefly the work by R. Dorfman, Paul A. Samuelson, R. M. Solow, *Linear Programming and Economic Analysis* (New York, Toronto, London, 1958). This work contains the fullest available description of the range of problems and also demonstrates that linear programming is in no conflict with marginal analysis: "It would be misleading to contrast the linear programming model with marginal analysis in general. Linear programming *is* marginal analysis, appropriately tailored to the case of a finite number of activities. Traditional marginal analysis is tailored to the case of a differentiable production function." (op. cit., p. 133.)

cf. also M. Beckmann, *Lineare Planungsrechnung*, 1959.

adjuster. The process of production yields two joint products $A$ and $B$ in the proportions of 1 unit of $A$ to 2 units of $B$. The price of the product $A$ is $p_a$, and that of the product $B$, $p_b$. The price of the complex unit is therefore $p_a + 2p_b$. If a sale of $x$ complex units consisting of $1A + 2B$ is planned, then the revenue will be:

$$R = (p_a + 2p_b) . x \qquad (9)$$

Let us call the costs of producing and of selling $x$ complex units $C(x)$, so that the profit will then be:

$$G = (p_a + 2p_b) . x - C(x) \qquad (10)$$

We are assuming that the cost function $C(x)$ is of the shape given in Fig. 41, so that we know, from our analysis of the profit plan of a

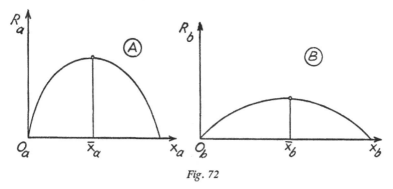

Fig. 72

single-product firm, that the maximum profit will be obtained with that level of sales at which the marginal cost of a complex unit of product is equal to the price. The seller will then plan that level of sales which satisfies the condition:

$$p_a + 2p_b = C'(x)^{(1)} \qquad (11)$$

(b) We now wish to assume that the seller is confronted with an expected price–sales function for both products and that they are both demanded independently. Let us call the quantity of good $A$ produced $x_a$, and that of good $B$ $x_b$. There then exists for each product a price–sales function and a revenue function corresponding to this. Figure 72 gives the two revenue curves (i.e. the revenue as a function of the sales).

Let us assume to start with that the seller has no costs, so that it is

(1) $C'(x)$ is the mathematical notation for "marginal cost of $x$ units". [Tr].

clear that it will be most profitable to offer that quantity of the two jointly produced goods at which the revenue is at a maximum and at which, therefore, the marginal revenue is nil. The seller will therefore plan a sales of $\bar{x}_a$ and $\bar{x}_b$ (Fig. 72). As the two products are being produced in a fixed unalterable proportion, it by no means follows that a production equal to $\bar{x}_a$ of $A$ also corresponds to a production of $\bar{x}_b$ of $B$.

We must here distinguish between the following cases:

($\alpha$) The proportion between the two most profitable levels of sales corresponds to the quantitative proportion in which the goods are produced:

$$\bar{x}_b = 2\bar{x}_a.$$

In this case the quantities produced correspond precisely with the planned levels of sales.

($\beta$) The proportion corresponding to what is the most profitable level of sales is not that in which the two goods are produced: i.e. either

$$\bar{x}_b < 2\bar{x}_a,$$

or
$$\bar{x}_b > 2\bar{x}_a.$$

If $\bar{x}_b < 2\bar{x}_a$, then the quantity $\bar{x}_a$, which yields the maximum revenue from good $A$, corresponds to a quantity of good $B$ larger than $\bar{x}_b$. If the seller sells the quantity $\bar{x}_b$ which is produced by this process, then he will not maximize the revenue he receives for $B$. If the maximum revenue is to be obtained, then the seller has to destroy the quantity of good $B$ which he produces in excess of $\bar{x}_b$ (i.e. the difference $x_b - \bar{x}_b$).[1]

If on the other hand $\bar{x}_b > 2\bar{x}_a$, then a larger quantity of $A$ will be produced than $\bar{x}_a$ and the excess quantity must be destroyed.

We can formulate these results as follows: the seller will plan that output of each good for which the marginal revenue is nil. If the technical conditions of production are such that the production of a good for which the marginal revenue is nil corresponds to the production of a quantity of a joint good for which the marginal revenue is negative, then part of the jointly produced good must be destroyed.

Similar considerations arise if we take into account costs of production and of selling. We have shown already, (a) that it is profitable for the seller of a good, in the case of a single-product firm, to increase the sales by one unit so long as marginal revenue is

[1] For simplicity we assume that the supplier does not have to reckon with costs of destruction. Where they arise they would have to be considered in his plans.

larger than marginal cost; (b) that the most favourable level of sales must satisfy the condition that marginal revenue equals marginal cost. The same propositions hold also in the case of joint production in constant proportions. It pays the seller to increase the sales by one complex unit if the marginal revenue of the complex unit is larger than the marginal cost; and it is profitable to increase the sales up to the point where the marginal revenue of a complex unit is equal to the marginal cost. We have here to notice also that, because of the fixed proportions in which the two goods are produced, an increase in the sales by 1 unit may lead to a negative marginal revenue from good $A$, while the marginal revenue from good $B$ is still positive. If that is the case, then it is profitable for the seller to destroy as much of the good $A$ as will make the marginal revenue from it equal to nil.

4. The analysis of this section has answered the question, when does it pay a firm to make certain changes in one or more of its action-parameters: when does it pay to lower the price of a product? When does it pay to increase the advertising effort in a given direction? When does it pay to alter the quality of a product? etc. The answer to these and similar questions reduces to a comparison of the expected changes in revenue and in cost. If we let $\alpha_1, \alpha_2, \ldots, \alpha_n$ stand, quite generally, without closer specification, for the action-parameters of the firm, then revenue, costs and profit can be presented as functions of these parameters:

$$G = R(\alpha_1, \alpha_2, \ldots, \alpha_n) - C(\alpha_1, \alpha_2, \ldots, \alpha_n).$$

A small, strictly speaking infinitesimal, change in parameter $\alpha$ by the amount $d\alpha$ will then be profitable if

$$\frac{\partial R}{d\alpha} > \frac{\partial C}{d\alpha} \tag{12}$$

i.e. when this change in parameters produces a marginal revenue which is greater than the corresponding marginal cost.

Beyond this we have enquired into the conditions which the parameters $\alpha_1, \alpha_2, \ldots, \alpha_n$ must satisfy at the profit maximum, provided such a maximum exists. The answer to this question led us to Cournot's point and its properties.

Of these two questions, it is undoubtedly the first which is most important in economic practice, since there the perennial problem is to determine when it becomes profitable to change an action-parameter. To this end, marginal revenue and marginal costs have to be compared with each other.

In concrete cases, condition (12) may be transformed in a definite manner. If it has to be decided, for instance, whether prices can profitably be lowered, condition (12) can, as we showed before, be re-written in the form:

$$p \cdot \left(1 + \frac{1}{\eta_{x,p}}\right) > m, \tag{13}$$

where $p$ is the price, $m$ the marginal costs, and $\eta_{x,p}$ the elasticity of sales with respect to price. It follows from (13) that

$$\frac{p}{p-m} < -\eta_{x,p}. \tag{14}$$

If price and marginal cost are known, it appears at once from (14) what is the minimum numerical value of the price elasticity of sales that would make a price reduction profitable.

If, to take a different example, one wishes to know whether with a given ruling price and known marginal costs $m$, an increase of advertising expenditure, $A$, in a particular direction would be profitable, then (12) can be re-written in the form

$$p \cdot \frac{dx}{dA} > m \cdot \frac{dx}{dA} + 1.^{(1)} \tag{15}$$

(15) can be transformed into

$$\frac{dx}{dA} > \frac{1}{p-m}$$

or into

$$\eta_{x,A} > \frac{A}{p \cdot x} \cdot \frac{1}{\dfrac{p-m}{p}}. \tag{16}$$

If, therefore, we know the price, marginal costs and the ratio of advertising costs to revenue, we can derive from (16) the minimum value for the elasticity of sales with respect to $A$ which would make profitable an increase in advertising cost.

But it must never be forgotten that the inequalities (14) and (16) are merely transformations of (12). *The transformation of (12) implies no change in the character of the argument.* It is always a matter of comparing marginal revenue with marginal costs.

---

[1] The left side of this inequality is the marginal revenue and the right side gives marginal cost. Total costs are the sum of production costs $C(x)$ and advertising costs $A$. Differentiating the sum $C(x) + A$ with respect to $A$, we obtain marginal costs with respect to $A$:

$$\frac{dC}{dx} \cdot \frac{dx}{dA} + 1 = m \cdot \frac{dx}{dA} + 1.$$

*Notwithstanding the primary importance of inequality (12) for economic practice*, the conditions that have to be satisfied by an existing profit maximum—the properties, that is, of the Cournot point—are nevertheless not without significance. They are significant first of all because they divide the area of rising profits from the area of falling profits if maximum profits are achieved *before* capacity is exhausted. They further enable theory to make statements about the results of the search for profits on the part of firms acting in fully transparent markets, and about the direction in which changes in the data influence the decisions of firms. To this we must return later on.

## Section E

## THE PRODUCTION FUNCTION AS THE BASIS OF COST PLANNING

The cost of producing the quantity $x$ of a given good in a unit of time equals the product of the quantities of the needed factors of production (factors, for short) and their prices. Let us assume that the production of the quantity $x$ requires $n$ factors in the quantities $v_1, v_2, \ldots, v_n$. If the dependence of the amounts of factors on the quantity $x$ of the output is denoted by

$$v_i(x) \qquad (i = 1, 2, \ldots, n),$$

and factor prices by $q_i$ $(i = 1, 2, \ldots, n)$, then the total costs of producing the quantity $x$ is defined as:

$$C = \sum_{i=1}^{n} q_i \cdot v_i(x).$$

This expression accords exactly with our definition of costs (see p. 79): $v_i(x)$ stands for the quantity structure of costs (tons of materials, number of man-hours, number of machine-hours, amount of kW-hours, etc.), $C$ for the quantity structure valued in terms of money.

The calculation of costs is therefore contingent on the technical relationships that exist between the amount of product and the required factor quantities. These technical relationships which are known as *production functions* (or *input–output relations*) must be known before money costs can be arrived at. We must therefore look more closely at these production functions. In so doing we can confine our analysis to the factors which vary in quantity with the size of output and which thus belong, when valuation is made in money terms, to the group of variable costs. In what follows, factors $1, 2, \ldots, n$ will refer solely to the factors that vary with the size of output.

## 1. Linear-Limitational Factors

If the quantities of the variable factors vary in proportion with the quantity of output, we have the simplest case of the production function (or input-output relation):

$$v_1 = \alpha_1 \cdot x$$
$$v_2 = \alpha_2 \cdot x \qquad\qquad (1)$$
$$\cdots\cdots\cdots$$
$$v_n = \alpha_n \cdot x$$

In (1), $\alpha_1, \alpha_2, \ldots, \alpha_n$ are constants which define the factor quantities that are needed for the production of one unit of output.[1] To every quantity $x$ of the output, there corresponds one and only one quantity combination of the $n$ factors which is wholly needed for the production of output $x$. The production of any one quantity $x$ always requires the application (the input) of the $n$ factors in the proportions $\alpha_1 : \alpha_2 : \ldots : \alpha_n$. For reasons that will appear presently, factors that possess these properties are called *limitational factors*.

Industrial production offers many examples of such limitational factor combinations. Some machines demand a specific amount of labour and of energy so that one will always find a constant proportion between the number of machine-hours, of man-hours and of kW-hours. Production is made possible only by the input of a *complex* of factors which stand to each other in a technically unambiguous relation of complementarity. Another example is afforded by mixing processes in which the mixture of factors in technically rigid proportions gives rise to a new product.

In the case of only two factors, it is easy to show by geometry the properties of production functions of type (1). Since in that case it is always true that

$$v_1 : v_2 = \alpha_1 : \alpha_2$$

all combinations of factor quantities which are wholly and without residue absorbed in the process of production, and which therefore are the minimum that must be available to produce a certain output, will lie in a system of co-ordinates $v_1$, $v_2$ on the straight line which goes through the origin and has the slope of $\alpha_2 : \alpha_1$ (the line $OQ$ in Fig. 73).

If the available combination of the quantities of factors lies above the line $OQ$, i.e. in area II, then some of the second factor of production is superfluous. For example, of the combination of factors given

---

[1] The factor quantities that are required for the production of one physical unit of output are also referred to as coefficients of production.

by the point $P$, the quantity $PQ$ of factor No. 2 is superfluous. Only the level of output corresponding to the point $Q$ can be produced. The quantity $OR$ of the first factor of production "limits" the feasible level of output. The quantity $RP$ of factor No. 2 will be completely

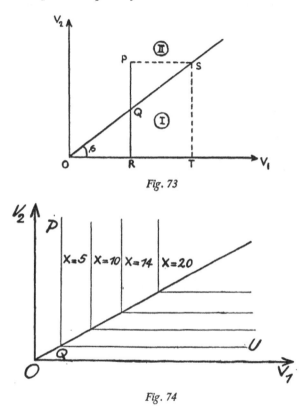

Fig. 73

Fig. 74

applied only if the quantity of the first factor is increased to $OT$, where a level of output designated by point $S$ will be feasible.[1] All combinations of the factors $v_1$, $v_2$ with which a level of output given by the point $Q$ (e.g. $x = 5$) can be produced, must obviously lie on the line $PQU$ (Fig. 74). We may describe this curve as the *isoquant* for that particular level of output. For each possible level of output there exists an isoquant of this kind (Fig. 74).

It was shown that if one has to do with linear limitationality of factors, there exists on each isoquant one and only one point which

---

[1] Production is thus limited by whichever factor is scarcest.

corresponds to the full employment of the factors: the point which lies on the ray $OQ$. This is the reason why factor combinations lying on the ray $OQ$ are also called *efficient* combinations: it is, for example, impossible to produce more than the quantity $x = 5$ with the combination given by the point $Q$; and it is equally impossible to produce the quantity $x = 5$ by using a smaller amount of one factor while holding all other factor quantities constant. Clearly only efficient combinations of factors will be considered in production. Inefficient combinations do not enter into economic decisions about the quantitative input of factors, whatever the level of factor prices. Efficient combinations can alone be minimal cost combinations. In the case of linear limitationality of factors, therefore, the ray $OQ$ is also the geometric locus of all minimum cost combinations. Be the level of factor prices what it may, the minimum cost combination of factors for a given level of output remains the same. For each level of output there exists by definition one and only one combination of factors which permits that output to be produced without leaving any residue of factors. There is thus, by definition, no possibility of substitution between factors. It is impossible to compensate for a reduction in the quantity of one factor by increasing the quantity of another factor in such a way as to keep the quantity of output constant.

Some of the observed properties of the production function (1) can now be put differently in terms of the concept of *marginal return* or *marginal product* and *marginal productivity*, which will become important in later discussion.

(a) If the quantity of factor No. $i$ undergoes an infinitesimal change $\partial v_i$ [1] while the quantities of the other factors remain constant, and if this causes the quantity of output to change by the infinitesimal amount $\partial x$ then one refers to the quotient $\dfrac{\partial x}{\partial v_i}$ as the *marginal productivity of factor No. 1*.

The absolute change in the quantity of output,

$$dx = \frac{\partial x}{\partial v_i} \cdot dv,$$

is referred to as the *marginal product* of, or the *marginal return* to, an infinitesimal change in the quantity of factor No. $i$.[2]

A glance at Fig. 74 tells us that for every efficient factor combination, i.e. one located on the ray $OQ$, marginal productivity and

---

[1] The looped $\partial$ denotes that the quantities of other factors remain constant.
[2] In the language of mathematics, marginal productivity is a differential coefficient while marginal product is a differential.

marginal product are nought for each factor. For inefficient combinations in area II (Fig. 73), however, the marginal product of factor No. 1 is positive and that of factor No. 2 equal to nought. For inefficient combinations in area I, it is the marginal product of the second factor which is positive, that of the first factor being nought.

(b) *The marginal product of a factor combination with respect to scale* is that change in the quantity of output which is caused by a small, strictly speaking infinitesimal, change in the factors while the ratios between their quantities are held constant. In the theory of Linear Programming, such a change in the factor compound, i.e. in the quantities of the factors but not in the ratios between those quantities, is referred to as a *change in the level of activity*.*

The level of activity (or scale of the productive process) in the two-factor case is indicated by the distance of the point $Q$ from the origin of the co-ordinate system. Changes of level are therefore indicated by shifts of $Q$ along the ray $OQ$. If one now asks about the marginal return to scale (or to the level of the activity)[1] one is in fact asking what change occurs in output when $Q$ travels a small distance on the ray $OQ$ (Fig. 74). This concept of marginal product is altogether different from that in the first case above. It appears from (1) that $\alpha_1$, $\alpha_2$ are those factor combinations which yield the quantity of output $= 1$. If $\alpha_1$ and $\alpha_2$ are multiplied by a non-negative number $\lambda$, one has thereby characterized a specific level of activity (or scale of the productive process). The marginal productivity with respect to scale is accordingly given by

$$\frac{\partial x}{\partial \lambda},$$

while the corresponding marginal product, or marginal return to scale, is:

$$dx = \frac{\partial x}{\partial \lambda} \cdot d\lambda.$$

If the factors are linear-limitational, marginal returns to scale will obviously be constant along the ray $OQ$. Since increases in output only take place along the ray $OQ$, it follows that marginal costs are constant if the factor prices are constant. Variable costs are therefore directly proportional to the size of output. The total cost function is linear:

$$C = A + (q_1 \cdot \alpha_1 + q_2 \cdot \alpha_2 + \ldots + q_n \cdot \alpha_n) \cdot x,$$

* This being the technical term in English, it will be used instead of the older phrase "change in the scale of the productive process" which chimes in more readily with the term "returns to scale." [Tr.]

[1] or the marginal product of the process with respect to scale.

where $A$ designates the fixed costs in the period, and $q_1, q_2, \ldots, q_n$ the constant prices of factors. Costs behave as in case $a$, Section C, para. 1.

2. If the firm behaves as a quantity-adjuster and seeks to maximize profits, the profit maximum will occur, as was shown earlier on, when capacity is fully utilized. An increase in factor prices will not displace the point of maximum profits; a change in factor prices will not cause the factors to be applied in different quantities.

Not so if the firm faces an expected price–sales function in the market for its product. A rise in the price of even one single factor will raise marginal costs. The marginal cost curve undergoes a parallel shift upwards, and the Cournot point will be found at a smaller output and a correspondingly higher price. The input of *every* factor will thus diminish. In this case, therefore, the quantities of the individual factors which get applied will depend on the prices of *all* variable factors and, *ceteris paribus*, diminish as the price of any one variable factor increases.

## 2. Continuously Substitutable Factors

1. In the linear-limitational case, a given good could be produced in one way only. Only one process was available. The firm's decisions related solely to the level of that activity (i.e. the scale of that process).

Let us now examine another and not very common case where a firm can in theory avail itself of an infinity of processes (or activities) for the production of a particular good, and where these processes can be continuously substituted one for another.

Two examples will serve to illustrate this case:

(a) In the manufacturing department of a firm a particular good is made from a particular raw material with the help of simple tools. If a given quantity is to be produced per unit of time, this can be done with more or less care. If much care is exercised, the waste of material per unit of output will be less than if little care is exercised, but production will take more time. One unit of the good can therefore be produced with more raw material and less labour time or with less raw material and more labour time. We may express such a condition by saying that the quantities of raw material and of labour time are, within certain limits, substitutes for one another, or that the two factors are substitute or compensatory factors. The possibility of substitution between two factors means that a decrease in the quantity employed of one factor can be compensated by a corresponding increase in the quantity of another factor so that the quantity of output remains unchanged. There will be a series of combinations of the quantities of these factors, all permitting the production of the same level of output, or, putting this differently, which are technically indifferent with respect to a particular level of output.

(b) Let us suppose that a firm produces a good with the aid of a machine which is attended by one worker. The machine is driven by a motor whose speed per hour is capable of being varied within given limits. Assume output per hour to be directly proportional to the motor's speed per hour—for simplicity we equate the level of output per hour with the speed—and it will follow that a particular daily output can be achieved by an infinitely large number of combinations of speed (= output) per hour and labour time per day (number of labour hours). Since the motor's speed per hour depends on the input of fuel (e.g. petrol), and since every speed is associated with a technically determined fuel consumption, we may equally well say that a given daily output can be produced by an infinitely large number of combinations of quantities of fuel and human labour. The two factors "fuel" and "human labour" are continuously substitutable for one another.

2. Following our convention, we shall designate the quantities of the two factors by $v_1$ and $v_2$, and the quantity of output by $x$. We then can write the production function as:

$$x = \phi(v_1, v_2) \tag{2}$$

where $v_1$ and $v_2$ are *continuously* variable and each quantity combination $v_1$, $v_2$ is associated with a particular value of $x$. In our example (b), the inputs of both fuel and human labour could be continuously varied, while a particular quantity of output per day corresponded to every quantity of fuel (speed per hour) and of labour time.

The isoquant for the level of output $x_0$ is then given by the equation

$$x_0 = \phi(v_1, v_2) \tag{2a}$$

which describes a curve in the system of co-ordinates $v_1$, $v_2$. The shape of the curve in any actual case needs to be determined empirically.

3. It is nevertheless possible to state some general properties of the isoquants for the case of continuously substitutable (compensatory) factors.

(a) If substitution between two factors is possible either without limit or within a limited area, then within the area of substitution the isoquant is a falling curve[1] (Fig. 75). Only in that case will it be

---

[1] The tangent to the isoquant must form an obtuse angle with the axis taken in the positive sense.

F

possible to replace the combination $v_1, v_2$ by the combination $v_1 - dv_1, v_2 + dv_2$ diminishing the quantity $v_1$ by the amount $dv_1$ and increasing the quantity $v_2$ by the increment $dv_2$ while leaving the quantity of output unchanged.

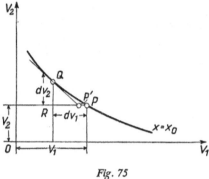

Fig. 75

If, for example, the isoquant is a straight line cutting the axes, or a rectangular hyperbola whose asymptotes coincide with the co-ordinate axes, then the two factors are *endlessly substitutable*, provided, of course, that the quantity of a factor can be enlarged without limit.

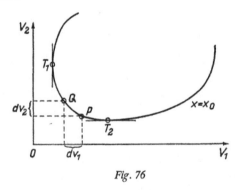

Fig. 76

If, however, the isoquant possesses the shape drawn in Fig. 76, it is evident that substitution is feasible only between $T_1$ and $T_2$, that is, between those points on the isoquant at which the tangents to the isoquant are parallel to the co-ordinate axes.

(b) In Figs. 75 and 76 it was assumed that within the area of substitution, the isoquants are convex to the origin of the diagram.

In theory and practice, this form of isoquant is alone relevant. It is easily seen that all points on the concave stretches of the isoquant in Fig. 76 are *inefficient points* according to our earlier definition.

The assumption of the convexity of isoquants within the area of substitution can be simply expressed in terms of the *marginal rate of substitution of the first factor for the second factor*.

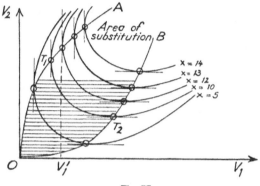

*Fig. 77*

*The marginal rate of substitution of the first factor for the second factor\** *is defined as the quotient* $\dfrac{|dv_1|}{|dv_2|}$ *that is, the quantity of the first factor the loss of which is exactly compensated by the increase by 1 unit of the second factor (leaving the quantity of product unchanged).* As the arc $PQ$ (Fig. 75) can be replaced in the case of small changes by the tangent to the isoquant at the point $Q$, the marginal rate of substitution of the first for the second factor is given by the *tan* of the angle $P'QR$. *A glance at Fig. 75 will tell that, if the isoquant is convex to the axis, the marginal rate of substitution of the first for the second factor declines as substitution is carried on.*[1]

(c) If isoquants are drawn for every possible level of production we obtain a family of isoquants covering the $v_1, v_2$ plane. It is immediately obvious that the isoquants for two different quantities of production can never cross[2] and that the isoquant corresponding to the larger level of output will lie further away from the origin of the co-ordinate system (Fig. 77). In contrast to the case of linear

---

* see Translator's note on p. 11 above.

[1] We are concerned here with precisely the same relationships which we discussed in the first chapter when analysing the indifference curves of a household.

[2] The reader should reflect on what would happen if two isoquants crossed.

limitationality, Fig. 77 also shows that in the area of substitution, the marginal productivity of a factor is positive for every combination of the quantities $v_1$, $v_2$:

$$\left[\frac{\partial x}{\partial v_1}\right]_{v_2=\text{const.}} > 0; \qquad \left[\frac{\partial x}{\partial v_2}\right]_{v_1=\text{const.}} > 0.$$

### a. Returns to Scale Functions. (Returns Functions when the Scale Varies.)
### (Proportional Variation of all Substitutable Factors.)

1. Further properties of the production function (or the isoquant diagram) when it allows continuous substitution are customarily

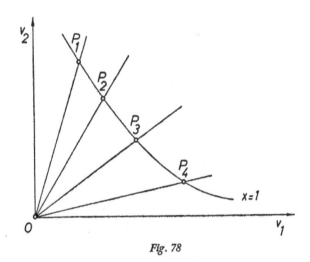

Fig. 78

explained with the aid of the concept of marginal returns to scale (or marginal product with respect to the level of activity) which we already used earlier on.

In the case of linear limitationality, only one process of production (one activity) was available. But in the case of continuous substitution there exists the choice between a theoretically infinite variety of processes. Every point on an isoquant represents a particular process (or activity). In our example (b) (on p. 145) the same quantity of output could be obtained by using either more fuel and less labour time, or less fuel and correspondingly more labour time. Each of these possibilities represents a different process of production. If there is continuous substitutionality, the production function contains infinitely many processes. In Fig. 78, four such processes are indicated by the points $P_1, P_2, P_3$ and $P_4$. One process differs from another in that the ratio $v_2 : v_1$ of the quantities in which the two factors are applied, changes from process to process.

Each process (activity) can be carried out on a different scale (level), meaning that the factors can be applied in greater or smaller quantities while yet the *ratios* between those quantities remain constant. All the various levels of an activity are, therefore, on a ray through the origin. For instance, all the levels of activity 4 lie on the ray $OP_4$.

Let us ask how the quantity of output changes as the level of activity varies along a ray through the origin of the co-ordinate system. The question is, how does the output $x$ vary as *all* the variable factor quantities undergo a proportional variation such that

$$v_1 = \lambda \cdot \bar{v}_1$$
$$v_2 = \lambda \cdot \bar{v}_2.$$

$\bar{v}_1$ and $\bar{v}_2$ designate the initial level of the two factors ($\lambda = 1$), while $\lambda$ indicates the level of activity (the scale of the process).

The variation in the quantity of output as the scale of process changes may then be described by the function:

$$x = \phi(\lambda \bar{v}_1, \lambda \bar{v}_2) = \psi(\lambda), \tag{3}$$

which is called the "returns function when scale varies," or briefly, the *returns to scale function*. Marginal productivity with respect to scale is then given by the differential quotient $\dfrac{dx}{d\lambda}$.

Theory distinguishes three cases:

(a) $\dfrac{dx}{d\lambda}$ is constant. In this case the quantity of output grows proportionately with the scale of process (the level of activity).

(b) $\dfrac{dx}{d\lambda}$ increases as $\lambda$ increases. In this case, $x$ grows more than in proportion with the scale of process.

(c) $\dfrac{dx}{d\lambda}$ diminishes as $\lambda$ increases. The quantity of product grows less than proportionately with the scale of process.

*One refers to these three cases as constant, increasing and diminishing returns to scale (Fig. 79).*

It is easily grasped that if factor prices are given, marginal costs with respect to changes in scale will be constant in case (a), diminish in case (b) and increase in case (c).[1]

2. Examples for these three cases are furnished by what are called *homogeneous production functions* which play an important part in the Theory of Production. A production function is said to be *homogeneous of the $r^{th}$ degree* if an alteration in the level of a process

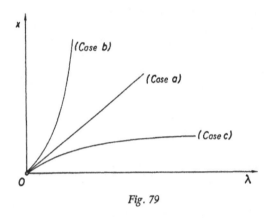

*Fig. 79*

changes the quantity of output in the proportion $\lambda^r$, i.e. when

$$\phi(\lambda \bar{v}_1, \lambda \bar{v}_2) = \lambda^r \cdot \bar{x} \qquad (r > 0) \qquad (4)$$

In this equation, $\bar{x}$ designates the output and $\bar{v}_1$, $\bar{v}_2$ the necessary quantities of the two factors when $\lambda = 1$.

If $r = 1$, marginal productivity with respect to scale (or "returns to scale") is constant. For $r > 1$, it increases and for $0 < r < 1$ it declines.

*It is easily seen that if the production function is homogeneous, knowledge of a single isoquant suffices to derive all other isoquants.* The curve $AA'$ in Fig. 80, for example, is the isoquant for $x = 1$. If the production function is homogeneous of the first degree, then each doubling (trebling, etc.) of the scale of process is associated with a doubling (trebling, etc.) of output. The isoquant for $x = 2$

---

[1] The total costs of the process at the level $\lambda$, when the factor prices $q_1$ and $q_2$ are given will equal:

$$C = (q_1 \cdot \bar{v}_1 + q_2 \cdot \bar{v}_2) \cdot \lambda.$$

Marginal costs are thus:

$$\frac{dC}{dx} = \text{constant} \cdot \frac{d\lambda}{dx} = \text{constant} : \frac{dx}{d\lambda}.$$

is accordingly obtained by doubling the length of all the rays $OS$ of the isoquant for $x = 1$.

3. The magnitude of the change in output consequent on an infinitesimal change in the scale of process (i.e. an infinitesimal proportional change in all substitute factors) can be indicated in

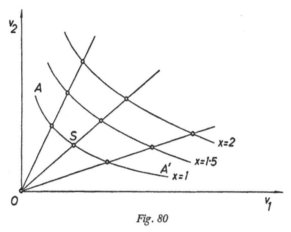

*Fig. 80*

yet another way which will become important in later discussion.

If the $n$ factors in the production function

$$x = \phi(v_1, v_2, \ldots, v_n)$$

undergo arbitrarily allotted infinitesimal changes $dv_1, dv_2, \ldots, dv_n$, then the change in $x$ will be given by

$$dx = \frac{\partial x}{\partial v_1} \cdot dv_1 + \ldots + \frac{\partial x}{\partial v_n} \cdot dv_n, \tag{5}$$

$\frac{\partial x}{\partial v_i}$ being the partial marginal productivities of the several factors.[1]

If the factor quantities $v_1, v_2, \ldots, v_n$ are all changed in the same proportion $\lambda$ then:

$$\frac{dv_1}{v_1} = \frac{dv_2}{v_2} = \ldots = \frac{dv_n}{v_n} = \frac{d\lambda}{\lambda}. \tag{6}$$

[1] For the continuous and differentiable function

$$y = f(x_1, x_2, \ldots, x_n)$$

it holds that

$$dy = \frac{\partial f}{\partial x_1} \cdot dx_1 + \frac{\partial f}{\partial x_2} \cdot dx_2 + \ldots + \frac{\partial f}{\partial x_n} \cdot dx_n.$$

In that case, and in that case alone, may we write the magnitude of the change in output as:

$$dx = \frac{d\lambda}{\lambda} \cdot \left( v_1 \cdot \frac{\partial x}{\partial v_1} + \ldots + v_n \cdot \frac{\partial x}{\partial v_n} \right). \tag{7}$$

This relationship can now be rewritten as follows:

$$x \cdot \frac{\dfrac{dx}{x}}{\dfrac{d\lambda}{\lambda}} = v_1 \cdot \frac{\partial x}{\partial v_1} + \ldots + v_n \cdot \frac{\partial x}{\partial v_n}. \tag{7a}$$

In (7a), the quotient $\dfrac{dx}{x} : \dfrac{d\lambda}{\lambda}$ designates the relation between the relative change in output and the relative change in the quantities of all factors. It thus represents the elasticity of output with respect to scale of process. The value of this elasticity is a function of the relevant factor combination. Given the isoquants, each point in a two-factor diagram corresponds with a particular numerical value of this elasticity. Let us name this elasticity the *scale-elasticity of a process*.[1]

If, for short, we write: $\dfrac{dx}{x} : \dfrac{d\lambda}{\lambda} = \varepsilon$, we may write (7a) also in the form:

$$v_1 \cdot \frac{\partial x}{\partial v_1} + \ldots + v_n \cdot \frac{\partial x}{\partial v_n} = \varepsilon \cdot x. \tag{7b}$$

Let us call this relationship the *Wicksell-Johnson Theorem*.[2] It holds for every combination $v_1, v_2, \ldots, v_n$, and will be useful when we come to derive the minimum cost combination (in sub-section 3 below).

### b. Returns Functions when Factors Vary Partially (Variation of One Substitute Factor by Itself)

1. In what preceded, we always allowed all substitute factors to vary together in proportion: we let the quantities of all the factors

[1] In my *Theorie der Produktion* (Vienna, 1934), I called this expression "the Degree of Productivity" (Ergiebigkeitsgrad). Frisch has called it "passus-coefficient," Johnson, "elasticity of production," and Carlson, "function co-efficient."

[2] I used the name in my *Theorie der Produktion* because these two scholars were the first to discover this relationship. (W. E. Johnson, "The pure theory of utility curves," *Economic Journal*, 1913.—Knut Wicksell, *Vorlesungen ueber Nationaloekonomie*, vol. 1, 1913, p. 187. (p. 127ff. of the English translation—*Lectures on Political Economy*, vol. 1, 1934.)

increase or diminish without changing the relation between the quantities of the factors. All changes were carried out in the framework of the same process. We changed the *scale of process* (the level of activity), not the *process* (the activity). Thus we moved in the two-factor diagram on a ray going through the origin. We asked how the quantity of output changes as one travels along such a ray. We found that the marginal product with respect to scale of process might be constant, diminishing or increasing, all according to the character of the production function.

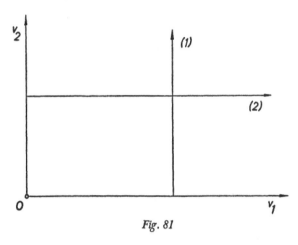

*Fig. 81*

We gain further insight into the form of the production function if we vary one single factor while holding constant the quantities of all the other substitute factors. In the two-factor diagram this corresponds to a movement along a parallel to one of the axes (line 1 or 2 in Fig. 81).

We are now concentrating on a problem which is wholly different from the one presented by a proportional change in all factors. Each isolated change in the quantity of one factor alters the ratio between the quantities of the factors used in production and thus implies a change of process. If in our earlier example of a motor we were to make successive increases in the speed per hour while keeping labour-time unchanged, the hourly input of human labour would get combined with steadily rising hourly quantities of fuel. But a *proportional* variation of all factors would cause one hour of labour to be always combined with one and the same quantity of fuel per hour.

If the system of isoquants (or rather, the production function) is known, the change of output can, of course, be determined irrespective of whether it is caused by a partial or by a proportional variation of factors. The system of isoquants being the embodiment of technical experience, it follows that the "returns functions", whether for proportional or for partial factor variations, are similarly empirical relationships.

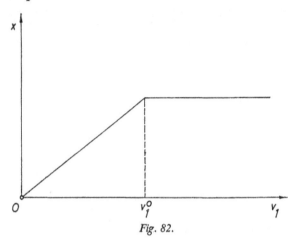

*Fig. 82.*

It follows directly from an inspection of Figure 74 that when the factors are linear-limitational the returns function will look as in Fig. 82. The partial marginal return for the first factor stays constant up to $v_1^\circ$ and is equal to nought from then on.

The earliest empirical investigations of the form of the returns function in the case when substitute factors are subjected to partial variation, originated in the field of agricultural production. We shall quote the classic example which J. H. von Thünen presented in *The Isolated State in Respect of Its Agricultural and Political Economy*[1] (first edition: 1826 and, of the second part, 1850), a work which is of fundamental importance for the development of economic theory.[2]

"Let us imagine an estate upon which above one hundred labourers are employed.

"The amount of labour required for the managing of these farms is by no means a fixed magnitude.

---

[1] *Der isolierte Staat in Beziehung auf Landwirtschaft und Nationalökonomie.* Rostock, 1842 and 1850.

[2] Quoted from Waentig's edition (Sammlung sozialwissenschaftlicher Meister, vol. XIII, 1910), p. 569 & sq.

"The fields may be tilled with greater care or with less, the grain may be threshed and the potatoes picked more or less thoroughly—and the necessary quantity of labour will vary accordingly.

"Let us choose for an example the lifting of potatoes.

"If only those potatoes are gathered which digging or hoeing brought to the top, then one person can pick more than 30 *Berlin Scheffel**\* in one day. But if the soil is also to be scratched with the hoe so as to gather further potatoes which the soil covers, then the product of a person's labour will at once fall very steeply. The more one insists on a full picking of the potatoes the smaller grows the product of labour, and if even the last *Scheffel* contained in a field measuring 100 square *Ruten*\*\* is to be gathered then that last *Scheffel* will demand so much labour that the person employed for that purpose will not be able to feed himself by the product of his labour, let alone satisfy his other needs."

Thünen then presents the following numerical example:

"Suppose that the quantity of potatoes which grows on a field of 100 square *Ruten* amounts to 100 *Berlin Scheffel*. Suppose further that of this quantity one harvests:

|  |  |  | The additional return due to the last man employed being: |
|---|---|---|---|
| 80 | *Scheffel* by employing | 4 persons | |
| 86·6 | *Scheffel* by employing | 5 persons | 6·6 *Scheffel* |
| 91 | *Scheffel* by employing | 6 persons | 4·4 *Scheffel* |
| 94 | *Scheffel* by employing | 7 persons | 3·0 *Scheffel* |
| 96 | *Scheffel* by employing | 8 persons | 2·0 *Scheffel* |
| 97·3 | *Scheffel* by employing | 9 persons | 1·3 *Scheffel* |
| 98·2 | *Scheffel* by employing | 10 persons | 0·9 *Scheffel* |
| 98·8 | *Scheffel* by employing | 11 persons | 0·6 *Scheffel* |
| 99·2 | *Scheffel* by employing | 12 persons | 0·4 *Scheffel* |

In this example, the marginal return declines continuously from the fifth labourer onwards.

Thünen gives yet another example in the *Isolated State*:[1]

"It is in the nature of agriculture—and this is a noteworthy circumstance—that the addition to product does not rise in direct proportion with the number of additional labourers employed, but each successive man employed yields a smaller product than his predecessor—the 22nd labourer less than the 21st, the 23rd less than the 22nd, etc.

\* 1 *Berlin Scheffel* = 1·5 bushels approx. [Tr.]
\*\* 100 Mecklenburgh *Ruten*² = ·535 acres. [Tr.]
[1] p. 416.

"By way of illustration let me draw up the following schedule:

> The 19th labourer produces 123 *Scheffel*
> The 20th labourer produces 111 *Scheffel*
> The 21st labourer produces 100 *Scheffel*
> The 22nd labourer produces 90 *Scheffel*
> The 23rd labourer produces 81 *Scheffel*
> The 24th labourer produces 73 *Scheffel*" ·

The decisive feature of all these examples from agriculture is the fact that beginning with a particular quantity of a factor, $v_1^0$, the

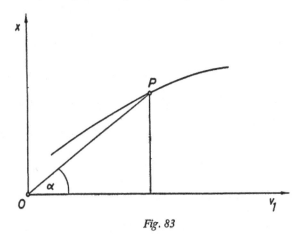

*Fig. 83*

marginal return of the factor declines. In the range $0 \leqq v_1 \leqq v_1^0$ there may occur constant, increasing or diminishing marginal returns.[1]

As is obvious—and will be shown in detail later on—the ratio of the price of the variable factor to its marginal product gives the marginal costs due to a partial factor variation. If the price of the factor remains constant, marginal costs will diminish, increase or remain constant according to whether partial marginal product diminishes, increases, or remains constant.

[1] If the production function is homogeneous of the first degree, a partial factor variation will cause the marginal return to diminish over the entire range of variation of the variable factor. If, for example,

$$x = v_1^{\frac{1}{3}} . v_2^{\frac{2}{3}}$$

then:

$$\frac{\partial x}{\partial v_1} = \text{constant} . \frac{1}{3 . \sqrt[3]{v_1^2}}$$

2. From the total product curve one may infer directly the behaviour of the average product. Average product is given by the quotient $\frac{x}{v_1}$ or, geometrically, by the *tan* of angle $\alpha$ in Fig. 83. To construct the average product curve we need merely ascertain how

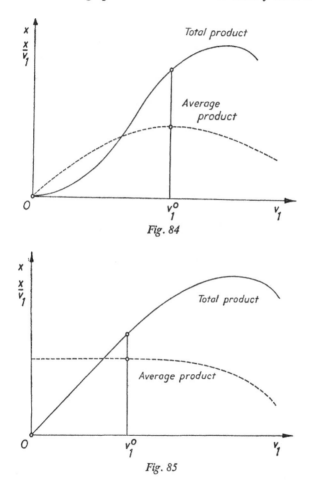

Fig. 84

Fig. 85

the angle $\alpha$ changes as $v_1$ grows. Figure 84 (85) shows the curves of total and average product for the case in which marginal product rises at first, (or, in Fig. 85, is constant at first) and then declines.

3. The fact observed in agriculture, that with partial factor

variation the marginal product diminishes after a certain point has been termed the "*law of diminishing returns*". But it must be stressed that this refers to a purely empirical regularity the validity of which can of course only be empirically established.

Similarly, the next section will make it apparent that if partial factor variation takes place in industrial production, the marginal product *may* diminish (and marginal costs increase, with given factor prices) from a particular point onwards. But in the field of industrial production one can equally well point to constant marginal product over the entire range of variation of a factor.

*The returns function in the case when factors vary partially can have different forms according to the type of the productive process, that is, according to the type of the production function.* A precise study of the technical characteristics of a particular process of production is alone capable of yielding information about the behaviour of the returns function in any concrete instance. *In this context—and this is often overlooked—one must carefully distinguish between returns functions for variation in the scale of process on the one hand, and returns functions for partial factor variations on the other hand.*

### c. The Minimum Cost Combination

If continuous substitution is possible, each of the factor combinations on the isoquant will furnish the same quantity of product. The firm has then to decide which of the technically possible factor quantities that lie in the area of substitution it ought to apply in the context of its plan. If the firm behaves economically, it clearly will choose the minimum cost combination, i.e., the combination which causes the least costs. We must now study the properties of this combination.

In Fig. 76 the isoquant for an output of $x = x_0$ has been drawn. The arc $T_1 T_2$ represents the range of substitutability for $x = x_0$. We have to ask under what conditions it will pay a firm to substitute the combination of factors represented by the point $Q$ for the combination represented by the point $P$, that is, to diminish the quantity $v_1$ of the first factor by the amount $dv_1$ and increase the quantity $v_2$ of the second factor by the quantity $dv_2$. The substitution of $dv_2$ for $dv_1$ is obviously profitable if a saving in costs is achieved, which will be the case if the costs represented by the combination $Q$ (i.e. the combination $v_1 - dv_1$ and $v_2 + dv_2$) are smaller than the costs represented by the point $P$. Let the prices of the two substitute factors be $q_1$ and $q_2$, so that the costs of the combination represented by the point $P$ are given by the expression $v_1 \cdot q_1 + v_2 \cdot q_2$. The question now is what change in costs will occur if the quantity of the factor $v_1$ is diminished by $dv_1$ and the quantity of the factor $v_2$ increased by $dv_2$.

1. We assume first that *the prices of the two factors are given to the firm*. The firm is behaving as a quantity-adjuster in respect of the sellers of factors of production. In moving from point $P$ to point $Q$ (Fig. 76) the costs diminish in respect of the first factor by the quantity $q_1 \cdot |dv_1|$, while the costs for the second factor increase by the amount $q_2 \cdot |dv_2|$. If $q_1 \cdot |dv_1| > q_2 \cdot |dv_2|$, then it obviously represents a saving in costs to move from point $P$ to point $Q$, for the saving on the first factor is larger than the increase in costs from the second factor. It is clear from Fig. 76 that the marginal rate of substitution of the first factor for the second decreases as the quantity of the second factor employed increases. Let us suppose that the substitution of the first factor for the second is continued from $T_2$ to $T_1$ by increasing the quantity of the second factor and correspondingly diminishing the quantity of the first factor, so that, to begin with, the saving on the first factor is greater than the increase in costs for the second factor. This saving on the first factor will decrease as the substitution proceeds, so that at some point between $T_1$ and $T_2$ it will be equal to, and with further substitution smaller than, the increase in costs from the second factor. This means that as we pass through the possibilities of substitution between the points $T_1$ and $T_2$, the total costs at first decrease, then reach a minimum at some point between $T_1$ and $T_2$, and with further substitution increase. The minimum cost combination must, therefore, satisfy the condition that the saving in costs on the first factor is exactly equal to the increase in costs on the second, i.e. that:

$$q_1 \cdot |dv_1| = q_2 \cdot |dv_2| \tag{8}$$

It follows from (8) that:

$$\frac{|dv_1|}{|dv_2|} = \frac{q_2}{q_1} \tag{9}$$

This says that for the minimum cost combination the marginal rate of substitution of the first factor for the second factor* must be equal to the ratio of the prices $q_2$ and $q_1$ of the two factors.

It is not difficult to show that the marginal rate of substitution of one factor for another is closely related to the partial marginal productivities of the two factors. Let us chose the factor combination $v_1, v_2$ to start from (point $P$ in Fig. 76). Let the two quantities of factors vary—strictly speaking, infinitesimally—by the amounts $dv_1$

---

* See translator's note on p. 11 above.

and $dv_2$. The corresponding change in output is then derived, according to a well-known mathematical proposition[1] as:

$$dx = \left[\frac{\partial x}{\partial v_1}\right]_{v_2 = \text{const.}} \cdot dv_1 + \left[\frac{\partial x}{\partial v_2}\right]_{v_1 = \text{const.}} \cdot dv_2.$$

As the increase $(dv_1)$ in factor No. 1 is to be compensated by a decrease $(-dv_2)$ in factor No. 2, the quantity of output remaining unchanged, it necessarily follows that $dx = 0$, i.e. it must hold that:

$$\left[\frac{\partial x}{\partial v_1}\right]_{v_2 = \text{const.}} \cdot dv_1 + \left[\frac{\partial x}{\partial v_2}\right]_{v_1 = \text{const.}} \cdot dv_2 = 0.$$

If $(MP)_1$ and $(MP)_2$ are the marginal productivities of the two factors, the last equation can be put as:*

$$(MP)_1 \cdot |dv_1| = (MP)_2 \cdot |dv_2|$$

or as:

$$\frac{dv_1}{dv_2} = \frac{(MP)_2}{(MP)_1} \tag{10}$$

The marginal rate of substitution of factor No. 1 for factor No. 2 is therefore equal to the ratio of the partial marginal productivity of the second to that of the first factor.

This proposition enables us to write condition (9) for the minimum cost combination of the two factors in the following manner:

$$\frac{(MP)_1}{(MP)_2} = \frac{q_1}{q_2} \tag{10a}$$

*For the minimum cost combination for a particular output, with two substitute factors of production, the marginal products of the two factors must be proportional to their prices.* This proposition can immediately be applied to cases of more than two factors. The general proposition holds that if there are $N$ substitute factors, and the prices of the factors are constant, the minimum cost combination for a particular level of output must be such that the marginal productivities of the substitute factors are proportional to their prices. *For the position of the minimum cost combination, therefore, it is simply the ratio of the prices of the substitute factors that is relevant.*

For the case of two substitute factors our argument can be presented more simply in a geometrical form. The method which we are applying is the same as that which we used to discover the most

---

[1] v. footnote (1) on p. 151 above.

* The vertical lines $|\ldots|$ mean that the sign of the enclosed expression is neglected. [Tr].

favourable distribution of a household's total consumption spending. In Fig. 86, $T_1T_2$ is the range of substitution on the isoquant for a particular level of output. Each combination of factors $v_1$, $v_2$ then corresponds (given the prices of the factors) to particular total costs for the two substitute factors. We now ask what line will give us the locus of points representing combinations of factors with the same

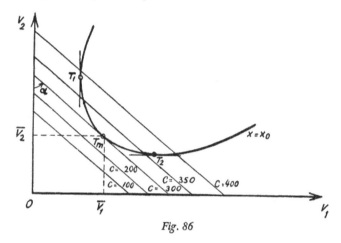

*Fig. 86*

total costs. If we take the total costs of a combination of substitute factors to be $C$, then clearly:

$$v_1 \cdot q_1 + v_2 \cdot q_2 = C \tag{11}$$

In this equation $q_1$ and $q_2$, the prices of the factors, are given constants. It is clear from equation (11) that all the combinations of factors for which the total costs are the same lie on a straight line which cuts the $v_1$ axis at a distance of $C/q_1$ from the origin, and the $v_2$ axis at a distance of $C/q_2$ from the origin. This line may be described as the *isocost* line and obviously lies further away from the origin the larger are the total costs, $C$. With given prices for factors the various isocost lines, corresponding to different levels of total costs, run parallel. We are concerned here with the same relationships which we discussed in connexion with the budget lines of a household. We can, therefore, fill in the whole plane $v_1$, $v_2$ with a number of parallel isocost lines (Fig. 86). Let us draw in, as is done in Fig. 86, the isoquant $T_1T_2$ for a particular level of output, along with the system of isocost lines. Then it is easily seen what the total costs are of each combination of factors lying on the isoquant. The study of Fig. 86 shows that the total costs of the two substitute factors are at a minimum where the isoquant touches an isocost line. In Fig. 86 this minimum cost combination is given by the coordinates of the point $T_m$. We know that the marginal rate of substitution of the first factor for the second, for the combination of factors given by the point $T_m$, is equal to the tan of the angle $\alpha$ (Fig. 86). On the other hand, the tan of the angle $\alpha$ is also equal to the ratio of the factor prices,[1]

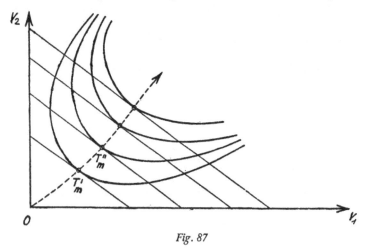

Fig. 87

so that for the minimum cost combination $T_m$ the marginal rate of substitution is equal to the ratio of the factor prices. For each level of output there exists a single uniquely determined minimum cost combination. The totality of these minimum cost combinations corresponding to different levels of output, are given, in the case of two substitute factors, by the curve $OT_m'T_m''$ (Fig. 87). To each level of output let us allot the corresponding minimum cost combination. Then we obtain the curve which shows the dependence, given the factor prices, of the minimum variable costs on the level of output. If the firm in its economic plan changes the level of output, then, with given factor prices, the quantities of substitute factors must always correspond to points on the curve $OT_m'T_m''$. We may describe this curve as the *factor-adjustment curve of the firm*, or its minimum cost curve.

---

[1] The intercept of the isocost line on the $v_1$ axis equals $\dfrac{C}{q_1}$, while that on the $v_2$ axis equals $\dfrac{C}{q_2}$. Hence:

$$tan\ \alpha = \frac{C}{q_1} : \frac{C}{q_2} = \frac{q_2}{q_1}.$$

The minimum cost combination corresponding to a given level of output tells us the quantities of the substitute factors which the firm will demand when producing a particular level of output. It follows from our argument that the minimum cost combination, and there-fore, *the quantity demanded of the substitute factors, depends on the level of planned output and the prices of the factors*. In our example,

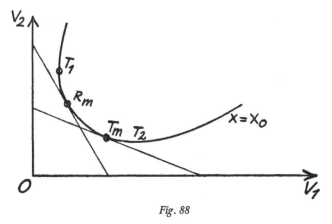

*Fig. 88*

limited to the case of two substitute factors, the demand for them is a function of the level of output $x$ and the factor prices $q_1$ and $q_2$:

$$v_1 = v_1(x, q_1, q_2)$$
$$v_2 = v_2(x, q_1, q_2) \tag{12}$$

These two functions represent the *demand functions of the firm for the two substitute factors*. From Fig. 87 it is clear that the demand for substitute factors, given their prices, grows with the level of planned output. We may now ask the further question as to how the demand for a substitute factor changes if its price changes, while the price of the other factor remains constant. Let us assume, for example, that the price $q_2$ of the second factor falls, while the price of the first factor $q_1$ remains constant. That would mean that the section which the isocost line cuts off on the $v_1$ axis remains unchanged, while the section it cuts off on the $v_2$ axis increases. The family of isocost lines will form a smaller angle than before with the $v_2$ axis. The point of tangency of the isoquant for the particular level of output, with the new family of isocost lines, will shift in the direction of an increased quantity of the second factor (Fig. 88). While previously the mini-mum cost combination was given by the point $T_m$, the same level of output now is produced by a minimum cost combination $R_m$. The reduction of the price $q_2$, with the price $q_1$ remaining the same, results in it being profitable for the firm to substitute the second factor for the first. If, therefore, with two substitute factors, one of them becomes cheaper in relation to the other, the substitution of the relatively cheaper for the relatively dearer will be profitable for the firm. This is what is understood by the *principle of substitution*. It must be noticed that the question of substitution first becomes relevant when the price relation between two substitute factors alters. If the prices of the factors both alter in the same proportion, then the minimum cost combination does not alter.

If the isoquants and the factor prices are known, then the minimum cost combination of the factors is equally known, and with it also the amount of variable costs and the behaviour of variable costs all along the factor-adjustment curve. It follows that when factor prices are given, the behaviour of the cost curve is determined exclusively by the technological basis of production as reflected in the isoquant diagram.

2. The enquiry into these relationships can now be carried further. It has already been shown that the minimum cost combination of the factors is characterized by proportionality between the partial marginal productivities of the different factors on the one hand, and their prices on the other hand. If there are $n$ substitute factors, we find that upon the minimum cost curve:

$$\frac{q_1}{\dfrac{\partial x}{\partial v_1}} = \frac{q_2}{\dfrac{\partial x}{\partial v_2}} = \ldots = \frac{q_n}{\dfrac{\partial x}{\partial v_n}} = \mu. \tag{13}$$

*This means that, given the quantity of output, the ratio of a factor's price to its marginal productivity is equal for all the factors in the minimum cost combination.*

Now the quotient

$$\frac{q_i}{\dfrac{\partial x}{\partial v_i}} \qquad (i = 1, 2, \ldots n)$$

is simply the marginal cost for the given quantity of output when a partial variation takes place in factor No. $i$. This is so because the change in costs corresponding to a partial factor variation amounts to $q_i \cdot dv_i$ (change in the quantity of factor times price of factor). The marginal costs of the change in output which is caused by this change in the factor quantity are therefore:

$$MC = \frac{q_i \cdot dv_i}{dx} = q_i : \frac{\partial x}{\partial v_i}. \tag{14}$$

Relation (13) can accordingly be put in the following terms:

*For every minimum cost combination of n substitute factors, partial marginal costs (i.e. the marginal costs corresponding to a partial factor variation) are equal for all factors.*

It can further be proved that in the minimum cost combination it is not only the partial marginal costs of each factor which are equal to one another, but marginal costs for any *random* (infinitesimal) variation in the quantities of factors are also the same, and equal to $\mu$.[1]

*More particularly, we find that marginal costs with respect to the scale of the process, which means marginal costs for a small proportional change of all substitute factors, are equal to partial marginal costs at every point on the minimum cost curve.*

3. We are now in a position to determine the level of costs for minimum cost combinations of factors. For any one combination of quantities, $v_1, v_2, \ldots, v_n$, costs will be:

$$C = q_1 . v_1 + \ldots + q_n . v_n. \tag{15}$$

[1] This is proved as follows:

$$\frac{dC}{dx} = \frac{q_1 . dv_1 + q_2 . dv_2}{dx}. \tag{X}$$

If it is now assumed that the combination of factors $v_1, v_2$ is the minimum cost combination, then the factor prices must be proportional to the marginal productivities of the two factors:

$$q_1 = \mu . \frac{\partial x}{\partial v_1} \quad \text{and} \quad q_2 = \mu . \frac{\partial x}{\partial v_2}, \tag{XX}$$

where $\mu$ is the factor of proportionality. If we introduce these expressions for the factor prices into (X), we have:

$$\frac{dC}{dx} = \mu . \frac{\frac{\partial x}{\partial v_1} . dv_1 + \frac{\partial x}{\partial v_2} . dv_2}{dx} \tag{XXX}$$

The numerator of the fraction on the right-hand side of this equation represents the sum of the marginal productivities of the individual factors multiplied by the small alteration in the quantities of those factors. This sum represents, simply, the total change in the quantity of product (strictly speaking this only holds for infinitely small changes in the quantities of the factors), and is, therefore, equal to $dx$, so that we obtain:

$$\frac{dC}{dx} = \mu. \tag{+}$$

This equation tells us that the factor of proportionaltity in (XX) or, which comes to the same thing, the quotient of factor price and marginal productivity for all substitute factors is equal to marginal costs, provided the minimum cost combination is realized.

If the combination $v_1, v_2, \ldots, v_n$ is a minimum cost combination then, as has just been shown:

$$q_1 = \mu \cdot \frac{\partial x}{\partial v_i}, \qquad (i = 1, 2, \ldots, n), \quad (16)$$

where $\mu$ is the marginal cost for minimum cost combinations. Substituting (16) in (15), this latter equation becomes:

$$C = \mu \cdot \left[ v_1 \cdot \frac{\partial x}{\partial v_1} + \ldots + v_n \cdot \frac{\partial x}{\partial v_n} \right], \qquad (17)$$

which holds for minimum cost combinations, but only for those!

According to the *Wicksell-Johnson* theorem (7b), it is true of any quantity combination $v_1, v_2, \ldots, v_n$ that:

$$v_1 \cdot \frac{\partial x}{\partial v_1} + \ldots + v_n \cdot \frac{\partial x}{\partial v_n} = \varepsilon \cdot x, \qquad (18)$$

where $\varepsilon$ is the scale elasticity of the combination $v_1, v_2, \ldots, v_n$. By substituting from (18) we now turn equation (17) into:

$$C = \mu \cdot \varepsilon \cdot x \qquad (19)$$

or:

$$\frac{C}{x} : \mu = \varepsilon. \qquad (19a)$$

We have thus obtained the interesting result that for *minimum cost combinations, the quotient of average costs and marginal costs is equal to the scale elasticity of the process.*

This result is interesting because it relates the quotient of two cost terms for minimum cost combinations to the purely technologically determined concept of the scale elasticity of a process.

By way of illustration we may consider two substitute factors. At every point in the factor diagram, the magnitude $\varepsilon$ assumes a certain numerical value. For points on the minimum cost curve—but only for those—we are now in a position to state the relation between the size of average and of marginal costs relating to the set of substitute factors:

If $\varepsilon > 1$ then $C/x > \mu$;

If $\varepsilon = 1$ then $C/x = \mu$;

If $\varepsilon < 1$ then $C/x < \mu$.

Thus, if average costs are greater (smaller) than marginal costs for a given output or for a given range, then $\varepsilon > 1$ ($\varepsilon < 1$). If marginal costs equal average costs, $\varepsilon = 1$. Let us emphasize again that this result only holds on the pre-supposition that given the prices of factors, every output is produced with the relevant minimum cost combination of factors.

Let us choose for example the case of a homogeneous production function of the $r^{\text{th}}$ degree:

$$\phi(\lambda\bar{v}_1, \lambda\bar{v}_2) = \lambda^r \cdot \bar{x}. \tag{20}$$

If $x$ is the quantity of product when $\lambda$ is the scale of process, it follows that

$$x = \lambda^r \cdot \bar{x}. \tag{20a}$$

$\bar{x}$ is therefore the output when the scale of process $\lambda = 1$. From (20a) we obtain immediately:

$$\frac{dx}{d\lambda} = r \cdot \lambda^{r-1} \cdot \bar{x}$$

and thus we get for the scale elasticity:

$$\varepsilon = \frac{dx}{d\lambda} : \frac{x}{\lambda} = \frac{r \cdot \lambda^{r-1} \cdot \bar{x}}{\lambda^{r-1} \cdot \bar{x}} = r. \tag{21}$$

*The scale elasticity is consequently equal to the constant index r of the production function.*

If $r = 1$, i.e. when there are constant returns to scale, then $\varepsilon = 1$. Marginal costs are constant and equal to average costs.

If $r > 1$, i.e. if we find increasing returns to scale, marginal costs are less than average costs. As scale increases, marginal costs diminish.

If $r < 1$, i.e. if marginal returns to scale diminish, marginal costs are greater than average costs. Marginal costs rise as scale increases.

Here we see clearly what rôle the technological form of the process of production plays in fixing the position of the minimum cost combinations, and in determining the behaviour of costs along the minimum cost curve. The basis of the theory of costs is technical in its nature. Technology has to provide us with the production functions and their properties from which the theory of costs will then proceed to its conclusions.

4. Let us explain the relationship just analysed with the help of our earlier example (p. 145) into which we now introduce some empirical data. Production per day, as measured by the number of miles per day (m.p.d.), is obviously equal to the mathematical product of speed per hour (m/hr.) and working time (as measured by the number of working hours per day, hrs.p.d.). Hence:

$$\text{m.p.d.} = \text{m/hr} \times \text{hrs.p.d.} \tag{22}$$

To each speed per hour (m/hr.) there corresponds a specific hourly

consumption of fuel. Figure 89 portrays the consumption by a petrol
engine of fuel in gallons per mile (gal./m) as a function of speed per
hour (m/hr.). From this curve we may read off the consumption in
gallons per hour (gal./hr.), which corresponds to the area of the

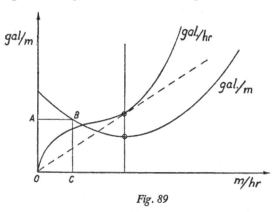

*Fig. 89*

rectangle *OABC*. By computing the area of this rectangle for
different speeds we can derive the gal./hr. curve as in Fig. 89, showing
fuel consumption in gallons for each different speed per hour.

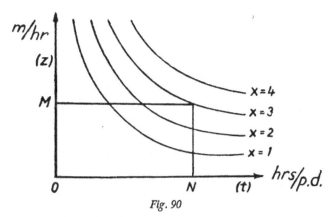

*Fig. 90*

Equation (22) implies that all combinations of speed per hour and
working time per day which result in the same output per day, will
lie on a rectangular hyperbola whose asymptotes are the co-ordinate
axes of Fig. 90. Note that these hyperbolas are *not* the isoquants:
the factors of production are human labour and gallons of fuel
rather than human labour and motor speeds. But it is not difficult

to re-draw Fig. 90 as an isoquant diagram. This task is left to the reader. Since fuel consumption in gallons per hour is not proportional to speed per hour, the production function is not homogeneous of the first degree. For our purposes it will be enough if we work with the diagram in Fig. 90 and imagine that each speed per hour (m/hr.) is labelled with its corresponding fuel consumption.

Note first of all that not all the combinations of speed and labour time are feasible. Only combinations which do not exceed maximum speed and maximum working time can be achieved. If in Fig. 90 maximum speed is denoted by $OM$, and maximum working time by $ON$, the aggregate of achievable combinations of speed and working time is represented by all the points inside and on the boundaries of the rectangle. Given the prices of factors (fuel price and wage) we now ask which combinations within the achievable area are the minimum cost combinations corresponding to the different feasible daily outputs.

If, to abbreviate, we write $z$ for speed per hour, $t$ for working time and $y$ for fuel consumption per hour, then $y$ is a function of $z$:

$$y = f(z), \tag{23}$$

of the form drawn in Fig. 89. If $q$ stands for the price of one gallon of fuel and $w$ for the wage, then the costs of any one combination within the achievable area are:

$$C = q \cdot y \cdot t + w \cdot t, \tag{24}$$

where $q$ and $w$ are given constants.

Substituting from (23), equation (24) becomes:

$$C = q \cdot f(z) \cdot t + w \cdot t. \tag{24a}$$

For a given output per day, $x_0$, all possible combinations of $z$ and $t$ are given by:

$$z \cdot t = x_0. \tag{25}$$

If $x$, $q$ and $w$ are given to us, we have so to determine $z$ and $t$ as to make $C$ as small as possible.

It follows from (25) that:

$$t = \frac{x_0}{z}$$

and substituting this into (24a) we get:

$$C = q \cdot x_0 \cdot \frac{f(z)}{z} + \frac{w \cdot x_0}{z}. \tag{26}$$

The first item in the sum to the right of the equation sign is represented by a curve of the form $AA'$, and the second item by a rectangular hyperbola $BB'$ (both in Fig. 91). The sum of these two curves yields $C$. It is easily seen that the aggregate curve has a minimum at $\bar{z}$, and that the position of $\bar{z}$ is independent of $x_0$.[1]

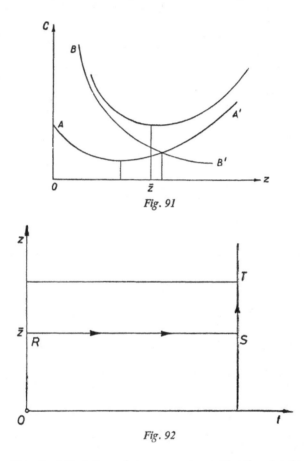

Fig. 91

Fig. 92

We thus find that the minimum cost combination in the region $0 \leqq x \leqq \bar{z} \cdot t_{\max}$ is characterized by constant speed per hour and varying working time. Larger outputs are therefore produced by a higher scale of process and not by a variation of the process.

[1] The equation $\dfrac{dC}{dz} = 0$ which serves for determining the minimum, is independent of $x_0$.

Up to $z \cdot t_{max}$ costs grow in proportion with the quantity produced. Marginal costs with respect to production are constant.

If the required daily output grows beyond $z \cdot t_{max}$, if, that is, it lies in the interval $z \cdot t_{max} < z \leqq z_{max} \cdot t_{max}$, then output can only

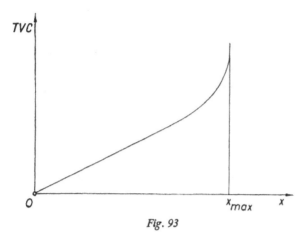

Fig. 93

be raised by increasing the speed (i.e. by using greater quantities of fuel per hour). Minimum costs in this interval are given by:

$$C = q \cdot f(z) \cdot t_{max} + w \cdot t_{max}, \qquad (27)$$

which is a curve whose marginal costs rise.[1]

The minimum cost curve in Fig. 90—which is not an isoquant diagram!—is a line $RST$ as in Fig. 92. The behaviour of costs along the minimum cost line is portrayed by the curve in Fig. 93, and corresponds to the type analysed as case (b) in Section 3, para. 1.

### d. The Profit Plan of a Firm Using Substitutional and Variable Factors

1. First we shall consider a firm which acts as a quantity adjuster in the sale of its products and which reckons in its plan with constant factor prices. *We further assume that as output rises, marginal returns as observed along the minimum cost curve will diminish from a certain point onwards. i.e. we assume marginal costs to increase.* On these assumptions, as we showed before, marginal costs along the

[1] Marginal costs are: $\dfrac{dC}{dz} = q \cdot t_{max} \cdot f(z)$, which is a multiple of marginal costs with respect to speed per hour.

minimum cost curve, at any-one of its points, are equal to the partial marginal costs of any one factor. Now we know that at the point of maximum profits, the price of the good must equal marginal costs. Partial marginal costs with respect to a variable factor, No. $i$, are given by the relation:

$$MC = q_i : \frac{dx}{dv_i}, \tag{28}$$

Therefore, the point of maximum profits is characterized by the condition *that for each substitute factor, marginal product multiplied by the price of the product must equal the price of the factor.* If we call the price of the product $p$, and the marginal product of the $i^{\text{th}}$ substitute factor $(MP)_i$ then we have:

$$(MP)_i \cdot p = q_i \qquad (i = 1, 2, \ldots, n) \tag{29}$$

The marginal product of a substitute factor multiplied by the price of that product simply signifies the value of the increase in the quantity of output resulting from an addition of 1 unit of the substitute factor. One may describe the expression on the left-hand side of equation (29) as *the value of the marginal product of the $i^{\text{th}}$ substitute factor.* Equation (29) can, then, also be written in the form:

Value of the Marginal Product = Price of a Substitute Factor

(30)

From the relationship in (29) we now have the answer to our question as to how large the demand of a firm for the $i^{\text{th}}$ unit of a substitute factor is, if the price of a factor is at a particular level: or, how the demand of a firm for the $i^{\text{th}}$ unit of a substitute factor varies with the price of this factor. On the present assumptions, the point of maximum total profit can only lie in the region of increasing marginal costs. Increasing marginal costs, according to the results arrived at earlier on, are identical (if factor prices are constant) with decreasing marginal product, so that we can also say that the point of maximum total profit must lie in the region of decreasing marginal product. With increasing prices for the substitute factor the left side of equation (29), i.e. the value of the marginal product of this factor, must increase. This says again that the quantity of a substitute factor which the firm will use will decrease as the price of this factor increases. *The relation (29), therefore, is simply nothing other than the demand function of the firm for the substitute factor concerned.* We can also arrive at this result by the following argument. If the price of a substitute factor increases while the prices of all other factors remain constant, then marginal costs increase. This rise in marginal costs, or this shift of the marginal cost curve upwards, makes profitable a reduction in the demand for *all* factors of production. But because of the possibility of substitution between substitute factors a second element enters in. By raising the price of a substitute factor, while the prices of all other factors remain constant, this factor becomes relatively dearer, so that it pays to substitute other relatively cheaper factors. The demand for the factor which has become relatively dearer will now decrease for reasons of substitution. The demand

| (1) Units of the variable factor | (2) Marginal product | (3) Value of the marginal product (shillings) |
|---|---|---|
| 1 | 1 | 2 |
| 2 | 2 | 4 |
| 3 | 3 | 6 |
| 4 | 4 | 8 |
| 5 | 5 | 10 |
| 6 | 6 | 12 |
| 7 | 7 | 14 |
| 8 | 6 | 12 |
| 9 | 5 | 10 |
| 10 | 4 | 8 |
| 11 | 3 | 6 |
| 12 | 2 | 4 |
| 13 | 1 | 2 |
| 14 | −1 | −2 |
| 15 | −3 | −6 |

for the factor which has become dearer declines in total because it pays both (a) to limit production and (b) to substitute the relatively cheaper factor for that which has now become relatively dearer. How the demand for other substitute factors alters with a rise in the price of one of them depends on whether the decrease in demand resulting from the higher marginal costs and the consequent effect on the level of output (*the quantity-of-product effect*) is greater or smaller than the increase in demand resulting from the substitution of the relatively cheaper factor for the relatively dearer factor (*the substitution effect*).

We shall now seek to clarify these important relationships by means of a simple example. Let us suppose that two substitute factors are used in the production of a good. The quantity of one of the factors is fixed and that of the other variable. The marginal products corresponding to the use of single successive units of the variable factor are given by the figures in Column 2 of the adjoining table. With the price of the product equal to 2s., the value of the marginal product will be given as in Column 3. We have shown how the firm (the price of the variable factor being given) will use that quantity of the factor at which its price is equal to the value of its marginal product. If, for example, the price of the factor is 6s., then it pays to employ 11 units of the variable factor, because the value of the marginal product of the eleventh unit is exactly equal to the price of the variable factor. If the price of the factor, on the other hand,

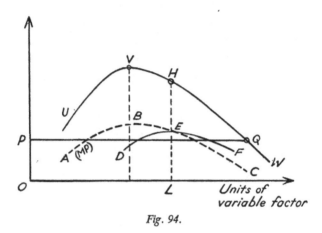

*Fig. 94.*

was 4s., then it would pay to employ 12 units of the variable factor. If we portray in a diagram the dependence of the marginal product on the quantity of the variable factor employed, then we obtain a curve (*ABC*) as drawn in Fig. 94. With a given price for the product one can obtain the curve for the values of the marginal products by multiplying the ordinates of the curve *ABC* by the price of the product. The curve *UVW* obtained in this way is the curve of the values of the marginal product if the price of the product is 2s. If the price of the factor is now equal to *OP*, then the firm will plan to employ the quantity *PQ* of the variable factor. It is clear that the quantity *PQ* demanded by the firm increases as the price of the factor falls. The entire falling part (*VW*) of the curve of the value of the marginal product does not, however, represent the demand curve of the firm for the variable factor. It was shown previously, in analysing the profit plan of a quantity-adjuster, that the firm will only become a supplier if the price of the product is not smaller than the minimum average variable cost. The short-period individual supply curve is, therefore, not the whole of the rising part of the marginal cost curve, but only the part of this curve beginning from the point of minimum average costs. With given prices for the factors, the minimum average variable cost will be where the average product of the variable factor (*DEF*) reaches its maximum, that is, in Fig. 94, at a level of output *OL*. We have shown earlier (Fig. 44) that the maximum for the average product of a variable factor lies on the marginal product curve. The firm will only demand any of the variable factor if its price is not greater than the value of the marginal product of the quantity *OL* of the factor. This proposition is simply another way of stating that the individual supply curve begins from the point of minimum average variable cost. *The demand curve of the firm for the variable factor will, therefore, be given by the section HQW of the falling part of the curve of the value of the marginal product.*

2. Up to now we have assumed that the firm behaves as a quantity-adjuster in selling the product it makes. We now want to study how our previous reasoning about the firm's demand for the factors is affected, *if the firm is confronted by an expected price-sales function.* It was shown previously that on the assumption that the firm is striving for maximum total profit it will decide to sell that quantity at which marginal revenue and marginal cost are equal. But we now know that for every minimum cost combination of factors, the marginal product of a substitute factor multiplied by the marginal cost is equal to the price of this factor. Taking account of the fact that at the Cournot point marginal cost and marginal revenue are equal, it follows that the level of output corresponding to the Cournot point must satisfy the equation:

$$(MP)_i \cdot (MR) = q_i \tag{31}$$

where $(MP)_i$ is the marginal product of the $i^{th}$ substitute factor, $MR$ is the marginal revenue, and $q_i$ the price of the factor. This relationship gives us the quantity of the factor demanded by the firm at each price for the factor. It represents the demand function of the firm for the $i^{th}$ substitute factor. As we can easily see, the expression on the left side of equation (31) simply represents the change in revenue corresponding to an additional unit of the $i^{th}$ factor. For the case of a quantity-adjuster marginal revenue is always equal to the price of the product, so that in this case the change in revenue brought about by an additional unit of the $i^{th}$ factor is equal to the value of the marginal product of this factor. The relation (28) is included in (31) as a special case.

We have already shown (page 73) that the marginal revenue is always smaller than the price of the product. Taking account of this fact, we may deduce from (31) that at the Cournot point the price of the factor *is always less than the value of its marginal product.*

While, therefore, for a seller acting as a quantity-adjuster, the price of the factor is always equal to the value of its marginal product, this equality no longer holds if the seller is faced by an expected price-sales function.

For the relation between the quantity of the factor demanded and the level of its price, the proposition remains true that the way in which the demand for a substitute factor depends on its price is "normal", i.e. *that a rise in the price of a factor will never lead to an increased quantity of the factor being employed.*

Following a method described by P. A. Samuelson,[1] the proof of this fact may be given in a very general way *without the assumption of continuity for the functions concerned.* For simplicity let us assume that there are only two substitute factors. With given prices $q_1$ and $q_2$ let $\bar{v}_1$ and $\bar{v}_2$ be the quantities of the factors demanded when profit is being maximized (at the Cournot point). The corresponding output will be $\bar{x}$, where the level of output is a technically and uniquely determined function of $v_1$ and $v_2$ (the so-called *production function*):

$$x = \phi(v_1, v_2) \tag{32}$$

Let the level of revenue from the sales $x$ be $R$, and the planned fixed costs for the period be $A$, then total profit $P$ will be:

$$P = R(\bar{x}) - A - (q_1 \cdot \bar{v}_1 + q_2 \cdot \bar{v}_2)$$

or, using (32):

$$P = R[\phi(\bar{v}_1, \bar{v}_2)] - A - (q_1 \cdot \bar{v}_1 + q_2 \cdot \bar{v}_2) \tag{33}$$

As $\bar{v}_1$ and $\bar{v}_2$ are, by our assumptions, those quantities of the factors (given their prices) with which maximum profit is obtained, then, at this level of factor prices, $P$ must be smaller for every other combination of factors $v_1'$, $v_2'$. It must hold that:

$$R[\phi(v_1', v_2')] - A - (q_1 \cdot v_1' + q_2 \cdot v_2') \tag{34}$$
$$< R[\phi(\bar{v}_1, \bar{v}_2)] - A - (q_1 \cdot \bar{v}_1 + q_2 \cdot \bar{v}_2)$$

Let us assume that $q_1'$ and $q_2'$ are those factor prices at which the quantities $v_1'$ and $v_2'$ give the maximum total profit. Then obviously:

$$R[\phi(\bar{v}_1, \bar{v}_2)] - A - (q_1' \cdot \bar{v}_1 + q_2' \cdot \bar{v}_2) \tag{35}$$
$$< R[\phi(v_1', v_2')] - A - (q_1' \cdot v_1' + q_2' \cdot v_2')$$

[1] P. A. Samuelson: *Foundations of Economic Analysis*, Cambridge, Harvard University Press, 1947, pp. 80–1.

By adding (34) and (35) we obtain:

$$- (q_1 \cdot v_1' + q_2 \cdot v_2') - (q_1' \cdot \bar{v}_1 + q_2' \cdot \bar{v}_2)$$
$$< - (q_1 \cdot \bar{v}_1 + q_2 \cdot \bar{v}_2) - (q_1' \cdot v_1' + q_2' \cdot v_2')$$

or

$$(q_1 - q_1') \cdot (\bar{v}_1 - v_1') + (q_2 - q_2') \cdot (\bar{v}_2 - v_2') < 0.$$

If we assume that the price of only one factor varies, say the first, then:

$$(q_1 - q_1') \cdot (\bar{v}_1 - v_1') < 0 \tag{36}$$

This inequality says that the alteration in the quantity of a factor must be negative if the alteration in its price is positive and *vice versa*; that is, simply, that the quantity of the factor demanded must (*ceteris paribus*) increase with a reduction in its price.

3. We have assumed up to now that the firm regards the prices of the factors as given, and that in buying the factors it behaves as a quantity-adjuster. We must now drop this assumption and assume *that the firm regards the price of the factor as depending on the quantity it demands of it.* In this case different possibilities may be imagined. The firm may assume that the price of the factor will be the higher the greater the quantity it demands. For example, it may have to pay a higher rate of wages if it wishes to obtain more workers of a particular quality, and the higher rate will have to be paid to all workers of that grade. Another case occurs if the firm assumes that the price of the factor will be lower the larger the quantity it demands. The reader will be able to call to mind plenty of examples from practical life of both cases. Let the price of the variable factor be $q_i$ and the quantity the firm demands $v_i$, then there will exist for this factor an expected relation between $q_i$ and $v_i$:

$$q_i = q_i(v_i) \tag{37}$$

We assume here that the price which the firm reckons with in its plans depends simply on the quantity of the factor demanded by itself. If the same factor is demanded by other firms, then the firm must take into account in its plans the influence of the demand of the other firms on the price. However, in this case, too, the relation between $v_i$ and $q_i$ can also be written in the form of (37). The firm's idea of the influence of the size of the demand of other firms can be expressed through the relation in (37).

If the firm plans to employ the quantity $v_i$ of the $i^{th}$ factor in a planning period, then the costs corresponding to this quantity are obtained by multiplying $v_i$ by the corresponding price given in (37). We now wish to ask by what amount costs alter if the quantity of the

G

factor demanded is increased by 1 unit. We are asking, that is, about the relation between the marginal cost of the variable factor and the quantity of it demanded. If the price of the factor is constant, this marginal cost is equal to the price of the factor. This relation obviously now holds no longer, because the price of the factor is varying with the quantity of it demanded. We have here similar relationships to those we discussed earlier (page 29ff.) when analysing the dependence of monetary demand on the level of the physical quantity demanded. The demand function corresponds here to the relation given in (37). The expenditure corresponds to the cost of the factors $v_i . q_i$, and the marginal outlay corresponds to the marginal cost of the variable factor with respect to the quantity of the factor purchased. The relationship (10) worked out on page 32 can, therefore, be directly applied in our present case. The marginal costs of the $i$th factor in relation to the quantity of the factor employed are given as follows:

$$\frac{d[v_i \cdot q_i]}{dv_i} = q_i \cdot \left(1 + \frac{v_i}{q_i} \cdot \frac{dq_i}{dv_i}\right) \tag{38}$$

The expression:

$$\frac{v_i}{q_i} \cdot \frac{dq_i}{dv_i} = \frac{dq_i}{q_i} : \frac{dv_i}{v_i}$$

gives the relation between the relative change in the price of the factor and the corresponding relative change in the quantity employed. Following H. L. Moore we may describe this as the *price flexibility of the factor*. If the price of the factor is independent of the quantity demanded, then price flexibility is obviously nil. By using the concept of price flexibility we can say that the marginal cost of a variable factor, in relation to the quantity employed, is equal to the price of the factor multiplied by its price flexibility plus 1. The price flexibility plus 1 multiplied by the price of the factor may be described as the "corrected" factor price. If the factor price increases as demand increases, then price flexibility is obviously positive, so that the marginal cost of a variable factor is then always larger than the price of the factor.

In expression (38) the marginal cost of the variable factor is related to the *quantity of the factor* employed. We can just as well relate the marginal cost of the variable factor to the *quantity of the product*. Increasing by 1 unit the quantity of a variable factor employed will result in that increase in the level of output which we have described as the marginal product of that factor. If we now divide the marginal cost of employing a particular factor by the marginal cost of employing a particular factor by the marginal product of the factor, then we obtain the corresponding marginal cost of an additional unit of product. It, therefore, holds that

The Marginal Cost of the Quantity of Product

$$= \frac{\text{The Marginal Cost of the Quantity of the Factor}}{\text{The Marginal Product of the Factor}} \quad (39)$$

or, taking account of (38):

$$MC = \frac{\text{The Price of the Factor} \cdot (1 + \text{Price Flexibility of the Factor})}{\text{Marginal Product}}$$

$$(39a)$$

With constant factor prices the relation (28) developed above holds as a special case:

$$MC = \frac{\text{Factor Price}}{\text{Marginal Product}} \quad (39b)$$

*We now wish to ask what combination of substitute factors the firm will demand if it is aiming, in the period for which it is planning, at maximum total profit.* Let us assume there are $n$ substitute factors in quantities $v_1, v_2, \ldots, v_n$. Given a particular plant, these quantities of the factors can be used to produce an output of $x$. If the output $x$ can be sold at a price of $p$, then the profit, as planned, will be:

$$P = p \cdot x - A - (q_1 \cdot v_1 + q_2 \cdot v_2 + \ldots + q_n \cdot v_n) \quad (40)$$

where $A$ represents the planned fixed costs for the period. In this expression the prices of the factors are *given* functions of the quantities employed. It will now obviously pay the firm to increase by 1 unit the quantity of a substitute factor, the quantities of the other factors remaining constant, so long as the marginal cost of this quantity of the factor is smaller than the increase in revenue from the increase in output resulting from the added unit of the factor. This increase in revenue is obviously equal to the marginal product of the factor multiplied by the marginal revenue. Let us call the marginal product of the $i^{\text{th}}$ factor $(MP)_i$ and the marginal costs of the $i^{\text{th}}$ factor $(MC)_i$, then it will pay the firm to employ a larger quantity of the $i^{\text{th}}$ factor so long as

$$MR \cdot (MP)_i > (MC)_i \quad (41)$$

On the other hand, it will pay the firm to decrease the quantity of the $i^{\text{th}}$ factor employed if

$$MR \cdot (MP)_i < (MC)_i \quad (41a)$$

The maximum profit will obviously be obtained if for each substitute factor the selling value of the marginal product is equal to its marginal cost; that is, when it holds for every factor that

$$MR \cdot (MP)_i = (MC)_i \quad (i = 1, 2, \ldots, n) \tag{42}$$

The quantities of factors which satisfy these $n$ equations represent the maximum-profit combination of factors, in so far as for every combination diverging from this either the relation (41) or (41a) will hold.

Equation (42) may also be written in the form:

$$MR = \frac{(MC)_i}{(MP)_i} \tag{43}$$

or, taking account of (24):

$$MR = (MC) \text{ with respect to quantity of product.} \tag{43a}$$

*From this form of the equation we can see that the equations in (42), which determine the firm's demand for substitute factors, can be directly arrived at from the equality of marginal revenue and marginal cost which is necessary for maximum total profits in all cases where a profit maximum exists within the range over which output varies.*

As those combinations of factors by which the maximum profit is obtained are also those giving the minimum cost combination, the equations (43, 43a) may also be interpreted in this way: *The minimum cost combination is such that the marginal costs of that level of output are the same for all substitute factors.*

We have already demonstrated this proposition for the case of constant factor prices. It is now clear that it has general validity.

Making use of (38), we may write (42) as follows:

$$(MR) \cdot (MP)_i = q_i \cdot \left(1 + \frac{v_i}{q_i} \cdot \frac{dq_i}{dv_i}\right). \tag{44}$$

As this equation holds for every substitute factor, it follows that *for the minimum cost combination it is necessary that the marginal products of substitute factors be proportional to their "corrected" prices (that is, to their prices multiplied by their price flexibilities plus 1).*

4. The equations (42) include all the previous cases as special cases. Let us now once more summarize the theorems we have worked out on the different assumptions:

*Main theorem: The demand for factors of production, assuming the aim of maximum total profits, follows from the proposition that marginal revenue and marginal costs must be equal at the output at which profit is a maximum (provided the profit maximum lies within the range of variation of output*). It, therefore, holds, for all substitute factors, that:

$$MR = \frac{(MC)_i}{(MP)_i}.$$

Case 1. The firm behaves as a quantity adjuster both in selling its product and in buying its factors.

In this case the marginal costs for the different quantities of factors are equal to the prices of the factors $q_i$; the marginal revenue is equal to price $p$. Therefore,

$$p = \frac{q_i}{(MP)_i}.$$

That is: (a) *the prices of the factors are equal to the marginal product multiplied by the price* (= *selling value of the marginal product*).

(b) *The minimum cost combination for a particular output is such that the marginal products of the substitute factors are proportional to their prices.*

Case 2. The firm in selling its product faces an expected price-sales function, but behaves as a quantity-adjuster in buying factors.

The proposition (a) from the first case now runs: *the prices of the factors are equal to the marginal revenue multiplied by marginal product* (= *selling value of the marginal product*). The proposition (b) remains unchanged.

Case 3. The firm behaves as a quantity-adjuster in selling its product, but in buying its factors assumes that their prices depend on the quantity demanded.

The proposition (a) of the first case now runs: *the marginal product multiplied by its price* (= *the selling value of the marginal product*) *is equal to the "corrected" factor price.*

Proposition (b) runs: *the minimum cost combination for a particular output is such that the marginal products of the substitute factors are proportional to the "corrected" factor prices.*

Case 4. The firm in selling its product faces an expected price-sales function, and in buying factors reckons that their prices are dependent on the quantity bought. Proposition (a) now takes the form: *the marginal product multiplied by the marginal revenue* (= *the selling value of the marginal product*) *is equal to the "corrected" factor price.* The proposition (b) is the same as in Case 3.

Demand functions which relate the demand for substitute factors to their prices may be arrived at in both the first two cases, because the firm is behaving as a quantity-adjuster in purchasing factors. A demand function which shows how demand for substitute factors depends on the selling price of the product can only be worked out in the first and third cases. In the fourth case no demand function for factors can be worked out at all in the usual sense. In this case the demand for factors depends on the shape of the curves and not on numerical values.

5. Our previous analysis can without much difficulty be applied to the case where in addition to substitute factors use is also made of limitational factors. The marginal costs due to the use of one more unit of a substitute factor are thus equal to the additional cost of this factor and the corresponding additional costs on account of the limitational factors. If the marginal costs of the limitational factors are deducted from the value of the marginal product, i.e. from the marginal revenue associated with the increase in output due to the use of another unit of the substitute factor, then one obtains a difference which is called the *value of the net marginal product of the substitute factor*. It is immediately obvious that the propositions which we discovered in the case when only substitute factors were used will now similarly apply to the value of the net marginal product. The analysis of the simultaneous use of substitute and limitational factors offers no particular difficulty.

6. These relationships were already perceived and described with unsurpassed lucidity by J. H. von Thünen. In continuation of the numerical example which we reproduced on p. 155 above, he goes on to ask:

"To what degree of thoroughness in the picking of his potatoes would the farmer be led by consistent behaviour (i.e. by the search for maximum net profits, E.S.)?"

and he replies:

"Doubtless up to the point where the value of the additional yield obtained is compensated by the costs of the labour applied to it.

"Supposing for example that the value of potatoes for feeding sheep amounts at some place to 5 *schillings* per *scheffel**  and the daily wage is 8 *schillings* per person: employment of the 9th person will then lead to an additional yield of 1.3 *scheffel* at 5 *schillings* each = 6·5 *schillings* while it costs 8 *schillings* and thus causes a loss of 1·5 *schillings*. But by employing the 8th person at a cost of 8 *schillings* one gains an additional yield of 2 *scheffel* at 5 *schillings* each = 10 *schillings*, hence a surplus of 2 *schillings*. It follows that

---

* v. Thünen reckons in terms of Mecklenburg money of his day (the money of the Lübeck Currency Union). The *schilling* (*leichter Schilling*) was worth about 1d of English money at the time he published his second volume (1850). The *Berlin scheffel* equals 1·5 bushels approx. [Tr.]

to obtain the highest net returns one would apply ca. 8·6 days' of one person's labour to the lifting of potatoes, and content oneself with a yield of ca. 96.8 *scheffel*.

"In circumstances, however, in which the daily wage rises to 15 *schillings*—as can easily happen where potatoes are cultivated on a very large scale because then people have to be drawn from afar—the additional yield due to the employment of the 7th person would just pay the wage, and of the 100 *scheffel* which have grown altogether one would, to act consistently, harvest only 94 *scheffel*.

"If, however, the potatoes can be made to yield 16 *schillings* per *scheffel*, being fed to horses or used for distilling spirits or for other products, then the employment of 11 days' work by one person at a wage of 8 *schillings* is still expedient, and of the 100 *scheffel* of potatoes that are in the ground 98·8 *scheffel* will be harvested.

"At a daily wage of 15 *schillings*, however, and at the value of 16 *schillings* per *scheffel* of potatoes the employment of the 11th person will no longer fully pay for itself.

"The extent to which the grain must be threshed out from the straw is subject to similar rules as the picking of potatoes.

"The loss of grain, often very considerable during the bringing in of the corn, can be markedly reduced through the employment of several labourers. This allows on the one hand the cutting, binding and bringing in to be done more nearly at the right time and, on the other hand, the introduction of cutting by sickle or slashing with the short scythe in the place of mowing by the long scythe. Here, too, one would, to be consistent, raise the number of labourers till the value of what is saved with their help just covers or slightly exceeds the outlay of wages.

"It follows from this:

"1. that a rise in wages, the value of the product remaining the same, will effect a reduction in the number of labourers to be employed and at the same time a diminution in the yield of corn to be gathered and threshed;

"2. that an increase in the value of the product, the wage remaining the same, will have the opposite effect in that more labourers will profitably be employed and the corn more carefully gathered and more cleanly threshed, thus bringing a greater yield;

"3. since it is in the interest of the entrepreneurs, be they farmers or manufacturers, to raise the number of their labourers so long as their increase still yields them an advantage, so the limit to that increase occurs where the additional product from the last labourer is absorbed by the wage paid to him; conversely, the wage of labour is equal to the additional product of the last labourer."

### 3. Substitution Between a Finite Number of Linear-Limitational Processes

1. In our analysis up to now the firm was able to substitute continuously between infinitely many processes. The firm's economic decision thus related to both the process *and* the scale of process (the activity and the level of the activity).[1] But the ability to chose

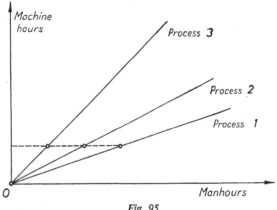

*Fig. 95*

among infinitely many processes which, through continuous substitution, shade into each other, is not often met with in the industrial production of a going concern. The rule is rather for firms with a given plant to be confined in their choice to a few, i.e. to a finite number of, processes, each of which consists of a combination of linear-limitational factors. A firm of printers, for example, may have three processes at its disposal side by side (i.e. in different departments): hand setting, linotype and monotype machines. A firm of civil engineers may move earth with the aid of shovels or with various types of mechanical excavators. Each process operates with a technically determined combination of factors which have to be applied in a technically and uniquely determined quantitative ratio. The several processes differ from each other in the quality of the factors and in the ratios in which they have to be employed.

Consider, for example, three processes. In Process 1, one machine of type I is attended by 3 workmen, In Process 2, one machine of type II is attended by 2 workers. In Process 3, one machine of type III is attended by 1 worker.

---

[1] If there exists only one process with linear-limitational factors, the economic decision will relate only to the scale of process.

In the first process, manpower and machinery are invariably employed in the ratio of 1 machine-hour : 3 man-hours. In the second process, 1 machine-hour : 2 man-hours. In the third process, 1 machine-hour : 1 man-hour. It must, of course, be remembered that the quality of the factors, and thus the prices of machine-hours and of man-hours in the three processes, need not, and as a rule will not be the same.

The diagrammatic picture of the three processes is drawn in Fig. 95 on the assumption that the type of machine is the same in each of the three processes.[1] Each of the processes is a linear-limitational process as described and analysed in the first section.

The quantities of factors which are required in the various processes to produce one unit of the good can be written in the form:

|          | Process I | Process II | Process III |
|----------|-----------|------------|-------------|
| Factor 1 | $a_{11}$  | $a_{12}$   | $a_{13}$    |
| Factor 2 | $a_{21}$  | $a_{22}$   | $a_{23}$    |

the first suffix designating the factor, and the second designating the process. The *production function* will consequently be:

$$v_{11} = a_{11} . x; \quad v_{12} = a_{12} . x; \quad v_{13} = a_{13} . x;$$
$$v_{21} = a_{21} . x; \quad v_{22} = a_{22} . x; \quad v_{23} = a_{23} . x,$$

where $x$ once again stands for the quantity of product and the $v_{ik}$'s stand for the amount of factor.

It is simpler to describe the available processes by the matrix:

$$\begin{bmatrix} 1 & 1 & 1 \\ -a_{11} & -a_{12} & -a_{13} \\ -a_{21} & -a_{22} & -a_{23} \end{bmatrix}$$

in which the negative elements of the columns denote the inputs, while the positive element denotes the output of the activity (or the process). *Each column is a complete and unique description of one activity (one process).* The matrix itself characterizes the firm's production function.

2. Suppose now that the firm wishes to produce the output $x_0$ within one time period. This calls for a decision about the manner in which $x_0$ is to be produced, what process or combination of available processes is to be used in production. The economic choice problem relates in this case to both the process and to the level of the process chosen.

[1] This must be assumed if the three processes are to be presented in the same co-ordinate system.

We shall treat this problem on the assumption that the quantities of all the factors can be continuously varied and that all the processes are mutually independent in the sense that the operation of one process in no way influences the operation of another. The simultaneous application of several processes will thus leave the input-coefficients of the matrix unchanged.

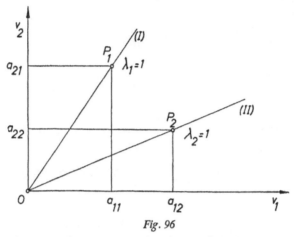

*Fig. 96*

Our first question concerns the shape of the isoquants of a production function characterized by a matrix of the above type. For simplicity we confine ourselves to a single-product firm whose production function consists of two processes and two factors, thus:

$$\begin{bmatrix} 1 & 1 \\ -a_{11} & -a_{12} \\ -a_{21} & -a_{22} \end{bmatrix}$$

or, putting it more explicitly,

$$[\text{I}] \quad \begin{matrix} v_{11} = a_{11} \cdot \lambda_1 \\ v_{21} = a_{21} \cdot \lambda_1 \end{matrix} \qquad [\text{II}] \quad \begin{matrix} v_{12} = a_{12} \cdot \lambda_2 \\ v_{22} = a_{22} \cdot \lambda_2 \end{matrix}$$

where $\lambda_1$ and $\lambda_2$ denote the outputs in process I and in process II respectively, so that the total output of the product is $x = \lambda_1 + \lambda_2$. Figure 96 shows the scale-line of the two processes. $P_1$ ($P_2$) denotes the *unit-scale* of the two processes (or the *unit-level* of the two activities): that quantity-combination of the two factors which, in each process, allows the production of one physical unit of the product. $P_1$ and $P_2$ are accordingly points on the isoquant for $x = 1$. It will easily be understood that the same output may be produced by each of an infinite number of combinations of the two processes.

For instance, output 1 can equally well be obtained by working both processes at the level of one-half, i.e. by using in the first process the factor quantities $\frac{1}{2}a_{11}$; $\frac{1}{2}a_{21}$, and in the second the quantities $\frac{1}{2}a_{12}$; $\frac{1}{2}a_{22}$; or, putting it generally, by operating the first process at the level $\lambda_1$ ($0 < \lambda_1 < 1$) and the second at the level $\lambda_2$ ($0 < \lambda_2 < 1$), where $\lambda_1 + \lambda_2 = 1$. This combination of processes will require the

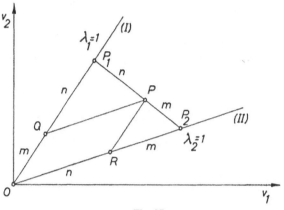

*Fig. 97*

quantities $\frac{1}{2}a_{11} + \frac{1}{2}a_{12}$ of the first factor and $\frac{1}{2}a_{21} + \frac{1}{2}a_{22}$ of the second; or, quite generally, the input $\lambda_1 . a_{11} + \lambda_2 . a_{12} = v_1$ of the first factor, and the input $\lambda_1 . a_{21} + \lambda_2 . a_{22} = v_2$ of the second. It can now be shown that all combinations like

$$v_1 = \lambda_1 . a_{11} + \lambda_2 . a_{12}$$
$$v_2 = \lambda_1 . a_{21} + \lambda_2 . a_{22}$$

which satisfy the condition $\lambda_1 + \lambda_2 = 1$ *will lie on the straight line joining the points $P_1$ and $P_2$.* (See Fig. 97.)

There are several ways of proving this. If we substitute

$$\lambda_2 = 1 - \lambda_1$$

into the above equations, we have

$$v_1 = \lambda_1 . (a_{11} - a_{12}) + a_{12}$$
$$v_2 = \lambda_1 . (a_{21} - a_{22}) + a_{22}$$

or:

$$\frac{v_2 - a_{22}}{v_1 - a_{12}} = \frac{a_{21} - a_{22}}{a_{11} - a_{12}}.$$

But this is merely the equation of the straight line passing through $P_1$ and $P_2$.

The following is a simple geometric proof.

Let $P$ be any point on the line $P_1P_2$. Let $P$ divide this line in the ratio $m:n$. Through $P$ we may draw $PQ$ parallel to $OP_2$, and $PR$ parallel to $OP_1$. The parallel line $PQ$ will then divide $OP_1$ in the ratio $m:n$, and the parallel $PR$ will divide $OP_2$ in the same ratio. Process I is, therefore, reduced to the level $\dfrac{m}{m+n}$, and process II to the level $\dfrac{n}{n+m}$.

$P_1P_2$ thus represents the isoquant for the output $x = 1$. It contains all the points that are efficient in the sense which we analysed when

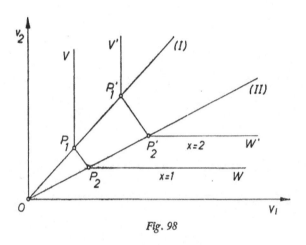

*Fig. 98*

dealing with the linear-limitational case. If we draw through $P_1$ a line parallel to the $v_2$ axis, and through $P_2$ the parallel to the $v_1$ axis (as in Fig. 98) then $VP_1P_2W$ includes all the points, efficient as well as inefficient ones, belonging to the isoquant for $x = 1$. All the points on $VP_1$ ($WP_2$) denote factor combinations in which there is an excess of factor No. 2 (factor No. 1).

Holding to our assumptions, we can now at once proceed to derive from the isoquant for $x = 1$ all the other isoquants. The isoquant for $x = 2$, for example, is constructed by doubling the factor combinations for the isoquant for $x = 1$ (see Fig. 98).

As we move from $P_1$ to $P_2$ along the isoquant for $x = 1$, a continuous substitution between processes I and II takes place: reductions in the scale of the first process get compensated by increases in the scale of the second process. Note the contrast between this and the earlier case when substitution was possible between infinitely many processes: there, any shift, however small, along any isoquant always indicated a transition to a completely new process, while here it is the *scale* of the two processes which changes.

Substitution between two processes is, obviously, only possible if the efficiency loci (the "efficient stretches") of the isoquants run from north-west to south-east. If the isoquant $P_1P_2$ in Fig. 97 were to run from south-west to north-east, $P_2$ alone would be an efficient point.

We are now equipped to deal with the case when there are more than two processes. In Fig. 99, four linear-limitational cases are illustrated. Let the points $P_1$, $P_2$, $P_3$ and $P_4$ denote the unit-level of

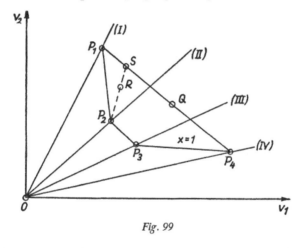

*Fig. 99*

the different activities (or processes), those combinations of factor quantities which allow an output $x = 1$ to be produced by a single activity (process). The line $P_1P_2P_3P_4$ will then represent the isoquant for $x = 1$, that is, the totality of efficient points to which corresponds an output of $x = 1$. Clearly, all the points (i.e. factor combinations) lying inside the quadrangle $P_1P_2P_3P_4$ and on the line $P_1P_4$ will equally permit an output of $x = 1$. Thus, for instance, point $Q$ represents a combination of processes I and IV to which corresponds an output of $x = 1$. But it is not an efficient combination: there always exists a combination on $P_1P_2P_3P_4$ which would permit the same output with less of one or of both factors. The same holds for any random point $R$ inside the quadrangle. The connecting line $P_2R$ cuts $P_1P_4$ in the point $S$. The combination $S$ is itself a combination of processes I and IV, yielding the output 1. $R$ is a linear combination of S and $P_2$. It follows that $S$ is a linear combination of processes I, II and IV, yielding output 1, but again not an efficient combination. To produce $x = 1$, only combinations on the line $P_1P_2P_3P_4$ can be considered, either a single one of those processes or else a combination of two neighbouring processes (I and II, II and III, III and IV) but never I and III, II and IV, I and IV.

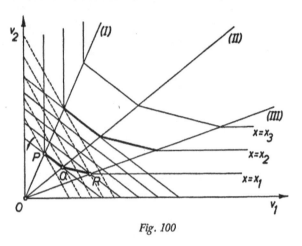

Fig. 100

From the isoquant for $x = 1$ we can once again derive the isoquant for $x = n$ simply by multiplying all the combinations on the isoquant for $x = 1$ by the factor $n$.

If more than two factors are considered, the shape of the isoquant changes from a convex line to a convex body.

3. We now have to ask what can be established about the minimum cost combination of the variable factors if substitution can be carried out as between a finite number of linear-limitational processes. To begin with it is obvious that non-efficient combinations can never be minimum cost combinations. The problem of economic choice relates exclusively to efficient combinations which, in the case of two factors, are the combinations on the convex line in Fig. 99.

The minimum cost combination is found, similarly as in case 2, by drawing the isocost curves into the isoquant-diagram. With given factor prices, the isocost curves may be represented by a set of parallel straight lines. In the present case there are only two possibilities: either the isocost curves pass through a vertex (a corner) of the family of isoquants (cf. the broken isocost curves in Fig. 100) or else the isocost curves have the same slope as a line joining two processes (cf. the solid isocost curves in Fig. 100).

If the isocost curves pass through a corner of the family of iso-quants, minimum costs will be achieved through the employment of one single process (Process I in Fig. 100).

If the isocost curves have the same slope as an isoquant segment, then all combinations on that isoquant segment are minimum cost combinations. In Fig. 100, for example, the output $x = x_2$ can be

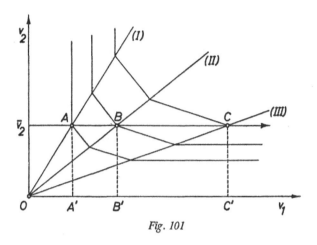

*Fig. 101*

produced either by employing Process I on its own, or by employing Process II on its own, or by any one of the combinations of those two processes which lie on the segment. It appears that in our example of two factors and three processes, every output can be produced at minimum cost by the use of only one process.

As the ratio of factor prices changes, so, we know, does the slope of the isocost curves change. In the case analysed in para. 2 we found that however small the change in factor prices, it yet caused a change of process. The minimum cost combination came to lie on a different ray through the origin. Not so if the firm is restricted in its choice to a finite number of processes. As the isocost curve through the point $P$ (in Fig. 100) turns anti-clockwise—as factor No. 1 becomes cheaper relative to factor No. 2—process I will still remain the "minimum cost process" so long as the isocost line remains steeper than the line $PQ$. Only when the isocost curve has become flatter than $PQ$, but still steeper than the segment $QR$, does process II become the "minimum cost process". In the case we are now examining, not every change in relative factor prices will cause a substitution between two processes. The explanation of this fact is that at the corners of the isoquants, the marginal rate of substitution of one factor for the other is not continuous.

It follows from our analysis that, if the prices of factors are given

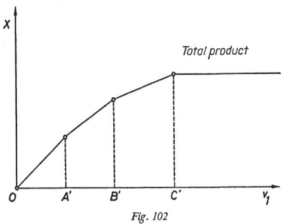

*Fig. 102*

and their quantities are variable without limit, the minimum cost combinations for every possible output will lie on one and the same process-ray. *Marginal returns, and hence marginal costs, are constant along the minimum cost curve.*

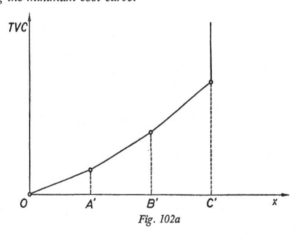

*Fig. 102a*

4. This is not so when factors are varied partially. In Fig. 101 let us, for example, vary the quantity $v_1$ of the first factor while holding that of the second factor constant, thus moving in the $v_1$, $v_2$-plane on a line parallel to the $v_1$-axis. The marginal product of the first

factor will then remain constant till point $A$ is reached; as soon as process-ray I has been crossed there occurs a discontinuous break in the marginal product of the first factor which will then stay on its lower level till point $B$ is reached; when crossing process-ray II (at $B$) the marginal product of the first factor declines further and remains constant till point $C$; and when crossing process-ray III the first factor's marginal product falls to zero. Figure 102 portrays the total product curve of the variable factor. Given the price of the variable factor, the total variable cost curve will then look as drawn in Fig. 102a. With a finite number of processes at its disposal, partial factor variation gives the firm a total cost curve which displays discontinuously rising marginal costs (this being our previous case $d$, see p. 83),

One should carefully consider the meaning of this sequence of discontinuities in the marginal product and the marginal costs which arises when factors are partially varied and which is characteristic of production with a finite number of processes. Increases in output, starting from nothing, will up to point $A$ be carried out by process I alone, the constant quantity $\bar{v}_2$ of the second factor being fully employed when point $A$ is reached. Till then, there always remains an unused residue of the constant factor. As production increases beyond the output denoted by $A$, it becomes necessary to combine process I with process II, reducing the level of process I and expanding that of process II. The reduction in the level of process I will release a portion of the constant factor $\bar{v}_2$ for use in process II. At point $B$, process II is employed on its own; between $B$ and $C$, process II is combined with process III, etc. One starts with that process which uses least of the variable factor, and thus has the smallest marginal costs (Process I in Fig. 101). If output is to be raised beyond the maximum obtainable from process I, the "second-best" process (i.e. process II) must be brought into operation and combined with process I. But that is possible only if the "fixed" factor is suitably shared out between the two processes, etc.

These relationships are sufficiently important to call for further analysis with the aid of an example. Let there be a firm with two departments or plants (hence two processes) whose variable factors are of the linear-limitational type. It follows, that with constant prices for the variable factors, marginal costs will be constant along any one process-ray. Let marginal costs be $m_1$ in plant I, and $m_2$ in plant II, so that $m_1 < m_2$. Let the capacity of plant I be $x_1$, that of plant II $x_2$. We now ask how a particular output $x$ is to be produced. So long as $0 < x \leq x_1$ the firm will only use plant I. If $x > x_1$, plant I will be fully employed and the quantity $x - x_1$ will be produced by plant II which is only feasible if the constant factor (say, a works

engineer) is shared between the two processes. Average variable costs
will be:

$$\text{if}\quad 0 < x \leq x_1 \qquad AVC = m_1$$

$$\text{and if}\; x_1 < x \leq x_2 \qquad AVC = \frac{m_1 \cdot x_1 + m_2 \cdot (x - x_1)}{x}$$

The marginal cost curve and the curve of average variable costs will
then run as in Fig. 103. If $x > x_1$, we conclude that average variable
costs rise.

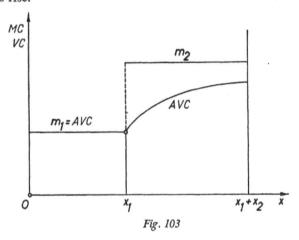

Fig. 103

The reader should note that if marginal costs are constant the
optimal allocation of output to the two plants, (from the point of
view of costs), cannot be determined by the methods of infinitesimal
calculus, any more than can the minimum cost combination of
variable factors for a given quantity of output.

5. Let us ask further what the conclusions will be if *all* the factors—
which in our example would mean factors No. 1 and No. 2—are
only available in limited quantities. Denoting the available quantities
of the factors as $\bar{v}_1$ and $\bar{v}_2$, it is only the factor combinations inside
or on the sides of the rectangle $OABC$ (in Fig. 104) that can be put
into practice. The rectangle, therefore, represents the possibility
region of the factors. Let us first enquire which factor combination
will yield the largest output. The answer appears at once from Fig.
104. If the point $B$ lies on the segment of an isoquant, as it does in
the figure, then maximum output is achieved by combining the two
processes (I and II, in our figure). If, on the other hand, point $B$
coincides with the corner of an isoquant, then maximum output will
be achieved by the employment of only one process. It follows that

if two factors are "fixed", i.e. limited in their quantity, one needs to combine at most two processes in order to reach maximum output. This result may be generalised: *To achieve maximum output, one needs, at most, to combine as many processes as there are fixed factors.*[1]

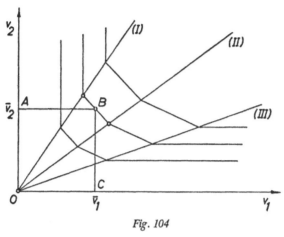

*Fig. 104*

6. The problem of the determination of the minimum cost combination can be formulated in a general manner as follows. Let the production function of a single-product firm consist of $n$ processes with the following matrix:

PROCESS

| | | 1 | 2 | . | . | . | . | $n$ |
|---|---|---|---|---|---|---|---|---|
| | Output | 1 | 1 | . | . | . | . | 1 |
| | Factor 1 | $a_{11}$ | $a_{12}$ | . | . | . | . | $a_{1n}$ |
| | Factor 2 | $a_{21}$ | $a_{22}$ | . | . | . | . | $a_{2n}$ |
| INPUT | . | . | . | . | . | . | . | . |
| | . | . | . | . | . | . | . | . |
| | Factor $m$ | $a_{m1}$ | $a_{m2}$ | . | . | . | . | $a_{mn}$ |

[1] The proof would lead us outside the limits of an introduction. The interested readers are referred to T. C. Koopmans, *Activity Analysis of Production and Allocation*, New York, 1951, or to A. Bordin, *La programmazione lineare nell'industria*, Torino (Unione Industriale de Torino), 1954. A more easily accessible rigorous proof is to be found in D. Gale and S. Danø, *Linear Programming: An introduction to the problems and methods* (Nordisk Tidsskrift for Teknisk Ökonomi, 1954). See also Dorfman, Samuelson, Solow, *loc. cit.*

If the process $k$ is carried out at the level $\lambda_k$ $(k = 1, 2, \ldots, n)$ i.e. if $\lambda_k$ units of the good are produced by the process $k$, then total output by all the processes together amounts to:

$$x = \lambda_1 + \lambda_2 + \ldots + \lambda_n = \sum_{k=1}^{n} \lambda_k.$$

The total input of the $i^{\text{th}}$ factor will then amount to:

$$v_i = a_{i1}\lambda_1 + a_{i2}\lambda_2 + \ldots + a_{in}\lambda_n \qquad (i = 1, 2, \ldots, m)$$

Total variable costs will therefore be:

$$C = \sum_{i=1}^{m} v_i \cdot q_i = \sum_{i=1}^{m} q_i \cdot (a_{i1}\lambda_1 + a_{i2}\lambda_2 + \ldots + a_{in}\lambda_n)$$

$$= \left(\sum_{i=1}^{m} q_i \cdot a_{i1}\right) \cdot \lambda_1 + \ldots + \left(\sum_{i=1}^{m} q_i \cdot a_{in}\right) \cdot \lambda_n,$$

where

$$\sum_{i=1}^{m} q_i \cdot a_{ik}$$

stands for the average variable cost in process $k$. With given factor prices, these unit costs are a uniquely determined magnitude. If, to abbreviate, we write:

$$\sum_{i=1}^{m} q_i \cdot a_{ik} = s_k \tag{45}$$

then the total variable costs will appear as:

$$C = \sum_{k=1}^{n} s_k \cdot \lambda_k. \tag{46}$$

If we are given the quantity of output $x$ (i.e. $x = \bar{x}$) then $\lambda_k$ has so to be determined that total variable costs (46) attain their minimum, subject to the side conditions that

$$\lambda_1 + \lambda_2 + \ldots + \lambda_n = \bar{x} \tag{46a}$$

and

$$\lambda_k \geqq 0 \qquad (k = 1, 2, \ldots, n). \tag{46b}$$

We have already shown the graphical solution of this problem when there are only two factors. If there are more than two factors the problem defies geometrical treatment. To determine the extreme values of a linear function, subject to linear side conditions of which some are in the form of inequalities, one needs to resort to the mathematical methods of linear programming. Their description would, however, take us outside the confines of this introduction.

7. The second problem which we examined for the case when there are two factors concerned the *maximisation of output*, given that the factors are available in limited quantities only. The general formulation of this problem may be stated as follows:

We have to maximise the linear function

$$x = \lambda_1 + \lambda_2 + \ldots + \lambda_n \tag{47}$$

subject to the side conditions:

$$\left. \begin{array}{l} a_{11}\lambda_1 + a_{12}\lambda_2 + \ldots + a_{1n}\lambda_n \leqq \bar{v}_1 \\ a_{21}\lambda_1 + a_{22}\lambda_2 + \ldots + a_{2n}\lambda_n \leqq \bar{v}_2 \\ \qquad \cdot \\ \qquad \cdot \\ \qquad \cdot \\ a_{m1}\lambda_1 + a_{m2}\lambda_2 + \ldots + a_{mn}\lambda_n \leqq \bar{v}_m \end{array} \right\} \tag{47a}$$

and

$$\lambda_k \leqq 0 \qquad (k = 1, 2, \ldots, n) \tag{47b}$$

8. If the firm wishes to maximise profits, the question needs to be formulated as follows:

*Which combination of $\lambda_1, \lambda_2, \ldots, \lambda_n$ will maximise profits, provided that the quantities of the factors must not exceed a given upper limit?*

The formulation of this problem is not difficult. It is clear, first of all, that we need concern ourselves only with gross profits (i.e. revenue less variable costs). If the price of the good is $p$, then the gross profits attained when quantity $x$ is produced are given by:

$$G = p \cdot x - (v_1 \cdot q_1 + v_2 \cdot q_2 + \ldots + v_m \cdot q_m), \tag{48}$$

or, using (46) and (47),

$$G = p \cdot \sum_{k=1}^{n} \lambda_k - \sum_{k=1}^{n} s_k \cdot \lambda_k = \sum_{k=1}^{n} (p - s_k) \cdot \lambda_k, \tag{48a}$$

where $(p - s_k) \cdot \lambda_k$ $(k = 1, 2, \ldots, n)$ denotes gross profits for the $k^{\text{th}}$ process, obtained when the quantity of output $\lambda_k$ is produced by process No. $k$.

The problem consists in maximising gross profits subject to the side conditions (47a, b).

If only two factors are used, we can once again produce a simple graphical solution. The isoquants are merely replaced by the iso-profit curves. Given the prices of the good and of the factors, this operation may be simplified by so choosing the technical coefficients of the factors, and the quantities of the factors, that for $\lambda_k = 1$ the gross profits from process No. $k$ will equal 1. In terms of geometry this means a parallel shift of the quantity isoquants since inputs and outputs are both directly proportional to gross profits.

So far we have been considering a single-product firm. Our analysis can nevertheless be applied quite readily to a multi-product firm. If two goods are produced, our earlier graphical solution (see p. 131) will apply.

## Section F

### THE LONG-TERM ECONOMIC PLAN OF A FIRM

1. Up to now we have considered the problem of the short-term planning of an entrepreneur working in the framework of an existing business: "short-term" meaning related to a single period of time. We must now turn our attention to the plans of an entrepreneur which extend over several economic periods. This sort of long-term planning is always involved when a decision is taken about founding a new undertaking. But even within the framework of an existing firm there are, in addition to the plans for the coming period, decisions to be made which relate to the course of economic events over several periods. Every purchase of a durable factor of production necessarily involves a long-term plan. Each planned extension of a plant, or each planned alteration in a production programme, necessarily requires planning for several economic periods. It is impossible in such an introductory account as this to deal with all aspects of the problems of long-term economic planning. We must confine ourselves to describing the fundamental relationships.[1]

2. In an exchange economy, in which money is used, the carrying out of a process of production is always accompanied by a stream of outlays necessary for the purchases of factors of production. This stream of outlays we may describe as the *investment process* accompanying a process of production (the outlays being "invested" in factors of production), or we may call it simply the *investment related to the process of production*. The process of production itself is the *object of the investment*. In manufacturing industry every investment has its counterpart in the sale of the resulting manufactured products and in the subsequent stream of receipts. As the object of the investment is to bring a profit to the entrepreneur, the relation between the series of outlays on the one hand, and the series of receipts on the other, is obviously of central importance in long-term economic planning.

[1] A fuller treatment of the problem of long-term planning will be found in my *Wirtschaftlichkeitsrechnung* (2nd ed., Tübingen, 1957).

The expected course of these two series must be such that the investor believes he can obtain the profit he is aiming at. For a complete description of a process of investment in a private-enterprise economy it is necessary, therefore, to know the series of outlays and receipts. It is generally convenient, in making plans, to add the total outlays and the total receipts for an economic period and to assume that they fall due either at the beginning or at the end of the period, disregarding, that is, how the outlays and receipts are distributed *within* the single economic period.[1]

A process of investment only comes to an end when the process of production is concluded, that is, if the factory is liquidated or in the case, for example, of a car-hire business if the vehicle is sold. Considerations of the profitability of a planned process of investment must, therefore, be based on an assumption about the course of receipts and outlays for the whole life of the investment. If one plans, at a particular point of time, a change in an already existing process of investment, one must form an idea of the entire remaining period of life of the investment, and of how the planned change will influence the course of outlays and receipts. It is always necessary to consider the series of outlays and receipts *in their entire temporal extent*. The two series may be finite or infinite according as to whether the process of investment extends over a finite or infinite number of economic periods. The case of processes of investment extending over an infinite number of economic periods is, in practice, of special importance because most investment processes are begun with the intention that they should be continued indefinitely.

3. Let us consider some simple examples:

Example 1: An entrepreneur plans at a particular point of time the purchase of a quantity of wine with the intention of storing and selling it after $t$ years. At the point of time at which he makes his plan, or, as we may call it, at the moment of calculation, the entrepreneur reckons with an outlay of $a$ (shillings) and with receipts of $b$ (shillings) after $t$ years ($b > a$). The picture of outlays and receipts for the investment he is planning may be given as follows:

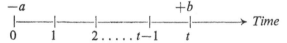

where negative numbers represent outlays and positive numbers receipts.

---

[1] For other problems, such as the drawing up of financial plans and providing for liquidity, it is important to know the exact moments at which outlays and receipts will occur.

Example 2: An entrepreneur is planning a bus service between two places for a period of $t$ years. At the moment of calculation the purchase of the buses cost $a$ (shillings), the average yearly running expenses (which we may assume here are equal to the running costs) are $b$ (shillings), and the average yearly receipts are $c$ (shillings), ($c > b$). Let the difference between the annual receipts and the running expenses, or the net annual receipts, be $d$, then this investment may be pictured, as regards its outlays and receipts, as follows (the value of the bus after $t$ years being assumed to be nil):

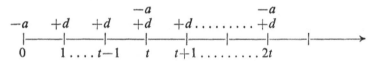

```
 -a    +d    +d    +d        +d    +d
  |-----|-----|-----|---------|-----|---------→ Time
  0     1     2     3 . . . . t-1   t
```

Example 3: If the bus service is planned to continue indefinitely, and if the length of life of a bus when used in accordance with the plans is estimated at $t$ years, then we have the following picture for the temporal distribution of outlays and receipts:

```
                      -a                    -a
  -a    +d    +d    +d    +d . . . . . . . +d
  |-----|-----|-----|-----|-----|-----|-----|------→
  0     1 . . t-1   t    t+1 . . . . . . . 2t
```

We are assuming here, as often happens in practice, that the investments repeated every $t$ years are identical.[1]

4. We now have to answer the question as to how it will be decided whether the investment is profitable for the entrepreneur. To do this we must first clarify what we understand by a profitable investment for the entrepreneur. *We shall say that an investment is profitable for an entrepreneur if the total receipts accruing from the investment represent a recovery of the total outlays including a rate of interest regarded as adequate by the entrepreneur.* This rate of interest regarded as adequate by the entrepreneur in making his plans we may describe as *the (adequate) "target" rate of interest.* It must be noticed that this (adequate) target rate of interest is not identical with the long-term rate of interest in the capital market. If we assume that the investment is financed exclusively by other people's capital, then it is clear that the target rate of interest must be higher than the rate of interest for the loan. The difference

[1] "In practice we have tacitly agreed, as a rule, to fall back on what is in truth a convention. The essence of this convention . . . lies in assuming that the existing state of affairs will continue indefinitely, except in so far as we have specific reasons to expect a change" (J. M. Keynes: *General Theory of Employment, Interest and Money*, London, 1936, p. 152).

between the target rate of interest and the rate of interest for long-term loans clearly depends on the size of the profit that is being aimed at, and on the degree of risk bound up with the investment. The greater (*ceteris paribus*) the risks involved in the investment, the higher will be the target rate of interest of the entrepreneur. On the other hand, if the investment is being financed with the entrepreneur's own capital, then the target rate of interest must obviously correspond with the rate of interest that could be obtained from some other investment involving the same risk. In the financing of an investment with the entrepreneur's own and with somebody else's capital, all these elements will affect the level of the target rate of interest. Often the target rate of interest is determined in the following way. If we describe the new capital necessary for an investment, own and borrowed, as $k_0$ or $k_b$ respectively, the rate of interest aimed at on his own capital as $i_0$,[1] and that on the borrowed capital as $i_b$, then in calculating the profitability of the investment the target rate of interest will be based on an average rate, according to the following formula:

$$i = \frac{k_0 \cdot i_0 + k_b \cdot i_b}{k_0 + k_b}$$

As the degree of risk involved, as well as the rate of interest regarded as normal for a particular kind of investment, rests on the subjective estimate of all the factors relevant for the investment, the target rate of interest is always a subjectively determined quantity. It may, therefore, also be described as the *subjective* rate of interest as contrasted with the *objective rate* of the capital market. It should be noticed that all the quantities involved in the investor's plans rest on estimates, and, therefore, contain a greater or lesser degree of uncertainty. On this ground a higher, rather than a lower, target rate of interest will be preferred. The high target rate of interest serves as a kind of insurance against mistakes in estimating the outlays and receipts from the investment.

5. Let us now apply our criterion for deciding whether or not a planned investment is profitable for an entrepreneur to the examples we described above. Let the target rate of interest be $i$, so that, in our first example, the receipts accruing after $t$ years (that is, $b$) will represent a recovery of the outlay $a$, plus a rate of interest equal to $i$, provided that the value of the outlays with interest added at the

[1] Throughout we express the rate of interest in the form of a fraction. If $p$ is the rate of interest expressed as a percentage, then as a fraction the rate is given by $i = \frac{p}{100}$. For $p = 4\%$, $i = 0.04$.

rate $i$ up to the point of time $t$ is not larger than the value of the receipts at the point of time $t$. This is to say that the *value of the receipts discounted at the target rate of interest to the moment of calculation at time zero must be not less than the value of the outlays at that point of time*. The planned investment is, therefore, profitable, assuming a particular target rate of interest, if

$$a(1 + i)^t \leqq b$$

or

$$\frac{b}{(1 + i)^t} \geqq a \qquad (1)$$

If the equality signs hold good in these expressions, then the investment yields exactly the target rate of interest. The condition (1) can now be expressed in another form, more useful in discussing long-term planning, if we introduce the concept of *the capital value of an investment*.

6. *By the capital value of an investment at a particular point of time* t, *and at a rate of interest* i, *we understand the sum of all the net receipts discounted to the point of time* t, *which will accrue after that point of time*.

Supposing the picture of outlays and receipts from the investment has the following form:

$$\begin{array}{cccccc}
+b_1 & +b_2 & +b_3 & & +b_n & \\
-a_0 & -a_1 & -a_2 & -a_3 & & -a_n \\
\end{array}$$

$$\begin{array}{ccccccc}
| & | & | & | & | & | & \longrightarrow \text{ Time} \\
0 & 1 & 2 & 3 & \ldots\ldots\ldots & n &
\end{array}$$

To abbreviate, let

$$b_t - a_t = c_t \quad (t = 1, 2, \ldots)$$

Then, at the moment of calculation which, following Fisher, we may designate as $0^-$ (the moment of time immediately before zero), the capital value of the investment will be:

$$C_{0^-} = \frac{c_n}{(1 + i)^n} + \frac{c_{n-1}}{(1 + i)^{n-1}} + \ldots + \frac{c_1}{1 + i} - a_0 \qquad (2)$$

Similarly, the capital value at the moment $0^+$ (i.e. the moment immediately after the planned start of the investment) will be:

$$C_0^+ = \frac{c_n}{(1 + i)^n} + \frac{c_{n-1}}{(1 + i)^{n-1}} + \ldots + \frac{c_1}{1 + i} \qquad (2a)$$

In planning the investment all calculations of capital value are taken from the moment of calculation $0^-$. The point of time to which they relate may be any moment between $0^-$ and $n^-$. In calculating the capital value of an investment we must therefore distinguish between the moment of time at which the outlays and receipts are estimated (the moment of calculation), and the moment of time for which the capital value is calculated (the discounting point of time). A precise statement about a capital value must distinguish between, and give, both these points of time. We shall, following Lindahl's procedure,[1] qualify the capital value $C$ with two indices, the first of which gives the moment of calculation, and the second the point of time to which the value is discounted. Thus, for example, $C_{0^-, \, 0^-}$, represents the capital value calculated from the moment $0^-$, and discounted to the moment $0^-$; $C_{0^-, \, 3^+}$ represents a capital value calculated from the moment $0^-$, and discounted to the moment $3^+$. $C_{1^+, \, 0^-}$ represents a capital value calculated from the moment $1^+$, and discounted to the moment $0^-$. Into such a capital value there enter the actual outlays and receipts from the first year, as well as the estimates of outlays and receipts in the second, third, etc., years following the first year. $C_{1^+, \, 0^-}$ represents, therefore, the corrected capital value of $C_{0^-, \, 0^-}$ after one year, making use of the facts and experiences of that first year. In the expressions (2) and (2a) only the index for the discounting point of time is given, because the moment of calculation is in those cases the same, i.e. the point of time $0^-$ immediately before the start of the investment.

7. Let us write condition (1) in the form:

$$\frac{b}{(1 + i)^t} - a \geqq 0 \tag{3}$$

We must notice that the left side of (3) represents the capital value at the moment of calculation and the value discounted to the same moment, so that we can also conclude that the investment in our first example is, at the chosen target rate of interest, profitable for the entrepreneur, *if the capital value of the investment discounted to the point of time immediately before its planned beginning is not negative.*

This proposition, as can easily be seen, possesses general validity. We may describe it as *the fundamental principle for long-period economic planning.* For our second example it holds that the investment will be profitable at the target rate of interest $i$ if:

$$\frac{d}{(1 + i)^t} + \frac{d}{(1 + i)^{t-1}} + \ldots + \frac{d}{1 + i} - a \geqq 0 \tag{4}$$

or

$$d \cdot \frac{(1 + i)^t - 1}{i \cdot (1 + i)^t} - a \geqq 0 \tag{4a}$$

---

[1] E. Lindahl: *Studies in the Theory of Money and Capital*, London, 1939, p. 101.

Similarly for the profitability of the investment in the third example:

$$\frac{d}{1+i} + \frac{d}{(1+i)^2} + \ldots + \frac{d}{(1+i)^t} + \ldots$$

$$- \left( a + \frac{a}{(1+i)^t} + \frac{a}{(1+i)^{2t}} + \ldots \right) \gtreqless 0 \qquad (5)$$

or

$$\frac{d}{i} - \frac{a(1+i)^t}{(1+i)^t - 1} \gtreqless 0 \qquad (5a)$$

8. Our fundamental principle may be expressed in another form which will be useful for our further problems. In order to arrive at this other formulation we introduce the concept of *the internal rate of interest of an investment*. We understand by this the *rate of interest* r *at which the capital value of an investment, immediately before it begins, is equal to nil.*

Let us consider, for example, an investment with the following outlays and receipts:

$$\begin{array}{cccc} -20{,}000 & +8000 & +8000 & +8000 \\ \vdash\!\!-\!\!-\!\!-\!\!-\!\!\vdash\!\!-\!\!-\!\!-\!\!-\!\!\vdash\!\!-\!\!-\!\!-\!\!-\!\!\vdash\!\!-\!\!-\!\!-\!\!\longrightarrow Time \\ 0 & 1 & 2 & 3 \end{array}$$

If r is the internal rate of interest, then:

$$\frac{8000}{1+r} + \frac{8000}{(1+r)^2} + \frac{8000}{(1+r)^3} - 20{,}000 = 0$$

or

$$8{,}000 \cdot \frac{(1+r)^3 - 1}{r \cdot (1+r)^3} = 20{,}000$$

or

$$\frac{r \cdot (1+r)^3}{(1+r)^3 - 1} = 0 \cdot 4.$$

From special tables for the expression on the left of this equation we can obtain as the solution for r:

$$r = 0 \cdot 1.$$

The internal rate of interest of the investment amounts, therefore, to 10%; that is, the receipts represent a recovery of the outlays with a rate of interest of 10%.

For our next example we shall take an investment as follows: The purchase is planned of a house to cost £a and to be rented out. The annual outlays for upkeep are £u. The annual receipts from rents £l. ($l > u$), so that the annual net receipts are £($l - u$). It is reckoned that the house could be sold again after $n$ years for £$a$ (i.e. at the purchase price).

The picture of outlays and receipts for the investment is, in this case, as follows:

$$-a \quad l-u \quad l-u \quad l-u \qquad l-u+a$$

|——|——|——|——|——|——$\longrightarrow$ *Time*
0   1   2   3.........$n$

The internal rate of interest is then given by the equation:

$$\frac{l-u}{1+r} + \cdots + \frac{l-u+a}{(1+r)^n} - a = 0$$

or:

$$r = \frac{l-u}{a}$$

In these examples we have considered the internal rate of interest as an *ex-ante* quantity, that is, a rate of interest as calculated in the process of planning. Of course, the internal rate of interest can also be calculated *ex-post* at the conclusion of an investment, or, in the course of an investment, calculated partly on *ex-post* and partly on *ex-ante* values for receipts and outlays. A share in a company may on 1.1.1930 have been sold for 3000s. The following dividends may have been obtained: 1930, 300s.; 1931, 150s.; 1932, 210s.; and 1933, 240s. At the end of the year 1933 the share was sold for 2500s. The internal rate of interest obtained is given by the equation:

$$\frac{300}{1+r} + \frac{150}{(1+r)^2} + \frac{210}{(1+r)^3} + \frac{240}{(1+r)^4} + \frac{2500}{(1+r)^4} - 3000 = 0.$$

The internal rate of interest may be discovered by trial to be slightly less than 4%.

The concept of the internal rate of interest which we have here introduced is identical with Irving Fisher's "rate of return over cost", J. M. Keynes' "marginal efficiency of capital" and K. E. Boulding's "internal rate of return".[1]

By using this concept of the internal rate of interest our fundamental principle can be expressed in the following way: *an investment is profitable if the internal rate of interest is not lower than the target rate of interest*. If the internal rate of interest is higher than the target rate of interest, then the capital value is positive, and if the internal rate of interest is equal to the target rate of interest, then the capital value is nil. A positive capital value, therefore, corresponds to an

[1] I. Fisher: *The Theory of Interest*, New York, 1930; J. M. Keynes: *op. cit.*, K. E. Boulding: "Time and Investment" in *Economica*, 1936.

internal rate of interest which is higher than the target rate of interest.

In order to decide whether an investment is profitable or not at a given target rate of interest, there are two methods available:

(a) Basing one's calculations on an assumed target rate of interest one may work out the capital value of the investment immediately before its beginning. If the capital value worked out in this way is not negative, then the intended investment is profitable. We may describe this procedure as the *method of discounting*.

(b) One may compare the internal rate of interest of the investment with the target rate of interest. If the internal rate of interest is not lower than the target rate of interest, then the planned investment is profitable. This procedure we may describe as the *internal-rate-of-interest method*.

9. Our investigation has shown that the capital value of an investment depends (a) on the level and distribution through time of the outlays necessitated by it; (b) on the level and distribution through time of the resulting receipts; and (c) on the level of the target rate of interest. It follows that whether an investor will demand a durable factor of production, whether it be a machine, a house, or a piece of land, depends simply on the stream of outlays necessary, if we take as given the stream of receipts and the target rate of interest. If we consider the series of outlays as given, with the exception of that necessary for purchasing the durable factor in question, then the sole element in deciding whether the investment is profitable, and whether, therefore, there will be a demand for the durable factor, is the price of acquiring it. From the condition that the capital value of the investment must not be negative, it may be discovered up to what price the investor is ready to pay for a durable factor. The lower the purchase price of the factor, the more profitable (*ceteris paribus*) is the investment for the entrepreneur making his plans. Every demander of a particular durable factor will obviously have his own subjective idea as to the course of the series of receipts and outlays (i.e. the outlays excluding the purchase price of the factor), as well as his own subjective target rate of interest. Each demander will, therefore, have a different maximum price. As the purchase price of the durable factor increases from nil upwards, so the total demand for the factor will decrease. Our fundamental principle, therefore, allows us to formulate and solve the problem of the demand for durable factors, and to show how the demand function for them can be obtained from the long-period economic plans of the entrepreneur.

Our conclusions show, further, that whenever higher receipts are expected (*ceteris paribus*) the demand for durable factors will increase. The purchase price is always only one of the factors which determine the demand for durable factors of production. *What are decisive are the expected outlays and receipts as a whole, in both their level and their temporal distribution, as well as the target rate of interest.* The target rate of interest is also only one of the many other elements determining the profitability of investments, and thereby the demand for durable factors of production. This fact must not be forgotten when we turn to the problem of the way in which changes in the target rate of interest influence (*ceteris paribus*) the investment decisions of the entrepreneur.

10. Let us consider a simple example. At a particular moment of calculation an entrepreneur is considering whether it pays to purchase a machine the use of which results in a saving of labour, and thereby of wages, of £$\Delta l$ per year, assuming a particular level of production per unit of time. The purchase price of the machine is $p$ and its length of life $n$ years. The annual running costs and costs of repairs of the machine are £$b$. We assume, further, that all other future expenses are not affected by the purchase of the machine. On the assumption that $b < \Delta l$, the purchase of the machine will result in an increase in the annual net receipts of the sum $\Delta e = \Delta l - b$. The purchase of the machine is, therefore, profitable (assuming that the entrepreneur has chosen a target rate of interest of $i$) if at the moment of calculaton the discounted present value of the annual increase in net receipts is not smaller than the purchase price of the machine; that is, if:

$$p \leqq \frac{\Delta e}{1 + i} + \frac{\Delta e}{(1 + i)^2} + \ldots + \frac{\Delta e}{(1 + i)^n}$$

or

$$p \leqq \Delta e \cdot \frac{(1 + i)^n - 1}{i \cdot (1 + i)^n} \qquad (6)$$

We now wish to ask what the result of the calculation will be if (*ceteris paribus*) the assumed target rate of interest changes. In relation (6) all the quantities with the exception of $i$ are constant. Only the rate of interest $i$ changes. We have, therefore, to study how the expression:

$$\frac{(1 + i)^n - 1}{i \cdot (1 + i)^n} \qquad (7)$$

changes with the rate of interest. It can easily be seen that expression (7) can also be written in the following form:

$$\frac{(1 + i)^n - 1}{i \cdot (1 + i)^n} = \frac{1}{i} - \frac{1}{i(1 + i)^n} = \frac{1}{i} \cdot \left[1 - \frac{1}{(1 + i)^n}\right] \qquad (8)$$

From (8) we can easily see that the value of expression (7) increases as the rate of interest falls. If, for example, $n = 10$, then if $i = 0\cdot1$ the expression (7) has a value of 6·144, if $i = 0\cdot08$ it has a value of 6·710, and if $i = 0\cdot06$ a value of 7·36. As the rate of interest falls the present value of the annual addition to net receipts, or, what is the same thing, the capital value of the investment, increases. The investment will, therefore, as the target rate of interest falls, become (*ceteris paribus*) more profitable. It follows directly from this that *a fall in the target rate of interest results* (ceteris paribus) *in an increase in the demand for durable factors of production*.

A fall in the target rate of interest will not influence the capital values of different planned investments in the same degree. The extent of the variation of the capital value of an investment that follows from a change in the target rate of interest depends, as we can see from expression (7), essentially on the expected duration of the investment (in our example, on the expected length of life of the machine). If the rate of interest falls from 4% to 2%, then we obtain the following values for expression (7):

|  | $i = 0\cdot04$ | $i = 0\cdot02$ | *Increase* |
|---|---|---|---|
| $n = \infty$ | 25 | 50 | 100% |
| $n = 100$ | 24·51 | 43·10 | 76% |
| $n = 50$ | 21·48 | 31·42 | 46% |
| $n = 25$ | 15·62 | 19·52 | 25% |
| $n = 10$ | 8·11 | 8·98 | 11% |
| $n = 5$ | 4·45 | 4·71 | 6% |
| $n = 1$ | 0·96 | 0·98 | 2% |

This table shows that a fall in the target rate of interest (*ceteris paribus*) increases the capital values of all planned investments, but not to the same extent. As may be seen from the table, the value of expression (7), and therefore the capital value of the investment, increases the more, the longer is the life of the investment. A fall in the target rate of interest will, therefore, make investments of a longer duration comparatively more profitable. *In general we may say that a fall in the target rate of interest will lead* (ceteris paribus) *to an increase in the demand for durable factors of production, and will make the use of durable factors comparatively more profitable than the use of short-lived factors*.

In applying these results it must be noticed that the rate of interest in question here is always the *subjective* target rate of interest of the entrepreneur in making his plans. As we have seen, this target rate of interest is usually above the long-term market rate of interest, the difference between the two being the greater, the greater the risk of the planned investment. This fact must always be borne in mind when we are trying to answer the question as to the extent to which it is possible (*ceteris paribus*) to influence the propensity to invest of the entrepreneur by changes in the long-term rate of interest. Experience, and inquiries recently undertaken, have shown that reductions in the long-term rate of interest are by no means generally effective in increasing the investment activity of the entrepreneur. This empirical fact finds a simple explanation in that the entrepreneur in his long-term calculations about investment is not reckoning with the long-term rate of interest, but with a subjective target rate of interest diverging from it upwards in accordance with the riskiness of the investment. Let us assume that the subjective rate of interest is 20%, and the market rate of interest 4%, so that 16% represents the subjective rate for the risk of the planned investment. If the market rate of interest is now reduced to 3%, then, the risk being estimated to be the same, this is a reduction in the target rate of interest from 20 to 19%. Such a reduction in the subjective rate of interest will have, as can easily be calculated, no appreciable influence on the capital value of the investment. An appreciable influence on the investment decisions of the entrepreneur will only be exercised by an alteration in the long-term rate of interest *in respect of investments which incur little risk, and in particular in respect of investments of long duration.*[1] It is, therefore, easily understandable that building activity will be especially influenced by changes in the long-term market rate of interest. It may be noticed, further, that as well as the rate of interest, the stream of outlays and of receipts is also relevant for the decisions of the entrepreneur. It is, therefore, clear that in times of uncertainty and pessimism the entrepreneur will hardly be stimulated in his propensity to invest by a reduction of the long-term rate of interest. This fact is of importance for the Theory of Employment which we shall study later on.

11. Up to now we have assumed that the entrepreneur is only considering a single investment plan. As a rule, the planning entrepreneur will always have a range of choice between several production possibilities, or methods of production, and, therefore, between several investment plans. The range and freedom of choice of the entrepreneur are, of course, the greater, the smaller the obligations imposed by already undertaken investments. Every plan carried out in the past restricts in some way the field of action of the entrepreneur in the present. Complete freedom of action in the choice of methods of production is only enjoyed when a completely new enterprise is being planned.

[1] See the important work of G. L. S. Shackle: "Interest Rates and the Pace of Investment" in *Economic Journal*, 1946, pp. 1 ff.

H

Let us take a simple example: an entrepreneur has the following possibilities to choose between:

(a) The purchase of a piece of land for £5000. The level of annual net receipts expected *ad infinitum* from the use of this piece of land is estimated at £300.

(b) The purchase of a piece of land at a price of £7,000. The level of annual net receipts expected *ad infinitum* from this piece of land being estimated at £480.

The question is, which of the two possibilities the entrepreneur will prefer at a target rate of interest of 5%. We may ascertain, first, that both of the possibilities are profitable for the entrepreneur at the given target rate of interest. The capital values of the two investments discounted to the moment of calculation are:

$$C_a = \frac{300}{i} - 5000 = 1000$$

and

$$C_b = \frac{480}{i} - 7000 = 2600.$$

The two capital values are positive and, therefore, both possibilities are profitable at the given target rate of interest. Which of the two possibilities is the more profitable? One might be inclined to say that the more profitable alternative is that of which the capital value is the larger. This conclusion is only correct on an important assumption, which in practice is always (though usually tacitly) made in such calculations as to investment possibilities, and which we shall be making in the following discussion: this is, that *it must be assumed that the investor is in a position to obtain and to make loans to an indefinite extent at the given target rate of interest*. It must be clear that if the problem of choice is to have any sense, it must, of course, be assumed that the investor is in a position to finance the different alternative choices. This means that in reality the investor has not only to choose between the two possibilities (a) and (b). If he chooses the possibility (b), then he is abandoning not only the possibility (a) but also a third investment possibility (x), for which the series of outlays is £2000 at the point of time zero. This is because the carrying out of possibility (a) only requires £5000 at the point of time zero. There is, therefore, a further £2000 for alternative uses. The choice between (a) and (b) rests in reality on a comparison between (a) and (x) on the one hand, and (b) on the other hand. The two alternatives (a) and (b) are, therefore, not completely defined until it is stated at what rate of interest any sums left over can be applied or obtained. If one makes the assumption that any sums left over can be invested at the target rate of interest, then it follows that the capital value of the third investment possibility (x) is nil, so that in comparing the possibilities (a) and (x) on the one hand, and (b) on the other, no attention need be paid to investments made possible by loans or credits.

The relation discussed here has, as can easily be seen, general validity. For the choice between several profitable investment possibilities the following criterion, therefore, holds: *on the assumption that the investor can obtain or make loans to an indefinite amount at the target rate of interest, that investment-possibility will be most profitable at a chosen target rate of interest of which the capital value is the greatest.*

This criterion is of fundamental significance in the practical calculation of investment possibilities. All the procedures applied in practice can be reduced to this principle.[1]

An entrepreneur who buys a machine for £a calculates, if he is acting rationally, not only that the capital value of this investment is positive, but also that it is larger than any alternative possibility known to him and available to him for the same sum, £a.

12. It was ascertained above that the capital value of a planned investment depends on the series of receipts and outlays, and on the target rate of interest. The receipts depend on the expected prices of the products and the expected levels of sales. The outlays depend, correspondingly, on the expected prices of the factors of production and on the quantities of factors employed.[2] All these quantities are to be treated as *variables* in calculating an investment, though not in the sense that the investor can in all cases fix the values of these as he pleases. It is quite possible that certain quantities (for example, prices) are given for the investor. But these quantities must be treated as variables determining the capital value of an investment in the sense that different alternative values can be given to them. One needs to ask what the result of the calculation will be if the quantities determining the capital values of the investment are different. We have already used such a procedure earlier in deducing the supply function of a quantity-adjuster and the demand function of a household. This procedure has shown itself especially useful in calculating investment possibilities because many of the quantities entering into the calculation rest on estimates and partake of a greater or lesser degree of uncertainty.

[1] Cf. my book *Wirtschaftlichkeitsrechnung* (2nd ed., 1957).
[2] In investment calculations it is usually assumed that the non-durable goods used in a period are equal in quantity to those purchased in the period so that the outlays for, and costs of, non-durable goods correspond.

Let us consider two investment possibilities I and II, of which the capital values are $C_I$ and $C_{II}$, depending in a particular way on the prices and quantities which determine outlays and receipts, and on the target rate of interest. Let us consider, now, a quantity which enters into the determination of both capital values, for example, the target rate of interest, the level of wages, or the quantity of the product, while all the other relevant quantities are treated as constant. The capital values of both the investments will then appear as functions of a single variable quantity. If there is a positive value for this variable quantity, for which the capital values of the two investments are equal, and in the neighbourhood of which the difference between the two capital values changes sign, then one may describe such a value of the variable as a *"critical"* value. If one knows the critical value of a quantity which is being treated as a variable, then one is at once able to give the range for which either investment I or investment II, as the case may be, is the more profitable. The points at which the entrepreneur "breaks even", described in Section IV, A, para. 1, when discussing the planning of profits, are examples of such "critical" values in planning for a single period.

To illustrate the theory and practice of this useful method, let us take the following example. In carrying out a particular process of production there is a choice of two methods: (a) a machine of type I at a price of £$a_1$ and an expected life of $n_1$ years; (b) a machine of type II at a price of £$a_2$ ($a_2 > a_1$) and an expected life of $n_2$ years ($n_2 > n_1$). The annual running costs will be a function of the annual production $x$, and with machine I these will be higher because of, among other reasons, higher wage costs than with machine II. Let the annual running costs be $b_1(x)$ and $b_2(x)$, then $b_1(x) > b_2(x)$. All the other outlays in connexion with the process of production, as well as the series of receipts, will be the same for the two methods of production.

In comparing the capital values of the investments we can therefore limit ourselves to a comparison of the capital values of the specific series of outlays for the two machine processes, that is, their purchase prices and running costs. The comparison may be made under the assumption that the two investment plans are identically repeated *ad infinitum*. The relevant series of outlays are, therefore:

Alternative I: At the point of time 0, $n_1$, $2n_1$, . . . , purchase of the machine I at the price $a_1$, and at the end of each year, running costs of $b_1(x)$.

Alternative II: At the point of time 0, $n_2$, $2n_2$, . . . , purchase of the machine II at the price $a_2$, and at the end of each year, running costs of $b_2(x)$.

The capital values of these two series of outlays will then be as follows:

$$C_{\mathrm{I}} = \frac{a_1 . (1 + i)^{n_1}}{(1 + i)^{n_1} - 1} + \frac{b_1(x)}{i} \qquad (a_1 < a_2)$$

$$C_{\mathrm{II}} = \frac{a_2 . (1 + i)^{n_2}}{(1 + i)^{n_2} - 1} + \frac{b_2(x)}{i} \qquad (b_1 > b_2) \qquad (9)$$

We now have to compare these two capital values with one another. Let us make a simplification by basing our comparison on the target rate of interest multiplied by the capital values, instead of on the capital values themselves; that is, the expressions:

$$C_{\mathrm{I}} . i = \frac{a_1 . i . (1 + i)^{n_1}}{(1 + i)^{n_1} - 1} + b_1(x)$$

$$C_{\mathrm{II}} . i = \frac{a_2 . i . (1 + i)^{n_2}}{(1 + i)^{n_2} - 1} + b_2(x) \qquad (10)$$

If $C_{\mathrm{I}} \gtrless C_{\mathrm{II}}$, then $C_{\mathrm{I}} . i \gtrless C_{\mathrm{II}} . i$ and *vice versa*.

The expression $\dfrac{a . i(1 + i)^n}{(1 + i)^n - 1}$ represents simply the sum which must be regained each year for interest and depreciation on the purchase price of the machine, that is, the sum which must be annually obtained in order to recover the purchase price after $n$ years allowing for a rate of interest of $i$. This sum may be described as the *capital service* of the machine. If the purchase price of the machine is, for example, £6000 the expected length of life four years, and the rate of interest 6% per annum, then the annual sum necessary for the capital service amounts to:

$$6000 . \frac{i . (1 + i)^4}{(1 + i)^4 - 1} = 6000 . 0 \cdot 28859 = 1731 \cdot 54.$$

This sum must be obtained annually if the £6000 is to be regained after four years with an interest of 6%. It will be distributed annually as follows between interest and depreciation:

| End of year | Interest | Depreciation | Capital service | Amount of purchase price not yet regained |
|---|---|---|---|---|
| 0 | — | — | — | 6000·00 |
| 1 | 360·00 | 1371·54 | 1731·54 | 4628·46 |
| 2 | 277·71 | 1453·83 | 1731·54 | 3174·63 |
| 3 | 190·48 | 1541·06 | 1731·54 | 1633·57 |
| 4 | 98·01 | 1633·57 | 1731·54 | — |
|  |  | 6000·00 |  |  |

In the two expressions in (10) we are comparing the sums necessary for the capital service and annual running outlays for the two machines. Let us consider the annual quantity produced by the two machines to be the sole variable, so that the capital service for the two alternatives is a given constant, and the sum of capital service and annual running outlays is a function of the annual quantity produced. For simplicity, let us assume that the dependence of the annual running costs on the quantity produced is linear, and let us assume that the capital service for the second machine is larger than that for the first machine, so that the dependence of the expressions in (10) on the quantity produced may be represented as in Fig. 105. From Fig. 105

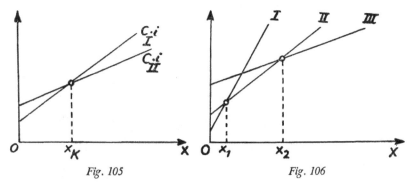

Fig. 105                                      Fig. 106

it can be seen that, on the assumptions we have made, there is a uniquely determined critical point $x_k$ for the level of output:

$$\text{if } x < x_k, \quad C_I . i < C_{II} . i;$$
$$\text{if } x = x_k, \quad C_I . i = C_{II} . i;$$
$$\text{if } x > x_k, \quad C_I . i > C_{II} . i.$$

So long as the planned annual production is below this critical quantity $x_k$, the first alternative will be more profitable than the second. If, on the other hand, the planned annual production is greater than this critical level $x_k$, then the second alternative, with the higher capital service, and the lower annual running outlays, will be more profitable than the first. Ceteris paribus, *therefore, it is the level of planned annual production which decides what method of production is the most profitable.* This argument can, of course, be extended to the choice between more than two alternatives. If, for example, one has to choose among three alternatives for which the dependence of the sum of capital service and annual running outlays on the level of output is as represented in Fig. 106 then a glance at this diagram shows that alternative I is the most profitable if the planned annual production is smaller than $x_1$. If, on the other hand, the planned annual production is between $x_1$ and $x_2$, then alternative II is the most profitable. If, finally, the planned annual production is larger than $x_2$, then the third alternative is the most profitable.

We may describe a method of production in which the capital service is larger, and the annual running outlays smaller than another method of production, as the *more mechanized*. This expresses what is usually meant in everyday speech when we talk of adopting a more mechanized method of production, that is, that the capital service increases and the running costs decrease. We may say that the advantages of the more mechanized of two methods of production first become effective above a particular level of production. This is the fact which Marshall describes as "economies of large-scale production".

The critical level of production, $x_k$ in Fig. 105 is, of course, not constant, but depends on the levels of the purchase prices of the machine, the levels of the annual running outlays of the different alternative machines, and the level of the target rate of interest. If (*ceteris paribus*) the rate of wages rises by a particular amount, then the running expenses of the less mechanized method increase relatively more than the running expenses of the more mechanized method which requires less labour. The critical level of output $x_k$ will decrease, which means that the application of more mechanized methods will be profitable above a lower annual level of production. This simply amounts to the fact, well-known in the real world, that increases in wages (*ceteris paribus*) lead to an increase in mechanization. Correspondingly, a simple calculation, which we may leave to the reader, will show that a fall in the target rate of interest (that is, of course, not necessarily a fall in the long-term market rate of interest) will work (*ceteris paribus*) in the same direction.

13. So far our analysis has been concerned with the discontinuous substitution of one method of production for another when there is a change in the level of output, in the price of a factor or in the rate of interest. If this is the case, and it alone is realistic, not every increase in output per unit of time would make it profitable to adopt another method of production. From Fig. 106 it appears, for example, that the transition from method I to method II, i.e. the substitution of II for I, only takes place as the critical level of output, $x_1$, is passed.

Let us now examine the case of continuous substitutability between different methods of production. This implies, for example, that even a small (strictly speaking, an infinitesimal) increase in output causes a more mechanized method of production to become profitable. Even though such continuous substitutability does not exist in practice, one gains important insights from studying this limiting case. For simplicity we shall allow the level of the annual running costs $b(x)$ of a given method of production to be proportional to the level of output. If the prices of factors and the rate of interest are known, the sum of capital service and annual running costs for a method of production is then given by the linear function

$$F = k + b \cdot x, \tag{11}$$

$k$ being the capital service and $b$ the running costs per physical unit.

To each method of production there corresponds a certain capital service $k$ and a certain (smallest) value of $b$; and conversely, each pair of values $(k, b)$ defines a certain method of production. We assume continuous substitutability between different methods of production having each a different degree of mechanization, and we know that the higher the degree of mechanization the higher will be the capital service and the lower the annual running costs per unit of output. This means that $b$ is a continuous function of $k$ or, which comes to the same thing, that $k$ is a continuous function of $b$, thus:

$$k = k(b), \tag{12}$$

and this function has the property that $k$ diminishes as $b$ increases.

Let us use (12) to re-write (11) as:

$$F = k(b) + b \cdot x. \tag{13}$$

If the quantity of output $x$ is given, (13) expresses the sum of capital service and annual running costs corresponding to different methods of production. We are looking for that method of production which minimizes the annual "expenses" (capital service + running costs) for a given quantity $x$. That method must clearly fulfil the condition

$$\frac{dF}{db} = \frac{dk}{db} + x = 0 \tag{14}$$

or:

$$x = -\frac{dk}{db} \tag{15}$$

If the value of $b$ which satisfies this equation is to make $F$ a minimum then it is further required that

$$\frac{d^2F}{db^2} = \frac{d^2k}{db^2} > 0 \tag{16}$$

which means that function (12) must be of the form drawn in Fig. 107.

Equation (15) immediately indicates that method of production which, when factor prices are given, will produce a *given* quantity $x$ with the least annual "expenses". In Fig. 107, the tangent to the curve representing the function $k(b)$ is drawn at $P$, and the method of production corresponding to point $P$ is the one which permits the quantity $x = \tan \psi$ to be produced with the least annual expenses.[1]

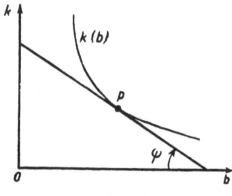

*Fig. 107*

Hence, when $x$ is given, we need only look for that point $P$ on the curve $k(b)$ for which $\tan \psi = x$.

Figure 107 teaches us at a glance that the greater $x$ the greater will be the corresponding angle $\psi$, and *vice versa*. But as the angle $\psi$ increases so the point $P$ shifts upwards. Hence, the larger the required quantity of output the more mechanized will be the method which allows that quantity to be produced with the least annual "expenses". Condition (15) expresses $b$—and hence, when (12) is used, the "cheapest" method—as a function of the size of the required output. In this way each quantity of output is unambiguously correlated with the least annual "expenses".

We designate the curve as the *annual expenses curve for total adjustment* (to changes in output).

These matters may be clarified with the help of a *numerical example*. Let function (12) have the following form:

$$k = \frac{10,000}{b}$$

---

[1] Because

$$-\frac{dk}{db} = \tan \psi = x$$

From this it follows that:

$$-\frac{dk}{db} = \frac{10,000}{b^2} = x$$

and also:

$$b = \frac{100}{\sqrt{x}}; \quad k = 100 \cdot \sqrt{x}. \tag{17}$$

For example, if $x = 100$, then $b = 10$ and $k = 1000$; while if $x = 10,000$, we have $b = 1$ and $k = 10,000$.

The annual expenses curve for total adjustment is therefore given by:

$$F = 100 \cdot \sqrt{x} + 100 \cdot \sqrt{x} = 200 \cdot \sqrt{x}. \tag{18}$$

and thus possesses the shape drawn in Fig. 108. For each quantity of output we can read off from this curve the corresponding least value

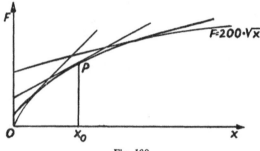

Fig. 108

of the annual expenses with which it is possible to produce that quantity, *given the state of technology and the prices of factors.* It can be shown that the curve in Fig. 108 will always be of that shape, provided only that the function $k(b)$ is of the form represented in Fig. 107. As $x$ grows so the rate of increase of the least annual expenses (the "marginal costs" for total adjustment) will diminish.

The method of production which allows output $x_0$ (in Fig. 108) to be produced with the least annual expenses corresponds to a particular capital service $k_0$ and a particular running cost $b_0$ per unit of output. Within the limits of this method of production as characterized by $k_0$ and $b_0$, annual "expenses" (the sum of capital service and running costs) are given as a function of the level of output $x$, thus:

$$F = k_0 + b_0 \cdot x \tag{19}$$

This curve we designate the *annual expenses curve for partial adjustment* (to changes in output). Adjustments to changes in output are made while retaining the method of production which is optimal for $x_0$. In our example, using the results of (17), we have:

$$F = 100 . \sqrt{x_0} + \frac{100}{\sqrt{x_0}} . x. \tag{20}$$

If, for instance, $x_0 = 100$,

$$F = 1000 + 10x. \tag{20a}$$

Equation (20) is simply the equation of the tangent at $P$ to the annual expenses curve for total adjustment (Fig. 108). It follows immediately that *average* annual "expenses" for $x \neq x_0$ when adjustment is partial will be greater than the corresponding average "expenses" when adjustment is total. Only if $x = x_0$ will annual "expenses" as derived from equation (20) coincide with the least annual expenses which, within the limits of technological knowledge will allow output $x_0$ to be produced.

In Fig. 108 we drew three curves for partial adjustment. If for *each* value of $x_0$ we imagine the corresponding partial adjustment curve drawn in, then the *total adjustment curve appears as the envelope of all partial adjustment curves.*[1]

14. From our investigation of the problems of long-term economic planning it can be seen that the theorems we have derived are simply extensions from the principles of single-period planning. We laid down as the main theorem for single-period planning that the entrepreneur (assuming he is out to maximize profit in a single-product firm) will plan that scale of production at which marginal revenue and marginal cost are equal. In long-term planning, instead of profit, there is the capital value of a planned investment, which is simply the receipts discounted to a particular moment of calculation, minus the outlays discounted to the same point of time. These discounted outlays are the discounted costs over all the periods over which the plans extend, so that the capital value is simply the difference between the discounted revenue and the discounted costs. The assumption of the objective of maximum profit is, therefore, replaced by the assumption of the objective of *maximum capital value, i.e. of maximum difference between discounted revenues and discounted costs.* The main theorem, repeated above for single-period planning, is, therefore, for the case of long-term planning: *on the assumption of the objective of maximum capital value the entrepreneur will choose*

[1] It appears from Fig. 108 that, whether adjustment is total or partial, average annual expenses $\left(\text{i.e. } \dfrac{F}{x}\right)$ always diminish with increasing output.

*that plan for which the discounted marginal revenue is equal to the discounted marginal outlays.*

For the demand for factors of production we obtain the following formula, which results from the same analysis as in Section V: *the entrepreneur will demand of each substitute factor of production, at the different points of time within the period of his plans, that quantity of the factor for which the discounted marginal costs are equal to the discounted value of its marginal net product.* So long as the discounted value of the marginal net product of an additional unit of a factor is larger than the discounted marginal costs of this unit, its employment will be profitable. By using the concept of the internal rate of interest we can express this proposition also in the following way: *any form of marginal change in the series of outlays of an investment is profitable, so long as the corresponding marginal change in the series of receipts is such that the internal rate of interest of this marginal investment is not smaller than the target rate of interest.*

15. We can use this analysis in order to decide whether it pays an entrepreneur to buy a particular piece of land at a particular price. The entrepreneur will investigate what average net return per year he can expect in the future from the use of the land. Let this net return, or the expected ground rent, be $g$, and the price the seller names for the land be $q$, then the purchase of the land will be profitable if the value (discounted at the moment of calculation at the target rate of interest) of the infinite series of ground rents, is not smaller than the price demanded, $q$. (The series of ground rents is infinite because of the infinitely long life of the land.) It must, therefore, amount to:

$$q \leqq \frac{g}{1+i} + \frac{g}{(1+i)^2} + \cdots \tag{21}$$

or

$$q \leqq g \cdot \frac{1}{i} \tag{22}$$

The factor $\frac{1}{i}$, that is, the reciprocal of the rate of interest, may be called the *capitalization factor*. Relation (22) shows that *the value which the demander will attach to the land is simply the capitalized ground rent.* The capitalized value of the rents is the highest price the demander will be ready to pay.

In the same way we can discover whether the purchase of a house is remunerative. If the sum of £$a$ is asked for a house, and the buyer or investor reckons with an annual net return of £$b$ for $n$ years, then, disregarding any eventual remaining value the house may have at the end of the $n^{\text{th}}$ year, the purchase will be profitable so long as:

$$\frac{b}{1+i} + \frac{b}{(1+i)^2} + \cdots + \frac{b}{(1+i)^n} \geqq a \qquad (23)$$

16. We have now set out the basic calculations necessary in long-term planning. Even more than in the case of single-period planning it has been necessary to remember that by far the majority of the quantities in the calculations rest on expectations, and, therefore, possess greater uncertainty the further they are in the future. The investor in making his plans must, therefore, be cautious in judging the series of receipts and outlays and will rather put the receipts too low than too high, and the outlay rather too high than too low. Furthermore, as we already know, the target rate of interest must be fixed higher the greater the degree of uncertainty. If the calculation shows that, on the assumptions we have made, an investment $X$ is more profitable than an investment $Y$, then this is by no means to say that the investor can now decide to make investment $X$. Only those factors can enter into the calculation which have a quantitative character. *But in judging between investments there are essential factors which are not of a quantitative character.* Such imponderables as, for example, the safety of the various alternatives, the liquidity of the firm, social or foreign exchange considerations, etc., may, in the final analysis, be decisive for the investor's choice. Nevertheless, such calculations are indispensable as the basis of the entrepreneur's dispositions. Even if one decides, on the basis of certain imponderables, to choose an alternative which, from the point of view of one's bare calculations, seems less profitable, one must realize the quantitative consequences of this decision. These calculations are, therefore, necessary in all circumstances, even if they do not provide the complete key to the entrepreneur's plans. Because of the uncertainty of the figures that are used, there must always be a continual revision of plans, including a revision of those parts of a plan which are still in the future, on the basis of the experience obtained and of new estimates concerning the future. From the point of view of the firm's calculations it is valid, if we assume an objective of maximum profit, that at every point of time the stream of future outlays and receipts will be so shaped that the maximum capital value will be obtained in the given conditions. The total of what is *in fact* obtained only emerges at the end of the final economic period, and at the end of the life of the firm.

17. It is in the nature of long-term planning that the variables in the important relationships (quantities of goods and prices) relate to *different* periods, as we have already discussed when we entered on

the subject of the long-term plan of the household. This fact has again come to our attention in considering the long-term planning of the entrepreneur. The position is quite different in short-term planning. In this case only relations between variables belonging to the *same* period are relevant. The essential difference between these two kinds of relationships has given rise to a distinction of fundamental importance for all economic theory. It is *the distinction between "static" and "dynamic" economic theory*. We must now examine this distinction before we can continue our analysis.

## BIBLIOGRAPHY

In addition to the works mentioned at the end of chapter 1.

E. Barone: *Grundzüge der theoretischen Nationalökonomie*, Bonn, 1927.

W. Eucken: *The Foundations of Economics*, Transl. T. W. Hutchison, London, 1950.

J. Meade: *Economic Analysis and Policy*, London, 1937.

*Specialist works on Sections I–V:*

L. Abbott: *Qualität und Wettbewerb*, Munich, 1958.

S. Carlson: *A Study on the Pure Theory of Production*, London, 1939.

E. Chamberlin: *The Theory of Monopolistic Competition*, 7th ed. Cambridge, Mass. 1956.

E. Chamberlin: *Towards a more General Theory of Value*, New York, 1957.

J. M. Clark: *Studies in the Economics of Overhead Costs*, Chicago, 1923.

B. Fog: *Priskalkulation og Prispolitik*, Copenhagen, 1958.

R. Frisch: "Monopoly—Polypoly—The Concept of Force in the Economy." (1933). *International Economic Papers*, vol. 1.

E. Gutenberg: *Grundlagen der Betriebswirtschaftslehre*, vol. 1, Die Produktion, 4th ed. Berlin, 1959. vol. 2, Der Absatz, 3rd ed. Berlin, 1959.

E. Küng: "Zur Lehre von den Marktformen und Marktbeziehungen." *Konkurrenz und Planwirtschaft*, Berne, 1946.

F. Machlup, "Tipi di concurrenza nella vendita." *Giornale degli Economisti*, 1941.

F. Machlup: *The Political Economy of Monopoly*, Baltimore, 1952.

F. Machlup: *The Economics of Sellers' Competition*, Baltimore, 1952.

H. Möller: *Kalkulation, Absatzpolitik und Preisbildung*, Wien, 1941.

J. von Neumann and O. Morgenstern, *Theory of Games and Economic Behavior*, 2nd ed. Princeton, 1947.

E. A. G. Robinson: *The Structure of Competitive Industry*, Cambridge 1937.

E. A. G. Robinson: *Monopoly*, London, 1946.

Joan Robinson: *The Theory of Imperfect Competition*, London, 1933.

E. Schneider: "Zur Konkurrenz und Preisbildung auf vollkommenen und unvollkommenen Märkten." *Weltwirtschaftliches Archiv*, vol. 48, 1938.

H. von Stackelberg: *Marktform und Gleichgewicht*, Wien, 1934.

H. von Stackelberg: *Grundlagen einer reinen Kostentheorie*, Wien, 1932.
H. von Stackelberg: "Probleme der unvollkommenen Konkurrenz." *Weltwirtschaftliches Archiv*, vol. 48, 1938.
P. M. Sweezy: "Demand under Conditions of Oligopoly." *Journal of Political Economy*, vol. 47, 1939.
J. Tinbergen: *Beperkte Concurrentie*, Leyden, 1946.
R. Triffin: *Monopolistic Competition and General Equilibrium Theory*, Cambridge, Mass. 1941.
P. Wiles: *Price, Cost and Output*, Oxford, 1956.
T. Wilson and P. S. Andrews: *Oxford Studies in the Price Mechanism*, Oxford, 1951.

*Specialist works on Section V, paragraph 3 (Theory of Linear Programming):*
R. G. D. Allen: *Mathematical Economics*, London, 1960.
M. Beckmann: *Lineare Planungsrechnung*, Ludwigshafen (Rhein) 1959.
A. Bordin: *La Programmazione Lineare*, Torino, 1954.
A. Charnes, W. W. Cooper and A. Henderson: *An Introduction to Linear Programming*, New York, 1953.
C. W. Churchman, R. L. Ackoff and E. L. Arnoff: *Introduction to Operations Research*, New York, 1957.
S. Danø: "Linear Programming i Produktionsteorien," *Nationaløkonomisk Tidsskrift*, Copenhagen, 1955.
R. Dorfman: "Mathematical or 'Linear' Programming," *American Economic Review*, vol. 43, 1953.
R. Dorfman: *Application of Linear Programming to the Theory of the Firm*. University of California Press, 1951.
R. Dorfman, P. A. Samuelson and R. M. Solow: *Linear Programming and Economic Analysis*, New York, 1958.
K. Förstner and R. Henn: *Dynamische Produktionstheorie und lineare Programmierung*, Meisenheim, 1957.
T. C. Koopmans: *Activity Analysis of Production and Allocation*, New York, 1951.
H. Makower: *Activity Analysis and the Theory of Economic Equilibrium*, London, 1957.
S. Vajda: *The Theory of Games and Linear Programming*, London, 1956.
S. Vajda: *Readings in Linear Programming*, London, 1958.

*Specialist literature on Section VI:*
K. E. Boulding: "Time and Investment," *Economica*, vol. 3, 1936.
W. Eucken: "Der Wirtschaftsprozess als zeitlicher Hergang," *Jahrbücher für Nationalökonomie und Statistik*, vol. 152 1940.
J. Fisher: *The Nature of Capital and Income*, New York, 1906.
J. Fisher: *The Theory of Interest*, New York, 1930.
E. Lindahl: *Studies in the Theory of Money and Capital*, London, 1939.
F. A. Lutz: *Zinstheorie*, Tübingen and Zurich, 1956,
J. R. Meyer and E. Kuh: *The Investment Decision*, Cambridge, Mass. 1957.
K. Rummel: "Wirtschaftlichkeitsrechnung," *Archiv für das Eisenhüttenwesen*, 10, 1936–37.

E. Schmalenbach: *Selbstkostenrechnung und Preispolitik*, 7th ed. Leipzig, 1956.

E. Schneider: *Wirtschaftlichkeitsrechnung*, 2nd ed. Tübingen, 1957.

G. L. S. Shackle: *Expectations, Investment and Income*, London, 1938.

H. von Stackelberg: "Kapital und Zins in der stationären Verkehrswirtschaft," *Zeitschrift für Nationalökonomie*, vol. 10, 1941.

J. Svennilson: *Ekonomisk Planering*, Uppsala, 1938.

K. Wicksell: *Lectures on Political Economy*, Transl. Classen, ed. L. Robbins, London, 1934. vol. 1.

# CHAPTER III

# Statics and Dynamics in Economic Theory

The economic process within a given economic system takes place in time. Like the physicist or the astronomer, we can by constant observation and measurement register all the quantities marking the course of the economic process, large or small, either in aggregates or in individual units. In the contemporary exchange economy we can follow the curves through time of prices, of the quantities of goods purchased, of the quantities of particular goods produced, of income, of the quantity of money, of the level of investment, of the number of unemployed, of the level of particular taxes, of the level of tariff revenue, etc., and follow, in each case, the course through time of each of these particular economic variables. In this way we obtain a description in as much detail as we wish of the course of economic variables through time. We can, if we like go back to the separate variables of the individual economic units engaged, or we may limit ourselves to registering the curve through time of macroeconomic aggregates. Which variables he registers depends on the problem in which the economist is interested. It is obvious that registering and describing variables simply for their own sake is senseless. One must be equipped with meaningful questions when approaching the real world, if one is to know what phenomena to observe. Such meaningful questions can only be obtained from a sound theoretical analysis of the real world which will enable us to form hypotheses as to the relationships between economic quantities. *One task of economic analysis is to explain the historical course of the economic process.* (For example, why did the prices of particular goods rise in a particular period, while the prices of other goods fell? Why has the national income of a country fallen in a particular period?) *Another task of economic analysis is to give an account of how the course of the economic process will develop from a particular initial condition under particular assumptions.* (For example, how will the course of a country's economy develop from today onwards if wages are raised by a particular amount?) Of the two tasks the second is undoubtedly the more important and one might even say the real task of economic analysis. Historical description for its own sake is not the task of economic science. Only in so far as the analysis of the past provides us with knowledge that is relevant to the shape of things to come is there any sense in the economist studying the past. The solution of the two problems requires, just as it does in the natural sciences, a close interaction between the theoretical and the empirical, or between the analysis and the exact observation of the real world.

2. In studying the course through time of an economic variable we must first distinguish between two sorts of phenomenon. The process of an economic variable through time appears either as *stationary* or as *changing* (evolving). An economic variable may be said to be stationary through time if the value of the variable does not change, that is, if the curve through time of the variable is parallel to the time axis.[1] Thus the prices of goods are behaving in a stationary way if they do not vary. The national income is stationary if its quantity does not change through time. On the other hand, the behaviour of an economic variable through time is non-stationary, or changing, or evolving, if its value is subject to changes. Correspondingly, we may say that an economy is stationary (or changing) if the values of all the variables are constant through time (or not constant). It is, of course, possible that many economic phenomena are changing from the micro-economic point of view, but stationary from the macro-economic point of view. Thus the population as a whole may be stationary when the size of individual families is by no means stationary. Similarly, the value of total net investment may be stationary even if the net investment of individual economic units is not stationary. We must notice, further, that particular variables may be stationary without the economy as a whole being stationary. The fact that positive net investment remains stationary at a particular level does not mean that the economy as a whole is stationary. With net investment at a constant rate and positive, the quantity of real capital in the economy is growing constantly per unit of time so that the total of capital is not constant.

3. It is the task of economic theory, as we have emphasised, to explain the course through time of a system of economic variables. *Such an explanation can be given in two different ways. If one is using an analysis where the relations between the relevant variables*

[1] Sometimes the behaviour of a variable is also characterized as stationary if the curve through time shows a periodically repeated fluctuation. We wish here to use the concept of the stationary behaviour of a variable only in the sense defined above in the text.

*relate to the same moment of time, or to the same period of time, then we may speak of a "static" analysis or "static" theory.* A relationship in which the values of the variables relate to the same point of time, or to the same period, may correspondingly be described as a "static" relationship. On the other hand, *if the explanation contains relationships between relevant variables the values of which do not all relate to the same point of time or period of time, then we may speak of "dynamic" analysis or "dynamic" theory.* The relationships themselves, if they possess this characteristic, may be described as "dynamic" relationships.

Examples of static relationships have occurred frequently in the previous sections. If we formulate the demand plans of a household in the following way:

"If the price of a good in the coming period is $p_1$, then the household (*ceteris paribus*) will buy the quantity $x_1$; if, on the other hand, the price in the coming period is $p_2$, then the household (*ceteris paribus*) buy an amount $x_2$, etc."

then the relationship described between the price and the quantity demanded is a static relationship.

If the savings plan of a household is formulated in the following way:

"If the income in the coming period is $e_1$, then, at the prices of goods expected in the period, a sum of $s_1$ will be saved; if, on the other hand, the income in the coming period is $e_2$, then (*ceteris paribus*) the sum $s_2$ will be saved, etc."

then, again, there is a static relationships between expected income and planned savings. The supply function deduced earlier for a supplier acting as a quantity-adjuster was similarly a static relationship. The reader will be able to work out further examples for himself.

We have noticed examples of dynamic relationships in discussing the problems of long-term planning. If one assumes that the demand of a household for a particular good depends in the coming period (*ceteris paribus*) not only on the price of the good in the coming period, but also on the expected prices in later periods, then there is a relationship between variables which relate to different points or periods in time.

If one assumes that the planned supply for the coming period depends on the actual price of the previous period, that is:

$$x_t = f(p_{t-1})$$

where $x_t$ is the planned supply for the coming period, and $p_{t-1}$ the price in the previous period, then we have a dynamic relationship between two variables.

If we assume that the value $C_t$ for total consumption in an economy in the period $t$ depends on the national income $y_{t-1}$ in the previous period $t_{-1}$, so that

$$C_t = f(y_{t-1}),$$

then again we are working with a dynamic relationship.

4. *For the understanding of modern theory it is necessary to maintain complete clarity as between the pair of concepts "static" and "dynamic" on the one hand, and "stationary" and "changing" on the other hand.* The concepts "static" and "dynamic" have been used in economics in many different ways, so that it is impossible to be clear unless a precise definition is given. The definitions used here were introduced into economic theory by Ragnar Frisch in 1928 and today have been accepted by the majority of theoretical economists in all countries.[1] It is essential to understand that in modern theory "statics" and "dynamics" refer to a particular *mode of treatment or type of analysis* of the phenomena observed, while the adjectives "stationary" and "changing" describe the actual economic phenomena. *A static or dynamic theory is a particular kind of explanation of economic phenomena; and, indeed, stationary and changing phenomena can be submitted either to a static or to a dynamic analysis.* We shall become acquainted in the next section with examples.

From the definition of the concept of dynamics it follows that a theory is not to be considered as dynamic simply because it introduces expectations. Whether that is the case or not depends simply on whether or not the expected values of the single variables relate to different periods, or points, of time.

5. In addition to the method of analytical dynamics for analysing the course of the economic process within a given economic system, there is also what, following Frisch, we may describe as "historical

---

[1] The fundamental work of Frisch which led to the final clarification of this complex of problems first appeared in Norwegian in the Danish *National-økonomisk Tidsskrift* in 1929. A shorter account is given in Frisch's article "On the Notion of Equilibrium and Disequilibrium" in *Review of Economic Studies*, Vol. III, 1935/36. See also J. Tinbergen: "Econometric Business Cycle Research" in *Review of Economic Studies*, Vol. II, 1939–40. P. A. Samuelson: "Dynamics, Statics and the Stationary State" in *Review of Economic Statistics*, 1943, now reprinted with a few changes in *Foundations of Economic Analysis* (1947) by the same author. Further, F. Zeuthen: *Economic Theory and Method*, Section III (Dynamics). A short and precise treatment is given by G. Haberler: *Prosperity and Depression*, 3rd ed., Geneva, 1941, p. 249. Also: Schneider, *Statik und Dynamik* in: Handwörterbuch der Sozialwissenschaften (15th instalment, 1957).

dynamics", which is concerned with the development of the economic system or its institutional framework, within which the economic process takes its course. This kind of historical dynamics lies outside the boundaries of economic theory. Its problems belong mainly to economic history and sociology. In historical dynamics one is interested in different types of environment, and in problems of the transition from one type of environment to another; in analytical dynamics one is interested in the course of the economic process within a given type of environment.

6. The necessity for, and significance of, a dynamic treatment in theoretical analysis depends on the fact that *the adjustment of the economy to changes in the data underlying economic plans takes time.* (We shall consider the concept of "data" in the next section.) Thus, changes in income in one period often only take effect in later periods on the decisions of households as to their consumption. Changes in prices influence the supply plans of the entrepreneur often only in subsequent periods, etc. It is these "*lags*" as they have been called in modern theory, with which the change of one variable works on another variable, which make necessary the use of dynamic relationships in explaining the economic world. In addition, there is the fact, as we have seen, that certain variables depend among other things on *the rate of growth* of other variables (for example, the demand for a good may depend on the rate of change of prices); and a speed is always a quantity in the calculation of which two different points of time are involved. Problems involving rates of growth therefore require the use of dynamic relationships.

The role of lags in the process through time of the economy has been presented in a very clear way in Tinbergen's "Arrow" diagram.[1] Let us assume that there are four variables, quantities $A$, $B$, $C$ and $D$, in the explanation of an economic process. In the adjoining diagram the points in horizontal rows represent the course through time of the single variables, that is, the values of the variables at the consecutive moments of time $t-1$, $t$, $t+1$, $t+2$, and $t+3$.

It is the business of theory to explain the observed development of these variables. It is therefore necessary to know how the change in the value of a variable at one point of time affects the values of other variables at different points of time. For this purpose the theory will assume particular inter-temporal relationships between the variables, and then will examine what the course through time of the four variables will be according to different assumptions, and will compare the theoretical results with the empirical facts. We may

[1] J. Tinbergen: "Econometric Business Cycle Research" in *Review of Economic Studies*, Vol. VII, 1939–40, pp. 74–5.

assume, for example, that changes in *A* affect the variable *B* in the same period, but affect the variable *C* one period later, i.e. with a lag of one period. In the Arrow diagram this is represented by the arrows from *A* to *B* and from *A* to *C*. We may assume, further, that changes in *C* bring about changes in *D* and *A* with a lag of two time-periods, as is portrayed in the Arrow diagram by the corresponding arrows from *C* to *D* and *C* to *A*. A change in *A* at the point of time *t* can

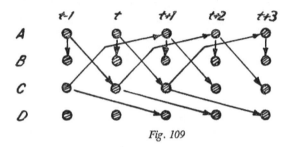

*Fig. 109*

then be the primary cause of a change in *C* at time *t* + 1, and a secondary cause of a change in *D* at time *t* + 3. On the other hand, a change in *C* results two periods later in a change in *A*. This causal interdependence between the relevant variables is graphically expressed in this Arrow diagram.

The Arrow diagram also makes it especially clear that *dynamic relations always involve propositions about inter-temporal causal relationships between economic variables. A dynamic theory shows how in the course of time a condition of the economic system has grown out of its condition in the previous period of time. It is this form of analysis which has central importance for the study of the processes of economic development, be they short-run or long-run processes. Sequence analysis (or process analysis) is only possible in the context of a dynamic theory, that is, of a theory which involves at least one dynamic relation.* Sequence analysis is not possible in static theory. because this type of theory works only with relations between variables which relate to the *same* period or point of time.

7. Now we have clarified this fundamental distinction between a static and a dynamic treatment of economic phenomena, we are in a position to turn to one of the main problems of economic theory: that of the interaction between the plans or dispositions of the individual economic units engaged. The relationships considered in this chapter will play an important role in the analysis of the problem of equilibrium, which we shall now discuss by means of a number of examples.

# CHAPTER IV

# The Problem of Equilibrium in a Closed Economy

## Section A

## THE CONCEPT OF ECONOMIC EQUILIBRIUM

In drawing up an economic plan each economic unit has to start from certain given conditions or *data*. These data relate in part *to the economy as a whole, and* in part *to the single economic unit*.[1] Among those which relate *to the economy as a whole* are:

(a) the tastes of the individual households, their nature and order;
(b) the resources of human labour of given types and quality at the moment of planning;
(c) the natural resources available at the moment of planning;
(d) the existing real capital at the moment of planning;
(e) the technical and organizational knowledge at the moment of planning;
(f) the existing legal and social order.

These six factors represent the data at the moment of planning "which determine the economic cosmos, without themselves being determined by economic facts" (Eucken).

It is important to notice that the data for the economy as a whole are not determined *directly* by economic facts. Indirectly, changes in economic phenomena can very easily lead to changes in the data. There may, therefore, be mutual interactions between the data and economic phenomena. But the investigation of these mutual relationships, and of the development through time of the data for the economy as a whole, is not a task of economic theory, but of the theory of population, of sociology, of legal history, of technology and other studies. Economic theory has to study the course of the economic process, given a particular constellation of data for the

---

[1] Cf. especially W. Eucken: *The Foundations of Economics*, pp. 213 ff.

economy as a whole. It has also to inquire what influence particular changes in data exercise on the course of the economic process. But it has not to analyse the data themselves or changes in the data.

In a centrally directed economy the system of data from which the directing planner of the economy starts is simply what we are calling the data for the economy as a whole. In the exchange economy the position is different. The individual economic unit, in drawing up its economic plan, reckons both with the data for the economy as a whole which are relevant, as well as with such data as are given to it but which do not relate to the economy as a whole, and which would have to be explained in a theoretical analysis of the course of the economy as a whole. This sort of data may be described as *data from the point of view of the individual unit*. Let us consider the economic plan of a household. The basis of its economic plan will be the legal and social order, the nature and order of tastes, the expected prices of goods, and expected income. These are the data for the household when it is making its plans. Of these data only the nature and order of tastes, and the legal and social order, belong among the data from the point of view of the economy as a whole. The expected prices of goods and expected income are quantities which the individual household has to reckon among the data when drawing up its economic plan, but which result from the course of the economic process as a whole. Prices and incomes are, therefore, in contrast to the data for the whole economy, phenomena which have to be explained by economic theory. Let us take as a further example the economic plan of a production unit which is facing an expected price–sales function. The following data are the basis for its economic plan: the expected price–sales function, the composition of its assets, the production function, the expected prices of factors of production, the quantity of labour available and its quality, and the legal and social order of which this firm is a part. Of these data, the state of its real capital and land, the production function, the quantity of labour available, and the legal and social order, belong to what are data from the point of view of the economy as a whole. The expected price–sales function, the prices of factors of production, and the composition of its monetary resources (cash, credits, and debits) are, on the other hand, data from the point of view of the individual unit, and are given quantities only for the individual supplier and not for the whole economic process. Prices, quantities sold, the level of cash holdings, and of debits and credits, are rather the results of the economic process, and can only be explained as a result of the interaction of all the individual economic plans. Also forming part of the data for the individual unit are the ideas which an oligopolist supplier has about the expected reactions of his competitors to changes in his own actions. How far these ideas belong also among the data for the economy as a whole we shall consider later in this chapter (Section B, para. 6).

2. The individual economic units draw up their plans on the basis of the relevant data—the data from the point of view of the economy as a whole and the data from the point of view of the individual unit—and make their dispositions on the basis of these plans. It is of decisive importance that some of the data for the individual planning unit are based on *expectations*, and are therefore vested with a certain lesser or greater degree of uncertainty. The future prices which the household inserts in its plans are anticipated quantities, which may to a greater or lesser extent diverge in the course of the economic period from the actually realized prices. The expected price–sales function of a monopolist supplier rests on estimates as to the quantities which the supplier believes he can sell at different prices. The sales expected at the price he fixes may not, therefore, coincide with the actually realized sales. What quantities of goods are sold at the price that is fixed are determined by the buyers. The quantities sold enter into the economic plan of the supplier as an expectation-parameter (Svennilson), but for the buyers they represent an action-parameter. The oligopolist supplier must, in drawing up his economic plan, assume a particular behaviour on the part of his competitors, which may very well diverge from the actually realized behaviour. These examples relate to the data from the point of view of the individual unit. Of course, the data for the economy as a whole may also be based on expectations, and as entered into the firm's calculations may subsequently diverge from the actual facts. It is easy to find examples. An entrepreneur assumes that in the period for which he is planning the existing stock of machines will remain the same as at the start of the period. In the course of the period some machines may unexpectedly be lost. Or a supplier may reckon that certain prices fixed by the authorities will also obtain in the coming period at the same level as they have at the moment he is making his plans. In the middle of the period these prices may be altered by the government. So long as it is simply a case of studying how the course of the economic process is shaped under given unchanging conditions, with the data from the point of view of the economy as a whole known to the economic units, it is only the surprises about the data for the individual unit (that is, divergencies between expectations and the subsequent facts) which have to be considered.

3. Given a particular set of data, there are two ways in which the economic plans of individuals may interact:

(a) *There may in a certain period of time be no complete harmony or congruence between the individual economic plans and the dispositions resulting from them, so that either some of, or perhaps all, the economic subjects are "surprised" at the end of the period. The system of exchange is then in a state of "disequilibrium".* The divergencies between expectations and facts will cause the individual subjects to revise their plans and dispositions. These divergencies between expectations and facts then determine the course of the system in the following period. We have already referred to these relationships in the introduction.

(b) *There may, on the other hand, be complete harmony between the individual economic plans, so that no one at the end of the period has reason to alter or revise his plans and dispositions, provided the set of data remains unchanged. The system then finds itself, given the particular set of data, in "equilibrium".* Every individual sees his expectations fulfilled, and, therefore, experiences no "surprises". There is complete adjustment to the existing set of data. *The values of the variables of a system in equilibrium are stationary, that is, the equilibrium values of the variables remain constant through time.*

4. As the economic plans of the individual economic subjects in the exchange economy are formulated independently, it is not to be expected that in any period chosen at random there will be agreement between the individual plans. Each economic unit will not behave in the way that it has been expected to behave by the other economic units when they made their dispositions. Any state of the economy taken at random will, as a rule, be a state of disequilibrium. From these facts two essential tasks emerge for theoretical analysis.

*First of all we have to ask what is the equilibrium position corresponding to a given set of data,* or what values the variables entering into the individuals' economic plans (prices, quantites of goods, income, etc.) must have, with a given set of data, if the dispositions of the individuals are to be brought into harmony and the system be in equilibrium. In this way of formulating the question the equilibrium condition is already assumed to exist at the start, and as all the variables have the same values in each period of time the answer can be given by analysing statically the equilibrium position corresponding to a given set of data.

There is, secondly, the question of *the nature of the equilibrium position corresponding to a given set of data*; that is, whether the equilibrium position, if it exists, is *stable or unstable. A position of equilibrium corresponding to a given set of data may be said to be stable if a disturbance of the position leads to a revision of economic plans, and therewith to a change in the dispositions of the individual economic units which leads the system back again in the course of time to the initial equilibrium position. On the other hand, if the revision of the individuals' economic plans, and of the resulting dispositions, does not lead back to the initial equilibrium position, then we may say that the equilibrium is unstable.* From these definitions of the stability and instability of equilibrium it follows that in order to find out whether a state of equilibrium is stable or not, assumptions must be made about the nature and manner of the reactions of the individual economic subjects to disturbances in the equilibrium conditions, causing divergencies between expectations and facts. Only then is it possible to say anything about the course of the economic process through time. A proposition of this kind can only be made as a result of a dynamic analysis which permits one to say how one condition emerges out of the previously existing one, that is, by means of the dynamic analysis of the equilibrium position corresponding to a particular set of data.

5. Closely connected with this second question is *the problem of the development through time of an exchange economy, starting from a particular position of disequilibrium, and given a particular set of data.* Again, the solution to this problem requires dynamic analysis. If there is one, and only one, set of data which corresponds to a stable equilibrium position, then such an analysis will describe the path from the initial position of disequilibrium to the final position of equilibrium. If the position of equilibrium corresponding to this set of data is unstable, then dynamic analysis can tell us the path which the values of the variables in the system go through from an initial position of disequilibrium. But in this case the path does not lead to an equilibrium position. It is, therefore, not permissible to describe the equilibrium position corresponding to a particular set of data as that position which a system in disequilibrium is tending towards. A tendency to equilibrium only occurs if the equilibrium position is stable. We shall shortly be considering an example (Section B, paras, 1 and 2).

6. Static and dynamic analyses of the equilibrium position corresponding to a particular set of data do not, however, make up the entire study of the course of the economic process in an exchange economy. The set of data undergoes changes in the course of time, and each new set of data has a new equilibrium position corresponding to it. It is therefore of great interest to compare the *different equilibrium positions corresponding to different sets of data.* In order to understand the effect of a change in the set of data on the corresponding position of equilibrium, we must only alter *a single datum at a time.* Only in this way is it possible to understand fully the effects

of alterations in the individual data. We ask, to start with, about Set I of the data, and the equilibrium position corresponding to it, and then study, next, the equilibrium position corresponding to Set II of the data, where Set II differs from Set I only in the alteration of a single datum. In this way we compare the equilibrium values for the system corresponding to the two equilibrium positions, with one another. This sort of comparative analysis of two equilibrium positions may be described as *comparative-static analysis*, since it studies the alteration in the equilibrium position corresponding to an alteration in a single datum.

This sort of comparative-static analysis of the influence of a change in one of the data on the equilibrium position in an exchange economy would be sufficient to explain the course of the economic system through time if it reacted and adjusted itself infinitely rapidly to an alteration in data. In reality, the reactions of economic individuals when there is a change in data do not take place instantaneously. A change in data will only work itself out *gradually* on the values of the variables in the system. We have, therefore, to study by means of a dynamic analysis how the system develops from an initial position of equilibrium when affected by a change in data. As soon as one datum alters, the compatibility of the individual plans is upset. A revision is undertaken which must be analysed through time. If the new set of data, with the equilibrium position corresponding to it, is stable, then the analysis will study the path of the system from the original position of equilibrium to the new position of equilibrium. This sort of dynamic analysis of the influence of a change in data is much more comprehensive and informative than the mere comparative-static analysis of two different sets of data and of the equilibrium positions corresponding to them. Nevertheless, the comparative-static treatment provides, as we shall see, some important insights into the mechanism of the exchange economy.

7. The movements through time which the variables of an economic system carry out from an initial disequilibrium position, through a succession of revisions of individual plans, may, *given a particular set of data*, be described as *the endogenous movements of an economic system*. On the other hand, a comparative-static analysis studies the movements in the equilibrium values of economic variables which correspond to changes in the data, that is, to changes which are solely the consequence of a change in *something outside the economic system*. Such movements may be described as *exogenous movements*. If an economic system is such that all adjustments to changes in data take place very rapidly, then all changes in economic variables may be explained by exogenous influences. The movements

then take place simultaneously, or almost simultaneously, with changes in the data. If, however, the adjustment to a change in data takes time, and the equilibrium position corresponding to the new set of data is stable, then only the final equilibrium position corresponding to the change in data is the result of an exogenous influence. The nature of the path to this equilibrium position, on the other hand, is solely determined by forces inside the economic system and is, therefore, determined endogenously. *Endogenous movements can only be explained by means of a dynamic theory.*

It is, of course, possible that certain variables may adjust themselves immediately to a change in data while the adjustment of other variables requires a short or long period of time. The change in the first kind of variables can then only be explained exogenously, while the change in the second kind only endogenously.

8. The static and dynamic analysis of an equilibrium position corresponding to a particular set of data can be carried out for an entire economy or for a section of an economy, and for one or for several partial groups of economic units. In the first case one may speak of *general analysis* and in the second case of *partial analysis*. The corresponding equilibrium position can be described as *general or partial equilibrium*. If one extracts, for example, from the totality of economic units simply those which are demanding and supplying a particular good, and studies the course of the economic process simply for this group of economic units, then one is engaged in partial analysis. Static partial analysis was treated in an especially masterly fashion by the great English economist *Alfred Marshall* (1842–1924). Marshall's partial analysis revealed both the great possibilities as well as the limitations of this method of approach. For practical problems it is indispensable because of its much greater simplicity as contrasted with general analysis. But it must never be forgotten that the totality of all economic dispositions and plans in an exchange economy forms one great interdependent system, and that, therefore, a genuine understanding of the course of the economic process as a whole is only possible by means of general analysis. This notwithstanding, the general interdependent system may be seen (to make use of an expression of the Danish economist F. Zeuthen) as a network of particular interdependencies, a point of view which provides a complete justification for partial analysis.[1] General

[1] See F. Zeuthen: "Der wirtschaftliche Zusammenhang—ein Netz von Teilzusammenhängen", *Weltwirtschaftliches Archiv*, 58, 1943, pp. 175 ff. Also: O. Lange, "Die allgemeine Interdependenz der Wirtschaftsgrössen und die Isolierungsmethode." *Zeitschrift für Nationalökonomie*, vol. 4, 1933, p. 52 ff.

analysis is, of course, much more complex. It has been developed in a masterly way by Léon Walras (1834–1910) and Vilfredo Pareto (1848–1923), who have analysed the position of general equilibrium by means of a static theory. The Walras-Pareto solution of the general equilibrium problem is one of the greatest achievements of theoretical economics. Recent study has taken an important step forward by attempting to answer the question as to the course of the economic process through time under certain assumed sets of initial data. In this treatment the Walras-Pareto analysis appears as a special case of a much more general and comprehensive problem. This development of modern dynamic theory has been furthered— to mention only a few of the more distinguished names—by the Norwegian R. Frisch, by J. Tinbergen of Holland, J. R. Hicks in England, C. F. Roos and P. A. Samuelson in America, and by the Swedes, Lindahl, J. Åkerman, Ohlin, Myrdal, Svennilson, and Lundberg, who have contributed their development of "sequence" analysis, or "process" analysis.

It must, however, be emphasized that static or comparative-static equilibrium analysis has in no way become superfluous through the development of dynamic theory.[1] Equilibrium analysis is, now as before, one of the chief instruments of economic theory. We shall accordingly demonstrate both forms of analysis by means of examples. We begin by considering problems in the field of partial analysis, and follow this with problems involving general analysis.

9. The concept of economic equilibrium is as old as economic theory itself. There is no economist in whose thought it did not have a place. No economic system exists which does not call for consideration of the problem of equilibrium because the problem of the consistency of economic plans occurs in every economic system. Particular (or partial) plans in a centrally directed and controlled economy must be made mutually consistent just as in the market economy. But the adjustment of economic plans for mutual consistency is simply an attempt to ascertain the economic equilibrium. It is true that this process of adjustment is different in a controlled economy from what it is in a market economy. But the problem exists here as there and needs to be solved in both systems. Whenever one considers disturbance-free economic growth, the reference is to a moving equilibrium, a form of growth in which individual dispositions are mutually compatible throughout.

Thus it is only natural that economic theory should have turned already in its very early stages to the solution of the problem of

---

[1] Cf. K. Boulding, "In Defense of Statics." (*Quarterly Journal of Economics*, Vol. 69, 1955, p. 485 *et seq.*)

equilibrium—and of the problem of disequilibrium, since disequilibrium has meaning only in the context of the notion of equilibrium—and that it continues to this day to circle around this problem, seeking new approaches and new aspects. What is the purpose of all the discussions of internal and external stability, of convertibility, etc., if not to search for ways of attaining or maintaining certain equilibria?

The Physiocrats had in mind a concept of equilibrium when they pointed to their Tableau Économique as a means for demonstrating "the order and the disorder which governments may cause". Adam Smith's doctrine of natural and of market price represents the first attempt to build a theory of the price mechanism as a means of establishing equilibrium in the market economy—an attempt which, not confined to static analysis, contained also the elements of a dynamic analysis of the path to equilibrium. A statement of the conditions for moving-equilibrium growth of an economy was first attempted by Karl Marx in his analysis of a progressive (accumulating) economy. These few examples from the history of our discipline must suffice. The history of economic doctrine must show in detail how thinking in terms of equilibrium developed in the course of time, and what rôle it played in the analyses of various scholars. Here it needs to be made clear that the concept of equilibrium is no phantom of an esoteric imagination but rather flows directly and necessarily from the observation and the intellectual penetration of economic reality and is indispensable for the understanding of economic problems. This will become apparent in the concrete examples of the following sections.

## Section B

## PARTIAL EQUILIBRIUM

### 1. The Equilibrium Price of a Good with a Constant Supply per Unit of Time

1. Let us consider the economic plans of an individual purchaser (household or firm) for the coming period, say for the coming day. The quantity which each household will demand of a particular good $A$ depends, as we saw in Chapter I, on the price of this good, on the prices of the other goods desired by the household, and on the level of its income. Let us suppose that the prices of all the goods with the exception of that of the good $A$, as well as the level of income of every household, are a fixed given quantity. Then the

planned demand of each household for the good $A$ may be taken as a function of the price of the good $A$, and normally the quantity demanded will decrease with a rise in price. We have already described this curve as the individual demand curve for the good concerned. By adding the individual demand functions, i.e. by adding up the individual quantities demanded at each alternative price, we obtain the total demand function for the good concerned

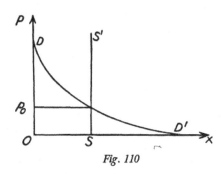

*Fig. 110*

(Fig 110). The curve $DD'$ is the demand curve of *the households*. It tells us what quantities the households altogether actually wish to buy (*ceteris paribus*) at a particular price. A corresponding demand curve of this "ceteris paribus" kind can, as we have shown, also be drawn up for each factor of production, from the individual demand curves of the individual entrepreneurs. We suppose that the group of demanders is facing a group of suppliers, who wish to supply and sell a fixed quantity $OS$ per unit of time (or per day) at a price which is the same for all suppliers. The demanders are indifferent between the various suppliers. The suppliers fix the price, and the demanders decide what quantities they will buy at the price fixed.

Our analysis is, therefore, a partial analysis. We concentrate our attention solely on the supply and demand relationships for the good $A$ and, using the "ceteris paribus" assumption, we disregard all other economic influences. The data of our problem are the total demand curve $DD'$ of the households and the quantity supplied per unit of time by the suppliers.

We want now, first of all, to make the assumption that the suppliers know the demand curve of the buyers, i.e. that the market is completely "transparent" to them. It is clear that on these assumptions, so long as the quantity supplied ($OS$) is smaller than the saturation demand of the households, there is one price and one price only ($p_0$)

at which the total quantity supplied ($OS$) will be purchased by the demanders (Fig. 110). At the price $p_0$ the economic plans of the suppliers and demanders are in harmony.

So long as the data (in this case, the demand curve $DD'$ and the quantity supplied per unit of time $OS$) remain unchanged, the quantity $OS$ will be supplied and sold at the price $p_0$ in each period. *At a price of $p_0$ there is equilibrium. Price and quantity will then be stationary through time.* On a graph, the curves through time of price and quantity sold will then run parallel to the time axis. Under the assumptions we have made, this equilibrium will only rule at a price of $p_0$. If the price fixed by the suppliers was higher or lower than $p_0$, then the quantity supplied would be greater or smaller than the demand. Assuming always that the quantity supplied per unit of time is constant, and is to be sold in its entirety, the suppliers will then in the first case reduce the price in order to avoid stocks piling up; and in the second case they will raise the price in order to limit the demand to the quantity supplied. On our assumption that the suppliers know the economic plans of the households, this sort of divergence from the equilibrium price is not possible. The equilibrium price will be fixed by the suppliers from the start.

2. *The explanation of the equilibrium price which we have given here is a static one. Stationary phenomena* (i.e. prices and quantities which are constant through time) have been explained by means of a static theory. In order to determine the equilibrium price, relations between economic variables (prices, quantities supplied and demanded) were used which related to the same period of time. If we denote the quantity supplied in the period $t$ till $t + 1$ as $s_t$, the quantity demanded in the same period as $x_t$, and the selling price in this period as $p_t$, then we have the data for the problem: first, the demand functions of the households:

$$x_t = f(p_t) \tag{1}$$

secondly, the supply curve of the suppliers:

$$s_t = \text{const.} \tag{2}$$

and further we have as a condition of equilibrium that the price will be so fixed that the quantity demanded will be equal to the quantity supplied:

$$s_t = x_t. \tag{3}$$

We have, therefore, three equations for three unknowns (two equations derived from the data, and one a condition), and these suffice in order to determine the values of the three relevant variables ($x_t$, $s_t$, and $p_t$) in equilibrium—their so-called equilibrium values.

I

This state of things is expressed by saying that the variables are determined by the three equations.[1]

3. The derivation of the equilibrium price on the assumptions we have made may seem to the reader highly unrealistic. But anyone acquainted with the different kinds of price formation in the real world will realize that the theory here worked out for the formation of an equilibrium price is directly applicable to the explanation of the

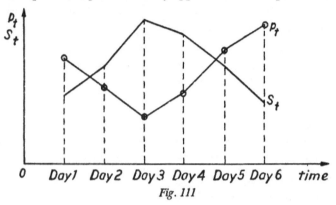

Fig. 111

formation of prices on a stock exchange or on other organized markets. A broker will derive the total demand function from the commissions he has received for buying shares at particular maximum prices, and if particular quantities of shares are also on offer for what they may fetch, the broker will be able literally to fix the equilibrium price (the price of the shares) in the way we have demonstrated. The purchases and sales all go through the hands of the broker, and the structure of demand and supply is completely transparent to him. He is therefore in a position at once to fix the equilibrium price.

4. *As soon as the data change, the equilibrium price will, as a rule, also change.* We shall deal with these relationships later, and here simply limit ourselves to one or two remarks on the subject. A change in data, in our example, is a change in the shape and/or position of the demand curve as a consequence of exogenous influences (for example, shifts in tastes, or in the level of prices of other goods, or in income).[2] Or it may mean a change in the quantity supplied per unit of time. Let us assume, for example, that as a consequence of fluctuations in the amount brought to market daily, the amount

[1] From school algebra the reader will remember that *n* equations are needed to determine *n* unknowns.

[2] In a partial analysis, as in this example, the levels of the prices of other goods, and of income, are for our problem exogenous factors.

actually supplied alters in the way portrayed in Fig. 111. The demand function is assumed to be the same each day (Fig. 110). It is then at once clear that the equilibrium price each day will change, and that it will fall as the amount supplied increases (that is, the line $SS'$ in Fig. 110 will move to the right), and as the amount supplied falls the price will rise (the line $SS'$ in Fig. 110 will then move to the left). The curve through time of supply, with the demand function unchanged, will correspond to a time curve for the equilibrium price like that of $p_t$ in Fig. 111. The series through time of quantities and prices will be negatively correlated. What are being compared here are the equilibrium conditions corresponding to the different sets of data. *The treatment is therefore one of comparative statics.* As the equilibrium prices and quantities change from day to day, we have here an example of *a comparative-static explanation of a non-stationary phenomenon.*

The answer to the question as to how the equilibrium values vary with changes in data is of fundamental importance. To find out that a particular set of data corresponds to a particular equilibrium position is by itself quite inadequate. *Equilibrium analysis only achieves real value by studying how changes in data influence the equilibrium values.* [1] Certainly, even this comparative-static treatment does not give us a complete picture of economic change. The picture would only be complete for the case where the adjustment to changes in data takes place immediately, that is, where there is an infinitely rapid reaction. This was the case given in our example, since we assumed complete "transparency", or perfect knowledge, for all parties in our partial system. In most cases there is not complete transparency of the market (or perfect knowledge on the part of those engaged), so that the adjustment to a change in data requires a greater or smaller amount of time. Nevertheless, the comparative-static

[1] "It is the task of comparative statics to show the determination of the equilibrium values of given variables (unknowns) under postulated conditions (functional relationships) with various data (parameters) specified. Thus in the simplest case of a partial-equilibrium market for a single commodity the two independent relations of supply and demand each drawn up with other prices and institutional data being taken as given, determine by their intersection the equilibrium quantities of the unknown price and quantity sold. If no more than this could be said, the economist would be truly vulnerable to the gibe that he is only a parrot, taught to say 'supply and demand'. Simply to know that there are efficacious 'laws' determining equilibrium tells us nothing of the character of these laws. In order for the analysis to be useful it must provide information concerning the way in which our equilibrium quantities will change as a result of changes in the parameters taken as independent data". (P. A. Samuelson: *Foundations of Economic Analysis*, Cambridge, Mass., 1947, p. 257).

treatment is of value because it tells us *how the equilibrium values change with a change in a single datum.* Whether the new equilibrium position corresponding to a particular change in data is actually reached is irrelevant in this case. But at each moment there will exist a tendency towards a new equilibrium position—provided always that it is a stable equilibrium—which corresponds to the new set of data. This continuous alteration in the tendency of

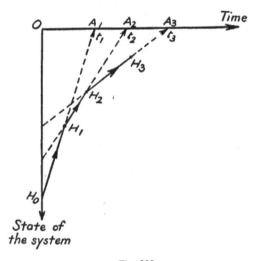

*Fig. 112*

an economic system under the influence of changing data may be represented by Pareto's *courbes de poursuite.*[1] In Fig. 112 $A_1$, $A_2$, $A_3$ represent the equilibrium positions corresponding to the different sets of data $D_1$, $D_2$, $D_3$ and are assumed to be stable. From the point of time 0 until $t_1$ the set of data $D_1$ obtains. The system then moves from its position at time 0, that is $H_0$, in the direction of the point $A_1$ (following the arrow $H_0A_1$). When it reaches the point $H_1$ there is a change in data. The new set of data $D_2$ obtains for the period $t_1$ to $t_2$. The system now changes direction towards $H_1A_2$. At the point $H_2$ on the path $H_1A_2$ there is a further change in data. The new constellation $D_3$ obtains for the period $t_2$ to $t_3$. The system again changes its direction towards $H_2A_3$. At $H_3$ yet another change in data occurs. And so on. The broken line $H_0H_1H_2H_3$ represents the changes in the direction of the economic system corresponding to the changes in

[1] V. Pareto: *Cours d'Économie Politique*, Vol. I, Lausanne, 1896, p. 18.

data that are taking place. It shows that at any moment a movement exists towards the equilibrium position corresponding to the existing set of data, but that this position is not reached owing to fresh changes in data. The direction in which it is moving alters before the equilibrium position is reached.

5. We have assumed up to now that the suppliers know the demand function of the buyers. In this case the equilibrium price

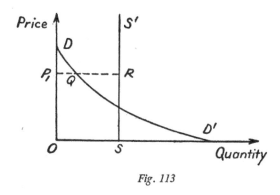

*Fig. 113*

can be fixed at once. As a rule in unorganized markets this is not possible. The demand function of the buyers is not known to the sellers. On the first day, therefore, the price fixing is more or less a "shot in the dark". We now want to show how the system develops through time, from such a random initial position, given a particular set of data.

Let us assume that on the first day the quantity $OS$ is supplied at the price $OP_1$ (Fig. 113). At this price the demanders will want to buy the quantity $P_1Q$. The sellers, therefore, at the end of the first day are "surprised" in that the quantity $QR$ remains unsold. At a price $OP_1$ there is no agreement between the economic plans of the sellers, and those of the buyers. The price $OP_1$ is not an equilibrium price. The sellers, therefore, will alter their price on the following day. The alteration in price will obviously be downwards. In order to know what the size of the alteration in price will be, we have to make an assumption about *the reaction of the sellers to divergencies between their planned sales and the actual sales* (i.e. between the quantity which they intended to sell and the quantity they actually sold). It is realistic to assume that the change in price in the following period depends on *the size of the divergence between planned and actual sales*. If we describe the prices in two successive periods as $p_t$ and $p_{t+1}$, the demand function as $x = x(p_t)$ and the constant quantity supplied as $s$, then the following functional relationship will obtain:

$$p_{t+1} - p_t = f[x_t(p_t) - s]. \tag{4}$$

This simply says that the change in price from one period to the next (i.e. the difference between $p_{t+1}$ and $p_t$) is a function of the difference between the quantity demanded and supplied in the period $t$ (or the difference between $x_t[p_t]$ and $s$). The function will possess the following characteristics:

(a) If $x_t(p_t) = s$, then $p_{t+1} = p_t$: that is, the sellers are not surprised in any way by the outcome and do not make any change in price. The system is in equilibrium.

(b) If $x_t(p_t) < s$, then there is an excess of supply and the sellers reduce prices, that is, $p_{t+1} < p_t$.

(c) If $x_t(p_t) > s$, then there is an excess of demand and the sellers raise prices, that is, $p_{t+1} > p_t$.

(d) The price alteration will be the smaller the smaller the excess either of demand or supply as the case may be.

If we know the functional relation (4), then we can find out what alteration in price will take place from period to period. If the price $p_t$ is known, then the relationship (4) enables us to calculate the price $p_{t+1}$ in the next period.

A simple numerical example will help to make this relationship clear. The demand function is:

$$x_t(p_t) = 10 - \tfrac{1}{2}p_t.$$

The constant quantity supplied is:

$$s = 6.$$

It is at once clear that the equilibrium price will be:

$$p = 8.$$

The functional relationship (4) is:

$$p_{t+1} = p_t + c(10 - \tfrac{1}{2}p_t - 6) = p_t + c(4 - \tfrac{1}{2}p_t) \tag{5}$$

From (5) we can see that if $p_t = 8$:

$$p_{t+1} = p_t$$

which is to say that the equilibrium price is such that it remains constant from period to period given the constancy of the data.

If the price fixed on the first day is $p_0 = 16$, i.e. above the

equilibrium price, and if we suppose that $c = \frac{1}{2}$, then it follows from
(5) that this price will be reduced by 2 on the following day to $p_1 = 14$.
It follows also from (5) that the price on the third day will be
reduced by 1·5, so that $p_2 = 12\cdot5$, etc. In general the price movement
will follow the formula:

$$p = 8(\tfrac{3}{4})^t + 8 \qquad (6)$$

From (6) it is clear that the price will fall from period to period and
approach increasingly to the equilibrium price:

$$\lim_{t\to\infty} p_t = 8 \qquad (7)$$

*Whether the equilibrium price is reached from a particular initial
position depends on the extent to which the suppliers alter their price
in the following period in reaction to a divergence between planned
and actual sales.* This extent is expressed by the coefficient $c$ in
relation (5). From (5) the price ruling at any moment of time $t$ is
given by the formula:

$$p_t = \alpha\left(1 - \frac{c}{2}\right)^t + 8 \qquad (8)$$

where $\alpha$ is a constant the value of which is determined by the initial
price. It is clear from (8) that the nature of the price movement from
a particular initial price depends essentially on the magnitude of the
constant $c$, which we may call *the reaction constant*. If $c = \frac{1}{2}$, then
starting from a given initial level the price approaches constantly
nearer to the equilibrium price, either decreasing or increasing
(Fig. 114). If, on the other hand, $c = 3$, with the suppliers reacting
more strongly to a divergence between planned and actual sales,
then equation (8) will be:

$$p_t = \alpha(-\tfrac{1}{2})^t + 8. \qquad (9)$$

From an initial price $p_0 = 16$ the following sequence of prices will
result (Fig. 115):

$$
\begin{array}{ll}
t = 0 & p_0 = 16 \\
t = 1 & p_1 = 4 \\
t = 2 & p_2 = 10 \\
t = 3 & p_3 = 7 \\
t = 4 & p_4 = 8\cdot5 \\
\end{array}
$$
etc.

Here the initial price is above the equilibrium price, and at this price supply is greater than the amount sold. The sellers react in the following period with such a large reduction in price that demand is greater than the quantity supplied. The sellers react to their "surprise" in the following period by raising the price to 10, at which the supply

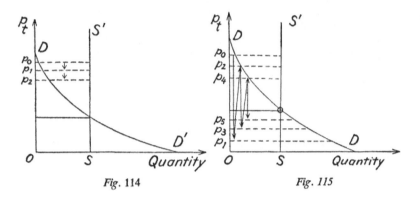

Fig. 114                         Fig. 115

is still in excess of the demand, though to a smaller extent. The sellers react then by a reduction of the price to 7, at which the demand is again larger than the supply, etc. The price fluctuates from day to day

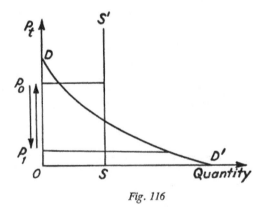

Fig. 116

with decreasing amplitude around the equilibrium price, which it successively approaches.

If the reaction constant is larger still, for example, if $c = 4$, then (8) will be:

$$p_t = \alpha(-1)^t + 8. \tag{10}$$

From an initial price of $p_0 = 14$ there will be the following movement of prices (Fig. 85):

$$t = 0 \qquad p_0 = 14$$
$$t = 1 \qquad p_1 = 2$$
$$t = 2 \qquad p_2 = 14$$
$$t = 3 \qquad p_3 = 2$$
$$\text{etc.}$$

Here the price only takes on the values of either 14 or 2. If the price on one day is at 14, then on the following day it will be 2, and *vice versa*. In this case the equilibrium price is never reached.

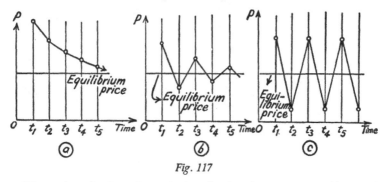

Fig. 117

The series of prices through time in the three cases we discussed are portrayed in the three adjoining figures in Fig. 117. It can be easily seen that "explosive" price movements, that is, movements which lead further and further away from the equilibrium price, are perfectly possible.

6. The analysis we have carried out here of price movements starting from an initial price position which diverges in each case from the equilibrium position is, as we have seen, only possible *if we make an assumption about the reactions of sellers to divergencies between planned and actual sales*. This assumption is expressed in the functional relation (4). The three equations:

$$x_t = x_t(p_t)$$
$$s_t = \text{const.} \qquad (11)$$
$$p_{t+1} - p_t = f(x_t - s_t)$$

i.e. the demand function, the supply function, and the reaction function of the sellers, determine the course through time of the variables in our example (price, quantity demanded, and quantity supplied), starting from a given initial position. To determine the course of the system through time we therefore need, exactly as in the static analysis, as many equations as there are unknowns. Only then is our problem determined in the sense that the course through time of the variables is then determined. Nevertheless, there is a fundamental difference between the static analysis expounded earlier on and the treatment expressed in the system of equations (11). While in the static analysis only those relations between variables enter which relate to the same period, an answer to the question of the course of the system through time, starting from an initial disequilibrium position, demands the introduction of *at least* one dynamic relationship. In the system of equations (11) this dynamic relation is the reaction function of the sellers. The two other relations are static. The introduction of a dynamic relation enables us to say how the position in one period develops out of the position in the preceding period, if the data remain unchanged. The movements which we have been considering are therefore endogenous. We have been able to show, in addition, under what conditions the economic process moves to the equilibrium position from a given position which diverges from equilibrium, or under what conditions the equilibrium position is stable. *The series of prices through time, given in Fig. 117, are therefore explained by means of a dynamic analysis.* If we consider the price movements before the equilibrium position is reached (Figs. 117A and B), we have then *an example of the explanation of a non-stationary phenomenon by means of a dynamic analysis.* As we have also in the cases portrayed in Figs. 117A and B explained the equilibrium price as *the result of endogenous movements,* we have here an example of *the explanation of a stationary phenomenon by means of a dynamic theory. It is clear, therefore, that a static theory only suffices if we are simply interested in the equilibrium position corresponding to a particular set of data.* If we wish to be able to say anything about *the nature of the equilibrium position,* or if we wish to know whether and when this position will be reached from a particular diverging initial position (which is fundamentally identical with the question of the stability of the *equilibrium position*) a dynamic theory is necessary, that is, a theory in which at least one of the relations between the relevant variables determining the economic process is dynamic.

## 2. The Equilibrium Price of a Good with a Variable Supply per Unit of Time

### a. *Variable Supply out of a Given Level of Stocks*

We assume that a group of suppliers behaving as quantity-adjusters possess a particular stock of a good at a particular moment of time.

This quantity is assumed to be unalterable by additional production within a particular period of time. For example, a corn merchant after the harvest has been gathered will be in possession of a particular stock of corn, and the quantity then existing will be sold throughout the coming year until the new harvest is brought in. We have to answer the question as to what quantity of corn the seller will offer, say, in a week at different prices. *Given the level of stocks, the amount offered each week will obviously depend on the price expected in the coming week, and on the development of prices expected in the future.* If a lower price is expected in the coming week, and a rise in prices in the future, then the quantity supplied will be reduced, assuming that the expected rise in price is sufficiently large in relation to the costs of storage. The quantity offered at an expected low price in the coming week will be the smaller, the higher the price which it is hoped to obtain in the future. If in the coming week a higher price is expected, and a fall in price is expected subsequently, then there will be an inclination to offer a larger quantity; and this quantity will be the larger the higher the price expected in the coming week and the steeper the fall in prices after that. If we describe the price expected in the coming week as $p_t$ and express the expected development of prices (or "price-tendency") by the differential quotient of the price with respect to time, that is, by $dp_t/dt$ then, given a particular stock, the following functional relationship will hold for the quantity offered $s_t$, in the coming week:

$$s_t = f\left(p_t, \frac{dp_t}{dt}\right) \tag{12}$$

This *dynamic supply function* corresponds precisely with the demand function (25) discussed in Chapter I. In this function the price expected in the coming week, $p_t$, and the expected price-tendency, $dp_t/dt$, are independent of one another. However, we do not wish here to treat this problem with this full degree of generality because that would require rather complicated analysis. We shall be assuming here that the expected price-tendency depends in a particular way on the price expected in the coming week: the lower (or higher) the price expected in the coming week the greater (or smaller) will the suppliers rate the probability that a higher price can be obtained later. If in this way we relate to each price $p_t$ a particular price-tendency, then the quantity supplied in the week in (12) can be represented simply as a function of the price expected in this week. The supply function (12) is then, in spite of the differential quotient $dp_t/dt$, a purely static relation. Just as in the static treatment of demand, we can find different alternative values for the prices expected in the coming week to correspond to the particular quantities supplied. Given our assumptions, we should find increasing supplies corresponding to increasing values of the future expected price level. For each individual supplier there exists a curve which tells us what quantity he will supply from his stocks in a week at particular alternative prices expected during the week, and with the particular price-tendencies corresponding to these prices. By adding the individual

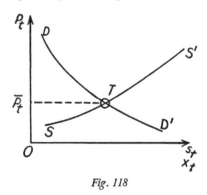

*Fig. 118*

supply curves we obtain the total supply as a function of the price expected during the week. If we put together the supply curve of the suppliers, and the demand curve of the buyers acting as quantity-adjusters (Fig. 118), then it is at once clear that there will be agreement between the plans of the suppliers and the plans of the buyers only at the price corresponding to the point of intersection, $T$, of the two curves, that is, the price $\bar{p}_t$. This price is then the equilibrium price for the coming week which would be forthcoming in an organized market, and calculated by the broker from the orders of buyers and sellers.

Of course, as we have already emphasized, not very much is discovered simply by ascertaining the existence of an equilibrium price. We have to know (a) whether the equilibrium price is stable or not, (b) how the equilibrium price varies with a change in the data. The problem of stability will be dealt with in the same way as in para. 1, so that we can refrain from discussing it further. Let us confine ourselves to the second problem: *the influence of a change in data on the equilibrium position.* This problem also has already been discussed in para 1. We showed by a comparative-static analysis how changes in the quantity supplied per unit of time influenced the equilibrium price, if the demand curve remained unchanged. We now wish to apply such a comparative-static analysis in our present example. Changes in data obviously express themselves either through changes in the demand curve and/or in the supply curve. *If the demand curve shifts from one period to another, that means that at each price a larger or smaller quantity will be demanded than in the previous period, so that we may say that demand has increased (or diminished).* An increase in demand will be represented in our diagram by a shift of the demand curve to the right, and a decrease in demand by a

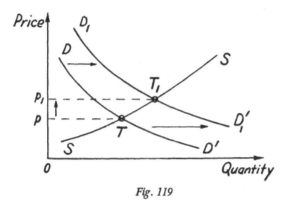

*Fig. 119*

shift to the left. *In the same way we may speak of an increase (or decrease) in supply from one period to the next if at every price a greater (or smaller) quantity is supplied than in the previous period.* An increase (or decrease) of supply will then be represented geometrically by a shift in the supply curve to the right (or left). Shifts in the demand curve can occur as a result of changes in tastes, or in the prices of other goods, or in the distribution of income. Changes in supply can result, for example, from changes in the prices of factors or in technique.

The effect of a change in demand on the equilibrium position can be seen at once from Fig. 119: *an increase (or decrease) in demand, if the supply conditions remain unchanged, will result in an increase (or decrease) in the equilibrium price and in the quantity sold.* The equilibrium position corresponding to the first set of data will be given by the coordinates of the point of intersection $T$, and the equilibrium position corresponding to the second set of data will be given by the coordinates of the point of intersection $T_1$. The proposition: "An increase in demand is followed *ceteris paribus* by an increase in price", which we are applying here, must be sharply distinguished from the proposition: "Rising prices correspond to falling demand". In the first case there is an alteration in the equilibrium price as the result of a shift in the demand curve. In the second case we are concerned with the relation between alternative levels of prices, and the demand corresponding to them, *given* a particular demand curve.

From Fig. 120 it is clear what the effect of an alteration in supply will be on the equilibrium position: *an increase (or decrease) in the supply, if the demand dispositions remain unchanged, will result in a fall (or a rise) in the equilibrium price and a rise (or a fall) in the*

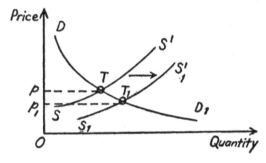

*Fig. 120*

*corresponding quantity sold.* The first set of data brings about an equilibrium price given by the coordinates of the point of inter- section $T$, and the second set of data a price given by the coordinates of the point of intersection $T_1$. In this case also the proposition: "With an increase in supply, *ceteris paribus*, the price falls", which is concerned with an alteration in the equilibrium price which takes place when the supply curve moves to the right, must be sharply distinguished from the proposition: "Rising prices result in increasing quantities supplied", which describes the relation between alternative levels of prices and the quantities supplied, *given* a particular supply curve.

If between one period and the next there is a simultaneous altera- tion both in the demand and in the supply, then the following pro- positions may be established.

If the supply increases and the demand decreases, then the equilibrium price will fall (Fig. 121). The set of data I corresponds to an equilibrium price $p_1$, and the set of data II to the equilibrium price $p_2$. As to the change in the quantity supplied no definite proposition can be arrived at. It may decrease, increase, or remain unchanged.

If the supply increases and the demand increases also, then the equilibrium quantity supplied increases (Fig. 121A). The set of data I gives an equilibrium quantity $x_1$, and the set of data II the equilibrium quantity $x_2$. No definite conclusion can be reached as to the change in the equilibrium price. The price may fall, rise, or remain unchanged.

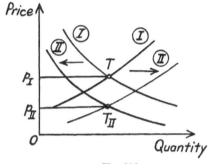

Fig. 121

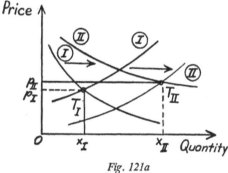

Fig. 121a

These conclusions have one or two interesting sequels. Firstly if it is assumed that the supply increases, while demand remains unchanged, because the supplier expects a fall in price in the future, then Fig. 120 shows that the equilibrium price actually falls. The expected future fall in price, therefore, leads by means of the resulting present behaviour of the supplier to a fall in the present price. *The pessimism of the supplier has the effect of bringing about what he himself expects.* The fall in price, as one can easily see, will be all the more marked if the demanders also expect a fall in price in the coming period in making their purchasing plans. The demand will then fall off so that instead of the system of curves I (in Fig. 121) the system II obtains. The equilibrium price will then fall more sharply than it would if simply the supply increased.

The cases we have examined are all examples of a comparative-static analysis of partial equilibrium problems. The equilibrium positions corresponding to different sets of data were compared with one another. We have already noticed in Chapter III that this method of treatment would suffice to explain the real world if the reactions of all the relevant variables in the system took place infinitely rapidly in the face of changes in data. This would require the complete

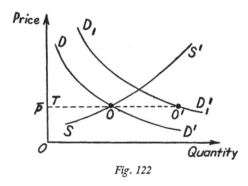

*Fig. 122*

transparency of all economic plans. On organized markets this assumption is fulfilled. On other markets the adjustment to changes in data requires time. Let us assume that equilibrium obtains in the market for a particular good (Fig. 122). At the equilibrium price $\bar{p}$ the quantity $TO$ is sold. In the coming period the demand increases. The demand curve shifts from $DD'$ to $D_1 D_1'$. The suppliers only learn of this change during, or at the end of, the period. They discover that the quantity demanded at the price $\bar{p}$ was greater than that supplied, and they will, therefore, alter their dispositions in the next period. If our assumption about the reactions of the sellers to divergencies between the quantity demanded, and that actually sold, is that they are such as we have described in para. 1, then it is possible to give a dynamic analysis of the course of the system through time, and to ascertain under what conditions, and by what paths, the new equilibrium position will be reached. This will be completely analogous to the analysis carried out in para. 1. We shall in considering the next case (that of variable supply from current production) examine more fully the problem of the path from one equilibrium position to another.

### b. Variable Supply from Current Production

1. Let us assume that the good is produced currently by $n$ producers employing a given productive equipment. All the suppliers are acting

as quantity-adjusters. At given prices for the factors of production there then exists, as was shown in Chapter II, Section D, (i), para. 1, for each supplier a particular short-term individual supply curve for a single economic period, which is given by the rising part of the marginal cost curve starting from the minimum point of the average variable cost curve (Fig. 51). By adding the individual supply curves of the $n$ suppliers we obtain the corresponding total supply curve

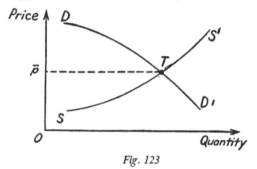

Fig. 123

(Fig. 57). Now, what is the full significance of this curve? The curve tells us what quantities per unit of time will be supplied by all the suppliers at different alternative prices out of current production, assuming a given productive apparatus. How many producers contribute to the total supply from current production depends, as we know, on the prices of the product (pp. 106 ff).

If we bring together the supply curve in Fig. 57 with the demand curve for the relevant period, which is made up of the individual demands of buyers acting as quantity-adjusters, it can be seen at once from Fig. 123 that in this period, equilibrium, or agreement between the dispositions of the suppliers and the buyers, can only be obtained at the point of intersection $T$ of the two curves, and at the price corresponding to it, $\bar{p}$.

2. Let us now assume that the demand and supply diagram in Fig. 123 has held good through several periods so that a complete adjustment of the producers to the prevailing equilibrium price has taken place. All the producers who do not obtain the minimum profit aimed at out of the equilibrium price will have closed down their plant. A producer will, as we know, only continue to supply if the price in the long run is sufficiently high to cover all the costs of his production and a certain minimum profit which he is aiming at. Let us say there are a hundred remaining producers who have discovered the minimum cost combination for their output at the prevailing price.

This condition of long-period partial equilibrium is now suddenly disturbed by an increase in demand, i.e. by a shift in the demand curve to the right (Fig. 124). The hundred suppliers, whose short-period supply curve is represented in Fig. 124 by the curve $SS'$, discover that, as a result of the increase in demand, the quantity demanded per unit of time is greater than the quantity supplied per unit of time. If the suppliers have no stocks at their disposal, then the

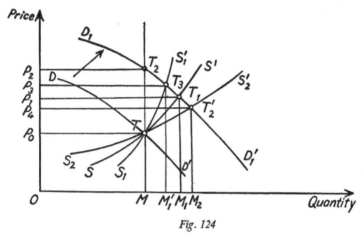

Fig. 124

new equilibrium position following the increase in demand is given by the point $T_2$ (the point of intersection of the line $TT_2$ parallel to the price axis with the new demand curve $D_1D_1'$), which corresponds to the higher price $p_2$. If, on the other hand, stocks are in existence then by drawing on those stocks supply may be raised somewhat above $OM$ which, for the time being, continues to be the supply from current production; and suppliers will be the readier to run down stocks the higher the price that can be obtained. Different prices will then correspond to different quantities supplied which will increase as price increases. The supply curve will be $S_1S_1'$ (Fig. 124). The equilibrium price $p_3$ obtained by drawing on stocks is then higher than the original price $p_0$ but lower than $p_2$. If the increase in demand is only a short-term phenomenon of a few days, after which the demand returns again to its former level $DD'$, then the question of the change in the equilibrium price is disposed of. We have dealt with a similar case when discussing that of supply with a given level of stocks in para. 1.

*The position is different if the increase in demand appears to be permanent.* The hundred existing suppliers will then adjust the current production to the new level of demand and raise it accordingly. The supply curve $SS'$ in Fig. 124 shows the quantities which the hundred existing suppliers are ready to supply at different prices per unit of time out of current production from the existing plants. The diagram makes it clear that in adjusting their current production the suppliers will come into equilibrium within the limits of their existing plants, only at the price $p_1$, which is higher than the price $p_0$ but lower than the price $p_3$. So long as the increased demand is satisfied from the previous level of current production ($OM$), and by drawing on stocks, the equilibrium price will be higher than if the demand is met by a higher level of current production, the existing plants having been adjusted to the new level of demand.

The hundred suppliers will adjust their current production from their existing plants by producing and supplying a larger output corresponding to the higher price. But this is not the end of the consequences of an increase in demand. By raising the equilibrium price from $p_0$ to $p_1$ and increasing the amount supplied from $OM$ to $OM_1$, the profits of the hundred suppliers increase. The marginal producers now obtain a higher profit than that which they had regarded as the normal minimum. This branch of production now becomes a lucrative field for new investment and new producers. On the other hand, it may be profitable for the hundred existing producers at the new equilibrium price $p_1$ to alter their methods of production and extend the scale of their plant, so as to be able to offer a larger output at the same price. The permanent rise in the equilibrium price from $p_0$ to $p_1$, after leading first to a *short-period* adjustment of current production within the limits of the existing plant, therefore brings about a *long-period* process of adjustment by altering and extending the existing plant and by leading to the appearance of new producers.

When the process of investment and readjustment brought about by the new equilibrium position $S_1$ has been concluded, and there has been complete adjustment in the sense that the number of producers and the size of their plants correspond to the price $p_1$, then the larger productive capacity will produce currently a larger output than $OM_1$. We now wish to consider the total supply offered at each price after there has been complete long-period adjustment to whatever the price may be. We obtain, then, a third supply curve $S_2 S_2'$ running through $T$ (a point of long-period equilibrium), which for prices above $p_0$ lies below the supply curve $SS'$, and for prices below $p_0$ lies above it. This supply curve, following Marshall, may be described as the *long-period supply curve*, as contrasted with the curve $SS'$ which may be described as the *short-period supply curve*. *It must be noticed*

*that there are two kinds of short-period supply curve: the supply curve
which is based on supply from a constant level of current production
and from stocks ($S_1S_1'$), and the supply curve based on a variable
supply from current production out of a given productive apparatus.*

The point of intersection $T_2'$ of the long-period supply curve $S_2S_2'$
with the demand curve $D_1D_1'$ represents the long-period position of

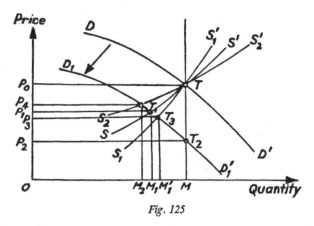

*Fig. 125*

equilibrium, i.e. at the price $p_4$, at which with complete adjustment of
productive capacity and equipment there will be agreement between
the dispositions of the suppliers and those of the demanders. As the
long-period supply curve, when $p > p_0$, is below the short-period
curve $SS'$, the long-period equilibrium price will necessarily be lower
than the short-period equilibrium price.

The same considerations apply for an increase in demand as for
a decrease in demand. In Fig. 125, $DD'$ represents the previous
demand curve and the point $T$ the previous long-period equilibrium.
If the demand now falls to $D_1D_1'$, the equilibrium price will fall to
$p_2$ if we assume that the previous current production of $OM$ per unit
of time is retained. If a part of the constant production per unit of
time is devoted to increasing stocks, so that the quantity devoted to
stocks increases as the price decreases, then the supply curve will in
the short run have the form $S_1S_1'$. It will diverge only slightly from
the line $TM$, as the suppliers will try to avoid a large accumulation of
stocks. The equilibrium price corresponding to this first short-
period reaction by the suppliers will be $p_3$. The fall in price causes the
suppliers to limit production from the existing plant. The quantities
supplied at different prices from current production from the existing
plant are given by the supply curve $SS'$. The equilibrium price

corresponding to this second short-period reaction of the supplier is $p_1$. It is lower than the original price $p_0$, but higher than $p_2$ or $p_3$ which results from the first short-period reaction. So long as the lower level demand continues, the equilibrium price $p_1$ does not represent a long-period equilibrium in the sense that none of the suppliers will have any further reason in the future to alter their dispositions. We know that in the long run the price for every supplier must be sufficiently high to cover all the costs including normal interest on capital invested. If the equilibrium price falls from $p_0$ to $p_1$, then there will be suppliers who are now not covering their total costs, and therefore will be closing down their plants and leaving that branch of production. With complete long-period adjustment to a price $p_1$, below the level of the original price $p_0$, the total quantity supplied will be smaller than that supplied from current production at the price $p_1$ with the productive capacity adjusted to the price $p_0$. The long-period supply curve has, therefore, for prices ranging from nil to $p_0$ the shape $S_2T$, so that the equilibrium price $p_4$, when the productive equipment has been adjusted in the long period, is higher than the price $p_1$ when there has only been short-period adjustment. *In general, the proposition holds that a rise (or fall) in demand has the tendency in the short period to bring about a larger change in price, and a smaller change in the quantity produced, than it does in the long period.*

3. Our argument has led us to distinguish between *three different sorts of supply curve:*

(a) *A short-period supply curve* which shows how a particular number of suppliers, with a given plant, change their dispositions in the short period when prices alter, when they have the possibility of adding to a constant output from current production by drawing on stocks, or by adding some of their current production to stocks.

(b) *A short-period supply curve* which shows how a particular number of suppliers, with a given plant, alter their supply in the short period in the face of price fluctuations, if their supply is always exactly to equal current production.

(c) *A long-period supply curve* which shows what quantities will be supplied at each particular price when there has been a complete adjustment of productive capacity and equipment, so that no existing supplier leaves that branch of production and no new supplier comes into it, and so that none of them have any reason for altering their productive equipment.

Of these three supply curves (b) and (c) are the most important, and generally when we speak of a short-period supply curve we mean curve (b).

We now want to consider more closely the interrelations between the long-period supply curve, given the technical "horizon" or the range of technical possibilities, and the theoretically infinitely large number of short-period supply curves of the type (b).

In Fig. 126 $S_L S_L'$ is the long-period supply curve for a particular good. At a price $p_1$, in the long run, after complete adjustment of

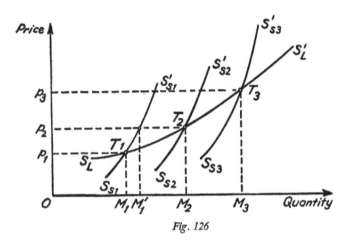

*Fig. 126*

supply to that price, the quantity $OM_1$ will be supplied. With short-period price changes the quantities supplied from current production, with productive equipment adjusted to a price of $p_1$, are given by the short-period supply curve $S_{S1} S_{S1}'$. This short-period supply curve is, as we have seen, steeper than the long-period supply curve. *The supply is, therefore, more elastic in the long period than in the short period.* As every point on the long-period supply curve corresponds to a particular scale of productive equipment adjusted to the particular prevailing price, a short-period supply curve runs through every point on the long-period supply curve. In Fig. 126 the short-period supply curves running through the points $T_1$, $T_2$ and $T_3$, on the long-period supply curve, are drawn in. When the suppliers have made their long-period adjustments to a change in price the short-period supply curve is correspondingly shifted.

4. This relationship between the long-period supply curve and the different short-period supply curves running through the various points on it is of fundamental importance for understanding the process by which supply is adjusted to changes in price.

Let us therefore carry a little further the reasoning that led to the concept of the long-period supply curve. In Fig. 127 the individual supply curves are represented by $F_1B_1$, $F_2B_2$, ... [1] The prices $p_1, p_2, \ldots$, corresponding to the points $F_1, F_2, \ldots$, mark the lower price limit in the long run, i.e. the price at which the firm concerned only just covers its costs including normal interest on invested capital.[2] If the firms aim at maximum profits then at the price $p_4$ firm 1 will supply the quantity $x_1 = OA_1$, firm 2 the quantity

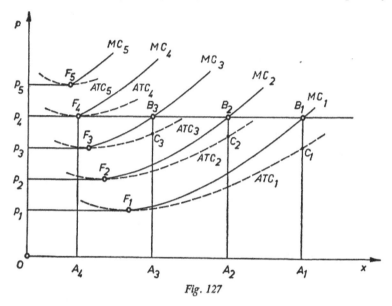

Fig. 127

$x_2 = OA_2$, firm 3 the quantity $x_3 = OA_3$ and firm 4 the quantity $x_4 = OA_4$. No supplies will be forthcoming from firm 5 nor from any other firm whose lower price limit is even higher. At the price $P_4$ firm 4 is therefore the marginal firm. Figure 127 shows not only the relevant portions of the marginal cost curves ($MC$) but also the average total cost curves ($ATC$) of the different firms from which one may straight away derive the profits which each firm obtains per unit of sales when the price is $p_4$: $B_1C_1$ for firm 1, $B_2C_2$ for firm 2, etc.

The total amount of a firm's profits at the price $p_4$ is found either as the product of profit per unit of sales and quantity supplied or else, directly from Fig. 127, as the difference between revenue and total costs. Thus, for instance, the revenue of firm 1 equals the area

---

[1] It is assumed that the marginal costs ($MC$) of the firms increase from a certain output onwards.

[2] Italian economic literature follows Amoroso in calling this the "escape price" (prezzo di fuga).

$Op_4B_1A_1$; the firm's total costs are given by the area $Op_1F_1B_1A_1$. It follows that the total profits of firm 1 are represented by the area $p_1p_4B_1F_1$. The profits of the other suppliers are found in a similar manner from Fig. 127.

The long period supply curve of the four suppliers, starting from $p = p_1$, is derived in the familiar manner by horizontal summation of the individual supply curves. We shall assume that equilibrium is reached with the price $p_4$ at which total supply ($= OA_1 + OA_2 + OA_3 + OA_4$) equals demand.

Now it is easily appreciated that this state of equilibrium cannot persist in the long run if there is unrestricted entry into this particular industry or, put in the language which was used earlier, if there is free competition and if newly arrived producers are also capable of producing the same good at the same costs as the first supplier. Given such circumstances, the new producers would eventually force the suppliers 2, 3 and 4 out of the market, thus causing the equilibrium price to fall finally to $p_1$, i.e. to what would now be the common lower price limit of all the suppliers. If the newly arrived suppliers had a lower price limit which was lower even than $p_1$ then the long period equilibrium price would be brought down to this lower limit through competition from the new suppliers. On the assumptions which were stated, free competition tends to remove profits that are greater than normal interest on invested capital and to reduce the price to the level of "costs".[1]

It follows from this reasoning that so long as supply can be expanded indefinitely under the same conditions of production it will in the long run be perfectly elastic with respect to price, this price being the lower price limit of the supplier who is most favourably placed as regards his costs.[2] Once production can be enlarged only through the entry of additional producers working at higher costs this perfect elasticity of the long period supply curve will disappear. In this case any supplier whose individual supply curve lies below that of the newly arrived suppliers will obtain profits above the normal interest on capital.[3]

5. The analysis we have carried out so far of changes in the position of equilibrium resulting from changes in demand has been exclusively of a comparative-static kind. All the relations which we

---

[1] This long period equilibrium price which results from the play of free competition was called by Adam Smith the "natural price".

[2] In Fig. 127 this is the price of supplier 1.

[3] The first to present a clear statement of these relations, with the aid of supply and demand curves, was H. v. Mangoldt in his *Grundriss der Volkswirthschaftslehre* (1863).

have used have been static relations: if the price in the coming period is $p_1$ instead of $p_2$ (Fig. 126), then in the same period there will be a short-period adjustment of the quantity supplied from $OM_1$ to $OM_1'$, and a long-period adjustment from $OM_1$ to the quantity $OM_2$, etc. We have started, therefore, from the assumption that the complete long-period adjustment to price changes takes place in one and the same period, or as the period can be indefinitely small that the reaction speed is infinitely great.

In the real world the transition from the position of long-term equilibrium $T$ (Fig. 124) to the new equilibrium position $T'$ (assuming that this is a stable position), does not, of course, take place with infinite rapidity. The short-period adjustment of supply will follow so rapidly on the change in demand that we can neglect the interval of time between the change in demand and the short-term supply reaction. But for the long-period adjustment of supply this assumption cannot be made. The alteration of the existing plant, the construction of new plant, or the closing down of old, requires time, so that a longer or shorter lag will occur, in accordance with the nature of the productive process, between the alteration in demand and the long-period adjustment of supply. The long-period supply curve must, therefore, be conceived as an essentially dynamic relationship if we are concerned to analyse realistically the course through time from one long-period equilibrium position to another: if *today* the price rises from $p_1$ to $p_2$, *tomorrow*, after a complete adjustment of the productive capacity to the new position, the quantity $OM_2$ will be supplied. We must now turn to this dynamic analysis of the process of transition from one long-period equilibrium position to another following a permanent shift in demand. The problem is known as the Cobweb Problem.

*c. The Cobweb Problem*

1. Let us start our argument with the following assumptions:
(a) Demand reacts immediately, i.e. in the same period, to price changes: if *today* the price is $p_1$, then *today* the quantity $x_1$ is demanded; if, on the other hand, *today* the price is $p_2$, then *today* the quantity $x_2$ will be demanded, etc. Let the demand in the period from $t$ to $t + 1$ be $D$, the price $p$, then the relation between price and demand will be a static one:

$$D_t = f(p_t). \tag{13}$$

(b) *Short-period reactions of supply to price changes are immediate, but long-period reactions follow with a lag* of one period, e.g. a year. If, then, the price *today* is $p_1$, *tomorrow* the quantity $x_1$ will be supplied and if, on the other hand, the price *today* is $p_2$, *tomorrow* the quantity $x_2$ will be supplied, etc. This assumption is based on the expectation of the supplier that today's price will also hold tomorrow. We can express this also in the following way: the supplier starts *today* an adjustment of the productive equipment to be used *tomorrow*, on the basis of the price expected to hold *tomorrow*. He reckons that the price tomorrow will be the same as the price today. If we describe the price expected tomorrow as $p_{t+1}^*$, and the quantity to be supplied tomorrow after the productive equipment has been readjusted as $s_{t+1}$, then the following relation holds for tomorrow's supply:

$$s_{t+1} = g(p_{t+1}^*). \tag{14}$$

If we now make the assumption that the price expected for tomorrow is the same as the price ruling today $p_t$:

$$p_{t+1}^* = p_t \tag{15}$$

then (14) becomes:

$$s_{t+1} = g(p_t) \tag{16}$$

It should be noticed that the supply relation as written in (14) is purely static. The variables in it relate to one and the same period. We have here an example which shows that the introduction of expected quantities does not of itself produce a dynamic functional relationship between economic variables. The long-period supply relation only becomes dynamic when we introduce in (14) the assumption (15). Only then does one obtain a relationship which links up quantities relating to different points of time, The relationship (16) must, therefore, be interpreted in the following way: *if today the price is $p_t$, and it is expected that this price will also hold tomorrow, then a process of production will be introduced today which will result tomorrow in a supply of $s_{t+1}$.* Relationships of this kind are always involved where there is a lag between the introduction of a process of production and the appearance on the market of the products ready for sale. A coffee tree planted today only yields its products after five years. The planter, therefore, must already, at the point of time when he starts production, have an idea of the price expected to rule five years later. He may start from the assumption which we are making here that the price ruling today will also be that ruling in the future. He therefore shapes his long-term production plans according to the price ruling today.

(c) For simplicity we will make the further assumption that supply in the short period is completely inelastic. This assumption does not prejudice in any way the general validity of our argument.

2. The two relations (13) and (16), of which (13) is static and (16)

dynamic, make it possible for us to describe the path of the transition from one long-period position of equilibrium to another. They make it possible for us to say how one position emerges out of the position immediately preceding it. In Fig. 128, $S_L S_L'$ is the long-period supply curve, $DD'$ the original demand curve, and $T$ the long-period equilibrium position corresponding to these demand and supply

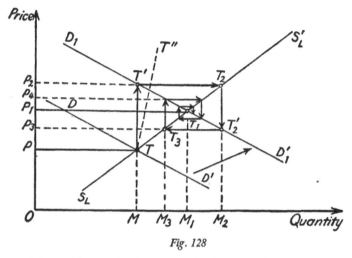

*Fig. 128*

conditions. The equilibrium price is then $p$. There now occurs an increase in demand, i.e. a shift in demand from $DD'$ to $D_1D_1'$, which is to be permanent. Employing a comparative-static analysis the new conditions of demand may be shown to give a long-period equilibrium position of $T_1$ where the demand curve $D_1D_1'$ intersects the supply curve $S_L S_L'$. The new long-period equilibrium price is, therefore, $p_1$. We now want to show, under the above assumptions, how the transition from $T$ to $T_1$ takes place through time. On our assumption that the supply in the short period is completely inelastic, the price directly after the increase in demand will rise to $p_2$. The point $T'$ represents the immediately resulting short-period equilibrium position. The suppliers produce from the existing plants as before the quantity $OM$, which is now bought by the demanders at the higher price $p_2$. If we had not made the assumption of the complete inelasticity of the short-period supply, then instead of the short-period supply curve $TT'$ there would be the curve $TT''$, with which we have previously been working in our static analysis (Fig. 128). The short-period equilibrium price would then be somewhat below $p_2$. The higher price $p_2$ would cause the suppliers, expecting that this price would also hold good in the future, to introduce at once a complete adjustment of their productive equipment to this price $p_2$. But on our assumption this long-period adjustment is only completed after one year, so that in the second year the quantity $OM_2$ is produced per unit of time at a price $p_2$. The demanders,

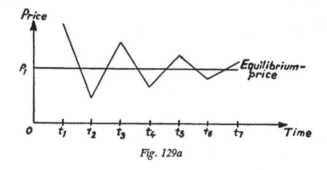

Fig. 129a

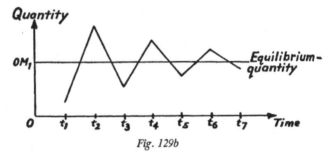

Fig. 129b

however, are only prepared to take this quantity at the lower price $p_3$. The price $p_2$ cannot, therefore, be maintained. It will immediately be reduced to $p_3$. At this lower price the suppliers, expecting that this price will also hold good in the future, will make a long-period adjustment in their equipment to the price $p_3$. After this adjustment has been completed the quantity $OM_3$ will be supplied at the price $p_3$. This quantity, however, will be bought by the demanders at the higher price of $p_4$, so that in the short period the price rises from $p_3$ to $p_4$. This process is repeated from period to period. From Fig. 128 it is clear that the series of prices and quantities converge through time on the new equilibrium position. A long-period stable equilibrium position is only reached when the quantity $OM_1$ is supplied at a price $p_1$. At this price neither of the parties has reason to alter its dispositions. The development of the prices and quantities supplied through time, from the long-period equilibrium position $T_1$, to the new long-period equilibrium position $T_2$, is shown in Fig. 129. It is represented by a fluctuating movement around the new equilibrium price and the new equilibrium quantity, the fluctuations being of gradually decreasing amplitude. Price and quantity are negatively correlated.

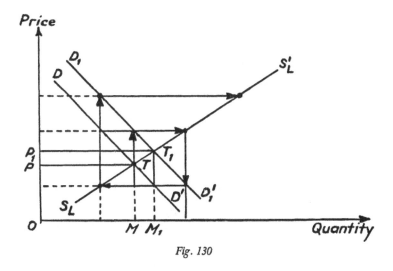

*Fig. 130*

The convergence of the prices and quantities on the equilibrium level occurs, as can easily be seen, only if the slope of the supply curve in relation to the quantity axis is steeper than that of the demand curve. If the slope of the supply curve is less steep than that of the demand curve (Fig. 130), then the amplitude of the fluctuations of price and quantity around the new equilibrium position $T_1$ will steadily increase. The adjustments of the suppliers to the ruling price will lead further and further away from the equilibrium position. The system "explodes". *The new equilibrium position is, therefore, unstable.* A continuous development of this kind is obviously impossible, because the price or quantity would in due course take on negative values. Sooner or later, therefore, there must be a change in the conditions determining this process. If the slope of the supply curve is equal to the slope of the demand curve (Fig. 130a), then the prices and quantities will move in a circle with fluctuations of a constant amplitude around the equilibrium price $T_1$. In this case, also, the equilibrium price $T_1$ will never be reached. *The new equilibrium position is again an unstable one.*

If, in the three cases we have dealt with, there had been an immediate adjustment of the plant following the change in demand, then
the new equilibrium position would have been reached in a single
period. The dispositions of the suppliers and demanders would then
have been in harmony. The equilibrium position would, however,
only have been stable in the first case. In both the other cases the

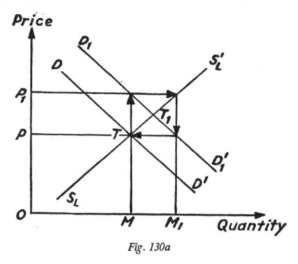

*Fig. 130a*

equilibrium position is unstable. A move away from the equilibrium
position is not followed by a move back.

3. An important objection can be made to the assumptions of the
cobweb theorem with which we shall be concerned later when
dealing with the dynamic aspects of price formation, and the important part played by expectations (see para. 6 of this section). We
assumed that the suppliers start from the expectation that today's
price will also hold good tomorrow, and that production for tomorrow is governed by the price ruling today. As our argument has
shown, experience should tell the suppliers, after only a single period,
that their price expectations were incorrect. It would then be reasonable to make the assumption that the suppliers, learning from
experience, would make their dispositions for the following periods
on the expectation of *price changes*. If they did this, and reckoned
that the expansion or contraction of their production undertaken
*today*, would lead to a fall in price or a rise in price tomorrow, then
the process would develop completely differently, and, in particular,
would show much less pronounced fluctuations around the equilibrium position. For the cobweb mechanism to work it is not

necessary to assume that the suppliers expect the price ruling today to hold good in the future. Our argument is also valid if the suppliers reckon that an expansion (or contraction) of production resulting from a higher (or lower) price *today*, will lead to a lower (or higher) price *tomorrow* (compared with today's price).[1] But in the cobweb problem it is nevertheless assumed in the analysis of the later periods of the process that the suppliers continue to act on the assumption given in (15). In other words it is assumed that the suppliers do not learn from experience. Behaviour of this kind by the suppliers cannot be dismissed as improbable *a priori*. Empirical studies have shown that American producers of potatoes, corn, and coal did behave approximately in this way.[2]

4. The classical example which can in essentials be explained with the aid of the cobweb mechanism is the pig cycle, described by Hanau for the period before 1914.[3] Hanau showed how the suppliers of fat pigs react with a lag of 14 or 15 months to changes in the price relationships between pork and pig fodder, and that a movement in prices and quantities corresponding with those of the cobweb mechanism takes place. Of course, a detailed explanation of the movement of pig prices must also take account of other factors. But the essential forces determining the movement can be explained by the cobweb theorem. Movements of the same kind can also be found for all productive processes with a long production period.

The assumptions which underline the cobweb mechanism can, of course, be invalidated by state action. By a suitable price policy, as can be seen from the diagrams in our example, it can be ensured that adjustments to changes in demand take place without such fluctuations.

### 3. The Equilibrium Price of a Good Available from Given and Unchanging Stocks

1. Let us imagine an economy in which a thousand copies of a particular book exist, distributed one each among a thousand individuals. In each period, let us say in each day, there is a particular demand for this book. Each of the demanders interested in the book

---

[1] The assumption (15) is then replaced by the assumption $p^{*}_{t+1} = p_t \pm \delta$ where $\delta$ is the expected divergence from today's price.
[2] H. Schultz: *The Theory and Measurement of Demand*, New York, 1938, p. 78.
[3] A. Hanau: *Die Prognose der Schweinepreise*, Berlin, 1930 (Sonderheft 18 der Vierteljahrshefte zur Konjunkturforschung). Also, E. Wagemann: *Konjunkturlehre*, Berlin, 1928, p. 123; Coase and Fowler: "Bacon Production and the Pig Cycle in Great Britain" in *Economica*, 1935, pp. 142 ff.

has a *subjective maximum price*. If the actual price is above his subjective maximum price, then his demand is ineffective. We can rank the demanders in order of their maximum prices, beginning with the demander whose maximum price is highest. The table might look somewhat as follows:

| Demander | Max. Price |
|---|---|
| I | 400 |
| II | 380 |
| III & IV | 350 |
| V, VI & VII | 320 |
| VIII | 300 |
| IX & X | 270 |
| XI, XII, XIII & XIV | 250 |
| XV | 210 |
| etc. | |

From this table of maximum prices one can draw up the demand schedule for the particular day, and the demand curve corresponding to it which shows how many copies will be demanded on this day at each of the prices from nil to 400 (see the adjoining table and Fig. 131):

| Price | Total Demand |
|---|---|
| 400 | 1 |
| 380 | 2 |
| 350 | 4 |
| 320 | 7 |
| 300 | 8 |
| 270 | 10 |
| 250 | 14 |
| 210 | 15 |

If we suppose that each price between 0 and 400 is the maximum price for one or other of the demanders, we obtain a continuous demand curve representing the state of demand on that day.

For each of those who already possess a copy of the book, there is on each day a *subjective minimum price* below which they are not ready to sell their copy of the book. For a possessor of a copy who is not ready at any price to sell his copy this minimum price is infinitely high. Just as we arranged the demanders in accordance with their maximum prices, we can now arrange the possessors of the book in the order of their subjective minimum prices at which they will sell

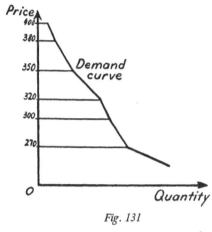

Fig. 131

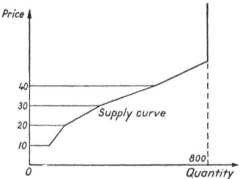

Fig. 132

their copy, starting from the one who has the lowest minimum price.
The table might look as follows:

| Minimum Price | Possessor |
|---|---|
| 10 | 1 |
| 20 | 2 |
| 30 | 3 & 4 |
| 40 | 5, 6 & 7 |
| 50 | 8 |
| 60 | 9 & 10 |
| . | . |
| . | . |
| . | . |
| ∞ | 800–1,000 |

K

From this table of minimum prices we can draw up a supply schedule for the day and the supply curve corresponding to it (Fig. 132). If we suppose that each price between 0 and infinity is the minimum price for one or other of the possessors, we obtain a continuous supply curve representing the state of supply on that day.

Let us bring together the demand curve and the corresponding

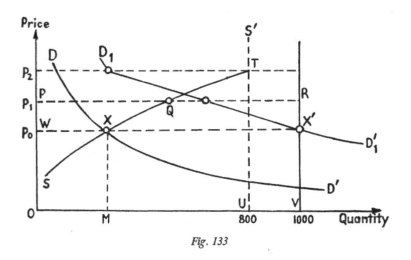

*Fig. 133*

supply curve (Fig. 133), and we can see that one and only one price $p_0$ exists at which the dispositions of the suppliers and of the demanders are in harmony and at which equilibrium will obtain on that day. On that day $OM$ copies of the book will be exchanged at a price $p_0$.

2. The equilibrium position can also be discovered in a different way, which enables us to treat the problem of the movement of the equilibrium position in the face of changes in demand and supply, particularly simply and clearly. A glance at Fig 133 shows that at a price of $p_1$ the quantity $QR$ of the existing stock will not be offered for sale by its possessors. This means that the possessors who are not ready to offer their copies for sale have a minimum price higher than the price $p_1$. In other words, at the price $p_1$ the quantity $QR$ is demanded by its present possessors. The horizontal distance between the supply curve and the vertical $VR$, which tells us the existing stock, can be interpreted as the demand of the present possessors for their own copies at the existing price. It represents, we may say, the *reserve demand* at the relevant prices, while the curve $DD'$ gives us the

demand of those who do not possess a copy of the book. Fig. 133 shows that the reserve demand remains constant as the price falls as far as $p_2$, and from that point onwards exactly increases with the new demand. If we add the *new demand* and the *reserve demand* at each price we obtain the curve $D_1D_1'$. This represents the *total demand* (*new demand* plus *reserve demand*) at each price. This total demand must obviously cut the vertical $VR$ at the point $X'$ corresponding to the equilibrium price $p_0$. By using the total demand curve $D_1D_1'$ we obtain the equilibrium price as given by the point of intersection of this curve with the vertical $VR$ representing the total existing stock. *The equilibrium price is then that price at which the sum of new demand and reserve demand is equal to the existing stock.* The distance $WX$ tells us the part of the existing stock which changes hands, while the distance $XX'$ represents that part of the stock which remains in the hands of its previous possessors.

*This method of presentation has a great advantage in that one obtains the equilibrium price simply by means of a single demand curve, which is made up of the curve of new demand and that of reserve, demand added together.* The supply curve $SS'$ is now replaced by the reserve demand curve which appears as a *reversed supply curve* (as Wicksteed called it). The advantage in this procedure will be clear if we inquire by means of a comparative-static analysis what influence changes in demand and supply have on the equilibrium price. *Changes in demand and in supply will then be expressed on one and the same curve, the total demand curve $D_1D_1'$.* If, for example, from one day to the next, there is an *increased "preference"* for the book, then the curve of new demand $DD'$ will rise and the supply curve $SS'$ will fall. The curve $DD'$ will, therefore, move to the right, and the curve $SS'$ to the left. By using the total demand curve (new demand plus reserve demand) this fact can simply be expressed by a shift in the total demand curve $D_1D_1'$ to the right. A generally increasing preference for the book, if the stock remains the same, will bring about a rise in the equilibrium price. Alternatively, a generally decreasing preference for the book will bring about a shift in the total demand curve $D_1D_1'$ to the left, and, with the stock remaining constant, a fall in the equilibrium price. By splitting up the total demand curve into the curve of new demand and the curve of reserve demand we can see at once what quantities will change hands at the new equilibrium price and what quantities will remain in the hands of their previous owners.

The use of the total demand curve as the sum of new demand and reserve demand enables us at once to discover what measures must be taken in order to prevent a rise in the equilibrium price following a general rise in preference for the book. From Fig. 134 it is clear that if the preference for the book increases there will be a rise in the equilibrium price, unless the existing stock $OV$ is increased at least by the quantity $VV'$. It is clear, further, that if preference for the book remains unchanged, and, therefore, the total demand curve

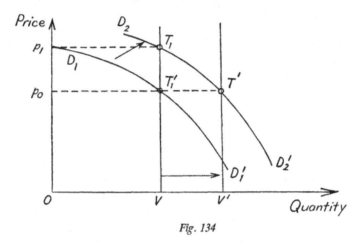

Fig. 134

remains unchanged, a larger stock can only be sold at a lower equilibrium price.

### 4. The Liquidity Theory of Interest as a Partial Equilibrium Theory

1. The relationships discussed in para. 3 are of fundamental importance in the formation of prices on stock exchanges and may be applied in the analysis of the formation of interest rates. Let us assume that there exists in an economy a total of a thousand fixed-interest-bearing bonds of equal nominal value, say government stock. Purchases and sales are only possible at a single stock-market. The demand and supply conditions existing on a particular day can be represented by a single demand curve $D_1D_1'$ (Fig. 134), which is composed by adding the curve of new demand to the curve of reserve demand. With the existing stock $OV$, the day's price will be $p_0$. This price is such that after exchange has taken place no holder of bonds will wish to sell them and no holder of money will wish to buy bonds. With a given nominal rate of interest for the bonds the level of the daily price determines the *effective rate of interest* (the yield) on the bonds; and this effective rate of interest or yield is higher (or lower), the lower (or higher) the day's price. *We can, therefore, also say that*

*the preference on a particular day for the bonds determines the effective rate of interest, or the long-term rate of interest.* If the preference for the bonds now increases, while the behaviour of the central bank remains unchanged, then the price of the bonds must rise, and the effective rate of interest fall. But a fall in the effective rate of interest, if it is permanent, influences certain of the investment decisions of the entrepreneurs (building activity). If the central bank wishes to bring about a decrease in investment activity, then it must make impossible a rise in the price of bonds. It can do this by neutralizing the rise in the public's and the banks' preferences for the bonds by increasing the quantities supplied at the existing prices. The central bank, therefore, has the power by means of a suitable purchasing or selling policy in respect of bonds, to enforce the long-term rate of interest it regards as desirable provided, of course, that it disposes of sufficient quantities of bonds. This sort of policy on the part of the central bank for influencing the level of the long-term rate of interest is known as *open market policy.* By means of the analysis we used in our example of the stock of books, we can see that if the preference for the bonds remains unchanged, though the central bank is in a position to increase their stock, a greater quantity will only be taken up by the public at a higher effective rate of interest.

Let us assume, for the purposes of a static treatment, that the total demand for a particular bond depends not only on the level of the rate of interest on this bond, but (*ceteris paribus*) also on the level of interest rates for all other kinds of interest-bearing claims: then the structure of the rates of interest obtaining on a particular day is given by a number of simultaneous equations of the following kind:

$$n_1(i_1, i_2, \ldots, i_k) = b_1$$
$$n_2(i_1, i_2, \ldots, i_k) = b_2$$
$$\ldots\ldots\ldots\ldots\ldots\ldots$$
$$n_k(i_1, i_2, \ldots, i_k) = b_k$$

where $n_1, n_2, \ldots, n_k$ are the total demand for the kinds of claims $1, 2, \ldots, k$ while $i_1, i_2, \ldots, i_k$ are the rates of interest, and $b_1, b_2, \ldots, b_k$ are the existing stocks of these types of interest-bearing claims, $1, 2, \ldots, k$. It follows that Fig. 134, which refers to the market for one type of claim only, presents only a partial description which assumes that rates of interest for all other types of claims are constant.

2. We now have to make an assumption that simplifies our arrival at a number of fundamental theoretical conclusions: that there is only a single rate of interest in the economy, and therefore that there is only a single kind of fixed-interest-bearing claim. The supply

curve of the claim, $SS'$ (Fig. 135), corresponds to a demand curve for cash. At the price $p$ ($= OB$) the amount of money demanded will be given by the area of the rectangle $OBCD$. It is clear that the demand for money increases as the price of the claim increases, or as the effective rate of interest falls. The demand curve for money, that is,

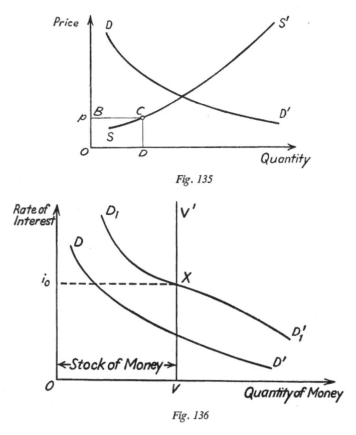

*Fig. 135*

*Fig. 136*

the curve which shows how the demand for money varies with the rate of interest, has the usual form $DD'$ (Fig. 136). Correspondingly, from the demand curve for claims $DD'$ (Fig. 135) the supply curve for money or cash can be derived, having the form shown in Fig. 137. If $OV$ is the quantity of money in the economy (central bank money plus current bank deposits), then, at a rate of interest $i$, the reserve demand for money is given by the distance $FG$. If one adds the new demand to the reserve demand for money at each rate of interest, then the total demand curve $D_1 D_1'$ will have the form shown in Fig. 136. The curve $D_1 D_1'$ represents the *liquidity preference* on the day concerned, i.e., the preference of economic individuals (excluding the central bank) for cash. The existing liquidity preference, and the stock of money existing in the economy on this day, give the corresponding equilibrium rate of interest, which, from our previous analysis, will be represented by the point of intersection $X$ of the line

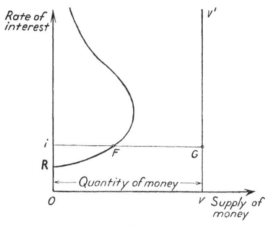

*Fig. 137*

$VV'$ (which denotes the total existing stock), with the total demand curve $D_1 D_1'$. On the assumption that there is in the economy only a single kind of fixed-interest-bearing bond, and therefore only a single rate of interest, we can reach the following conclusions:

(a) *The rate of interest on a particular day will be determined by the liquidity preference and the existing stock of money.*

(b) *If the quantity of money is constant, the rate of interest will rise if liquidity preference rises.*

(c) *With a given liquidity preference a larger quantity of money will correspond to a lower rate of interest.*

These propositions give the content of the *Keynesian liquidity theory of interest. Our treatment shows that it is simply another way of expressing the proposition that the supply and demand for claims, i.e. the supply and demand for credit, determine the level of the rate of interest.*

This account, however, makes it clear that the Keynesian formulation of the determinants of interest is only applicable if one starts by assuming that only a single rate of interest exists in the economy.

*If one wishes to explain the different levels of different rates of interest, then one must go back to the demand and supply conditions for the separate kinds of claims and to the preferences for these different kinds.*

### 5. The Problem of Equilibrium under a Supply Monopoly

1. If the supplier of a particular good in drawing up his economic plan assumes that his sales depend only on his own price (more generally, on his own action-parameters), and on the behaviour of

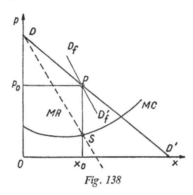

*Fig. 138*

$DD'$—*expected price–sales curve.*
$D_fD_f'$—*actual (or factual) price–sales curve.*

the buyers, that is, if he assumes that the prices (or the action-parameters) of the suppliers of other goods have no influence on the level of his sales, then we say that the supplier is acting as a monopolist (see Chapter II, Section A, para. 2). In Chapter II (Section D(i), 2) it was shown how a supplier acting as a monopolist, assuming that he is aiming at maximum profit, discovers what is the price–quantity combination most favourable for him. We found that a supplier faced by an expected price–sales function will choose that price–quantity combination for which marginal revenue and marginal cost are equal (the Cournot point). If the price–sales curve and the marginal cost curve are of the form shown in Fig. 138, then the supplier will offer in the period for which he is planning a quantity $x_0$ at a price $p_0$.

2. Now the price–sales curve, as well as the marginal cost curve, is *conjectural* or "expected". This conjectural element is of particular importance in the price–sales curve. The quantities which the supplier in making his plans assumes that he will sell at alternative prices are *estimated* quantities. They represent the sales which the supplier

believes he can most probably sell at alternative prices. But the determination of the quantity which will actually be sold at a particular price in any period of time is in the hands of the buyers. The actual price–sales function will in general diverge from the expected price–sales function on which the supplier's dispositions in the period concerned are based. The supplier, usually, will be "surprised" at the end of a period, and will be moved to revise his

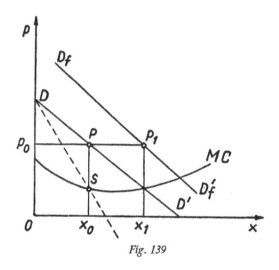

Fig. 139

calculations. This process of revision must now be studied more closely. We shall assume that the supplier has no reason for revising his marginal cost plan.

Case 1: The supplier ascertains at the end of a period that at the price $p_0$, expected sales were equal to actual realized sales. This fact does not, of course, necessarily mean that the expected price–sales curve, or that part of the curve which the supplier was considering, was identical with the actual price–sales curve. The actual price–sales curve could, for example, be of the form of $D_f D_f'$ in Fig. 138. Nevertheless, the agreement between expected and actual sales at the price $p_0$ may cause the supplier to believe that his estimate of the price–sales curve corresponds with the facts, so that in so far as no other factors cause him to draw up new plans, he will continue in the next period to offer the quantity $x_0$ at a price $p_0$.

Case 2: The supplier ascertains at the end of a period that at a price $p_0$ expected sales are smaller than the actual sales $x_1$ (Fig. 139). He knows now that the actual price–sales curve diverged from the expected price–sales curve in the previous period, and on the basis of the actual realized price–quantity combination will carry out a revision of his plans. The planning of prices and sales in one period

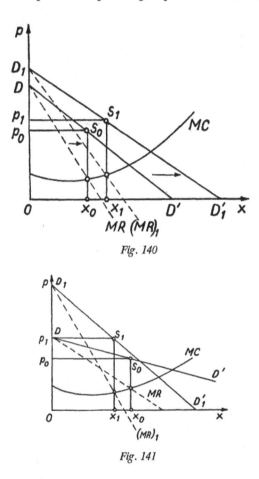

Fig. 140

Fig. 141

follows always on the actual price–sales combination of the previous period (following the principle of "price continuity", as it was called by von Zwiedineck-Südenhorst). As the whole price–sales curve is never actually included in his plans, but always only a particular section of it in the neighbourhood of the previous price, the supplier will consider how a small variation from the previous price, taking account of the new situation, will influence his profit. This revision, in the case where the actual sales were larger than those expected, may lead to the following results:

(a) The supplier may offer a larger quantity at a higher price (Fig. 140).

(b) The supplier may offer a smaller quantity at a higher price (Fig. 141).

(c) The supplier may offer a larger quantity at a lower price (Fig. 142).

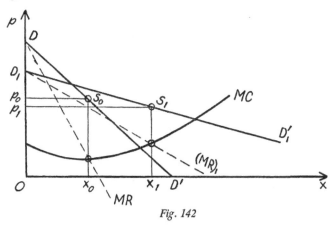

*Fig. 142*

Corresponding propositions may be deduced for the case where actual sales were smaller than expected sales.

It is also possible[1] that the surprise at the end of the period in the shape of a divergence between actual and expected sales only leads to a change in the quantity supplied and not to a change in price. We have shown above (page 113) that it holds for the price–quantity combination at the Cournot point that:

$$\text{Price} - \text{Marginal Cost} = -\frac{\text{Price}}{\text{Elasticity of Sales}}$$

or, in other words:

$$\text{Price} = \text{Marginal Cost} \cdot \frac{\text{Elasticity of Sales}}{\text{Elasticity of Sales} + 1}$$

If the marginal costs to the supplier are constant (and this assumption would often hold of a range of outputs in the neighbourhood of full capacity of the plant), and if the supplier assumes that the elasticity of his sales in relation to the price is the same, at the existing price,

[1] See Harald Dickson and A. Östlind: "Prisstabiliserande Egenskaper hos en Säljares Efterfrågaföreställningar" in *Ekonomisk Tidsskrift*, 1943, pp. 238 ff.

for the new price–sales curve, then it follows from the above relation that it is most profitable for the supplier to retain the previous price in the coming period, and only to alter the quantity supplied. The assumption about the constancy of the elasticity of sales at the existing price even where there are divergencies between actual and expected sales may well be realistic in many cases. If, at a price of 50, instead of the expected 1000 units, 1200 units were sold, and if the supplier reckons that a reduction in price from 50 to 48 will increase the sales by 10%, and that an increase in price from 50 to 52 will diminish sales by 10%, then it can scarcely be assumed that the fact of a divergence of the actual from the expected sales will change his estimate of the elasticity of sales at the price 50. With constant marginal costs the price 50 will remain the most profitable in the coming period. We have here a possible explanation for the often-observed phenomenon of the rigidity of prices under a supply monopoly.

### 6. The Problem of Equilibrium under Heterogeneous Competition between Two Suppliers

1. Let us consider two suppliers of whom No. 1 supplies a good $A$ and No. 2 supplies good $B$, and who are faced by a number of buyers acting as quantity-adjusters. The suppliers name their price and the buyers decide the quantities they want to buy at that price. Both goods are assumed to be "substitute" or competing goods. It is also assumed that heterogeneous competition exists between the suppliers and that each supplier in drawing up his economic plan reckons with the competition only of the other. This assumption amounts to saying that the buyers are not indifferent between the two suppliers, so that each supplier in planning his prices and sales reckons that his sales depend both on his own price and on the price of his competitor. It is finally assumed that neither of the suppliers engages in an active sales policy. The sole action-parameter of each supplier is his selling price.

Let the sales obtainable in the planning period by the two suppliers be $x_1$ and $x_2$, and the prices they fix $p_1$ and $p_2$, so that there will exist for each supplier a particular relation between his sales, the level of his own price, and the level of the price of his competitor:

$$\text{(a)} \quad x_1 = f_1(p_1, p_2)$$
$$\text{(b)} \quad x_2 = f_2(p_1, p_2) \tag{17}$$

These two price–sales functions are conjectural or expected, that is to say, the first supplier *believes* that in the planning period he can sell the quantity $x_1$ if he fixes his own price at $p_1$ and his competitor fixes his price at $p_2$. In order not to complicate our problem unduly we may assume that the quantity which it is estimated will be sold at a combination of prices $p_1$ and $p_2$ actually corresponds with the realized sales at these prices. The essential characteristics of the equilibrium problem under heterogeneous competition are not affected by this simplification.

The total costs corresponding to any particular level of output are given by the two functions:

$$C_1 = \phi_1(x_1)$$
$$C_2 = \phi_2(x_2)$$

(18)

If the prices of the two suppliers in the planning period are given, then it is possible to calculate from (17) and (18) the profit that each supplier will obtain. It can be seen at once that the profits of each supplier in the period depend on the level of his own price and level of the price of his competitor. If we call the two profits $G_1$ and $G_2$, then:

$$G_1 = G_1(p_1, p_2)$$
$$G_2 = G_2(p_1, p_2)$$

(19)

We must understand fully the significance of these two functions. They tell us that if the first supplier in the period under consideration fixes his price at $p_1$, and the second supplier fixes his price at $p_2$, the first supplier will make a profit of $G_1$ and the second supplier of $G_2$. But each supplier at the moment of planning can only fix his own price. The fixing of the other price is in the hands of the competitor. If, therefore, the supplier at a particular moment is considering whether a change in his price is profitable for him, he has to formulate an idea as to the expected behaviour of his competitor. His profit depends *both* on $p_1$ and on $p_2$. He can, therefore, only make his calculations if he takes account of the expected reaction of his competitor to the intended price change. The assumptions of each supplier about the expected behaviour of his competitor belong to the *data* of the problem. They must be regarded as independent data like the price–sales function (17) and the cost function (18). *It is this fact, that the profit of each supplier depends on both prices and, therefore, that an intended change in price must be based on an assumption about the competitor's expected behaviour, which is at the root of the essential difficulties of the problem of price formation under heterogeneous competition between suppliers.*

2. We shall now show how the solution of the equilibrium problem

under heterogeneous competition between suppliers is arrived at under particular assumptions about the behaviour of the two competitors. Let us start first from the assumption that each supplier acts as a *polypolist*. In making his economic plan he takes the price of his competitor as given. Our question then must be: *how are the equilibrium prices and quantities determined, with given price–sales functions and cost functions, under the assumption that each supplier is aiming at the maximum profit in the planning period, and is acting as a polypolist*? In other words, what will the prices and quantities be, under these assumptions, if there is to be harmony between the economic plans of the two suppliers?

Let us first treat the problem statically. If the price of the second supplier is given, then the first supplier can tell on the basis of (17) what quantities he can sell at alternative levels of his own price. The nature of this sort of price–sales relationship between his own price and his sales depends, of course, on the level of his competitor's price. The higher the price of the second supplier the greater will be the sales of the first supplier, at any particular price. To each given price of the second supplier there will correspond a particular relationship between prices and sales for the first supplier. If, for example, the function (17a) has the form previously adopted (page 52):

$$x_1 = 10 - 2p_1 + \tfrac{1}{2}p_2$$

then, for different alternative levels of $p_2$ the following are the price–sales functions of the first supplier:

$$\begin{array}{ll} \text{for } p_2 = 0 & x_1 = 10 - 2p_1 \\ \text{for } p_2 = 2 & x_1 = 11 - 2p_1 \\ \text{for } p_2 = 4 & x_1 = 12 - 2p_1 \\ & \text{etc.} \end{array}$$

In this example the various demand functions of the first supplier are represented by the series of parallels in Fig. 143. The distance of the demand curve from the origin is the greater the higher the price $p_2$ of the competitor's good.

At a given level of the price $p_2$ the first supplier is now in a position to work out the price most favourable for him, and the quantity corresponding to it. We know that this most profitable price–quantity combination (the Cournot point) is given by the condition that marginal revenue = marginal costs. In Fig. 143 it has been assumed for simplicity that marginal costs are constant. At a price $p_2 = 0$, the price $p_1'$ will be the most favourable price for the first supplier. Correspondingly, there results, for every other level of the price $p_2$, a price most profitable for the first supplier. For $p_2 = 2$, for example, $p_1''$ will be the most favourable price for the first supplier, and so on. The Cournot points corresponding to each particular price of the second supplier are $C_1$, $C_2$, $C_3$, $C_4$, etc.

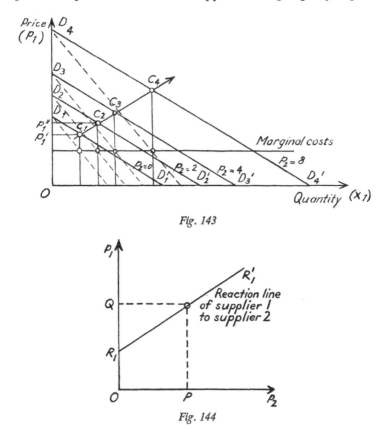

Fig. 143

Fig. 144

(Fig. 143). We can now, for each given price of the second supplier, give the most profitable price for the first supplier. From Fig. 143 it is clear that the most profitable price for the first supplier will be higher, the higher the price of the second supplier. In Fig. 144 this relation, between the price of the second supplier and the corresponding most profitable price for the first supplier, is represented diagrammatically by the straight line $R_1 R_1'$. This line may be called the *reaction line* of the first supplier, and it is important to understand what this line signifies. It tells us what price is most favourable to the first supplier when the second supplier adopts a particular price. If the second supplier fixes his price at $OP$ (Fig. 144) and the first supplier, in making his price–sales plan, reckons that the second supplier will still hold to this price if he (the first supplier) alters his

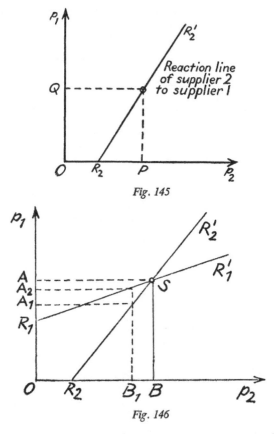

Fig. 145

Fig. 146

own price $p_1$, then for the first supplier the most profitable price to fix is $OQ$. The line $R_1R_1'$ shows how the first supplier when making his plans reacts to a given price on the part of the second supplier.

Exactly the same analysis can be carried out for the second supplier. We only need to substitute $p_2$ for $p_1$ and $x_2$ for $x_1$. Similarly for the second supplier there will be a reaction line $R_2R_2'$ which will give the most favourable price for the second supplier, given the price of the first supplier (Fig. 145). If, for example, $OQ$ is the price of the first supplier, and if the second supplier reckons that his competitor will retain this price if he (the second supplier) alters his price, then $OP$ is the most favourable price for the second supplier. Let us now draw the reaction lines of the two suppliers on the same diagram, and let us assume that they are of the shape represented in Fig. 146, then it can be seen at once that equilibrium only obtains at the point $S$ where the two reaction lines intersect, and with the price combination given by that point. If they act as polypolists, it is only when the first supplier fixes his price at $OA$ and the second at $OB$ that the economic plans of the two suppliers will be in harmony so that neither of them has reason to alter his price. If, for example, the first supplier fixes his price at $OA_1$, it is easy to see that this price is not an equilibrium price. At a price of $OA_1$ for the first supplier it would be most profitable for the second supplier to fix a price of $OB_1$. At a price of $OB_1$ on the part of the second supplier it would be profitable for the first supplier to raise his price from $OA_1$ to $OA_2$, which in turn would cause the second supplier to alter his price in accordance with his reaction line, and so on.

Whether there is an equilibrium depends on the shape of the price–sales functions (17) and the cost functions (18). Demand and cost functions are conceivable which would result in reaction lines that did not intersect, so that no equilibrium position could exist. But we do not wish here to enter further into this problem.

The determination of the equilibrium position in the case of polypolistic behaviour on the part of two competitors competing heterogeneously was first propounded by Launhardt, and was later carried further by Hotelling. The problem which we have just treated may, therefore, be described as the Launhardt-Hotelling problem.[1]

The derivation of the reaction lines of the two suppliers, which make it possible to discover the equilibrium position, may be carried out in another way which we may briefly indicate here. As was shown above, the profit of each supplier depends on the prices of the two suppliers [relation (19)]. We could now ask what are all the possible combinations of prices with which a supplier would obtain the same profit. The totality of all these combinations of prices lies in a diagram having the two prices as axes on curves which we may call the *isoprofit curves*. For each level of profit there will be an isoprofit curve of this kind. It can be shown mathematically that this isoprofit curve for the second supplier, given the demand and cost

[1] W. Launhardt, *Mathematische Begründung der Volkswirthschaftslehre*, Leipzig, 1885, pp. 161–163. And: H. Hotelling, "Stability in Competition," *Economic Journal*, vol. 39 (1929), pp. 41 *et seq.*

functions, will have the shape portrayed in Fig. 147. If now the first supplier fixes a price $OA_2$, and the second supplier reckons that the first supplier will hold to this price $OA_2$, even if he changes his price $p_2$, then the second supplier will clearly look for the point on the horizontal line $A_2A_2'$ at which his profit is largest. Points on the horizontal $A_2A_2'$ represent all the combinations of prices $p_1p_2$ for

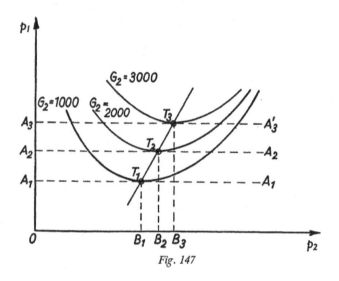

*Fig. 147*

which the price of the first supplier is at the constant level of $OA_2$. It is clear from the figure that the most profitable price for the second supplier is the point of tangency $T_2$ of an isoprofit curve with the horizontal $A_2A_2'$. If the first supplier fixes his price at $OA_2$, the price $OB_2$ will be the most profitable for the second supplier. In the same way the most profitable price for the second supplier can be discovered if the price of the first supplier is $OA_1$, $OA_3$, etc. The locus of the points of tangency $T_1$, $T_2$, $T_3$, etc., represents the reaction line of the second supplier. If the second supplier is acting as a polypolist, the reaction line will be the locus of all the points of tangency of the isoprofit curves to lines parallel to the $p_2$ axis. Correspondingly, the line of reaction of the first supplier can, if he is acting as a polypolist, be discovered in the same way.

3. Polypolistic behaviour is, as we know, only one of many possible modes of behaviour under heterogeneous competition between two suppliers. Let us consider briefly the case where the two suppliers are behaving as *oligopolists*, that is, where each supplier expects

a certain alteration in the price of his competitor with an alteration of his own price. The view which a supplier takes about the
expected price reaction of his competitor will generally depend upon
the initial price combination. Fig. 148 gives a geometrical picture of
the ideas of a supplier about the reactions of his competitor, given an
initial price combination $P$. If the second supplier reckons (as a
polypolist) that if he alters $p_2$ his competitor will not react, then the

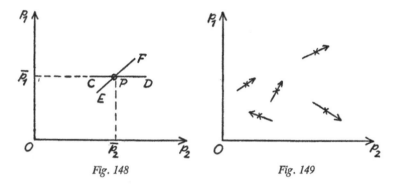

Fig. 148              Fig. 149

expected reaction of the first supplier is expressed by the parallel $CD$.
If, on the other hand, the second supplier reckons that his competitor
will react to a rise in his price by a similar rise in price, and will react
to reductions in price by corresponding reductions, then this expected
reaction will be represented by the line $EF$. The slope of the line $EF$
depends on the strength of the expected reaction of the competitor.
If the second supplier reckons that the competitor will *not* react to a
rise in price, but *will* reduce his price in the face of a price reduction,
then these expected reactions will be portrayed by the discontinuous
line $EPD$, etc. Through every point on the diagram there passes a line
which represents the ideas of the supplier about his competitor's
reaction at the particular combination of prices represented by that
point (Fig. 149). This family of lines, which correspond to particular
possible initial price combinations, may be described as the *structure
of expectations* of a supplier in respect of the reactions of his
competitors.

With given price–sales functions, cost functions, and structures of
expectations for both suppliers, we are now able to discover the
equilibrium position corresponding with these data, if one exists.
We have to ask about the combination of prices $p_1, p_2$ at which, given
these data, and in particular the structure of expectations of the two
suppliers, equilibrium will rule. As we are simply concerned here to

give the essential elements of the solution, we may assume for simplicity that the second supplier expects, at each initial combination of prices, that the competitor will react to a rise (or fall) in the price $p_2$ by 1 unit, with a corresponding rise (or fall) of the price $p_1$ by $a$ units. A corresponding assumption may be made for the second supplier. The structure of expectations of the second supplier will then be given by a family of parallel lines which have a slope of $a$

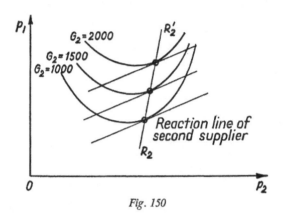

*Fig. 150*

in relation to the $p_2$ axis. A corresponding family of parallels will express the structure of expectations of the first supplier. If we now bring together the structure of expectations of a supplier with his family of isoprofit curves, then, given the structure of expectations, the most profitable $p_1$, $p_2$ combinations can at once be discovered. They will be given by the points of tangency of the parallels representing the structure of expectations, with the family of isoprofit curves. In Fig. 150 we have portrayed the locus of the most profitable $p_1$, $p_2$ combinations for the second supplier, which, following Ragnar Frisch, may be called the *attraction line*. In the same way we may discover the *attraction line* of the first supplier. If the two attraction lines of the two suppliers intersect, then the point of intersection is the position of equilibrium, given the particular price–sales functions, cost functions, and the structure of expectations.

4. Special attention should be given to the problem of the equilibrium position under the assumption that each supplier assumes that if he raises his price his competitor will not alter his price, but, on the other hand, that if he reduces his price his competitor will correspondingly make a reduction in price. The structure of expectations of each supplier will, given an initial price combination, be represented

by the broken line *EPD* (Fig. 148). We have shown earlier (page 115, Fig. 62) that it may be profitable for a supplier under these circumstances not to alter his price. *Any initial price combination may then be a position of equilibrium.*

5. *Our previous analysis has led us to the result that if the suppliers are acting as oligopolists, the position of equilibrium, if one exists, given the demand and cost structures, depends on the structure of expectations of the suppliers. The equilibrium position changes with changes in the structure of expectations.* This conclusion holds for all forms of markets which with given demand and cost structures permit of different modes of behaviour on the part of those engaged. Only when the structure of expectations is given can the equilibrium position, if one exists, be determined. *As, however, the structure of expectations under heterogeneous competition between suppliers does not result in any definite way from the objective forms of supply and demand, it is not possible (given the demand and cost functions), to deduce a determinate position of equilibrium simply from the aim of the suppliers alone (maximum total profit). In this sense the form of market we have analysed has no equilibrium; or, in other words, the equilibrium position in this form of market is indeterminate.* The indeterminacy disappears as soon as a particular structure of expectations for each supplier is introduced as a datum. This is the decisive difference from the form of market where there is homogeneous atomistic competition on the supply and demand sides. With homogeneous atomistic competition on the supply and demand side of a market for a particular good each individual *must*, as we have shown above (page 60), behave as a quantity-adjuster. In this case, the mode of behaviour of the individuals is uniquely determined by the form of the market. This is not the case in all other forms of market. Then no unique mode of behaviour can be deduced from the form of market alone, nor can any particular structure of expectations on the part of those engaged in the market.[1] Rather the structure of expectations

---

[1] "The difficulty is simply that under oligopolistic conditions there is no one clear and unambiguous answer to the question 'How would a sensible man act in such a situation?' His action depends on his necessarily imperfect expectations about the conduct of other people. Though one can argue vaguely *a priori* that some assumptions are more reasonable than others, if one wants to find out how, or on what expectations, oligopolists in fact behave, the only way is 'to look and see'. It cannot be directly deduced from some 'Fundamental Principle', any more than except in a very few cases, one can deduce how a hand of bridge will be played with given cards simply from the principle that all the players are out to maximize their points." (T. W. Hutchison: "Expectations and Rational Conduct", *Zeitschrift für Nationalökonomie*, Bd. 8, 1937, pp. 644 ff.)

of each individual has to be introduced into the analysis as an independent datum. Only when an assumption of this kind has been made can a position of equilibrium, if such exists, be deduced.

6. Up to now we have asked simply about the position of equilibrium corresponding to a particular structure of demand, costs, and expectations. We have shown earlier, however, that any real understanding of the *process* of price formation can only be arrived

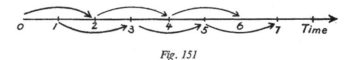

*Fig. 151*

at by a *dynamic analysis*. Further, only a dynamic theory can tell us anything about the nature of an equilibrium position, about its stability or instability. In order to show clearly the role played by the expectations of the suppliers in the process of price formation, we shall make the assumption that the planned price–sales functions and cost functions of the suppliers agree with the actual functions, so that divergencies between the expected and actual sales of a supplier depend simply on divergencies between the expected and actual price of the competitor. We shall assume also that the buyers react immediately to changes in price, and that a supplier reacts to changes in the price of his competitor with a lag, as represented in Fig. 151: the first supplier fixes his price at time 0, the second supplier reacts at point of time 1, the first supplier reacts in turn with a change in price at time 2, and so on. The first supplier, therefore, in planning his price at the point of time $t$ must reckon with the possible reaction of his competitor at the point of time $t + 1$.[1] We must assume, in the most general case, that his expectation about the price his competitor fixes depends not only on the price he himself fixes at the point of time $t$, but on the whole previous development of prices. If we describe the competitor's price expected by the first supplier at the point of time $t + 1$ as $*p_2^{t+1}$, then the following dynamic relation holds:

$$*p_2^{t+1} = F(p_1^t, p_2^{t-1}, p_1^{t-2}, p_2^{t-3}, p_1^{t-4}, \ldots) \tag{20}$$

For a fully realistic analysis of the development of prices through time it is also necessary to consider that the individual supplier can choose the point of time at which he reacts to a competitor's price

[1] "It is thus that a chess-player when making his move takes account of the move which his adversary will probably make." (F. Y. Edgeworth: "The Pure Theory of Monopoly", *Papers relating to Political Economy*, Vol. I, p. 137.)

changes. This is of special significance if the buyers do not immediately react to changes in prices. The supplier has then to consider, in planning a change in price, not only *how* his competitor will probably react to a price change, but also *when* this reaction will take place. The expected *speed* of reaction of the competitor will then be as important a datum in a supplier's planning of a change in price is as the *nature* of the expected reaction. For our present analysis it is sufficient to assume that the mutual reactions take place at fixed intervals of time as represented in Fig. 151. The essential aspects of dynamic analysis with which we are concerned here are not affected by this simplifying assumption. At the point of time 0 a particular combination of prices exists resulting from a particular historical process. We assume that the two suppliers behave as polypolists. Each supplier reckons that his competitor will hold to his previous price, if he alters his own price. The structure of expectations of the two suppliers is therefore as follows:

$$\text{(a)} \quad {}^*p_2^t = p_2^{t-1}$$
$$\text{(b)} \quad {}^*p_1^t = p_1^{t-1} \tag{21}$$

The first equation tells us that the first supplier at time $t$ reckons that his competitor will retain his previous price at time $t-1$. Correspondingly, the second equation is to be interpreted in the same way for the second supplier. We assume, further, that the initial price combination at the point of time 0, given the price–sales functions, cost functions and structure of expectations, is not an equilibrium combination.

The first supplier at time 0 will, taking account of (21a), fix his price $p_1^0$ so that in the coming periods from 0 till 2 he will obtain the maximum profit. As, however, the initial price combination, according to our assumptions, is not an equilibrium combination, the second supplier at time 1 will adjust his price $p_2^1$ to the new price $p_1^0$ of the first supplier, expecting that the first supplier will leave his price $p_1^0$ unchanged in the future. The price change of the second supplier at time 1 will also cause the first supplier to alter his price at time 2, on the assumption that the second supplier will be keeping to his price $p_2^1$ and so on. The first supplier, therefore, meets with "surprises" at times 1, 3, 5, 7, etc., and the second supplier at the points of time 2, 4, 6, 8, etc. Each supplier discovers that the actual price of his competitor at the relevant points of time does not correspond with his expectations. If we were now to assume that, in spite of this divergence between expectations and reality, each supplier in fixing his further prices started from the same structure of expectations, then the equilibrium position corresponding to this structure of expectations, in so far as it could be said to exist, would theoretically be reached after an infinite number of such steps.

The following *numerical example* may assist in explaining this argument. The demand functions of the two suppliers are as follows:

$$x_1^t = 46 - 4p_1^t + 2{}^*p_2^t$$
$$x_2^t = 63 + 4{}^*p_1^t - 7p_2^t \tag{22}$$

Let the cost functions be:

$$C_1 = c_1 + \tfrac{1}{2}x_1 \qquad (c_1 > 0)$$
$$C_2 = c_2 + x_2 \qquad (c_2 > 0) \tag{22a}$$

According to the structure of expectations given in (21), a static analysis shows that the following equilibrium prices would be arrived at for the two suppliers:

$$p_1 = 7\tfrac{21}{26}; \qquad p_2 = 7\tfrac{3}{13}.$$

Analysing dynamically the process of the development through time of the two prices from an initial combination of prices $p_1 = 14$ and $p_2 = 8$, we would obtain a table as follows:

Initial Price Combination $p_1 = 14$; $p_2 = 8$

| Point of time | $p_1^t$ | ${}^*p_2^{t+1}$ | $p_2^t$ | ${}^*p_1^{t+1}$ |
|---|---|---|---|---|
| 0 | 8 | 8 | — | — |
| 1 | — | — | $7\tfrac{2}{7}$ | 8 |
| 2 | $7\tfrac{23}{28}$ | $7\tfrac{2}{7}$ | — | — |
| 3 | — | — | $7\tfrac{23}{98}$ | $7\tfrac{23}{28}$ |
| . | | | | |
| . | ↓ | ↓ | ↓ | ↓ |
| . | $7\tfrac{21}{26}$ | $7\tfrac{3}{13}$ | $7\tfrac{3}{13}$ | $7\tfrac{21}{26}$ |

*However, the assumption of an unchanged structure of expectations in the face of divergencies between expectations and the facts is highly unrealistic.* If it appears to a supplier that his competitor fixes a different price from that which he had expected, then the next time he fixes his price he will do so on the basis of changed expectations, taking into account what he has since found out. Such a process in itself brings about changes in the originally assumed conditions. A particular structure of expectations at a particular moment of planning gives rise to a movement, which in turn at the next moment of planning, on the basis of an alteration in the structure of expectations, takes on a different direction. It is not sufficient for an explanation of the process of price formation through time simply to know the initial structure of expectations. It is also necessary to know in what way the two suppliers revise the expectations on which their calculations are based when divergencies appear between expectations and facts.[1] *The important conclusion follows from this that the static equilibrium analysis of heterogeneous competition between suppliers has little significance compared with the dynamic analysis of the process of price formation, and that it is doubtful even whether the question as to what equilibrium position corresponds to a particular set of data has any sense at all.*[2]

As the possible reactions of a supplier to divergencies between the actual and the expected behaviour of his competitor are very numerous, and no *a priori* generalizations are possible, the course of the economic process through time under conditions of heterogeneous competition is indeterminate and unstable in a way in which it is not under homogeneous atomistic competition. *This is true for all economic events the explanation of which is only possible on the basis of the expectations of those engaged, and on the basis of a knowledge of the divergencies between these expectations and the facts, i.e. for all economic events in a world in which the assumption of complete transparency of market conditions, or complete knowledge of them, is not fulfilled.*

7. The mode of behaviour which we have assumed in studying the problem of price formation under conditions of heterogeneous competition on the supply side was that the supplier adjusted his plans to the given situation, in particular to the given prices of competitors. We have seen already that even this kind of peaceful adjustment to a given situation causes considerable instability in the course of the economic process through time. This instability is markedly increased under conditions of oligopoly by the fact that the oligopolist supplier may not limit himself to peaceful modes of behaviour. If there are on the supply side only a few relatively large

---

[1] "... it is not, in general, sufficient to possess merely the initial anticipations of each duopolist concerning his rival's reactions; data must also be provided to determine revisions of these anticipations." (G. J. Stigler: "Notes on the Theory of Duopoly" in *Journal of Political Economy*, Vol. 48, 1940, p. 528.)

[2] The conclusion we have come to has been put very clearly by P. M. Sweezy: "... it becomes very doubtful, whether the traditional search for the equilibrium solution to a problem in oligopoly has very much meaning. ... The theorist should attempt to develop an analysis which will make him understand the process of change which characterizes the real world rather than waste his time in chasing the will-o'-the-wisp of equilibrium." ("Demand under Conditions of Oligopoly" in *Journal of Political Economy*, Vol. 47, 1939, pp. 572–73.)

suppliers, then there is a possibility for each supplier of changing to his advantage, by means of economic warfare, the existing market conditions, i.e. the present form of market and the modes of behaviour applied in it. He may, by economic warfare, force his competitors from the market, or force them into negotiations as to their future rules of action. A full account of the principles of oligopolistic warfare would far exceed the scope of this volume. The problems have been too little studied for a systematic treatment to be possible. Only a few suggestions can be made here. Any study must start from the empirical fact that the individual oligopolist supplier can at any time make an attempt to alter the existing market situation by economic warfare, for example, by a price war. *Behind all the decisions of an oligopolist supplier there rests a threat of open conflict with his competitors.*[1] Certainly, economic war in the form of a price war will only break out occasionally. But the mere possibility of such an outbreak at any moment affects the actions of the individual oligopolist by causing him to aim not simply at the maximum profit, but at as secure and unassailable a position as possible. These two objectives are both opposed to a policy of short-period changes in prices adjusted to changes in demand, costs, and expectations. Frequent price changes attract the attention not only of existing competitors to the supplier who makes them, and therefore bring about counter-measures, but they may arouse the interest of those previously outside that branch of industry. The individual supplier aims at making his profit as large as possible *in the long run*. He must, therefore, avoid all manoeuvres which jeopardize his security and existence. Here is an additional ground (in addition to the factors we have already mentioned which work in the same direction) for the phenomenon of rigid prices which is particularly important under conditions of oligopoly and monopoly.[2] The rigidity of prices over long periods of time does not mean, of course, that the suppliers have ceased to fight for their positions in the market. It only means that the struggle for customers is now carried on by other means than that of price. Instead of price competition there is competition by advertising, by sales organization, by quality, and so on. However, from time to time, important changes in the data for all suppliers

[1] "The background to oligopoly . . . is . . . a struggle. But this is, of course, not a continuous struggle. . . . It is the continuous existence of potential struggle." (K. W. Rothschild: "Price Theory and Oligopoly" in *Economic Journal*, Vol. 57, 1947, pp. 310 and 313. We should like particularly to draw attention to this important article.)

[2] "The existence of a stable price instead of a fluctuating one will deter rivals from starting panicky price-reduction campaigns, and it will not induce newcomers to enter a booming market." (K. W. Rothschild: *Op. cit.*, p. 311.)

may bring about a reduction in prices by all the suppliers, though not by the same amount in every case. A price war may result, which leads either to the destruction of the weaker opponent or to agreements between the suppliers. The history of cartels in Germany supplies sufficient examples. But it is also possible that the stronger of two oligopolist competitors may succeed in getting the weaker supplier, without price warfare, to accept the price he fixes or to confine himself to a particular mode of behaviour. The problems arising from this kind of *"price leadership"* by a particular supplier, or from the different possible kinds of agreements, have an important place in the study of industrial and commercial policies. They belong partly in the field of sociology, because a change in the form of market may come about not only by means of economic warfare, but also by political measures. "The oligopolistic struggle for position and security includes political action of all sorts right up to imperialism. The inclusion of these 'non-economic' elements is essential for a full explanation of oligopolistic behaviour and price."[1] Equilibrium analysis, as it has previously been conducted, has little significance for such problems as these, and it is therefore all the more necessary to build up an analysis of the economic process in close cooperation with empirical studies.

### 7. The Problem of Equilibrium under Bilateral Monopoly

1. *Let us consider the supply and demand relation between a single supplier and a single demander*. The supplier considers himself to be a monopolist and estimates the cross-elasticity of demand in relation to the price of the goods offered by other economic individuals to be nil. The demander is equally a monopolist and assumes that there will be no competition from other demanders for the good offered by the supplier. This sort of supply and demand relation, or market form, may be described as *bilateral monopoly*.

2. The simplest case of bilateral monopoly is that of *isolated exchange* or exchange between two individuals cut off from every economic connexion with others.[2] Let us assume that No. 1 is in possession of a quantity of $a_0$ of good $A$ and that No. 2 possesses the quantity $b_0$ of the good $B$. The tastes of the two individuals can then be described by a system of indifference curves, as we know from

---

[1] Cf. K. W. Rothschild: *Op. cit.*, p. 319.
[2] This section is reproduced with a few modifications from my article "Zielsetzung, Verhaltensweise und Preisbildung" (*Jahrbücher für National-ökonomie und Statistik*, Bd. 157, 1943, pp. 410 ff.).

the theory of the household. In Figs. 152A and 152B quantities of good $A$ are measured along the horizontal axis and quantities of good $B$ on the vertical axis. Fig. 152A relates to No. 1 and Fig. 152B to No. 2. In Fig. 152A $OM$ is the quantity $a_0$ possessed by No. 1 of the good $A$, and in Fig. 152B $O'N$ correspondingly represents the quantity $b_0$ in the possession of No. 2 of the good $B$. The indifference curve $MM'$ divides the field $OBMY$ into two areas I and II. Field II

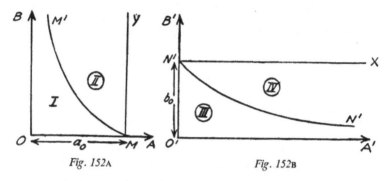

Fig. 152A                              Fig. 152B

contains all the combinations of quantities of the two goods which are preferred by No. I to the possession of the combination $a_0$. Field I contains all combinations which No. 1 finds less satisfactory than the quantity $a_0$. Those equivalent to $a_0$ are the combinations lying on the curve $MM'$. Correspondingly, the indifference curve $NN'$ passing through $O'N$ divides the field $A'O'NX$ into two fields III and IV. Field IV contains all the combinations of quantities which are preferred by No. 2 to the combination $b_0$. Field III contains all the combinations which No. 2 finds less satisfactory than $b_0$. Those equivalent to $b_0$ are the combinations lying on the curve $NN'$. Following the procedure of Pareto let us bring together the two systems in Figs. 152A and 152B in Fig. 153.[1] $BOA$ represent the system of coordinates for No. 1 and $B'O'A'$ those for No. 2. $OM$ ($= ON$) represents the quantity $a_0$ of the good $A$ in possession of No. 1; $O'M$ ($= O'N$) represents the quantity $b_0$ in possession of No. 2 of the good $B$. Let us take any point $P$ within the rectangle. Then $PP'$ and $PP''$ represent the quantities possessed by No. 2, *after* the exchange of $MP''$ of the good $B$ against $MP'''$ of the good $A$; and the coordinates $OP'''$ and $PP'''$ of this same point $P$ represent No. 1's situation after the exchange of the same quantities. In short, we may say that $P$ represents the situation for the two individuals as a result

[1] V. Pareto: *Manuel d'Économie Politique*, Paris, 1927, Ch. III, Sect. 116 (Modes et formes de l'équilibre dans l'échange).

of the exchange of the quantity $MP'''$ of the good $A$ against the quantity $MP''$ of the good $B$.

It is clear that only those combinations of quantities will be exchanged which are represented by points lying within or on the boundaries of the shaded area. None of the points in this area is one of positive disadvantage to either of the parties as compared with

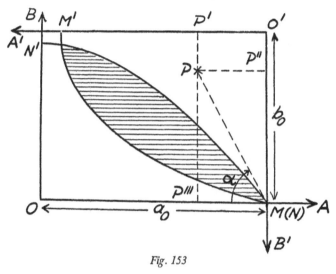

*Fig. 153*

their initial positions. A point within this *area of possibilities* represents for each of them an advantage as compared with their initial position. Every point within or on the boundaries of this area represents a possible act of exchange and may conceivably be a position of equilibrium. Which of these possible equilibrium positions will actually be realized can only be discovered if the objectives and modes of behaviour of the two parties are known. From a knowledge simply of the objective, it is not possible to derive the equilibrium position. If we simply take as objective the maximum gain, that is, in the case of isolated exchange the maximum ophelimity, then the amount exchanged is indeterminate. *Only when we make an assumption about the mode of behaviour of the two parties, in addition to an assumption about their objective, can we discover what point within the area of possibilities will be reached.*[1] This dependence of the

[1] This was clearly expressed by Wicksell: "Price formation in the case of isolated exchange is essentially an indeterminate problem, which is not soluble *simply on the assumption that the two parties are aiming at the largest possible profit.*" (*Lectures on Political Economy*, Vol. I, p. 51—our italics.)

equilibrium position on the mode of behaviour of the two parties to the exchange must now be examined more closely.

Let us now supplement Fig. 153 by drawing in further indifference curves on the same two systems of coordinates in addition to the curves $MN'$ and $MM'$. If we connect the point $M$ with any point $P$ within the two systems of coordinates, then the slope of the line $MP$

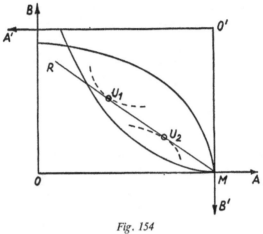

Fig. 154

represents the relation between the quantities of goods exchanged. For example, tan $\alpha$ represents simply the price of $A$ in terms of $B$, when the two parties exchanging are at the point $P$. All points $P$ lying on the same straight line through $M$ represent points of exchange at that same price. The straight line through $M$ may, therefore, be described as a *price line*. With given price lines each party will exchange those quantities which will maximize his ophelimity, and will seek to arrive at that point on the given price line. This point will clearly be that where the price line is tangential to one of his indifference curves. At a price corresponding to the line $MR$ (Fig. 154) No. 1 will aim at the point $U_1$ and No. 2 at the point $U_2$. The point $U_1$ corresponds to a particular supply of the good $A$ and a particular demand of the good $B$; point $U_2$ corresponds to a particular supply of the good $B$ and a particular demand of the good $A$. If we now vary the price, that is, rotate the price line on the point $M$, the points $U_1$ and $U_2$ will trace out the curves $MV_1$ and $MV_2$ (Fig. 155), which may be described as "offer curves" or "curves of exchange" (Pareto's *courbes des échanges*). The point of intersection of the curve $MV_1$ (or $MV_2$) with a price line is the point of exchange aimed at by No. 1 (or No. 2) at this price. Its coordinates give the quantities demanded and supplied at this price.

(a) *If the two parties behave as quantity-adjusters*, then the equilibrium position corresponding to this mode of behaviour will be represented by the point of intersection $T$ of the two offer curves $MV_1$ and $MV_2$.[1] Only at the price given by this point will supply

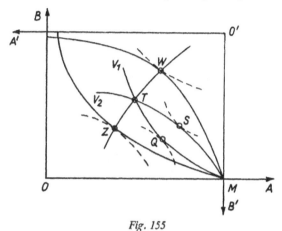

*Fig. 155*

and demand be equal, and only at this price will both individuals simultaneously maximize their ophelimity, which of course will only be a relative maximization.

(b) *If No. 1 acts as a monopolist and No. 2 as a quantity-adjuster*, then No. 1 can determine the price. Let us suppose that he fixes the price so that his ophelimity is maximized, taking into account the fact that No. 2 will only select points lying on his offer curve. Then the price he chooses will be that corresponding to the point at which an indifference curve is tangential to $MV_2$. In Fig. 155 this point is given by $S$. It corresponds to the Cournot point in the usual theory of monopoly. Correspondingly, the Cournot point $Q$ may be derived for No. 2. These two points again only represent relative maxima.

(c) Another equilibrium position will result if one of the two parties fixes an *option* and the other acts as the taker or leaver of the option. An individual, as we know (page 54), acts as the fixer of an option if he fixes both price and quantity, and only leaves to the other party the choice of accepting or rejecting the option he has fixed.

[1] On the case where the curves, $MV_1$ and $MV_2$ intersect at several points, see V. Pareto: *Op. cit.*, Ch. III, Paras. 120–25.

If No. 1 now fixes an option, and No. 2 is accepting or rejecting it, then, given the objective of maximum ophelimity, the point $W$ represents the resulting equilibrium, being the point at which the indifference curve of No. 2 passing through $M$ is tangential to an indifference curve of No. 1 (Fig. 155). The point $W$ may be described as the *exploitation point* of No. 1. If, on the other hand, No. 1 acts as the taker of the option and No. 2 as the fixer of it, then point $Z$

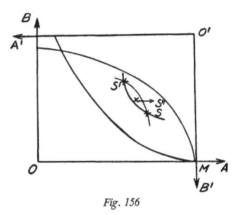

*Fig. 156*

will be the equilibrium point, which may be described as the *exploitation point* of No. 2.

(d) It has been assumed, under the modes of behaviour dealt with so far, that equilibrium is reached *uno actu*. The process of exchange will develop differently if it is assumed that exchange takes place in single successive steps, and that on each day the terms of exchange reached on the previous day are revised. This case was studied by Edgeworth and Marshall.[1] It represents a particular form of strategy in negotiation, under which the price and the quantities to be exchanged are determined in a succession of negotiations between the exchanging parties. Let us take, for example, the Cournot point $S$ for No. 1 (Fig. 155) and draw in on our diagram the indifference curve of No. 2 passing through $S$. From the theory of the household we know that only one indifference curve passes through any particular point in the indifference field of an individual. For simplicity of presentation the construction is put in a separate diagram (Fig. 156). The two indifference curves passing through $S$ intersect again

[1] F. Y. Edgeworth: *Mathematical Physics*, London, 1881, and "On the Determinateness of Economic Equilibrium" in *Papers relating to Political Economy*, Vol. II, pp. 313 ff. A. Marshall: *Principles of Economics*, 8th ed., pp. 791 ff., and Note XII to the Mathematical Appendix, p. 844.

at $S'$, and enclose an area of the same shape as that enclosed by the indifference curves passing through $M$. Any point in this area will afford a greater ophelimity to the exchanging parties than the point $S$. It therefore pays the two parties to choose any point $S''$ within this area as the point of exchange. For the point $S''$ we can now carry out the same analysis as we did for the point $S$. Clearly it is profitable for the two individuals to continue altering their position of exchange until a point is reached at which the indifference curves of the two parties running through it are touching. Every movement from this point reduced the ophelimity of both parties. *The locus of all the points of tangency between the indifference curves of the two parties represents all the possible possible results of successive transactions.* The locus ($ZTW$) of these points has been called by Edgeworth the *contract curve* of the two parties (Fig. 155). As can be seen at once, the bargaining objectives of the two parties are the two end points of the contract curve. The point $T$, the equilibrium point for two quantity-adjusters, also lies on the contract curve. Which of the infinite number of points between $Z$ and $W$ (Fig. 155) on the contract curve will be the resulting equilibrium position cannot be discovered without a knowledge of the tactics in negotiation of the two parties. Any path leading from $M$ to the contract curve will be a possible path leading to a point of equilibrium on the contract curve.

(e) In addition to the previous possibilities there are other positions of equilibrium depending on the mode of behaviour which may result, for example, from oligopolist strategies.[1] We cannot study this problem further here. *The cases we have dealt with suffice to show that under bilateral monopoly in the form of isolated exchange the final point of exchange (or point of contract) depends on the mode of behaviour of the parties, and will be indeterminate if simply the objectives, and not also the mode of behaviour, of the two parties are given in the data of the problem.*

It may be noticed that the two Cournot points $S$ and $Q$ for the two parties may be improved upon by moving on to the contract curve, so that as a general result we have the proposition discovered by Edgeworth *that only points lying on the contract curve are possible as positions of equilibrium.* But all these points are equally possible as equilibrium positions. Which of the many possible modes of behaviour will be applied can no more be decided by the theoretical economist than they can in the case of oligopoly considered in previous sections. The solution of the problem of equilibrium is therefore indeterminate.

3. These results remain valid when, instead of isolated exchange,

---

[1] Cf. A. C. Pigou: *The Economics of Stationary States*, London, 1935, Ch. XVII and Appendix V.

we consider other forms of bilateral monopoly. *Let us take the example of an entrepreneur who in producing a particular good requires a factor of production of which he is the sole demander and which is only supplied by a single other entrepreneur.* No substitutes exist for this factor of production. Fundamentally we have the same situation as that of isolated exchange and the problem can be treated in exactly the same way. In place of an objective of maximum ophelimity let us suppose that of maximum profit on the part of the two parties. In place of ophelimity indifference curves we now have the *isoprofit* curves of the supplier and the demander.

Let us take two firms 1 and 2 at successive "vertical" stages in one industry. Firm 1 produces a single product $X$ and requires as the sole demander of this input a factor of production $Z$ which is only produced and supplied by Firm 2. Firm 2 is the sole supplier of this factor. For producing one unit of the final product one unit of the factor of production is required. The prices of the other factors used by Firm 1 in making its product, as well as the prices of the factors required by Firm 2, are given constants. Let us write:

$p$ for the price of the product $X$ of Firm 1;

$x$ as the planned sales of Firm 1 in the period;

$q$ as the price of the factor of production $Z$ supplied by Firm 2;

$K_1(x)$ as the relation of the costs of Firm 1 to the planned sales, excluding the costs of the factor of production $Z$ supplied by Firm 2;

$K_2(x)$ as the relation of the costs of Firm 2 to the quantity sold;[1]

then clearly the profit $G_1$ of Firm 1 for the period will be:

$$G_1 = p . x - q . x - K_1(x) \qquad (23)$$

Correspondingly, the profit $G_2$ for Firm 2 will be:

$$G_2 = q . x - K_2(x) \qquad (24)$$

As we are concerned simply to study the transactions between the two Firms 1 and 2 we may assume for simplicity that the price $p$ for Firm 1 is a given constant, that is, that Firm 1 acts as a *quantity-adjuster* in supplying its product, $X$.[2] The profits of the two firms, therefore, depend alone on the level of the planned sales $x$ of the good $X$ (which on our assumptions is equal to the demand for the

---

[1] According to our assumptions one unit of the factor $Z$ is required to produce one unit of the product $X$, so that $x$ represents both the quantity of the product $X$ and of the factor $Z$.

[2] If Firm 1 faces an expected price–sales function, then $p$ is a function of $x$. This does not alter any of our results.

factor of production $Z$) and on the price $q$ of the factor:

$$G_1 = G_1(q, x) \tag{25}$$

$$G_2 = G_2(q, x) \tag{26}$$

Let us consider now all the combinations of the price $q$ of the factor and the quantity of the product $x$ (= quantity of the factor) for which

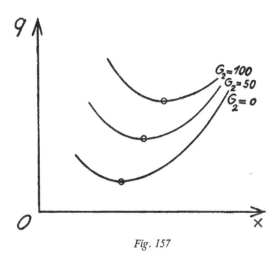

Fig. 157

the profit of a firm is a given quantity. For Firm 2 we have from equation 24:

$$q = \frac{K_2(x)}{x} + \frac{G_2}{x} \tag{27}$$

or, if we separate the total costs $K_2$ into the fixed costs $f_2$ and the variable costs $v_2(x)$:

$$q = \frac{f_2 + G_2}{x} + \frac{v_2(x)}{x} \tag{27a}$$

Given the profit $G$, we can now derive from (27a) what combinations of $q$ and $x$ will yield this profit $G_2$. If $G_2 = 0$, then the isoprofit curve is simply the curve of total unit costs. If $G_2 > 0$ then a higher iso-profit curve results having the same shape as the curve of total unit costs. The larger $G_2$ is, the larger will be the quantity of $x$ at the curve's minimum point. The family of isoprofit curves for the second firm, therefore, has the form portrayed in Fig. 157.

For Firm 1 we obtain from (23) the equation for the isoprofit curve:

$$q = p - \left(\frac{K_1(x)}{x} + \frac{G_1}{x}\right) \tag{28}$$

where $G_1$ is a particular level of profits. From (28) it is clear that the family of isoprofit curves for the first firm has the shape portrayed in

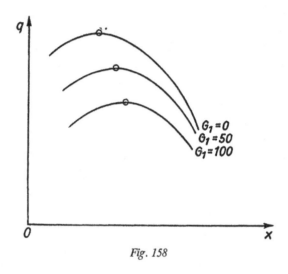

*Fig. 158*

Fig. 158.[1] We must notice the opposite shape of the two families of isoprofit curves. For Firm 1 (the demander of the monopolized factor), given the demand, the profit increases as the price of the factor falls. An isoprofit curve, corresponding to a higher profit, in this $(q, x)$ diagram lies below one corresponding to a lower profit. For Firm 2 (the supplier of the monopolized factor of production) the profit from a given output decreases as the price of the factor falls. An isoprofit curve corresponding to a higher profit lies, therefore, on this diagram above one corresponding to a lower profit.

Let us now draw the two sets of isoprofit curves for the two firms on the same system of coordinates. We then have a diagram such as

[1] For the case of $G_1 = 0$ the isoprofit curve is derived by subtracting from the sales price of the product the total unit costs corresponding to the various quantities of output. For $G_1 = 50$, the sales price $p$ has in each case to be reduced by the ordinal values of a curve which lies above the curve of total unit costs (see Fig. 157) and which reaches its minimum at a higher level of output.

in Fig. 159. The area enclosed by the isoprofit curves of the firms corresponding to zero profit represents all the combinations of price and quantity of the factor $Z$ which may possibly result from the transactions between the demanding and supplying firms.[1] Only

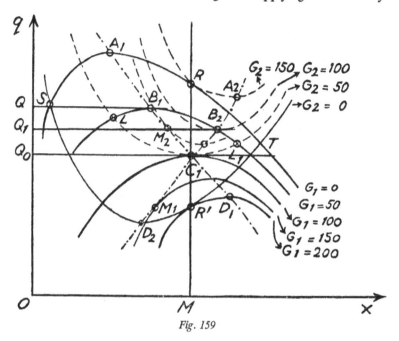

*Fig. 159*

price and quantity combinations within this area yield a positive profit to both firms. The area between the two zero-isoprofit curves corresponds exactly to the area of possibilities between the two indifference curves passing through $M$ in the case of isolated exchange (Fig. 153). Which of the price and quantity combinations within the possible area is realized depends, just as in the analysis of isolated exchange, on the modes of behaviour of the two parties.

(a) Let us take first the case where demander and supplier behave as *quantity-adjusters*. At a given price $q$ for the factor of production, Firm 1 (or 2) will demand (or supply) the quantity $x$ at which its

---

[1] In the short period the lower limit for the price is set, not by the total unit cost, but by the variable unit cost, because losses will be smaller at prices slightly above average variable cost than they will be if the plant is closed down. In the short period the fixed costs in (23) and (24) can be disregarded, so that the area of possibility is correspondingly larger and is bounded by two "iso-loss" curves for which the loss is exactly equal to the fixed costs.

profit will be maximized. The quantity demanded by Firm 1 at a particular price $OQ$ is given then by the point at which the parallel to the $x$ axis from $Q$ is tangential to an isoprofit curve of Firm 1. At a price of $OQ$ Firm 1 demands the quantity $QB_1$ of the factor. At every price $q$ one may obtain in this way the quantity demanded by Firm 1. All these quantities lie on the curve $A_1B_1C_1D_1$ which passes through the maxima of the isoprofit curves of Firm 1. This curve represents *the demand curve of Firm 1* for the factor $Z$. At a price $OQ_1$ Firm 2 will offer the quantity given by the point where the parallel to the $X$ axis from $Q_1$ is tangential to an isoprofit curve of Firm 2. The price $OQ_1$ corresponds to a quantity supplied of $Q_1B_2$. For every price we can arrive in this way at a particular quantity supplied by Firm 2. All these quantities supplied lie on a curve $A_2B_2C_1D_2$ which passes through the minima of the isoprofit curves of Firm 2. This curve is the *supply curve of Firm 2*. The equilibrium price will be given by the point of intersection of the demand curve and the supply curve. In Fig. 159 it is at a level of $OQ_0$. At this price the quantity $Q_0C_1$ will be supplied and demanded. At the point of intersection $C_1$ of the supply and demand curve the corresponding isoprofit curves of the first firm and of the second firm are tangential. The common tangent to the two curves at this point is parallel to the $x$ axis.

(b) *If Firm 1 acts as a quantity-adjuster and Firm 2 as a monopolist*, then Firm 2, confronted by the demand curve $A_1B_1C_1D_1$ of Firm 1, will choose the Cournot point on this curve, and will fix the price $q$ where marginal revenue and marginal costs are equal. This Cournot point for Firm 2 will be given by the point of tangency $M_2$ of the demand curve $A_1B_1C_1D_1$ with an isoprofit curve of Firm 2. The Cournot point for Firm 2 gives, as can easily be seen, a higher price than $OQ_0$, the price where both parties behave as quantity-adjusters. If Firm 2 behaves as a quantity-adjuster and Firm 1 as a monopolist, so that Firm 1 fixes the price $q$, then Firm 2 will offer at different levels of price $q$ the quantities given by its supply curve $A_2B_2C_1D_2$. Firm 1 will then fix the price $q$ at that level at which it obtains the maximum profit. This price is clearly that where the supply curve of Firm 2 is tangential to an isoprofit curve of Firm 1. This price in Fig. 159 is given by the point $M_1$ and, as can be seen, is smaller than the price $OQ_0$ which obtains when both parties behave as quantity-adjusters.

(c) *If Firm 1 fixes an option and Firm 2 is the taker*, then Firm 2 will be forced on to its zero-isoprofit curve and Firm 1 will try to realize the price and quantity combination on this curve at which its profit is highest: that is, at the point $R'$ where the zero-isoprofit curve of Firm 2 is tangential to an isoprofit curve of Firm 1. The *point R' represents the exploitation point of Firm* 1. If Firm 2 fixes the option and Firm 1 is the taker, then Firm 2 will force Firm 1 on to its zero-isoprofit curve and try to arrive at that point where its profit is at a maximum. This point will be given by $R$, at which the zero-isoprofit curve of Firm 1 is tangential to an isoprofit curve of Firm 2. *The point R is the exploitation point of Firm* 2.

It can be shown that the two exploitation points lie on a line parallel to the $q$ axis; that is, that *the two points correspond to the same quantities of the factor of production (in Fig.* 159 *the quantity OM).*[1] The parallel $RR'$ is simply the locus of the points of tangency of all the isoprofit curves. The point $C_1$, which is the equilibrium point when both parties act as quantity-adjusters, also lies on this straight line $RR'$. *We, therefore, come to the interesting conclusion that if both parties behave as quantity-adjusters the equilibrium position will*

[1] This can only be proved mathematically. The bargaining objectives $R$ and $R'$ are points at which two isoprofit curves from the two sets are tangential. We therefore enquire as to the locus of all the points of tangency between two curves belonging to the two firms' sets of isoprofit curves. These points of tangency have the characteristic that the slope of the tangents is the same for both curves. The equation of the set of isoprofit curves for Firm 1 is given by (23):

$$(p - q) \cdot x - K_1(x) = G_1,$$

where $G_1$ is any constant. According to the rule for the differentiation of implicit functions we have for the first derivative:

$$\frac{dq}{dx} = \frac{p - q - K_1'(x)}{x}$$

The equation for the set of isoprofit curves for the second firm is given by (24):

$$q \cdot x - K_2(x) = G_2,$$

where $G_2$ is any constant. From this we obtain:

$$\frac{dq}{dx} = -\frac{q - K_2'(x)}{x}$$

The combinations of $q$ and $x$ which represent points of tangency between the isoprofit curves (23) and (24) must therefore satisfy the condition:

$$\frac{p - q - K_1'(x)}{x} = \frac{K_2'(x) - q}{x}$$

or

$$p = K(x)_1' + K_2'(x).$$

As $q$ does not occur in this condition, the abscissa of the points of tangency is independent of $q$; that is, it is the same for all the points of tangency. The locus of all the points of tangency between members of the two sets of isoprofit curves is therefore a line parallel to the $q$ axis. As $R$ and $R'$ (Fig. 159) are points of tangency, this parallel must go through $R$ and $R'$.

*be such that the same quantity will be exchanged as when the two parties behave as the fixer and taker of an option. It is simply the price that is different in the case of the fixing of an option, as compared with what it is when both parties behave as quantity-adjusters. It can further be shown that the most favourable quantity of the factor OM for the two parties, both in the case of fixing an option, and if they both behave as quantity-adjusters, is equal to that at which both parties would arrive if they combined together and sought the maximum profit.*[1] If Firm 1 (or Firm 2) succeeds in arriving at its bargaining objective R' (or R) then it obtains the whole of this maximum profit.

(d) Let us consider now the case where the firms try to arrive at the equilibrium position in a series of successive steps by negotiation. One of the firms takes the point L, and the price and quantity combination corresponding to it, as the basis for negotiations. It is then clear that every point enclosed by the two isoprofit curves passing through L ($LB_1L_1$ and $LC_1L_1$) is more profitable for both parties than the point L. Both parties will be ready to accept a move from L, for example, to $M_2$. The same analysis may be applied to the point $M_2$ as for the point L. It is clear that a change in the price and quantity combination is profitable for both firms until a point is reached at which the isoprofit curves passing through it are tangential, that is, until a point is reached on the line RR'. The line RR' is *Edgeworth's contract curve*, which we have already met in our statement of the problem of isolated exchange. What point on the contract curve will be reached at the end of the negotiations depends on the initial position and the tactics in negotiation of the two parties. Every point on the contract curve RR' (on which, as we know, lie the two points corresponding to either party's exploitation points, as well as the equilibrium point when both parties behave as quantity-adjusters) is equally possible as an equilibrium point. Without additional information about the modes of behaviour and of negotiation we cannot say anything further about the position of this equilibrium point. Pigou, Zeuthen, and Denis, among others, have attempted by an exhaustive analysis of different forms of strategy to narrow the

---

[1] From (23) and (24) the total profit of the two firms is:

$$G_1 + G_2 = p \cdot x - K_1(x) - K_2(x).$$

On our assumption that Firm 1 treats the price of the product p as constant, the maximum total profit will be obtained at that output where marginal costs equal the price p. This quantity must satisfy the equation:

$$p = K_1'(x) + K_2'(x)$$

which agrees with the equation for the locus of the points of tangency of the isoprofit curves of the two firms (see p. 311, Note 1).

zone of indeterminacy on the contract curve. We do not wish here to enter further into these important problems of the theory of economic policy and simply refer the reader to the important writings on the subject.[1]

If one or other party fixes an option, only points lying on the contract curve are possible equilibrium positions. As the quantity of the factor is the same for all points lying on the contract curve, the struggle between the two firms over the equilibrium position *simply relates to the price fixed for the quantity OM of the factor. As, also, the total profits of the two firms are constant, given the quantity of the factor exchanged, and are, therefore, independent of the price of the factor, the struggle over the price for the quantity OM is identical with the struggle over the distribution of the corresponding total profit.* It is interesting to note that the resulting price may very well be that which would result if both parties acted as quantity-adjusters.

## 8. The Problem of Equilibrium in the Labour Market

1. In the exchange economy a wage is the price for the services of labour, or for the performance of work by all those who are not entrepreneurs. The wage paid for one hour's labour services may be described as the hourly wage-rate. A non-entrepreneur is paid a time rate of wages if his income in a period is reckoned simply by multiplying the hourly wage-rate by the number of hours worked, without regard to his performance in the time he is employed. A non-entrepreneur is paid by results (or by piece-rates) if his income in a period is reckoned by multiplying the performance, measured by the number of pieces of work performed, by the rate paid for a piece of work (the piece-rate). The piece-rate is calculated in firms employing modern methods of time and motion study by multiplying the hourly wage-rate for that quality of labour by a "normal" time for the job fixed on the basis of time studies. Therefore:

Piece-rate = Wage-rate per hour × "Normal" time (in hours) for the piece of work or "job".

If the wage-rate is 6s. per hour, and the normal time for the "job" (or carrying out of a particular operation) is fixed at 15 minutes, then the piece rate is 1/6d. The worker receives this rate independently of

[1] F. Zeuthen: *Problems of Monopoly and Economic Warfare*, London, 1931; H. F. Denis: *Le Monopole Bilatéral*, Paris, 1943. Also A. C. Pigou: *Principles and Methods of Industrial Peace*, London, 1905, and "Equilibrium under Bilateral Monopoly" in *Economic Journal*, 1908, Vol. XVIII, pp. 205–20. Also J. Marchal: *Le Mécanisme des Prix*, 2nd ed., Paris, 1948.

how long the actual time is that he spends on a piece of work. In the equation fixing the piece-rate the normal time per piece is determined technically and physiologically. Only the hourly rate for that quality of performance is an economic quantity. The same holds for all other wage systems, for example, "premium bonus" wage systems. Economic theory is interested in the problem of wages mainly from the point of view of the determination of the hourly wage-rate. It is the hourly wage-rate which must be the starting point for any economic treatment of the wage problem. When in the following discussion we examine the factors determining the level of wages and the problem of the equilibrium wage, then we are concerned simply with the hourly wage-rate.

2. The demanders of the services of labour are the entrepreneurs, and the suppliers are members of households who are not entrepreneurs. The demand of entrepreneurs is not simply for labour services in general, but for one particular quality of services. An entrepreneur in order to produce a good requires, for example, 1000 hours of unskilled labour, 600 hours of skilled labour of a particular quality, 400 hours of skilled labour of another quality, and so on. Similarly, the suppliers of labour and the members of households dispose of services of different qualities and grades. It follows from this that we have as many markets for labour services as we have qualities of performance. We cannot, therefore, speak simply of a rate of wages. Rather there is a particular market, and a particular rate of wages, for each quality of labour. The market for the services of labour is a good example of an imperfect market because of the many differences of quality. The imperfection is increased by the facts that the owners of the services are firmly tied by local connexions, while transition from one grade to another is scarcely possible, as a rule, in a short period. If we consider the transactions between demanders and suppliers of a particular grade of labour in a particular geographical area, then, at least in the short period, the markets for the different separate grades are completely isolated. This was what Cairnes means when he described them as "non-competing groups". But even the market for a particular quality of service is imperfect, because of the impediments in the way of complete freedom of movement, so that here, too, differences in hourly wage-rates may exist as between different localities. We must therefore consider each particular rate of wages in a particular place for a particular quality of labour by itself, and seek to explain it individually. We shall try to do this here by means of a partial analysis studying the transactions between suppliers and demanders for hours of labour of a particular quality at a particular place.

3. This task has already been achieved by the paragraphs in this section devoted to partial analysis. The demand for the services of labour is the demand for a factor of production, and the supply of them is the supply of a factor of production. What we have previously said about the formation of the prices of goods in our partial analysis holds in the same way both for consumption goods and for factors of production. The special characteristics of the problem of the formation of wages lie simply in the fact that a human being who supplies the services of labour is not only a factor of production, but also has desires and objectives of his own which are both the starting point and the final purpose of all economic activity. As a result, there are essential differences in the position of suppliers of labour as compared with that of suppliers of material goods.

The fundamental proposition that the equilibrium price for a good depends on the actions of the supplier and the demander in a particular form of market holds, of course, also in this case. The progress which has been made by modern analysis of the problem of wages has been particularly in the more exact study of the influence of different possible modes of behaviour under different possible forms of supply and demand. The classical theory had confined itself mainly to the case of homogeneous atomistic competition on both sides of the market. We can, therefore, confine ourselves to summarizing briefly the problem of the formation of the equilibrium price, and beyond that limit our discussion to a few special characteristics. A thorough treatment of the whole theory of wages is a task for the theory of social policy.[1]

4. *Let us assume, to start with, homogeneous and atomistic competition on both the supply and demand side.* Suppliers and demanders must then behave as quantity-adjusters. The demand for a factor of production is always, as we have seen, a derived demand. The household buys goods in order to satisfy its needs directly. The entrepreneur, on the other hand, uses the services of labour for carrying out a process of production. What is decisive for the value he puts on labour of a particular quality is simply the contribution which the performance of the labourer makes to his profit. We have discussed this already in our analysis of the demand for factors of production (Chapter II, Section E). It was shown there that the decision whether to employ a new worker is always based on a comparison between the value of the marginal product of this worker

---

[1] See F. Zeuthen, "Arbejdsløn og Arbejdsloshed," in: *Socialpolitik*, vol. 1, Copenhagen 1939. Also: J. R. Hicks, *The Theory of Wages*, London, 1932; and K. W. Rothschild, *The Theory of Wages*, Oxford, 1954; E. Arndt, *Theoretische Grundlagen der Lohnpolitik*, Tuebingen 1957.

and the corresponding marginal costs. If the entrepreneur demanding the services of labour acts as a quantity-adjuster, then at a given rate of wages for a particular quality of labour he will demand that number of hours of labour at which *the value of the marginal product of one hour of labour is equal to the rate of wages* (assuming that the factors of production can be substituted for one another). From this condition we obtain the individual demand curve of the single

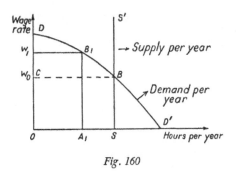

*Fig. 160*

entrepreneur, which, as we have seen earlier, is of the normal shape for all factors of production. By summation of the individual demand curves of the entrepreneurs we arrive at the total demand curve of all the entrepreneurs.

The total supply of hours of labour of a particular grade, at a particular rate of wages and in a particular period of time, is the mathematical product of the number of workers of that grade ready and able to work at that rate of wages in that locality, and of the number of working days in the period and the number of hours of labour per day supplied.

Let us take first the case where the number of men ready to work at any rate of wages is equal to the total number of able-bodied men, and that the number of working days in a period is a given constant (25 days per month and 300 days per year). Similarly, let us suppose that the number of working hours per day is independent of the level of the wage-rate, being, for example, fixed by law. In this case the total supply of hours of labour is completely inelastic in relation to the level of the wage-rate. If the saturation demand is greater than the total supply, then there will be a wage-rate above nil at which the total supply will be absorbed by the demanding entrepreneurs (Fig. 160). The equilibrium wage $w_0$ is here equal to the value of the marginal product of one hour of labour. At a wage $w_1$, which is above the equilibrium wage, only that number of hours will be demanded which is represented by the distance $OA_1$, so that at the wage $w_1$ there will be an under-employment of $AA_1$ hours of labour, of that particular quality and at that particular place. With free atomistic competition this state of affairs will not be maintained. In order to see this we simply need to carry out a dynamic analysis such as we made in Section I of this chapter. This analysis showed that the wage-rate will fall until the equilibrium wage is reached. The limitations of

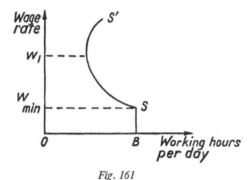

Fig. 161

partial analysis become particularly clear at this point. Every fall in wages brings about a change in the total income of the workers, so that it is possible that a change in the demand for consumption goods and a shift in the demand curve $DD'$ may result. To decide whether the equilibrium wage $w_0$ is stable is only possible by means of a total analysis. If we are to continue with a dynamic partial analysis of the above form, we have to assume that the position of the demand curve $DD'$ is independent of the level of the wage-rate.

We may now drop the assumption of a constant daily labour time, and assume that the individual worker has the possibility of deciding the number of hours of labour he will supply per day at a particular rate of wages. The daily supply curve of the individual worker will then, as a rule, have the form portrayed in Fig. 161. At a wage-rate $w_{min}$ which simply supplies a physiological subsistence minimum the worker will supply a high number of hours of labour, $OB$. If the rate of wages rises above $w_{min}$, then the worker, *ceteris paribus*, will at first cut down his supply of labour hours in order to have more free time. Above a particular rate of wages $w_1$ he may possibly again increase his supply. But as the rate of wages rises above $w_1$ other reactions are possible: the supply may further decrease or it may remain constant. The total supply function obtained by adding up the individual supply functions will have the same shape as the individual supply function.

The fact that the total supply curve may, within a particular range, have an abnormal shape may lead to interesting conclusions for an unorganized labour market, which we are still examining. If the

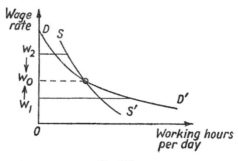

*Fig. 162*

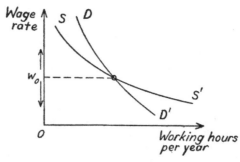

*Fig. 163*

supply and demand curves for a particular economic period have the form portrayed in Fig. 162, then a fall in wages will correspond both to an increase in demand and to an increase in supply. If the wage-rate was below the equilibrium wage, then the demanders would compete for workers by raising their wage-rate. The wage-rate would rise again to $w_0$. If the wage-rate was above $w_0$, then supply would be greater than demand and the competition of the workers would bring the rate back to $w_0$. By means of a dynamic analysis it can be shown precisely that the equilibrium wage $w_0$, in the case illustrated in Fig. 162, is stable. If, on the other hand, the supply and demand curves are of the shape illustrated in Fig. 163, then the equilibrium wage is unstable. Any wage other than $w_0$ will set off a movement which will not lead back to the equilibrium wage. We may leave the proof of this to the reader. In the case illustrated in Fig. 164 there are two equilibrium wage-rates $w_0$ and $w_1$. It can easily be seen that the wage-rate $w_1$ is stable, while $w_0$ is unstable.

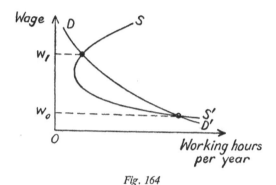

*Fig. 164*

In this discussion we have assumed that the number of workers willing to work is constant. The number of men willing to work in the short period depends on the level of the wage-rate, particularly for unskilled work, so that if the wage-rate falls the amount of labour forthcoming increases. If the wage-rate falls and the hours of labour are constant, then, perhaps, women who previously worked in the home will come on to the labour market. In analysing the form of supply, particularly for unskilled labour, this element must be borne in mind. For long-period changes in wages, or in the structure of wage-rates in a particular locality, an alteration in the number of men able to work is, of course, a particularly important factor. But any definite relationship between changes in the level of wages and changes in the population, and therefore in the labour force, cannot be demonstrated.

5. The market conditions discussed so far are much less important than the case where both parties in the market (or one of them) are organized and in a position to adopt other modes of behaviour than that of the quantity-adjuster.

(a) If the workers of a particular grade are organized in a trade union, but free homogeneous and atomistic competition exists between employers, and if we assume that the trade union prescribes a minimum wage for their members, then the supply curve of labour will have the shape given in Fig. 165. If the demand curve of the entrepreneurs is $DD'$, the equilibrium wage will be $w_0$. If we compare the equilibrium position at $w_0$ with the equilibrium position corresponding to the higher supply curve $S_1S_1'$, then we can see that it will

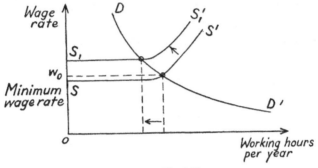

Fig. 165

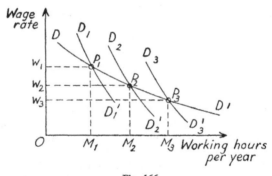

Fig. 166

be profitable for the workers to raise their wage claim as employment in the short period only slightly falls if there is a not too large increase in the wage-rate.

The position is different when we consider the long-period reaction of the employer to a rise in wages. We have distinguished already (Fig. 126) between the short-period and long-period supply curves. Correspondingly, we have distinguished between the short-period and long-period demand curves of the employer for a factor of production. The short-period demand curve tells us the demand in a particular economic period at different rates of wages, given a particular plant or apparatus of production. The long-period demand curve, on the other hand, tells us the demand for hours of labour of a particular quantity in an economic period at different rates of wages, when the apparatus of production has been completely adjusted to the existing wage-rate so that the technique adopted is the most economical. In Fig. 166, $DD'$ represents the long-period demand curve of the employer. At a wage-rate of $w_1$ the number of hours of labour $OM_1$ will be demanded, when the plant has been adjusted to

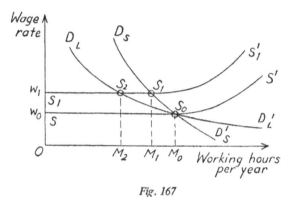

Fig. 167

the price relations between the factors of production at this rate of wages. If the wage-rate now changes, and there is only a short-period adjustment to the wage change within the limits of the existing plant, then the demand of the entrepreneurs will be represented by the demand curve $D_1D_1'$. Through every point on the long-period demand curve there passes a particular short-period demand curve. The long-period demand curve is more elastic than the short-period demand curve for the reasons we discovered when dealing with the problem of long-period planning. *It follows from this fact that in the long period a higher wage will lead to a greater fall in employment than in the short period.* In Fig. 167, $M_1M_0$ is the amount of under-employment when the demand of the employers has been adjusted in the short period to a rise in wages from $w_0$ to $w_1$. $M_2M_0$ is the amount of under-employment when a long-period adjustment of demand to the wage increase has been made.

(b) If the workers are of a particular grade and organized in a trade union, and if the employers who demand this quality of labour are similarly organized in an employers' organization, then in place of an individual contract of labour between a particular worker and a particular employer, the collective contract between workers' and employers' organizations will be the rule. The supply and demand conditions now follow those of bilateral monopoly which we have already studied. All the conclusions as to the formation of prices in this form of market are directly applicable to the case of collective wage bargaining. Bilateral monopoly can, of course, also occur in the case of individual contracts. The value of the marginal product of the supplier of labour for the demanding firm is then always the upper limit for the demand price of the firm. The lower limit which the supplier fixes for the wage depends on the costs of his training, on the standard of living he claims, and on all sorts of subjective elements. The actual level of the wage will as a rule be the result of negotiations between the two parties in which tactics and bargaining skill on the part of the supplier and the demander will ultimately determine the result.

### 9. The Problem of Equilibrium in the Market for Land

1. In considering the demand for and supply of land we must distinguish precisely between the demand for and supply of a piece of land of a particular size, situation, and quality, and the demand and supply for *the use* of such a piece of land. We have, therefore, two questions to answer: (a) how the price of a precisely defined piece of land is determined when it is bought or sold, and (b) how the price for the use of this piece of land is determined. The price for the use of land is usually described as ground rent.

The first question we have already touched upon in Section F of Chapter II. It was shown there that a particular relation exists for buyer and seller, between the price of land and the price of the use of the land. At a particular target rate of interest the price of the land can be arrived at by capitalizing the price of its use or service. The seller of a particular piece of land calculates his minimum price by capitalization of the prices of the use which he expects from it, and the buyers calculate their maximum price in the same way. The price is then formed according to the mode of behaviour adopted in the particular form of market.

We have, therefore, only to answer the second question as to how the price of the use of a piece of land of a particular size, situation, and quality is determined. For this purpose we simply need to apply the results of our partial equilibrium analysis, and we may do this here quite briefly.

2. In treating the problem of the determination of ground rent we must remember that *each piece of land is different from every other piece*. All pieces of land differ from one another in size, situation,

or quality. In this sense every possessor of a piece of land is a sole
supplier of the services of his piece, and is therefore a monopolist.
Of course, the differences within a group of pieces of land may be so
small in size, situation, or quality that the individual pieces are
regarded as homogeneous and substitutable by the buyers.

Let us assume that the use of a hundred acres of land similar in type
is offered by a number of competing suppliers. If the buyers behave as

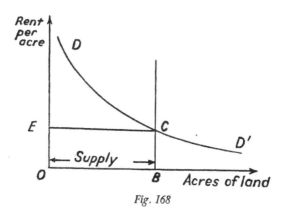

Fig. 168

quantity-adjusters there will be a falling demand curve which will
tell us how many acres the demanders wish to purchase at a given
price for the use of an acre for one year. If the quantity of land available is greater than the saturation demand, then obviously the rent
will be nil. There will only be a rent above nil if the quantity available
is smaller than the saturation demand, i.e. if land is scarce. If the use
of a total quantity of land, equal to *OB* is supplied, and if the demand
curve has the form illustrated in Fig. 168, then the equilibrium rent
will be represented by *OE*. *It is the shortage of land which results in
rent being above nil. Differences between the rents for different groups
of substitutable pieces of land are explicable simply from the differences
in the kind of land or from differences in the structure of demand.*[1]

The simple explanation of the level of rents which we have given
here is, of course, only applicable under the assumptions we have
made. It is only one of many different possibilities among the various
market situations. Because every piece of land is an individuality,
the form of market may well be that of bilateral monopoly, or one

---

[1] The importance of differences in fertility for the level of rent was studied
   particularly by David Ricardo (1772–1823), and differences in situation by
   J. Heinrich v. Thünen (1783–1850).

where the sellers face a small number of buyers. As we know, different modes of behaviour are applicable in such forms of markets. Some form of negotiating strategy will usually be adopted. Anyone who wishes to hire a particular piece of land for the purpose of production will calculate from his production plan the upper limit up to which he is willing to pay for the use of the land. On the other hand, the seller will calculate the lower limit for his supply price, which will be equal to the most lucrative of the other possible uses for the land. Where the price will be fixed within these limits cannot be discovered simply by theoretical analysis.

3. Rent, in the strictest case, does not comprise the whole payment for use of, or the whole return from a piece of land. In so far as the land has been subject to improvements in the past of one kind or another, it has taken on the characteristics of a piece of material capital. In the total "rent" there will be included elements of interest and depreciation on the sums invested in the past. Only when the sum for interest and depreciation has been subtracted from the total rent will we have the so-called "pure rent" as the price of the services of "the original and indestructible powers of the soil" (Ricardo). But it is hardly possible in practice to make such a division. Modern theory considers the difference between land and capital goods more as a distinction of degree than of kind. Much of modern land must be regarded as a *produced* good. On the other hand, the powers of the soil are not always indestructible (for example, mines), and must be subject to depreciation by the firm using them just like any other piece of capital equipment. The difference between land and other pieces of capital equipment simply consists in the fact that land, as contrasted with capital, is not reproducible at will.

## Section C

## TOTAL EQUILIBRIUM IN A CLOSED ECONOMY

### 1. Partial versus Total Equilibrium

1. Up to now we have been discussing partial equilibria. We have taken out a section of the total economy and made it the subject of a static, and in some cases also of a dynamic, analysis. We have studied what values the variables relating to this section of economic events must have, given certain data, if the economic plans of the individuals engaged in this sector are to be in agreement or harmony with one another. The influences of variables not belonging to this sector of the economy have been excluded from the relationships we

have been studying. To do this we have made the assumption that variables outside our sector of the economy do not change their value in the course of the analysis of these partial relationships. This is the well-known "*ceteris paribus*" *clause*, which we had to introduce in order to be able to study the economic process undisturbed by influences external to the partial sector we are examining. The surrounding world is regarded as fixed or frozen over the period for which it is being studied. A partial analysis cannot be pursued by any other methods. Just as we have to study the course of the economic process as a whole on the basis of a certain set of data for the whole economy, similarly we have here to treat as given and unchanging everything outside these partial relationships.[1] The results of partial analysis, therefore, are only valid on the assumption that the outside variables have given values. If the exogenous variables have other values, then the conclusions of partial analysis, and in particular the equilibrium values of the variables in the partial relationships, are altered, just as the economic process as a whole is different if the data for the total economy are changed. This shows us the limits of partial analysis. *Because of its dependence on the values of variables outside it, the existence of a partial equilibrium does not in any way guarantee a total equilibrium for the whole economy, where, given certain data for the economy as a whole, the variables have values such that no individual has reason to alter his dispositions.* Let us assume, for example, that for the description and analysis of the economic process as a whole four variables $x$, $y$, $z$, and $u$ are necessary. Given certain data for the total economy, the following

[1] "The concept of an equilibrium system . . . is applicable as well to the case of a single variable as to so-called general equilibrium involving thousands of variables. Logically the determination of output of a given firm under pure competition is precisely the same as the simultaneous determination of thousands of prices and quantities. In every case *ceteris paribus* assumptions must be made. The only difference lies in the fact that in the general equilibrium analysis of, let us say, Walras, the content of the historical discipline of theoretical economics is practically exhausted. The things we are taking as data for that system happen to be matters which economists have traditionally chosen not to consider as within their province. Among these data may be mentioned tastes, technology, the governmental and institutional framework, and many others.

It is clear, however, that logically there is nothing fundamental about the traditional boundaries of economic science. In fact, a system may be as broad or as narrow as we please, depending upon the purpose at hand; and the data of one system may be the variables of a wider system depending upon expediency. The fruitfulness of any theory will hinge upon the degree to which factors relevant to the particular investigation at hand are brought into sharp focus." (P. A. Samuelson: *Foundations of Economic Analysis*, Cambridge, Mass., 1947, pp. 8–9.)

four functional relationships may exist between these four variables:

$$f(x, y, z, u) = 0$$
$$g(x, y, z, u) = 0$$
$$h(x, y, z, u) = 0$$
$$j(x, y, z, u) = 0.$$

The variables $x$ and $y$ and the first two of the above equations may relate to the (partial) market 1, and the variables $z$ and $u$ along with the other two equations, relate to market 2. If one is engaged in a partial analysis of market 1, then in addition to the data for the economy as a whole, the values of the variables relating to market 2, i.e. $z$ and $u$, must be treated as given. Let us call the values of $z$ and $u$, to be regarded as constant, $\bar{z}$ and $\bar{u}$, then we have the following equations for the partial analysis of market 1:

$$f(x, y, \bar{z}, \bar{u}) = 0$$
$$g(x, y, \bar{z}, \bar{u}) = 0$$

in which only the two quantities relating to market 1, i.e. $x$ and $y$, are now variables. The values of $x$ and $y$ which satisfy these two equations then represent the equilibrium values for the (partial) market 1. As can be seen, these equilibrium values are only valid if the values for the external variables $z$ and $u$ are treated as constant. If these variables are given other values, then, if the data for the economy as a whole remain unchanged, there will be a new partial equilibrium on market 1. Let us take a numerical example in the form of the following four equations:

$$2x + y + z + u = 9$$
$$x + 3y - z + 2u = 8$$
$$-6x + y + 2z - u = 14$$
$$x - 2y - z - u = -22.$$

For $z = 2$ and $u = 1$ we have from the first two equations equilibrium values of $x = 2$ and $y = 2$; for $z = 3$ and $u = 2$ the equilibrium values are $x = 1$ and $y = 2$.

The equilibrium values $x = 2$ and $y = 2$ corresponding to the values $z = 2$ and $u = 1$ do not, as can easily be seen, give a total equilibrium because the system of values $x = 2, y = 2, z = 2, u = 1$ does not satisfy the second two equations. If $x$ and $y$ have the values $x = 2$ and $y = 2$, there is only equilibrium in the second two equations if $z = 14\frac{2}{3}$ and $u = 5\frac{1}{3}$. But with these values for $z$ and $u$ the equilibrium values for $x$ and $y$ change in the first partial system, and so on. There is only total equilibrium with those values of the four variables which satisfy simultaneously all four equations.

Equilibrium, therefore, on one partial market may directly lead to disequilibrium in other markets. *To understand the essential character of the position of total equilibrium, and in fact the whole of economic theory, it is of fundamental importance to grasp this mutual interdependence of all quantities in an economy.* An especially clear formulation of these decisive relationships was given by Cournot in his great work which appeared in 1838 entitled *Investigations of the Mathematical Foundations of the Theory of Wealth:*

"So far we have studied how, for each commodity by itself, the law of demand in connection with the conditions of production of that commodity, determines the price of it and regulates the incomes of its producers. We considered as given and invariable the prices of other commodities and the incomes of other producers; but in reality the economic system is a whole of which all the parts are connected and react on each other. An increase in the income of the producers of commodity *A* will affect the demand for commodities *B*, *C*, etc. and the incomes of their producers, and, by its reaction, will involve a change in demand for commodity *A*. Its seems, therefore, as if, for a complete and rigorous solution of the problem relative to some part of the economic system, it were indispensable to take the entire system into consideration." (A. Cournot, loc. cit., English translation by Nathaniel T. Bacon, London, 1897, p. 127.)

From an understanding of the interdependence of all economic variables it is a long way, however, to solving the problem of total or general equilibrium. Cournot believed that the problem of total equilibrium would be too much for mathematical analysis.[1] It was Léon Walras who first succeeded in solving with complete generality the static problem of total equilibrium in a closed economy, taking account of the general interdependence of all variables.[2] In honour of this great work, one of the supreme achievements in the development of economic theory, a bronze plaque was unveiled on the 10th June, 1909, at the Academy of Lausanne celebrating the jubilee of Léon Walras and bearing the following inscription:

"To Léon Walras, born at Evreux in 1834, professor at the Academy and at the University of Lausanne, who was the first to establish the general conditions of economic equilibrium and was

---

[1] Loc. cit., p. 127.
[2] The solution to the problem of total equilibrium was given in his *Eléments d'Économie politique pure* which appeared for the first time in 1874, and in its final version in 1926. (English translation: *Elements of Pure Economics*, transl. Jaffé, London, 1954.)

thus the founder of 'the School of Lausanne'. In honour of 50 years of disinterested work."

2. We shall now examine Walras' static solution of the total equilibrium problem. A complete analysis of Walras' exposition would exceed the limits of this volume. We shall, therefore, make a few simplifications and confine ourselves to working out the essential features of his solution. In doing this we shall proceed somewhat differently from Walras, in order to show what contribution static equilibrium analysis can make to the problem of the level of employment which we shall discuss in vol. III.

The question which we are asking is: *what levels must prices and quantities of goods have, given particular data for the economy as a whole, if the economic plans of individuals are to be in agreement?* Our answer will in the first place be for a pure exchange economy; that is, for an economy in which stocks of goods given at the beginning of a period are to be exchanged between the individual members. We are not concerned with the origin of these stocks of goods. The stocks are data, so far as we are concerned. If we have got a grasp of the total equilibrium problem for this kind of pure exchange economy it will be easier to understand subsequently the problems of production.

## 2. Total Equilibrium in a Stationary Exchange Economy without Production (The Case of a Pure Exchange Economy)

### a. Exchange between Two Parties

1. Let us take an economy in which only two individuals are engaged. No. 1 disposes in each period of *a* units of good *A* and No. 2 disposes of *b* units of good *B*. We are not interested in the question of how these individuals came to possess these quantities of goods. Good *A* has no ophelimity for No. 1, and good *B* none for No. 2. But good *A* has ophelimity for No. 2, and good *B* for No. 1. An exchange is therefore clearly profitable for both individuals. The quantities *a* and *b* are assumed to be less than the saturation quantities of the good for the two individuals. The prices of the two goods are to be expressed in a unit of account recognized by both parties, let us say shillings. The price of *A* or *B* is, therefore, $p_a$ or $p_b$ shillings. The two parties are assumed to be treating the prices as given quantities. Our question is, what levels the two prices must have if the existing stocks of goods are to be completely exchanged in a period of time.

2. Let us call the income of the two subjects expressed in the unit

of account as $y_1$ and $y_2$. Then at a price of $p_a$ the quantity $x_a$ of the good $A$ demanded by No. 2 will be:

$$x_a = \frac{y_2}{p_a} \tag{1}$$

Correspondingly, at a price of $p_b$ the quantity $x_b$ demanded by No. 1 of the good $B$ is:

$$x_b = \frac{y_1}{p_b} \tag{2}$$

These two relations represent in our simplified case the *demand functions* of the two parties.

For the incomes of the two parties the following equations hold:

$$y_1 = p_a \cdot a \tag{3}$$

$$y_2 = p_b \cdot b \tag{4}$$

On our assumption, the quantity demanded by one party is to be treated as equal to the constant quantity supplied in the period. It must, therefore, hold:

$$x_a = a \tag{5}$$

$$x_b = b \tag{6}$$

It can easily be seen that equations (1) to (6) reduce to a single equation:

$$p_a \cdot a = p_b \cdot b \tag{7}$$

so that we have a single equation for determining the two prices. Equation (7) can also be written in the form:

$$\frac{p_a}{p_b} = \frac{b}{a} \tag{8}$$

This equation represents the condition which the two prices must satisfy if the quantities supplied in the period are to be equal to the quantities demanded. The equation contains the two prices as unknowns, so that in order to determine the two unknowns we only have a single equation. This fact may be expressed by saying that *the system possesses one degree of freedom.* That is to say, *we can choose the level of one of the two prices arbitrarily. Only if the level of one price is arbitrarily fixed will the level of the other price be determined.*

*The degree of freedom of the system, that is, the number of variables which can be chosen at random, is of great importance for the analysis of economic systems.* The reader must therefore be completely clear about this concept of the degree of freedom and its content. If, for example, there exist between ten variables only seven equations, or relationships, then the system possesses three degrees of freedom. The system is only determined if the values of the three variables are arbitrarily chosen.

3. *The assumptions of our simple problem do not, as we have seen, allow us to derive the absolute level of the two prices.* The indeterminacy in the solution of the problem lies in the existence of the one degree of freedom. This result can also be expressed as follows: *The assumptions of our problem only allow us to derive the relation between the two prices.* If the quantities demanded are to be equal to the quantities supplied, and the quantities supplied to be exchanged without remainder, then the price relationship must be as in (8). It must be the inverse of the ratio of the quantities supplied. For the existence of equilibrium it is only the *price relation* that is relevant, not the absolute level of prices. We may also say that the equilibrium prices, and therewith the equilibrium income, are determined up to (i.e. except for) a single multiplicative constant. In the exchanges themselves there is nothing that can determine the actual prices of the goods. This is the first important conclusion which the analysis of this simple case gives us.[1]

If the price relation is other than $b/a$, then the existing quantities of goods will not all be exchanged without a remainder. These relationships can be very clearly displayed by a geometrical method of R. Frisch.[2] In Fig. 169 the quantity $x_a$ of the good $A$ is measured along the horizontal axis, and the quantity $x_b$ of the good $B$ along the vertical axis. The distance $OR$ (or $OP$) gives the available quantity of good $A$ (or good $B$). If we draw in the rectangle $OPQR$, with the sides $OR = a$ and $OP = b$, then all the points lying within or on the sides of the rectangle represent a possible relation of exchange. An exchange of the quantity $OS$ of the good $A$, against the quantity $ST$ of the good $B$, will be represented by the point $T$. The exchange relation $x_b/x_a$ will then be given by the tan of the angle $TOS$ ($= \alpha$). All points of exchange with the same exchange relation therefore lie on a ray from the origin the slope of which, measured by $\tan \alpha$, is

[1] "Hence we arrive at an important, if self-evident, fact, the neglect of which has constantly resulted in false conclusions. The exchange of commodities in itself, and the conditions of production and consumption on which it depends, affect only exchange values or *relative* prices: they can exert *no direct influence on the absolute level of money prices.*" (K. Wicksell: *Interest and Prices* (1898), translated by R. F. Kahn, p. 23.)

[2] R. Frisch: "Circulation Planning: Proposal for a National Organization of a Commodity and Service Exchange" in *Econometrica*, Vol. II, 1934, pp. 258 ff.

equal to the exchange relation or the price relation $p_a/p_b$. It must always hold that:

$$\frac{x_b}{x_a} = \frac{p_a}{p_b}$$

If the price relation has exactly the equilibrium value, then:

$$\frac{x_b}{x_a} = \frac{b}{a} = \frac{p_a}{p_b} = 0{\cdot}8.$$

Then all the points of exchange at this price ratio lie on the line $OQ$. If $A$ is dearer in terms of $B$ than in the equilibrium condition (if,

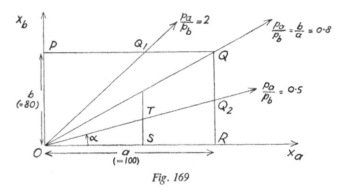

Fig. 169

say, $p_a/p_b = x_b/x_a = 2$) then two units of $B$ must exchange for one unit of $A$ and the exchange line will be steeper than $OQ$. It will now be represented by $OQ_1$. If $A$ measured in terms of $B$ is cheaper than in the equilibrium position (if, say, $p_a/p_b = x_b/x_a = \frac{1}{2}$) then only half a unit of $B$ exchanges for one unit of $A$, and the exchange line will be less steep than $OQ$. It may now be represented by $OQ_2$. From Fig. 169 it is clear that only for an exchange line passing through $Q$, that is, only if the exchange relation is $b/a$, can the existing quantities be exchanged without remainder. For any other price relation either a part of the stock of good $A$, or a part of that of good $B$ will remain over. At a price relation of $p_a/p_b = 2$, if $B$ is to be entirely exchanged, a quantity $QQ_1$ of $A$ will remain over; at a price of $p_a/p_b = 0{\cdot}5$, if $A$ is to be entirely exchanged, then a quantity $QQ_2$ of $B$ will remain over. This diagram supplies us with a second important conclusion: *that divergencies of price relationships from equilibrium relationships result in the under-utilization or under-employment of the existing quantities of the goods.*

### b. Exchange between Three Parties

1. Let us extend our analysis to the case of an economy with three economic individuals engaged. No. 1 has in the period under consideration $a$ units of good $A$, No. 2 has $b$ units of good $B$, and No. 3 $c$ units of good $C$. None of the three goods have any ophelimity for their possessor. Each of the three parties desires the goods in the possession of the other two, and each tries to exchange their entire stock against the goods they desire. The entire stock of a good is smaller than the total of the "saturation" quantities of the subjects desiring it. The prices for the three goods are expressed in a unit of account, "shillings", and are $p_a$, $p_b$, and $p_c$. We assume that the subjects consider the prices to be for them given constants, and behave as quantity-adjusters. Our question is: *what levels must the prices have, given the tastes of the three subjects, if the existing stocks are to be exchanged without remainder, that is, if the existing (constant) supply is to be completely absorbed by the demand?* The data of our problem, therefore, are the quantities of goods existing in a period in the hands of the three parties, their tastes, and their mode of behaviour.

2. Let us make use of the following symbols:

$x_{1b}$ or $x_{1c}$ quantity demanded by No. 1 of good $B$ or $C$

$x_{2a}$ or $x_{2c}$ quantity demanded by No. 2 of good $A$ or $C$

$x_{3a}$ or $x_{3b}$ quantity demanded by No. 3 of good $A$ or $B$

$y_1$, $y_2$ or $y_3$ incomes in shillings of Nos. 1, 2 and 3.

These nine variables, together with the three prices $p_a$, $p_b$ and $p_c$, represent the 12 unknowns of our problem. We have to discover what conditions these variables must satisfy in equilibrium, and how their equilibrium values are determined.

The dispositions to exchange of the parties are expressed as part of the data by the individual demand functions. We know from the analysis of the household that the demand of the household for the goods it desires in a period depends on the prices of these goods, and the income of the household. For example, for the demand $x_{1b}$ of No. 1 for the good $B$ we have the functional relation:

$$x_{1b} = x_{1b}(p_b, p_c, y_1). \tag{9}$$

We now suppose that the demanders are free of any money illusion,[1] which means that the quantity demanded depends not on absolute prices and absolute levels of income but upon the relation of incomes

[1] See above, p. 6.

to prices, in other words on the household's real income. The demand function above has, therefore, the form:

$$x_{1b} = x_{1b}\left(\frac{y_1}{p_b}, \frac{y_1}{p_c}\right) \tag{9a}$$

The six demand functions of the three parties are, therefore, as follows:

$$\left.\begin{aligned} x_{1b} &= x_{1b}\left(\frac{y_1}{p_b}, \frac{y_1}{p_c}\right) \\ x_{1c} &= x_{1c}\left(\frac{y_1}{p_b}, \frac{y_1}{p_c}\right) \end{aligned}\right\} \text{Demand functions of No. 1} \tag{10a}$$

$$\left.\begin{aligned} x_{2a} &= x_{2a}\left(\frac{y_2}{p_a}, \frac{y_2}{p_c}\right) \\ x_{2c} &= x_{2c}\left(\frac{y_2}{p_a}, \frac{y_2}{p_c}\right) \end{aligned}\right\} \text{Demand functions of No. 2} \tag{10b}$$

$$\left.\begin{aligned} x_{3a} &= x_{3a}\left(\frac{y_3}{p_a}, \frac{y_3}{p_b}\right) \\ x_{3b} &= x_{3b}\left(\frac{y_3}{p_a}, \frac{y_3}{p_b}\right) \end{aligned}\right\} \text{Demand functions of No. 3} \tag{10c}$$

*The incomes of the three parties,* on our assumption that each party exchanges the entire stock in his possession, are given by the three equations:

$$\begin{aligned} y_1 &= p_a \cdot a \\ y_2 &= p_b \cdot b \\ y_3 &= p_c \cdot c \end{aligned} \tag{11}$$

Finally, in equilibrium, *the total quantities of a good demanded must be equal to the total quantity supplied.* The following equations must, therefore, hold:

$$\begin{aligned} x_{2a} + x_{3a} &= a \\ x_{1b} + x_{3b} &= b \\ x_{1c} + x_{2c} &= c \end{aligned} \tag{12}$$

While the total demand depends on the price relations and income, the total supply is, on our assumption, independent of the levels of prices.

Between the 12 variables or unknowns in the system, six representing quantities of goods, three prices, and three incomes, we have 12 relations: six demand functions, three income equations, and three equations expressing equality between total demand and supply in equilibrium. It appears, therefore, that the number of equations corresponds to the number of unknowns, and that the 12 equations determine the 12 variables. But this is not the case. It is not difficult to see that *one of the three equations in* (12) *is not independent of all the other equations*, and that it can be derived from the other 11 equations. From equations (10), (11), and two of those in (12), the third equation in (12) automatically follows. We can show that the third of the equations (12):

$$x_{1c} + x_{2c} = c$$

is automatically fulfilled if the other equations (10), (11) and (12) are given. If we multiply the first of the two equations in (12) on both sides by $p_a$, and the second of the two equations in (12) on both sides by $p_b$, then we have:

$$p_a \cdot a = p_a \cdot x_{2a} + p_a \cdot x_{3a} \qquad (13)$$
$$p_b \cdot b = p_b \cdot x_{1b} + p_b \cdot x_{3b}$$

As, in a stationary economy, the total income of an individual is used for consumption, the total monetary demand of an individual must be equal to his income. It must hold that:

$$p_a \cdot a = p_b \cdot x_{1b} + p_c \cdot x_{1c} \qquad (14)$$
$$p_b \cdot b = p_a \cdot x_{2a} + p_c \cdot x_{2c}$$

These two equations are in a stationary economy implicitly contained in the demand functions, and represent conditions which the demand functions in the stationary economy must always satisfy. They do not represent additional independent equations. If we add together the equations in (13) we have:

$$p_a \cdot a + p_b \cdot b = p_a \cdot x_{2a} + p_a \cdot x_{3a} + p_b \cdot x_{1b} + p_b \cdot x_{3b}.$$

But according to (14):

$$p_a \cdot a + p_b \cdot b = p_b \cdot x_{1b} + p_c \cdot x_{1c} + p_a \cdot x_{2a} + p_c \cdot x_{2c}$$

so that the equation holds

$$p_a \cdot x_{2a} + p_a \cdot x_{3a} + p_b \cdot x_{1b} + p_b \cdot x_{3b}$$
$$= p_b \cdot x_{1b} + p_c \cdot x_{1c} + p_a \cdot x_{2a} + p_c \cdot x_{2c}$$

or

$$p_a \cdot x_{3a} + p_b \cdot x_{3b} = p_c \cdot (x_{1c} + x_{2c}) \qquad (15)$$

The left side of this equation represents the total of the monetary demand of No. 3 which is equal to his income. It holds, therefore that:

$$p_a \cdot x_{3a} + p_b \cdot x_{3b} = p_c \cdot c$$

so that equation (15) can also be written in the form

$$p_c \cdot c = p_c \cdot (x_{1c} + x_{2c})$$

or
$$c = x_{1c} + x_{2c}.$$

But this is the third of the three equations in (12). This shows that the third of the equations in (12) is not an independent equation, but depends on the other equations in (10), (11) and (12).

We, therefore, have in all only 11 independent equations for determining the equilibrium values of the 12 variables. Our system of 11 equations again has one degree of freedom; that is, the values of one variable, for example, a price or an income, can be chosen arbitrarily. Our system of equations only permits the determination of *relative prices and incomes, but not the absolute level of prices and incomes.* This conclusion will be still clearer if we introduce the expressions (11) for the incomes in the demand functions in (10). Then we have:

$$
\left.
\begin{aligned}
x_{1b} &= x_{1b}\left(a \cdot \frac{p_a}{p_b}, a \cdot \frac{p_a}{p_c}\right) \\[2mm]
x_{1c} &= x_{1c}\left(a \cdot \frac{p_a}{p_b}, a \cdot \frac{p_a}{p_c}\right) \\[2mm]
x_{2a} &= x_{2a}\left(b \cdot \frac{p_b}{p_a}, b \cdot \frac{p_b}{p_c}\right) \\[2mm]
x_{2c} &= x_{2c}\left(b \cdot \frac{p_b}{p_a}, b \cdot \frac{p_b}{p_c}\right) \\[2mm]
x_{3a} &= x_{3a}\left(c \cdot \frac{p_c}{p_a}, c \cdot \frac{p_c}{p_b}\right) \\[2mm]
x_{3b} &= x_{3b}\left(c \cdot \frac{p_c}{p_a}, c \cdot \frac{p_c}{p_b}\right)
\end{aligned}
\right\} \qquad (16)
$$

In these equations the following price relations appear as independent variables:
$$\frac{p_a}{p_b}, \frac{p_b}{p_a}, \frac{p_c}{p_a}, \frac{p_a}{p_c}, \frac{p_b}{p_c}, \frac{p_c}{p_b}$$

Actually, these six price ratios are made up of three pairs of reciprocal ratios. It follows that only three price ratios appear as variables which need to be determined, namely:
$$\frac{pa}{pb}, \frac{pa}{pc}, \frac{pb}{pc},$$

Moreover, in general equilibrium it must hold that
$$\frac{pa}{pc} = \frac{pa}{pb} \cdot \frac{pb}{pc}$$

Hence we are left with only two price ratios, i.e. the rate at which each of two goods exchange for the third good, as variables independent of each other. All the quantities demanded in (16) can, therefore, be expressed as functions of the two price ratios $\frac{p_a}{p_c}$ and $\frac{p_b}{p_c}$ .[1]

We have now reduced our eleven equations in (10), (11) and (12) to eight for eight unknowns (or variables): six demand functions representing the quantity demanded as a function of the two price relations, and the two equations (12) expressing the equality between the total quantity demanded and the total quantity supplied of the two goods. These eight equations determine simultaneously the two price relations and the six quantities demanded. *If the quantities supplied of the goods a, b and c are to be disposed of in the period, without remainder, then the price relations must have the particular values given by this system of equations.*

This solution for three-sided exchange can be extended to the exchange of *n* goods between *m* different subjects. (*n, m,* >3).

By ascertaining that the number of equations agrees with the number of unknowns we have not, of course, disposed of the problem. We still have to examine whether any solution at all exists to the system of equations, i.e. whether an equilibrium position exists[2] and also whether such an equilibrium is stable or unstable. The second question can only be decided by means of a dynamic theory. The problems of the existence and stability of equilibria are outside the limits of this introductory volume.[3]

3. The following numerical example may help to make still clearer the analysis of the preceding paragraph. In order not to complicate the calculations unduly we are assuming that the demand of an individual for a good depends simply on the price of this good and on his income, and that this dependence is of the simple form:

$$x = \alpha . \frac{y}{p} \quad (0 < \alpha < 1)$$

---

[1] "When the market is in a state of general equilibrium, the $m(m-1)$ prices which govern the exchange between all possible pairs drawn from $m$ commodities are implicitly determined by the $m-1$ prices which govern the exchange between any $m-1$ of these commodities and the $m^{th}$." (L. Walras, *Elements of Pure Economics*. English translation by William Jaffé, London, 1954, p. 185).

[2] See A. Wald, "Ueber einige Gleichungssysteme der mathematischen Oekonomie", *Zeitschrift fuer Nationaloekonomie*, vol. 12, 1936, pp. 649 ff.

[3] See J. R. Hicks, *Value and Capital*, London, 1939, part II: "General Equilibrium."

We are therefore, assuming that the monetary demand for the good represents a constant fraction of income. Individual No. 1 disposes of 36 units of good $A$, No. 2 disposes of 20 units of good $B$, and No. 3 of 50 units of good $C$.

The six demand functions of the three individuals are:

$$x_{1b} = 0 \cdot 6 \cdot \frac{y_1}{p_b}; \quad x_{1c} = 0 \cdot 4 \cdot \frac{y_1}{p_c}$$

$$x_{2a} = 0 \cdot 6 \cdot \frac{y_2}{p_a}; \quad x_{2c} = 0 \cdot 4 \cdot \frac{y_2}{p_c} \tag{17}$$

$$x_{3a} = 0 \cdot 3 \cdot \frac{y_3}{p_a}; \quad x_{3b} = 0 \cdot 7 \cdot \frac{y_3}{p_b}$$

The three income equations are:

$$y_1 = 36 \cdot p_a; \quad y_2 = 20 \cdot p_b; \quad y_3 = 50 \cdot p_c \tag{18}$$

Making use of (18) we may write the demand functions:

$$x_{1b} = 21 \cdot 6 \cdot \frac{p_a}{p_b}; \quad x_{1c} = 14 \cdot 4 \cdot \frac{p_a}{p_c}$$

$$x_{2a} = 12 \cdot \frac{p_b}{p_a}; \quad x_{2c} = 8 \cdot \frac{p_b}{p_c} \tag{19}$$

$$x_{3a} = 15 \cdot \frac{p_c}{p_a}; \quad x_{3b} = 35 \cdot \frac{p_c}{p_b}$$

Using (19) the first two equations in (12) become:

$$12 \cdot \frac{p_b}{p_a} + 15 \cdot \frac{p_c}{p_a} = 36$$

$$21 \cdot 6 \cdot \frac{p_a}{p_b} + 35 \cdot \frac{p_c}{p_b} = 20 \tag{20}$$

To abbreviate:

$$\frac{p_a}{p_b} = u; \quad \frac{p_c}{p_b} = v.$$

Then (20) becomes:

$$\frac{12}{u} + 15 \cdot \frac{v}{u} = 36$$

$$21 \cdot 6 \cdot u + 35 \cdot v = 20.$$

The solution of these equations gives us:

$$\frac{p_a}{p_b} = \frac{5}{11}; \quad \frac{p_b}{p_c} = \frac{55}{16}$$

or

$$p_a : p_b : p_c = 25 : 55 : 16.$$

*The three prices are, therefore, determined up to a multiplicative constant*, and can be written in the form: $p_a = 25 \cdot \gamma$; $p_b = 55 \cdot \gamma$; $p_c = 16 \cdot \gamma$, where $\gamma$ represents any constant factor of proportionality.

For all combinations of prices which fulfil these conditions our system of exchange will be in equilibrium. From (18) the equilibrium incomes are:

$$y_1 = 900 \cdot \gamma; \quad y_2 = 1110 \cdot \gamma; \quad y_3 = 800 \cdot \gamma$$

From the individual incomes we obtain the total (national) income:

$$y = y_1 + y_2 + y_3 = 2800 \cdot \gamma$$

and these are determined up to a multiplicative constant.

From (17) we obtain the quantities of goods exchanged in equilibrium:

$$x_{1b} = 9\tfrac{9}{11}; \quad x_{1c} = 22\tfrac{1}{2}$$
$$x_{2a} = 26 \cdot 4; \quad x_{2c} = 27 \cdot 5$$
$$x_{3a} = 9 \cdot 6; \quad x_{3b} = 10\tfrac{2}{11}.$$

The quantities of goods are uniquely determined given the price relation. In order to obtain absolute levels for the prices various procedures are possible. We could, for example, choose one price at random. If we take, say, $p_a = 1$, then we have:

$$p_a = 1; \quad p_b = 2 \cdot 2; \quad p_c = 0 \cdot 64.$$

For the incomes we have:

$$y_1 = 36; \quad y_2 = 44; \quad y_3 = 32.$$

Instead of a price we could choose at random an income, or the total (national) income, and the absolute prices and incomes would then again be uniquely determined. If, for example, we take $y_1 = 900$, then we have:

$$y_1 = 900; \quad y_2 = 1100; \quad y_3 = 800$$
$$p_a = 25; \quad p_b = 55; \quad p_c = 16.$$

4. Let us consider once more the nature of the equations which determine the equilibrium position of our system of exchange. The demand functions (10), which, like the quantities of the goods supplied, belong to the data of the system, express the dispositions to purchase of the individuals at given prices and given incomes.

They are relations representing the behaviour of the individuals as buyers. We may describe them, therefore, as *behaviour equations*. The income equations (11) are simply definitions of the incomes of the individuals. They may be described as *definitional equations*. The equations in (12) contain the equilibrium conditions. They say that in a position of equilibrium the total quantity demanded of a good is equal to the total quantity supplied. They may be described, therefore, as *equations for the equilibrium conditions*.

5. The theory of economic equilibrium in a stationary closed economy, which we have now expounded, tells us nothing as to whether the exchanges take the form of barter, where money simply has the role of a unit of account (Walras' *numéraire*), or whether a generally recognized means of payment is employed for purchases and sales. Both forms of exchange are possible and Walras left this question open.[1]

If the exchange takes the form of *barter* it follows essentially from the theory of exchange that the equilibrium position will generally not come about by direct exchanges between the original possessors of the goods. The direct transactions have to be combined with *indirect transactions*, in which some individuals obtain goods by exchange, not in order to use or consume them, but in order with their aid to obtain indirectly the quantity of the good they desire.

The quantities exchanged between the three individuals when the position of equilibrium has been reached, following the numerical examples above, are given in the adjoining table.

The exchange relations are:

1 unit of good $B$ against 2·2 units of good $A$

1 unit of good $C$ against 0·64 units of good $A$

1 unit of good $C$ against 0·29 units of good $B$

1 unit of good $B$ against 3·44 units of good $C$.

It can easily be seen that the process of exchange between the two individuals, if it takes the form of barter, necessarily requires that some of the individuals obtain goods, not for their own consumption, but for further exchange transactions:

For the $9\frac{9}{11}$ units of good $B$ which No. 1 obtains from No. 2, No. 1 has to give, at the ruling rate of exchange, $21\frac{3}{8}$ units of good $A$, so that No. 2 is short of $4\frac{4}{5}$ units of good $A$.

No. 1 wishes to obtain $22\frac{1}{2}$ units of good $C$; the quantity of good $A$ which has to be given in exchange for this is 14·4 units, while No. 3 only wants 9·6 units of $A$.

[1] L. Walras, *op. cit.* [Engl. transl.], p. 190.

With barter, the exchange can only be carried out indirectly by means of intermediate trading. In the first place the following direct exchange transactions will be carried out:

(1) No. 1 gives to No. 2: $21\frac{3}{5}$ units of $A$ in return for $9\frac{9}{11}$ units of $B$.

(2) No. 1 gives to No. 3: $9\frac{3}{5}$ units of $A$ in return for 15 units of $C$.

(3) No. 2 gives to No. 3: 8 units of $B$ in return for $27\frac{1}{2}$ units of $C$.

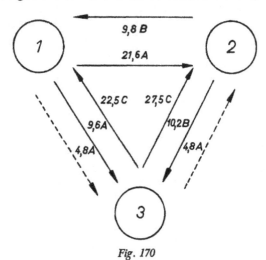

Fig. 170

After these direct-exchange transactions the situation will be as follows:

| | Has obtained by exchange | Still desires | Still possesses |
|---|---|---|---|
| No. 1 | $9\frac{9}{11}$ units of $B$<br>15 units of $C$ | $7\frac{1}{2}$ units of $C$ | $4\frac{4}{5}$ units of $A$ |
| No. 2 | $21\frac{3}{5}$ units of $A$<br>$27\frac{1}{2}$ units of $C$ | $4\frac{4}{5}$ units of $A$ | $2\frac{9}{11}$ units of $B$ |
| No. 3 | $9\frac{3}{5}$ units of $A$<br>8 units of $B$ | $2\frac{9}{11}$ units of $B$ | $7\frac{1}{2}$ units of $C$ |

No. 3 now exchanges $7\frac{1}{2}$ units of $C$ against $4\frac{4}{5}$ units of $A$ bringing No. 1 to his equilibrium position. The $4\frac{4}{5}$ units of $A$ which No. 3 has thereby received he now exchanges with No. 2 for $2\frac{9}{11}$ units of $B$, which thereby brings Nos. 2 and 3 into their equilibrium positions. No. 3 therefore obtains the $4\frac{4}{5}$ units of $A$ simply for purposes of intermediate trading (Fig. 170).

The exchanges take place much more simply if money is used, or some generally recognized means of payment. As means of payment let us assume that an intrinsically valueless form of money is used which has no ophelimity for its possessors. The quantities of the means of payment necessary for carrying out the exchange transactions required to reach equilibrium depend obviously on the level of prices and the income velocity of circulation. Let us suppose that the income velocity of circulation is 1, then the prices in terms of the unit of account, which for simplicity we may assume to be identical with the means of payment, will be as follows:

$$p_a = 1; \quad p_b = 2 \cdot 2; \quad p_c = 0 \cdot 64.$$

The demand for money or means of payment will be as follows for the three individuals:

No. 1: 36 units

No. 2: 44 units

No. 3: 32 units.

Let us assume, further, that all the payments are made at the end of the period (that is, all purchases and sales within the period are performed on credit), then we have the following table of payments:

|  | No. 1 | No. 2 | No. 3 | Total |
|---|---|---|---|---|
| No. 1 pays to | — | 21·6 | 14·4 | 36 |
| No. 2 pays to | 26·4 | — | 17·6 | 44 |
| No. 3 pays to | 9·6 | 22·4 | — | 32 |
|  | 36·0 | 44·0 | 32·0 |  |

The total income $y$ of the economy (112 units of money) is, therefore (as must be the case in a stationary economy), equal to the value of consumption $C$:

$$y = C.$$

If the income velocity of circulation is 1, the quantity of money required will be 112 units. This sum represents the demand for money of the stationary economy at the prices $p_a = 1$; $p_b = 2 \cdot 2$; and $p_c = 0 \cdot 64$, these being the equilibrium prices, and the money being distributed among the three individuals in the manner given above.

It appears from the above "matrix" that the payment by No. 1 to No. 2 is 4·8 monetary units less than No. 2's payments to No. 1; while the amount paid by No. 1 to No. 3 is exactly 4·8 monetary units greater than the payment from No. 3 to No. 1. No. 1 uses his "export surplus" with No. 2 to settle his "import surplus" with No. 3 The same goes for the transactions between No. 2 and No. 3.

It thus becomes clear that general equilibrium in no way implies equilibrium in each of the three partial markets.

Were one to insist on equilibrium in each of the three partial markets, so that the value of the purchases of individual $i$ from individual $k$ equals the value of the purchases of $k$ from $i$, "then the problem would have given us more independent equations than unknowns and would thus have become over-determined; unless at the same time we had foregone the demand for correlation between the commodity prices, in which case the possible exchange ratios between $n$ goods would be not $n - 1$ only, but $\frac{1}{2}n(n - 1)$, i.e. for three commodities 3, for four 6, etc."[1] The processes of exchange which so far were multilateral in character would in this case become bilateral transactions. In our example it would then follow that: "as between each pair of commodities, the price ratio would be determined in a separate market, isolated from the other two, and the resultant three relative prices would not usually be correlated, i.e. they would not be such that each would be the ratio (or product) of the other two".[2]

The theory which we have now considered, concerning the exchange of more than two goods between more than two parties, is basic to the understanding of the problem of equilibrium in international trade. The reader need merely substitute three countries for the three individuals whom we considered. By our analysis we have demonstrated that in the case of three countries, general equilibrium is only possible if the three currencies are freely convertible.

6. The relation between the total income $y$ (or national income) in a period, the quantity of means of payment $M$, and the income velocity of circulation $v$ obviously has the form:

$$Y = M \cdot v \tag{21}$$

where $v$ is an institutionally determined constant. Bearing in mind that

$$Y = p_a \cdot a + p_b \cdot b + p_c \cdot c \tag{22}$$

we can write (21) in the form:

$$p_a \cdot a + p_b \cdot b + p_c \cdot c = M \cdot v \tag{23}$$

[1] K. Wicksell, *Lectures on Political Economy*, volume I, "General Theory," Jena, 1913 [English translation by E. Classen, edited by L. Robbins, London, 1924, p. 67.] On p. 63 of this classical work the reader will find a very lucid exposition of these matters which are fundamental for an understanding of the processes of exchange.

[2] K. Wicksell, *loc. cit.* [Engl. translation], p. 63.

This equation is known as *the equation of exchange, or quantity equation*, for our stationary economy. It amounts to the tautological proposition that the total amount of payments in a period is equal to the quantity of means of payment multiplied by the institutionally given income velocity of circulation. If this income velocity of circulation is not given institutionally, then (23) is the definitional equation for the income velocity of circulation.

In equilibrium, as we have shown, prices stand in a particular relation to one another. In our numerical example:

$$p_a : p_b : p_c = 25 : 55 : 16.$$

Generalising, we may say:

$$p_a : p_b : p_c = k_a : k_b : k_c$$

or

$$p_a = k_a \cdot \gamma; \quad p_b = k_b \cdot \gamma; \quad p_c = k_c \cdot \gamma \qquad (24)$$

where $\gamma$ represents the undetermined multiplicative constant the value of which fixes the absolute level of prices. If we insert in (23) the expressions given for the prices in (24), then the equation of exchange (23) takes on this form:

$$(k_a \cdot a + k_b \cdot b + k_c \cdot c) \cdot \gamma = M \cdot v \qquad (25)$$

From this equation in which $k_a$, $k_b$ and $k_c$, the three quantities of goods $a$, $b$ and $c$, and the income velocity of circulation $v$, are given constants, it emerges that the size of the multiplicative constant, i.e. the absolute level of prices, depends on the quantity of money $M$; or, inversely, the quantity of money depends on $\gamma$, i.e. the absolute level of prices. We can, therefore, lay down the following two propositions which fundamentally say the same thing:

(1) *In a stationary exchange economy, given the income velocity of circulation, the quantity of money determines the absolute level of prices in a position of equilibrium. If, therefore, in a stationary exchange economy in equilibrium a particular quantity of money is to be held, then the equilibrium prices must have the levels given in (24) and (25).*

(2) *In a stationary exchange economy the absolute level of equilibrium prices determines the quantity of money necessary for carrying through the process of exchange.*

The formulation of these propositons must be closely examined if we are to understand the rôle which the quantity of money plays in our stationary exchange economy. We are *not* saying that an increase in the quantity of money is the *cause* of a rise in the equilibrium prices in accordance with equation (24). We are only saying that *if* a larger amount of means of payment is to be used in our system, the prices in equation (24) *must* correspondingly be raised. *Our treatment is simply a comparative-static one. We are comparing two equilibrium positions which differ simply as to the quantities of money existing, and we are asking how high the equilibrium levels of prices must be in the two cases.* We are *not* asking how a system moves from one position of equilibrium, with a particular quantity of money, to a new position of equilibrium when the quantity of money, let us say, has doubled. The answer to this question, as we are aware, is only possible in terms of a dynamic theory, or a "process" analysis, by which we can work out by what paths the additional quantity of money will flow through the system, and how the individuals engaged will react through time to this change. If it emerged as the result of such a dynamic analysis that a new position of equilibrium, with prices twice as high, was the final result of the process of transition, then, but only then, would we be justified in saying that the doubling of the quantity of money is the *cause* of the doubling of prices. Then there would be a causal connexion between a change in the quantity of money (the cause), and a change in the absolute level of prices (the effect). These relationships will be discussed in Vol. III in the context of the Quantity Theory which asserts the existence of a causal nexus of this sort.[1] Here, in the comparison of two equilibrium positions for a stationary system, they do not concern us. The rôle of money in our analysis is a very modest one. It is, as Wicksell said, purely formal.[2] We have introduced money as a means of payment *after* the equilibrium price relations were determined, simply for the purpose of giving an absolute level to the prices, and in order to determine the multiplicative factor left indeterminate in equations (10), (11) and (12). The quantity equation was, as it were, fitted on subsequently as an appendix to the "essential" equations (10), (11), and (12). It is important to emphasize that the equilibrium relative prices are completely independent of the monetary resources of the system. They result from equations (10), (11) and (12), which have nothing to do with monetary factors. The addition of the equation of exchange to the equations determining relative prices and quantities demanded does not alter the fact that our system, as before, possesses one degree of freedom. If a price or an income is chosen at random, then the quantity of money is uniquely determined. If the quantity of money

[1] The reader must beware of falling into the common error of confusing the Quantity Theory with the Quantity Equation stated above in (23). See also Vol. III (*Money, Income and Employment*), p. 172.

[2] K. Wicksell, *op. cit.* [Engl. transl.], vol. I, p. 67.

is chosen arbitrarily, then the absolute levels of prices and incomes are uniquely determined.

7. It is now possible for us to compare the equilibrium analysis of a stationary economy that starts from micro-economic processes, with a corresponding macro-economic treatment. In a macro-economic static analysis of a stationary system the position of equilibrium is expressed simply in the equation:

$$y = C \tag{26}$$

which simply tells us that in the position of equilibrium the value of the consumption of all the economic individuals must be equal to the total of their incomes. Making use of the symbols we adopted in the case of an exchange economy, we have:

$$y = p_a \cdot a + p_b \cdot b + p_c \cdot c$$

and

$$C = p_b \cdot x_{1b} + p_c \cdot x_{1c} + p_a \cdot x_{2a} + p_c \cdot x_{2c} + p_a \cdot x_{3a} + p_b \cdot x_{3b}$$

so that the macro-economic condition of equilibrium, expressed in terms of the individual prices and quantities demanded, is:

$$p_a \cdot a + p_b \cdot b + p_c \cdot c = p_a \cdot (x_{2a} + x_{3a}) \\ + p_b \cdot (x_{1b} + x_{3b}) + p_c \cdot (x_{1c} + x_{2c})$$

or

$$a + \frac{p_b}{p_a} \cdot b + \frac{p_c}{p_a} \cdot c = x_{2a} + x_{3a} \\ + \frac{p_b}{p_a} \cdot (x_{1b} + x_{3b}) + \frac{p_c}{p_a} \cdot (x_{1c} + x_{2c}) \tag{26a}$$

The macro-economic quantities $y$ and $C$, from the equation $y = C$, contain the price relationships and the quantities demanded by the individuals, the equilibrium values for which can only be obtained from a system of equations which contains the dispositions of the individuals, that is, from a total system of "micro-economic" equations. Equation (26) represents, as E. Lindahl has put it, simply *a condensed expression of the Walrasian system of equations for a stationary economy. When, therefore, we say that in a stationary economy the total value of consumption is equal to the total income, it must always be remembered that the prices and quantities contained in these aggregates must have the particular values required by the Walrasian system of equations.*

### 3. Total Equilibrium in a Stationary Exchange Economy with Production

1. We shall now drop the assumptions made in the preceding analysis of a pure exchange economy, since we wish to study how the

N

solution to the equilibrium problem in a stationary economy is arrived at, if the quantities of goods supplied by an economic individual in any period are obtained by him by means of a process of production. This problem cannot be studied here in its full generality. We shall confine ourselves to the analysis of a simplified case, which will not, however, leave out of account any essential aspects of the problem.

2. Let us consider a closed economy in which two firms exist. Firm 1 produces consumption good No. 1 in a vertically integrated plant, and Firm 2 similarly produces consumption good No. 2. Both the firms have at their disposal all the raw materials and land they need, so that it is only labour which they have to obtain by purchase from non-entrepreneurial households. All the necessary material capital (buildings, machines, tools) is produced within the individual firm. It does not affect the general validity of the conclusions we shall come to if we assume that the length of life of all the material capital used by a firm is infinitely long.

In our exchange economy there are households of workers (or non-entrepreneurs) who obtain their income by working for the two firms, and there are two entrepreneurs' households. The workers' households we may divide, for simplicity, into two groups: the households of workers obtaining their income from Firm 1 and the households of workers obtaining their income from Firm 2.

The economy described here is to be taken to be in a position of stationary equilibrium. *Our question is what level will the prices of the goods have under a particular set of given conditions, what wages the workers will receive, what incomes the households of the entrepreneurs and non-entrepreneurs will obtain, what quantities of each consumption good will be bought by the households, and what will be the level of employment measured in hours.*

The data for our problem are clearly the tastes of the individual households, the technical conditions for the production of the two consumption goods (the production functions), the quantity of labour available, the natural resources available, the productive equipment available, the modes of behaviour employed by the individuals engaged, and the social and legal structure of the economy.

3. Let us make use of the following symbols:

$Y_1, Y_2$   Incomes of the two groups of workers' households
$G_1, G_2$   Incomes (residual) of the two entrepreneurs' households
$x_1, x_2$   Production = Sale of the two consumption goods
$t_1, t_2$   Employment in man-hours in the two firms
$t_d$   Demand for man-hours

$t_s$ Supply of man-hours

$p_1, p_2$ Prices of the two consumption goods

$w$ Wage-rate per hour

$x_1^{a1}, x_2^{a1}$ The quantities demanded of the two consumption goods by the workers' households drawing their income from Firm 1

$x_1^{a2}, x_2^{a2}$ The quantities demanded of the two consumption goods by the workers' households drawing their income from Firm 2

$x_1^{u1}, x_2^{u1}$ The quantities of the two consumption goods demanded by entrepreneur's household No. 1

$x_1^{u2}, x_2^{u2}$ The quantities demanded of the two consumption goods by the entrepreneur's household No. 2.

These 21 variables are the relevant quantities for our problem. We have to ask first, what relations exist between these properties in our stationary economy.

4. (a) *The incomes of the workers' households* are by definition equal to the hourly wage-rate multiplied by the employment:

$$Y_1 = w \cdot t_1; \quad Y_2 = w \cdot t_2 \tag{27}$$

We assume that workers and entrepreneurs consider the wage-rate in their calculations to be a given quantity.

(b) *The employment of the workers* in each firm depends in a technically determined manner (given the productive equipment and the productivity of the workers) on the quantity of consumption goods to be produced in the period:

$$t_1 = \Phi_1(x_1); \quad t_2 = \Phi_2(x_2) \tag{28}$$

These functions have the characteristic that employment increases as the output of consumption goods increases, but that the marginal product of labour falls, i.e. above a particular output of consumption goods the amount of employment increases more rapidly than the output of goods. The technical functions (28) represent simply the well-known law of returns for the variable factor of production, labour.

(c) *The residual incomes of the entrepreneurs' households* result, by definition, from the difference between revenue and costs, which here consist simply of the wages of the workers:

$$G_1 = p_1 x_1 - Y_1; \quad G_2 = p_2 x_2 - Y_2. \tag{29}$$

(d) We are assuming that the demanders of consumption goods (workers' and entrepreneurs' households) act as quantity-adjusters, so that the dispositions to purchase of the demanders, given their tastes, are expressed by the individual demand functions. As there are four groups of buyers (two of entrepreneurs' households and two of workers' households) and two consumptions goods, we have altogether eight individual demand functions:

The demand functions of worker's households No. 1:

$$x_1{}^{a1} = x_1{}^{a1}\left(\frac{Y_1}{p_1}, \frac{Y_1}{p_2}\right); \quad x_2{}^{a1} = x_2{}^{a1}\left(\frac{Y_1}{p_1}, \frac{Y_1}{p_2}\right)$$

The demand functions of workers' households No. 2:

$$x_1{}^{a2} = x_1{}^{a2}\left(\frac{Y_2}{p_1}, \frac{Y_2}{p_2}\right); \quad x_2{}^{a2} = x_2{}^{a2}\left(\frac{Y_2}{p_1}, \frac{Y_2}{p_2}\right)$$

The demand functions of entrepreneurs' household No. 1:     (30)

$$x_1{}^{u1} = x_1{}^{u1}\left(\frac{G_1}{p_1}, \frac{G_1}{p_2}\right); \quad x_2{}^{u1} = x_2{}^{u1}\left(\frac{G_1}{p_1}, \frac{G_1}{p_2}\right)$$

The demand functions of entrepreneurs' household No. 2:

$$x_1{}^{u2} = x_1{}^{u2}\left(\frac{G_2}{p_1}, \frac{G_2}{p_2}\right); \quad x_2{}^{u2} = x_2{}^{u2}\left(\frac{G_2}{p_1}, \frac{G_2}{p_2}\right)$$

As our economy is assumed to be stationary the whole income of each household is spent on consumption, so the above demand functions automatically fulfil this condition.

(e) We have to know, further, *how the entrepreneurs determine the quantities they supply (= produce) in a period.* From our analysis of the economic plan of the entrepreneur we know that any conclusion on this is only possible if his mode of behaviour and objective are known. We wish to assume here that the entrepreneur considers the prices of consumption goods and the wage-rate to be, for him, given quantities, and therefore behaves, both as purchaser and seller, as *a quantity-adjuster.* We assume, further, that the entrepreneur is aiming at the maximum profit in the period. We have shown, in studying the economic plan of the firm, that on these assumptions it will produce and supply that quantity at which marginal costs are equal to the price of the product. The marginal costs for a firm which is acting as a quantity-adjuster in purchasing the factors of production are, as we learnt above (page 171 ff.), equal to the quotients of the prices and the marginal products of the factors concerned. The quantities supplied by the two firms, are, therefore, in our model given by the two equations:

$$p_1 = w: \frac{dx_1}{dt_1} = w \cdot \frac{dt_1}{dx_1}$$

$$p_2 = w: \frac{dx_2}{dt_2} = w \cdot \frac{dt_2}{dx_2}$$

(31)

where the marginal products $dx_1/dt_1$ and $dx_2/dt_2$ and their reciprocals are determined by the production functions (28).

(f) As further conditions we have those following from the condition that in a position of equilibrium *the total quantities of goods demanded must be equal to the total quantities of goods supplied:*

$$x_1 = x_1{}^{a1} + x_1{}^{a2} + x_1{}^{u1} + x_1{}^{u2}$$

(32)

$$x_2 = x_2{}^{a1} + x_2{}^{a2} + x_2{}^{u1} + x_2{}^{u2}$$

One of these two equations is not independent of the equations we have previously set out (just as in the case of the pure exchange economy).[1] The second equation in (32) can be derived from (27) to (31) and from the first equation in (32). In reality, therefore, we simply have a *single* equation in (32).

(g) A further equation in the shape of the supply function for work is obtained when we introduce an assumption about the supply of manpower. The nature of the assumption made about the form of the labour supply function is of crucial importance for what follows. Let us begin by considering the following assumption:

On the labour market there rules free atomistic competition. Workers regulate their offer of man-hours with reference to the *real wage*, in such a way as to raise the supply as real wages rise. We thus suppose the workers to be free from money illusion.[2]

The *supply function of work* (measured in man-hours) will then have this form:

$$t_s = t_s \left( \frac{w}{p_1}, \frac{w}{p_2} \right),$$

(33)

where $t_s$ stands for the supply of man-hours, $w/p_1$ for the real wage in terms of good 1, and $w/p_2$ for the real wage in terms of good 2.

---

[1] The proof is exactly the same as in the case of the pure exchange economy, and there is no need to repeat it.

[2] Cf. p. 6.

(h) In equilibrium, total demand for man-hours ($t_d$) must equal total supply of man-hours ($t_s$). This condition yields the equation

$$t_s = t_d, \tag{34}$$

where, by definition,

$$t_d = t_1 + t_2. \tag{35}$$

The system expressed in (27)–(35) is composed of equations which, except for the production functions, are identical in character with those required in the analysis of the pure exchange economy. We have *definitional equations*—(27), (29) and (35); *reaction* (or *behaviour*) *equations*—(30), (31) and (33); and equations stating *equilibrium conditions*—(32) being the equilibrium condition for the market of goods and (34) being the equilibrium condition for the labour market. In addition, we have now the two equations (28) which are of a purely technological character and are, therefore, known as *technological equations*. All the equations that are met with in static and dynamic economic analysis are of these four types.

5. We have, therefore, altogether 20 independent relations between 21 variables:

4 income equations,
2 production functions,
8 demand functions for the two goods,
2 supply functions for the two goods,
1 supply function for labour,
2 equilibrium conditions (equilibrium in the market for goods and equilibrium in the labour market), and
1 definitional equation for the demand of labour.

The number of variables is greater by one than the number of relations. Our system therefore possesses one degree of freedom; that is, we can choose at random the value of one variable. Once we have chosen it, the values of all the other variables have been determined.[1] The conclusion that our system possesses one degree of freedom has general validity, given our assumptions about the form of the demand and supply functions. It will apply, irrespective of the number of firms, households, consumption goods and means of production that may be brought into the analysis.

On closer examination it appears—just as in the case of a pure exchange economy—that the sytem of equations (27)–(35) will only

---

[1] In this case, also, the existence of a solution of the system of equations needs to be proved. But this proof, as also the examination of the stability or instability of an existing equilibrium, would take us outside the limits of an introduction like the present one.

allow us to work out the price ratios, which means, in our simple model, the ratios between the prices of two goods and the wage rate. First we eliminate from the system of equations the incomes of workers and entrepreneurs, by substituting the expressions for $Y_1$, $Y_2$, $G_1$ and $G_2$ from (27) and (29) into the demand functions.[1] Then, using (31) we note that the levels of employment $t_1$ and $t_2$ can similarly be expressed as functions of $w/p_1$ or $w/p_2$. We then conclude that the quantity demanded depends only on the price ratios $w/p_1$ and $w/p_2$.

We furthermore learn from (31) that the supply of consumption goods equally depends solely on $w/p_1$ or $w/p_2$, and we may accordingly write the equilibrium condition (32) for the market for goods in the form:

$$x_1^s\left(\frac{w}{p_1}\right) = x_1^d\left(\frac{w}{p_1}, \frac{w}{p_2}\right). \tag{36}$$

where $x_1^s$ designates the supply and $x_1^d$ the demand for good 1.

The equilibrium condition (34) for the labour market similarly reduces to an equation of the form:

$$t_s\left(\frac{w}{p_1}, \frac{w}{p_2}\right) = t_d\left(\frac{w}{p_1}, \frac{w}{p_2}\right). \tag{37}$$

We have thus found that the system of (27)–(35) reduces to the two equations (36) and (37) in the two unknowns $w/p_1$ and $w/p_2$. Supposing these two equations to possess a unique positive solution, (36) and (37) will determine the two price ratios:

$$w : p_1 : p_2.$$

This result we may rephrase as follows: the structure of supply and demand in the markets for the goods and for labour determine the *ratios* of the prices.[2] The prices of goods and the wage rate are

---

[1] E.g. the first demand relation (30) becomes, when $Y_1$ has been eliminated,

$$x_1^{a1} = x_1^{a1}\left(\frac{w}{p_1} \cdot t_1, \frac{w}{p_2} \cdot t_1\right).$$

The demand function for $x_1^{u1}$ assumes the form:

$$x_1^{u1} = x_1^{u1}\left(x_1 - \frac{w}{p_1} t_1, \frac{p_1}{p_2} \cdot x_1 - \frac{w}{p_2} t_1\right)$$

Remembering that because of (28), $x_1$ is a technologically determined function of $t_1$, it follows here also that $x_1^{u1}$ depends solely on the price ratios $w/p_1$, $w/p_2$ and on the levels of employment $t_1$ and $t_2$.

[2] This result is predicated on the assumption that the suppliers and buyers of goods and of labour are free of any money illusion.

therefore only determined up to a multiplicative constant, indicating that our system possesses one degree of freedom. *The level of one price can be fixed arbitrarily.* By choosing, for example, one particular money wage rate, we would simultaneously have determined the absolute level of the prices of the goods. The level of employment, however, and similarly the quantities exchanged of the goods, depend on the price ratios alone. *It follows that an alteration in the absolute prices which yet leaves the price ratios unchanged, will have no influence on employment and the quantities of goods.*

If we incorporate the quantity of money as an explicit variable in our system of equations, which is done exactly as in our earlier analysis of the pure exchange economy by adding the equation of exchange

$$p_1 . x_1 + p_2 . x_2 = M . v^{(1)} \qquad (38)$$

then we might also say:

*Our system determines the amounts of the goods and of employment; given the level of the wage rate, it further determines the absolute equilibrium values for the prices of goods and for the incomes and also (given the velocity of income circulation) the required quantity of money.*

Or: *If a particular quantity of money is to be held in our system and the system is to stay in equilibrium, then the prices of goods and the wage rate must be of a particular absolute value while the price ratios and the amount of employment emerge independently of the quantity of money from equations* (27)–(35).

If "full employment" is defined as that state of the system in which the supply of man-hours at ruling prices and wage rates equals demand, then we might characterize the equilibrium condition (37) as the "full employment condition." The equilibrium (assuming always it exists) which is determined by the system of equations (27)–(35) would in this case by definition always be a state of full employment. In equilibrium, on the assumptions adopted, there can by definition be no involuntary unemployment.

Finally, the state described by the system of equations (27)–(35) may also be expressed as follows:

*Equilibrium on the market for goods corresponds to an equilibrium on the labour market. The market for goods and the labour market are simultaneously in equilibrium. Our system of equations is consistent.*

6. The logic inherent in the system becomes especially clear if the relevant equations are replaced by *macro-economic relationships,*

---

[1] The value of consumption, which, as we know, equals total income, comes in our model to: $C = p_1 . x_1 + p_2 . x_2$.

i.e. by relations which link together variables referring to groups rather than to economic individuals.[1]

We adopt the following notation:

$Y$—Money income of the economy.

$p$—price index of goods.

$X_d$—index of the quantity of aggregate demand of households for consumption goods.

$X_s$—aggregate supply of consumption goods.

$t$—total employment.

$t_d$—entrepreneurs' demand for labour (in terms of man-hours).

$t_s$—workers' supply of man-hours.

$w$—rate of wage per man-hour.

If a macro-economic analysis is carried out, the equations of our system (27)–(35) (*System I*) will assume the following form:

In the place of the individual *demand function* for consumption goods (30) we have the equation:

$$X_d = \frac{Y}{p} \tag{39}$$

which simply says that the entire income is spent on goods. The *production functions* (28) are replaced by the single production function

$$X_s = \phi(t_d). \tag{40}$$

The equilibrium condition for the commodity market reads:

$$X_d = X_s \tag{41}$$

The equations (31) are replaced by:

$$\frac{dX_s}{dt} = \frac{w}{p} \tag{42}$$

This equation represents the entrepreneurs' demand for man-hours as a function of real wages. It may also be written thus:

$$t_d = t_d\left(\frac{w}{p}\right) \tag{43}$$

The supply function will assume the following form:

$$t_s = t_s\left(\frac{w}{p}\right) \tag{44}$$

Lastly we have the equilibrium condition for the labour market:

$$t_d = t_s = t. \tag{45}$$

Altogether 6 equations are available for determining the equilibrium

[1] Macro-economic models as examined in what follows will occupy our attention at length in Vol. 3.

values of the seven variables $Y$, $p$, $X_s$, $X_d$, $t_d$, $t_s$ and $w$. The three equations (39)–(41) relate to the market for goods and the three equations (43)–(45) to the labour market.

The supply function for consumption goods is implied in the system. Merely introduce the expression for $t_d$ from (43) into the production function (40), and the supply of consumption goods is obtained as a function of real wages. The definitional equation of income:

$$Y = p \cdot X_d = p \cdot X_s$$

is similarly contained in the system (39)–(41) and (43)–(45).

To solve the system one proceeds thus: the equilibrium value for the rate of real wages $\dfrac{w}{p}$ results from the three labour market equations (43), (44) and (45). To this rate of real wages there corresponds a particular demand for man-hours and, from (40), a certain supply of consumption goods. Using the equations (39) and (41) one then finds the real income and, equal to it, the demand for consumption goods. *The equilibrium in the labour market thus corresponds with an equilibrium in the market for goods.* Our system of equations is consistent. The plans of individuals as expressed in the behaviour equations are all mutually compatible. *All the equations can be fulfilled simultaneously.*

7. This ceases to be so if we drop the assumption that households consume their entire income *irrespective of its amount*[1] and replace this by the more realistic assumption that equation (39) possesses the form of the consumption function (23) in Chapter 1[2]. Retaining our symbols, and writing for the sake of brevity

$$\frac{Y}{p} = Y_r,$$

we now work with the following system of equations (*System II*):

$$X_d = \psi(Y_r) \qquad (46)$$

$$X_s = Y_r \qquad (47)$$

$$X_d = X_s \qquad (48)$$

$$X_s = \phi(t_d) \qquad (49)$$

$$t_d = t_d\left(\frac{w}{p}\right) \qquad (50)$$

$$t_s = t_s\left(\frac{w}{p}\right) \qquad (51)$$

$$t_d = t_s \qquad (52)$$

[1] This assumption is the real content of Say's Law.
[2] V. p. 43.

The system now consists of seven equations. The first three of them again relate to the market for goods and may be combined into a single equation:

$$Y_r = \psi(Y_r), \tag{53}$$

which says that the demand for consumption goods corresponding to the income $Y_r$ should exactly equal the real income: we assume a stationary economy.[1]

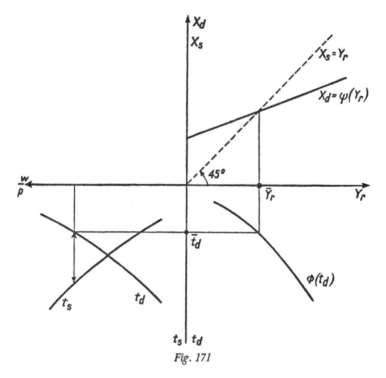

Fig. 171

*The production function forms the link between the market for goods and the labour market.*

The last three equations determine, here as before, the equilibrium for the labour market.

It is easily seen that *this system of equations is inconsistent.* Equation (53) determines $Y_r$ $(= X_s)$. In accordance with (53) we determine $Y_r$ by means of the graph in the first (north-east) quadrant of Fig. 171. With the postulated consumption function there exists only one

[1] This income corresponds to the basic income discussed in Chapter I, p. 38.

particular income which is spent entirely on consumption. To this real income there corresponds, according to the production function (49) a particular level of employment $t_d$ (see fourth quadrant, south-east, in Fig. 171). On the other hand, however, employment and the rate of real wages are together determined by the equations (50)–(52) relating to the labour market (see the third, south-west, quadrant in Fig. 171). Employment as determined by the conditions of the labour market will not as a rule be identical with the level of employment resulting from the conditions on the market for goods. Hence: *If equilibrium obtains in the market for goods, the labour market will not as a rule be in equilibrium and vice versa, which is another way of saying that the system of equations is inconsistent.*

The assumption that only real magnitudes (real incomes and real wages) are relevant for the decisions of the economic agents in the markets for goods and labour can also, as we know, be expressed by saying that all the parties involved are free from money illusion. The conclusion that we reached may accordingly be stated thus:

*If we abandon Say's Law and also assume absence of money illusion on the part of all parties in the market, i.e. in the markets for goods and labour, then the system is inconsistent. Equilibrium in the market for goods is in this case compatible with disequilibrium in the labour market and hence with involuntary unemployment (excess supply of labour at the rate of real wages corresponding to equilibrium in the market for goods).*

8. The inconsistency of the static system will disappear if we drop, for instance, the assumption that the suppliers of labour are free of money illusion, but rather treat the supply of labour as a function of, say, the rate of wages alone:

$$t_s = t_s(w) \tag{54}$$

The system of equations (46)–(52) will thus become (*System III*):

$$Y_r = \psi(Y_r) \tag{55}$$

$$Y_r = \phi(t_d) \tag{56}$$

$$t_d = t_d\left(\frac{w}{p}\right) \tag{57}$$

$$t_s = t_s(w) \tag{58}$$

$$t_s = t_d \tag{59}$$

Equation (55) determines $Y_r$, just as in the previous model (see the first quadrant in Fig. 172). Equation (56) determines $t_d$ (fourth quadrant of Fig. 172). The rate of real wages will then result from equation

(57) (see third, south-west, quadrant of Fig. 172). Because of (58) $t_s = t_d$ ($OB = OA$ in Fig. 172). The wage rate $w$ is then determined from the relationship (58) which is drawn in the second (north-west) quadrant. System III is evidently consistent.

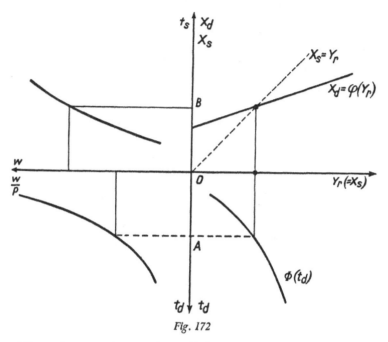

Fig. 172

The system remains consistent if *the supply of labour is taken as a function of the wage rate and of the price of consumption goods* (*System IV*):

$$t_s = t_s(w, p). \tag{60}$$

An inconsistent system will, however, result from the assumption that the wage rate $w$ is fixed by negotiation or through state intervention and that the workers are ready to supply their entire labour at this fixed wage rate (*System V*). The system of equations will now look as follows:

$$Y_r = \psi(Y_r) \tag{61}$$

$$Y_r = \phi(t_d) \tag{62}$$

$$t_d = t_d\left(\frac{w}{p}\right) \tag{63}$$

$$w = \bar{w} \tag{64}$$

The first three equations determine the real magnitudes, real income, employment and real wages. Price and money income are given through the fourth equation. Demand for labour in this system does not as a rule equal supply and involuntary unemployment is thus possible. It follows from the structure of the system *that the size of involuntary unemployment depends solely on the demand for consumption goods* $[\psi(Y_r)]$ *and the production function* $[\phi(t_d)]$. *Full employment cannot therefore be secured by changing the money rate of wages* but, given the production function, *only through an increase in the demand for consumption goods.*

We will content ourselves with these examples. In the third volume we shall have to concern ourselves closely with such macro-economic models, including in them private investment and the state budget. In the context of our present enquiry the following results are important:

(a) The systems all consist—exactly like the detailed Walrasian system on a micro-economic basis—of two distinct groups of equations: one group of equations relating to the market for goods and the other relating to the labour market.

(b) The market for goods and the labour market are linked by the production function.

(c) Systems I and II contain exclusively real magnitudes: real income, real wages and employment. One can accordingly only determine the ratios of money income and money wage rates to the prices of consumption goods. Suppliers and demanders in the two markets are free from money illusion. It follows that money incomes and absolute prices are determined only when the amount of the wage, of the price or of the money income has been arbitrarily fixed.

(d) In Systems III, IV and V the market for goods and the demand side of the labour market are characterized by the absence of money illusion. Money illusion exists, however, on the supply side of the labour market. One absolute price—the wage rate—thus enters into the determination of the supply of labour and in consequence the system determines directly the level of money incomes and of prices. It is therefore only the absence of money illusion, assumed throughout the Walrasian system, which causes incomes and prices to be determined only up to a multiplicative factor. This assumption is the sole reason why happenings in the monetary sector are without influence on happenings in the real sector, why in equilibrium the real magnitudes of incomes and prices are independent of the level of the monetary magnitudes such as the level of the wage rate. If we cease to assume freedom from money illusion and allow it to exist if only at a single point of the system, real incomes and real wages will no longer be independent in equilibrium from, e.g. the level of wages. The world of real magnitudes is then no longer independent of the world of monetary magnitudes. Equilibrium in the world of real magnitudes can no longer be discovered by "drawing back the veil of money".

(e) If System I, where consumption is equal to income whatever the level of income, is in equilibrium full employment will exist. At the equilibrium value for real wages, the supply of labour is always equal to demand. In System II, however, where consumption depends on the level of real income, involuntary unemployment is possible in spite of the general absence of money illusion because of the inconsistency of this system.

Involuntary unemployment is similarly possible in System V where the suppliers of labour are not free of money illusion. Because of the fixing of money wage rates the equilibrium in the market for goods is not as a rule associated with equilibrium in the labour market.

Finally, one point must be stressed. All the models examined were static in character. If such a system has been found to be consistent, so that equilibrium in the market for goods is associated with equilibrium in the labour market, and vice versa, *this will not mean that consistency persists after the system is disturbed*. We know that time is needed for an adjustment to a new set of data. Some of the parties involved in the markets must during the process of adjustment necessarily experience surprises, and this means that the system is no longer consistent. These problems will have to be discussed in Vol. III.

## 4. A Scheme of the General Interdependence between Economic Variables and the Data for the Whole Economy

The general interdependence between economic variables and data relating to the total economy which we considered in the last paragraph is a key to the understanding of economic processes. We shall, therefore, recapitulate in words the fundamental relationships of this system of interdependence which is reflected in the Walrasian system of equation. To do this we use an idea of B. Ohlin.[1]

The boxes in Fig. 173 denote the data relating to the total economy: structure of demand, technical knowledge, amounts of factors (available resources) and distribution of ownership. We have to show

[1] B. Ohlin, "A Note on Price Theory." *Essays in Honour of Gustav Cassel.* London, 1933, pp. 471 *et seq.* The arrangement in our Fig. 173 diverges from Ohlin's presentation.

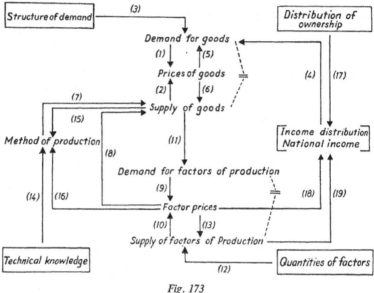

Fig. 173

how the prices of goods and of factors, the incomes and quantities of goods get determined, given the data for the total economy.

The prices and quantities of goods are formed in the markets for the various goods in the familiar manner through the interaction of supply and demand (arrow 1 and 2).[1]

The demand for goods depends on the structure of demand (arrow 3), the level of national income and the distribution of income (arrow 4) and the level of the prices of goods (arrow 5).

The supply of goods is determined by their prices (arrow 6) and production costs. But since the costs of production depend on the chosen method of production and on the prices of factors we might equally well say that the supply of goods depends on the chosen method of production (arrow 7), the prices of goods (arrow 6) and of factors (arrow 8).

The chosen method of production, given the state of technique (arrow 14), in its turn depends on the quantity of goods to be produced (arrow 15) and the prices of factors (arrow 16).

[1] The arrows point to those economic variables which are determined, in the context of the whole, by the element from which the arrow starts. Arrows 1 and 2 ought therefore to be read thus: the demand for goods and the supply of goods determine the prices of goods.

The prices of factors result from the demand for factors (arrow 9) and the supply of factors (arrow 10).

The demand for factors of production is a function of the supply of goods (arrow 11) or of the data and magnitudes that determine the supply of goods.[1]

The supply of factors of production is either a datum (arrow 12) or else a function of the factor prices (arrow 13) and in some circumstances of the prices of goods (no arrow drawn).

Total income as well as its distribution are determined by the distribution of ownership (arrow 17), factor prices (arrow 18) and the quantities of factors put to work (arrow 19).[2]

This scheme presents in its simplest outlines the picture of the extremely complicated network of interdependence between economic variables and data relating to the total economy.

The formation of prices is seen to take place in the markets for goods and factors. Both groups of markets are linked directly with one another by arrow 11, and indirectly via the incomes and other variables. The equality signs across the broken lines connecting supply and demand for each market are the expression of the equilibrium conditions for the commodity and factor markets.

The scheme further demonstrates that in the *last analysis* it is the data for the total economy that determine the equilibrium values for economic variables (prices, incomes and quantities of goods). The equilibrium values corresponding to specific data for the whole economy, once determined, will only change if one or more of these data undergo a change. The real merit of static equilibrium analysis consists in the possibility of carrying out such comparative-static analyses, to analyse, for instance, how a change in the structure of demand or in technical knowledge reacts on the equilibrium values of the economic variables.


## BIBLIOGRAPHY

*To Section A:*

R. Frisch: "On the Notion of Equilibrium and Disequilibrium," *Review of Economic Studies*, vol. 3, 1935–36.
V. Pareto: *Manuel d'Économie politique*, Paris, 1927.
H. L. Moore: *Synthetic Economics*, New York, 1929.

[1] The influence of factor prices on the demand for factors is therefore not direct but works through the supply of goods.
[2] The square brackets indicate that total income and distribution of income are determined *uno actu*.

P. A. Samuelson: *Foundations of Economic Analysis*, Cambridge, Mass. 1947.

To Section B, in addition to the works mentioned in connection with Sections A–F of Chapter II:

A. Cournot: *Researches into the Mathematical Principles of the Theory of Wealth*, (1838), translated by Nathaniel T. Bacon, New York, 1897.

H. Denis: *Le Monopole Bilatéral*, Paris, 1943.

W. Fellner: *Competition among the Few*, New York, 1949.

R. L. Hall and C. J. Hitch: "Price Theory and Business Behaviour." *Oxford Economic Papers*, No. 2, 1939.

H. D. Henderson: *Supply and Demand*, London and Cambridge.

L. Hurwicz: "The Theory of Economic Behaviour," *American Economic Review*, vol. 35, 1945.

W. A. Jöhr: *Theoretische Grundlagen der Wirtschaftspolitik*, vol. 1, St. Gallen, 1943.

W. A. Jöhr: *Die Konjunkturschwankungen*, Tübingen and Zurich, 1952.

P. S. Labini: *Oligopolio e Progresso Tecnico*, Milano, 1957.

F. Lutz: *Zinstheorie*, Zurich and Tübingen, 1956.

H. von Mangoldt: *Grundriss der Volkswirtschaftslehre*, Stuttgart, 1863.

J. Marchal: *Le Mécanisme des Prix*, 2nd ed. Paris, 1948.

A. Marshall: *Principles of Economics*, 8th ed. 1949.

A. J. Nichol: *Partial Monopoly and Price Leadership*, New York, 1930.

A. J. Nichol: "L'Oligopole," *Économie Appliquée*, vol. V, 1952.

J. Pen: "The General Theory of Bargaining." *American Economic Review*, vol. XLII, 1952.

A. C. Pigou: *The Economics of Stationary States*, London, 1935.

R. Richter: *Das Konkurrenzproblem im Oligopol*, Berlin, 1954.

E. Schneider: "Zielsetzung, Verhaltensweise und Preisbildung," *Jahrbücher für Nationalökonomie und Statistik*, vol. 157, 1943.

E. Schneider: "Eine dynamische Theorie des Angebotsdyopols," *Archiv für mathematische Wirtschafts- und Sozialsforschung*, vol. 8, 1942.

E. Schneider: "Wirklichkeitsnahe Theorie der Absatzpolitik," *Weltwirtschaftliches Archiv*, vol. 56, 1942.

E. Schneider: "Der Realismus der Marginalanalyse in der Preistheorie," *Weltwirtschaftliches Archiv*, vol. 73, 1954.

G. J. Stigler: *The Theory of Prices*, New York, 1946.

L. Tarshis: *The Elements of Economics*, New York, 1937.

H. Winding Pedersen: "Omkring den moderne Pristeori," *Nationaløkonomisk Tidsskrift*, 1939.

F. Zeuthen: *Economic Theory and Method*, London, 1955.

O. von Zwiedineck-Südenhorst: "Kritisches und Positives zur Preislehre," *Zeitschrift für die gesamte Staatswissenschaft*, vol. 64–65 (1908–09).

The Problem of Wages (in addition to works mentioned in the text and in connection with Chapter I):

J. T. Dunlop: *The Theory of Wage Determination*, London, 1957.

O. von Zwiedineck-Südenhorst: "Die Lohnpreisbildung," *Grundriss der Sozialökonomik*, vol. 4, 1, Tübingen, 1925.

*The Liquidity Theory of Interest:*

G. v. Haberler: *Prosperity and Depression*, London and New York, 1946. Also the literature mentioned there.

J. M. Keynes: *General Theory of Employment, Interest and Money*, London, 1936.

J. Pedersen: *Pengeteori og Pengepolitik*, Copenhagen, 1944.

Joan Robinson: *Introduction to the Theory of Employment*, London, 1937.

*To Section C:*

G. Cassel: *The Theory of Social Economy*, Transl. Joseph McCabe, London, 1923.

J. R. Hicks: *Value and Capital*, 2nd ed. London, 1946.

V. Pareto: *Manuel d'Économie Politique*, 2nd ed. Paris, 1927.

V. Pareto: *Cours d'Économie Politique*, Lausanne, 1896–97.

H. Peter: *Grundprobleme der theoretischen Nationalökonomie*, vol. 1, Stuttgart, 1937. vol. 2, Stuttgart, 1934. vol. 3, Stuttgart, 1937.

L. Walras: *Elements of Pure Economics*, Transl. from the last edition, W. Jaffé, London, 1954.

K. Wicksell: *Lectures on Political Economy*, Trans. E. Classen, ed. L. Robbins, London, 1924. vol. 1.

F. Zeuthen: *Economic Theory and Method*, London, 1955.

F. Zeuthen: "Der wirtschaftliche Zusammenhang—ein Netz von Teilzusammenhängen," *Weltwirtschaftliches Archiv*, vol, 58, 1943.

# Further Problems

1. Together with the insights that are to be gained from the static or the comparative-static equilibrium analysis we also discover the limitations of this approach. The mutual interdependence of all economic variables must always work itself out through time (cf. *Tinbergen's* Arrow Scheme, p. 230 above). Only in a stationary economy can we abstract from the "time quality" (*Morgenstern*) of the individual variables, and assume to be synchronized what in the real world takes place as a successive process. Only on this assumption can we regard the total development as though the economic process took place in a *single* period of time. In an evolving economy this is not possible. Its course through time can only be understood in the context of a dynamic analysis. Moreover, a dynamic analysis is already essential if we are to examine the problem of the stability of equilibrium even in a stationary economy. Only if we know whether the new equilibrium position corresponding to a change in data is stable, can we describe this position as that towards which the economic system is tending, given the change in data. But the path that leads to this new final position can only be discovered by means of a dynamic analysis. We have met with examples in our treatment of partial equilibrium problems. *We are now left with the considerable task of analysing the process of the economy as a whole through time, of carrying through a total process analysis which would show how the economic system as a whole develops through time from a particular given initial position, under particular conditions.*[1] *Such a general theory of the expansion and contraction of the economy as a whole* will contain as a special case the problem of how a system in equilibrium will develop through time under the influence of a change in the data. We shall be dealing with these problems in Vol. III.[2] The analysis of the economic plans

[1] *E. Lindahl* has accordingly considered it the task of economic theory "to provide theoretical structures showing how certain given initial conditions give rise to certain developments." (*Studies in the Theory of Money and Capital*, 1939, p. 23).

[2] *Money, Income and Employment*, London, George Allen & Unwin, 1962.

of households and firms which we carried out in this present volume was a necessary preparation.

2. The initial position of an economy at a particular point of time is given by the distribution of assets, that is, by the initial balances of the individuals engaged. If we know the structure of assets held by individuals, and if we know how they dispose of them and how they react to surprises or to divergences between their expectations and the facts, then the course of the whole economic system through time is determined. In this connection we have especially to investigate how purely monetary events influence the economic process and, in particular, production and consumption. We may describe this question, which we have to study in the third volume, as the specific task of monetary theory. It will be particularly clear, when we analyse the course of the economic process in this way, that there is no separate realm of monetary phenomena. The theory of money, prices, and public finance is indissolubly unified and makes up a comprehensive single body of economic theory. This conclusion becomes obvious if we employ dynamic analysis in studying the problems and processes of the economy. Only so long as we confine ourselves to a Walrasian type of static analysis of the position of equilibrium, with a general absence of money illusion, and regard this analysis as the central task of economic theory, can the theory of price and the theory of money be treated as though not fully coordinated, and be developed independently. We have shown in our analysis of the total equilibrium of a stationary economy that the Walrasian system of equations only permits the determination of *relative* prices. Prices are determined except for a single multiplicative factor. Only when we know the quantity of money in the system can the magnitude of this multiplicative factor, and therewith the *absolute* level of prices, be ascertained. It is, therefore, the quantity of money which here determines the absolute level of prices. The explanation of the absolute level of prices is therefore, in the static equilibrium analysis of the stationary economy, a monetary problem; and from this standpoint the task of the theory of money obviously appears to be the explanation of the absolute level of prices, or "the general price level", or "the value of money".[1] That is, the explanation of the factors determining the quantity of money is the task of monetary theory, while the task of price theory is to explain the relative prices

[1] *Gustav Cassel* expressed this very clearly: "In the general pricing problem a multiplicative factor of all prices remains indeterminate. The determination of this factor, and consequently the final solution of the problem of prices, belongs to the theory of money." (*The Theory of Social Economy*, translated by Joseph McCabe, London, 1923, vol. 1, p. 152.)

of goods. *In this way a complete separation is effected between price theory and monetary theory.* Monetary theory appears to be simply an appendix to the central problems of price theory. Attention will then be mainly concentrated on the equation of exchange which has to be added to our static system of equations.

But as soon as we depart from the static treatment of the equilibrium position of a stationary economy, and by means of a dynamic analysis attack the problem of the course of the economy through time from a given initial position, this dualism between price theory and monetary theory becomes impossible. *Monetary theory and the theory of public finance now appear as inseparably connected parts of a general theory of the process through time of the economy as a whole.* This approach, which coordinates the theory of money and the theory of price, and which has been of such revolutionary importance in the working out of a more realistic and serviceable body of economic theory, was introduced by Wicksell in his path-breaking work on *Interest and Prices* (1898). It has been carried on especially by the Swedish followers of Wicksell (J. Åkerman, B. Ohlin, E. Lindahl, and G. Myrdal), and by Lord Keynes. "The Fundamental Problem of Monetary Theory," said Keynes, "is not merely to establish identities or statical equations relating (e.g.) the turnover of monetary instruments to the turnover of things traded for money. The real task of such a theory is to treat the problem dynamically, analysing the different elements involved, in such a manner as to exhibit the causal process by which the price-level is determined, and the method of transition from one position of equilibrium to another."[1] We shall be devoting ourselves to these tasks and questions in our third volume. They will find their place as part of a general theory of the processes of expansion and contraction which will include also the modern theory of employment.

[1] *A Treatise on Money*, Vol. I, p. 133. Ohlin has formulated this problem in a similar way: "Until recently it was regarded as the task of monetary theory to explain the factors which determined the value of money. A static price theory, like that of Walras and Cassel, leaves this question unanswered and needs to be supplemented by a separate theory of money. From this point of view it is obviously logical to base this theory on the scarcity of means of payment . . . . In recent years the main task of monetary theory has come to be regarded more and more as the explanation of changes in absolute prices. The theory of money is then coordinated with the dynamic theory of price" (B. Ohlin, *Penningspolitik, Offentliga Arbeten, Subventioner och Tullar som Medel mot Arbetslöshed*, Stockholm, 1934, p. 5).

# Index of Authors

# SUBJECT INDEX